J. King 5/89

Bro. Guidera

CALIFORNIA
The Irish Dream

Patrick J. Dowling

GOLDEN GATE
PUBLISHERS

Patrick Dowling
Golden Gate Publishers
173 Cerritos Avenue
San Francisco, CA 94127
Telephone: (415) 585-8091

First edition 1988
First printing 1988

Printed in the United States of America

1 2 3 4 5 6 7 8 9 10

ISBN 0-9620974-1-1

Cover design created by **John Cody** and executed by **Jose Barbosa**.

Dedication

To my dear mother,

who never lost faith
in her wandering minstrel boy.

*To my wife Maureen
and to my family*

for their forbearance
during this protracted literary project.

And to the Dowlings,

both living and dead,
vigilant and tenacious in Ireland,
triumphant in America.

California: The Irish Dream

Table of Contents

Contents

Contents

Acknowledgments

This work is my joyful effort to chronicle the Irish success story in California. My own life for well over half a century has been a small part of the larger story. This saga of Irish achievement might never have reached fruition had it not been for the many devoted friends who came into my life before this book was even a glimmer in my mind, and others of like interest who volunteered their expertise and guidance when I launched this project. For their continuous support over many years, my heartfelt thanks to:

Don Cahalan, Professor Emeritus, University of California at Berkeley for his interest and timely encouragement

Irene Moran, Archivist supreme of the Bancroft Library, University of California, Berkeley

Tom Harrison, Renowned educator, a gentleman of the highest order, and long-time friend and confidant

Eileen Murphy, San Francisco educator, whose diligence has improved my manuscript in many ways

Professor Florence Elon of San Francisco State University for her stylistic inspiration

William J. Miller for sharing his family history and rare photographs, which provide the missing link in California history

Coleen Dowling, my charming daughter, whose diligent assistance and proofreading greatly improved my manuscript

Father Joseph O'Reilly, Pastor of St. Stephen's Parish, whose knowledge and interest in early California and Nevada history was invaluable

Timothy Kessler, Political Science, Berkeley

John Coll, Principal Librarian of the Merced Branch of the San Francisco Public Library

Gladys Hansen, Archivist, San Francisco History Room, authority on Old San Francisco

John Cody, Educator and Editor, for valuable stylistic suggestions, and for his many technical contributions that have improved the editorial content of my manuscript

In addition, my sincere appreciation to the following organizations for the privilege of using their archives:

The Bohemian Club, San Francisco

Society of California Pioneers

Treasure Island Archives, U.S. Navy

I was also greatly encouraged by the many expressions of support from all over Ireland and particularly from my native County Laois, through the medium of the *Leinster Express* of Portlaoise (**Teddy Fennelly**, Editor) and the **Laois Heritage Society**, which honored me with a lifetime membership.

As a life-long member, I warmly acknowledge the **Ancient Order of Hibernians** for keeping alive the flame of Irish lore.

A warm thanks also to the many loyal friends and supporters who steadfastly encouraged me, little knowing what would be the outcome. I would like to single out for special thanks the following:

Jeffrey Burns, Archivist of the Archdiocese of San Francisco

James (Jim) Cummins, San Francisco business executive and Irish-American community leader

John Riordan, Commissioner of the San Francisco Community College and former President of its Board of Directors

Rev. William Treacy (Diocese of Seattle), who in a deep sense inspired this book. It was my fortunate discovery of Hilary Walsh's history of an Irish parish (*Borris-in-Ossory*), a study sparked by Father Treacy, that inspired in me the idea of founding an All-Irish Library and Archives.

"Insula California": California romantically depicted as an island in Henricus Hondius' 1642 map. [Compliments of the Bancroft Library, University of California, Berkeley]

Prologue

This is a chronicle of the dramatic success story of the Irish in California. Surprisingly, Irish contributions to American history, culture, and economy have been given but scant mention in our history books. This oversight I learned firsthand as a longtime student of American history. Both to make amends for this historical silence and to highlight the wholehearted Irish participation in all things American were what inspired my literary balancing of the scales of history.

Historically, it was especially in California—America's Western Land of Youth and Promise—that the Irish transformed their proverbial image as impractical romantics and "dreamers of dreams" into practical and famous achievers with fully realized visions of fabulous fortunes and extravagant success in every field. It would, in fact, be no overstatement to call California the *"New Ireland."* The enormous number of Irish descendants—nearly four million Irish-Americans—currently living in California equals the total population of the Republic of Eire. In California, the New Ireland, the native Irish genius for creativity and achievement—long stifled or repressed by an inhospitable political, social, economic, and cultural environment in Ireland— was given free rein. This unprecedented explosion of pent-up Irish energies resulted in spectacular successes over many fields of endeavor. Even in the mid-19th century this Irish-American ferment excited the wonder of the otherwise sober native Irish social historian John Francis Maguire (*The Irish in America*, 1868), who came as a inquiring Celtic Tocqueville to analyze the roots of why the Irish were getting on so splendidly in America. In his *The Irish Race in California* (1878), another 19th-century observer, the Irish-born padre, Dr. Hugh Quigley, also traced the dynamic energies that the American and Californian free society fostered and spawned. In California, as we shall see, the optimistic legends about a New Ireland in a Golden Land to the West became flesh-and-blood realities for the transplanted Irish and their millions of descendants.

Throughout all of American history, the Irish have been second to no other national group in their patriotism and loyalty to America's ideals of freedom and democracy. One colorful example will make this point. Moving testimony as to the Irish contribution to American independence was voiced by George Washington's adopted son, George Washington Parke Custis. Custis in fact acknowledged that at the time of the American Revolution, "Ireland supplied one hundred men for any one man from any other nation. America bears eternal gratitude to the Irish." Custis admired the Irish combined traits of bravery and joviality that were conspicuously displayed during the war. Shortly before his death, Custis expressed his wish that the Irish, whom he had loved in life, would remember him in death. Custis' love of things Irish is chiseled on his own epitaph: "Though years after my mortal body has been laid in the bosom of our common Mother, some honest Irish heart may come and dropping a shamrock on my grave, cry, 'God bless him.'" Even down to the present day the Irish proudly conduct an annual march to Arlington National Cemetery to plant fresh shamrocks on the grave of their long-departed hero, George Washington Parke Custis.

The annual planting of shamrocks on the grave of George Washington Custis. [Courtesy of the Irish Embassy, Washington, D.C.]

Although Americans today may know little of the Irish participation in the War of Independence, they might be more familiar with the Irish role in building a greater America. Evidences of such Irish achievements are everywhere present for all to see: the early canals, the railroads, highways and bridges, mills and mines, the great cities, and schools and churches—these are all enduring monuments to American-Irish creative energy.

The Irish in California

These historic feats distinguished the Irish in the Eastern and Midwestern states. But equally significant and often more illustrious were the Irish contributions to the American West. When the Irish settled in California, their centuries-long pent-up and shackled energies were tremendously liberated by a freer environment, and they were consequently blessed with exceptional good fortune.

In the more fluid and open frontier society of Spanish California, any discrimination or prejudice the Irish pioneers might possibly have feared because of their race or religion was negligible. Indeed, the Irish vanguard to California was welcomed with open arms by the Spanish, who professed the same Catholic religion. This freer society meant more opportunities for the Irish. Their tragedy of centuries of persecution in Ireland, their cautious acceptance in Canada, the discrimination and outright hostility against them in eastern Puritan America were now but memories as the Irish trekked westward to the promised "land of youth," poetically foretold by Oisin, the ancient and legendary Irish bard.

Thus began the romance of two old-world cultures, the Spanish and the Irish, who were united by a common bond: the cross of Christianity. The Irish were to leave their stamp on every epoch of California history: from Spanish hegemony to Mexican rule to the first (pre-Gold-Rush) settlers to the Gold Rush influx, on to the 1890s and continuing down to the present day.

California for her part encouraged the Irish to turn their dreams and ambitions into reality and even flamboyant successes. A voice or say-so in the affairs of state, which had eluded earlier Irish immigrants for almost a century, became unexpectedly theirs in California. For example, the Irish-American David Broderick, after being disillusioned in his struggles to gain a foothold in New York's established political arena, journeyed to California in 1849 and swiftly rose to become a leading political figure in less than two years. Broderick inaugurated an era of Irish political power in California which lasted for over a century. Broderick's notable success opened the way for others, men like John Downey (from County Roscommon) who distinguished himself not only as the first Irish-born Governor of California, but also as the very first Irish governor in the United States. Fortunately, too, the California Irish enjoyed a most favorable press to tell their side of the story while lambasting their adversary Britain at the slightest provocation. Irish Californian weeklies included the *Irish News, Daily Herald, Mooney's California Express*, the *Monitor*, and the *Catholic Guardian*. In addition, the California Irish had sympathetic journalists and friends (like Dan O'Connell) staffing the leading daily papers, who saw to it that the Irish got their due and then some.

Irish Contributions and Success Stories

In California, the Irish-American's success story was repeated in every field. The state's entire history bears witness to Irish participation in California architecture, business, education, cultural creativity, religion, popular entertainment, and competitive sports.

It was just nine years after California became a state in 1850 that the Hibernia Savings and Loan was founded by John Sullivan (who himself had immigrated to California in 1844), John McHugh, and others. This banking success story symbolized the more general Irish achievement. The Hibernia Bank, which boasted assets far beyond any of its competitors, made it financially possible for the more ambitious California "Hibernians" to own land and property.

In 1871, when certain banks required redemption on their certificates in gold, the Irishman James Phelan, a pioneer merchant, organized the first gold bank in San Francisco (the second in the nation) and took over as its president. Within a decade, Phelan's bank had amassed such lavish assets that it could bankroll even the dredging of the Panama Canal.

The Gold Rush bonanza turned the envious eyes of the entire world to California. Within the short span of some 20 years following 1848, the Golden State had grown to become a colossus of wealth and prestige. With economic power now in their hands, the Irish never looked back. They boasted of their own tycoons: American silver barons like the "Big Four": Fair, Mackay, Flood, and

O'Brien; and Irish-American financiers such as the Tobins, Sullivans, Murphys, and Phelans.

The Irish success story in California was perhaps most brilliant in San Francisco, historically one of the most Irish of all American cities. San Franciscans are constantly reminded of their Irish heritage by the very streets they walk, which bear the names of Irish pioneers: O'Farrell, Hayes, O'Shaughnessy, McCoppin, Phelan, and Downey. Buildings and monuments everywhere continue to echo the names of other Irish greats from the past: the Flood Building, the Phelan Building, and the Fairmont Hotel, to mention a few.

Indeed, the Irish prospered and succeeded everywhere in California. For example, in contrast to the lackluster economic participation of the Irish in other American cities, San Francisco nurtured battalions of Irish merchants, hotel owners and tradesmen, not to mention the socially important saloonkeepers—all copiously listed in the early San Francisco city directories and advertisements. Even though San Francisco had its share of poorly paid Irish day-laborers, the bulk of the better-paying trades and merchandising was also in Irish hands. In the advertisements we read of representative Irish businesses: J.J. O'Brien Co. (dry goods), Murphy, Grant and Co. (wholesale grocers), the Hibernian Brewery, and J.J. O'Connor (the friendly Irish undertaker).

While most of the early trailblazers were lured by the earthly prospects of gold, Irish priests like Pat Manogue, though fewer in number, measured their wealth in giving glory to God and sharing His love with their fellow men. These youthful apostles left home, family and friends to share life with brawny miners and earthy settlers in the wilds of California. Their saintly story forms one of the most heart-warming and inspiring chapters in the early history of this state, a tale that would challenge the drama of the Gold Rush itself. Along with Irish bankers and tradesmen, Irish priests performed a stabilizing and humane role in the Irish-American community. During the turbulent period when authority over California was being transferred from Mexico to the United States, and the rule of law was in disarray, these godly Irishmen were much sought out for their spiritual guidance and practical advice. They cheered the lonely, gave solace to the troubled, and inspired hope in the less fortunate. They counselled both plaintiff and defendant and acted as judge and jury to the satisfaction of all concerned.

Historians such as Professor Kerby A. Miller in *Emigrants and Exiles: The Irish Exodus to North America* (New York: Oxford University Press, 1985) have celebrated the mass exodus of millions of Irish emigrants to America, the brave men and women exiles who abandoned their rural upbringing to begin a new life in the big cities of the East Coast. What may come, therefore, as a surprise is that this off-the-farm trend was reversed among many of the Irish who settled in California. Many indeed were the Irishmen who, having struck it rich in the gold fields, proceeded to invest in land and take up farming, dairying, and stock raising. Frequently, it was the Irish who were the pioneer farmers in clearing the land and planting the first crops in the virgin California soil.

Irish Exemplars as the Inspiration for This Chronicle

A more detailed account of Irish exploits appears in the following chapters. My chronicle of the Irish in California is not, of course, the last word since it focuses chiefly on the 19th-century Irish. However, it is my hope that this saga will offer inspiration to serious-minded students of California history and more particularly to those with Irish roots. Irishmen and Irishwomen of today—whatever your present station in life, be it business, trade, or politics, farming, mining, or manufacturing—you will find a counterpart in one or more of the Irish characters in this book, someone to model yourself after in moments of doubt. These earlier Celtic exemplars were men and women of impressive character and ability, who guided the destiny of California and who helped lay the foundation for a great state in the greatest nation in the world. Get to know them: you will come to love and revere them.

Enthusiasm is truly God's gift. In this divine joy I have been abundantly blessed. Following a lifetime in business, I have been privileged to channel some of my own enthusiasm into my duties as Library Director of the United Irish Cultural Center in San Francisco. After participating in founding the United Irish Cultural Center in 1972, I focused my energies to help preserve the culture and traditions of Ireland for Americans, and provide Irish-Americans with a sense of their own unique heritage, history, and roots in Ireland and America.

Prologue

This present book has evolved from my conviction that Americans, and particularly Irish-Americans, should be more history-minded in order to appreciate the many contributions of the Irish to America and California. I am delighted to share my enthusiasm with you, my readers, in the hope of encouraging you to join in fostering a new renaissance of Irish achievement. When I took up this literary challenge to record the Irish experience in California, it was with the same exuberance as I enjoyed while hunting rabbits on the Slieve Bloom Mountains in my native County Laois, over sixty years ago.

Memories not only of the old Ireland of my birth but also the heartfelt inspiration that I imbibed in the "New Ireland" of California have animated my enthusiasm to record the Irish pioneering saga for Americans. My personal transition from the old to the New Ireland—with all its opportunities—was quite congenial. In my new home of San Francisco I found to my astonishment more Irish than lived in the whole of my native Irish County of Laois. In Irish San Francisco I everywhere saw more "Irishness" about: more Irish activities, more Irish music, song, and dance, more festive parties sparkling with Celtic merriment, and every Sunday the round of Gaelic sport and celebration. Still vivid in my recollections was my first night at the old K.R.B. (Knights of the Red Branch) Hall. How well I remember that first dance call, "Choose your partners for a set of quadrilles." Since there were usually more girls than boys, it was easy for an Irish immigrant "greenhorn" to choose a spirited partner. Amid the high-stepping square dances, we heard the many announcements of the Irish doings for all of northern California, which tended to alleviate any gut feeling of homesickness.

In addition to these inspirations, many fond personal memories of carefree days spent in my native Ireland have also sustained me during my youth, helped lighten my load as a man, and now cheer me on in my golden years when the going gets tough. In a similar vein, I hope the story of the early pioneers in California will help inspire and challenge the reader in his or her own life.

These Irish-American pioneers bestowed on us a rich legacy, inspiring pride and emulation. Their foresight and honest endeavor have made life more abundant for us who have followed in their footsteps.

Introduction

by

*Kerby A. Miller**

In a sense Patrick J. Dowling is one of the last Irish *seanachai* (Shaun'-a-kee), the famed oral storytellers of pre-famine Ireland who preserved and transmitted to posterity their people's history, legends, and traditions. Of course, the *seanachai* were primarily concerned with the local lore of their native districts and preserved that lore through the power of prodigious memories, while Pat Dowling—an Irish-American living thousands of miles from his birthplace—tells the story of the early Irish settlers in California and relies largely on written documents, typewriters, and even word-processing computers to reconstruct and convey that story.

Nevertheless, the comparison is apt, for like the old *seanachai* Pat Dowling's mission has been to record his people's experience and convey its meanings and lessons to the younger generations before memory of that experience has become irretrievably lost. Like the ancient storytellers, Pat instinctively understands that even the third- and fourth-generation Irish-American stands on the shoulders of those who came and struggled before, and that people who have forgotten from whence they came have lost an invaluable sense of identity and direction. It is entirely fitting, then, that Pat Dowling should have undertaken to piece together and tell the story of the Irish in California.

Born four score and three years ago on a farm at the foot of the Slieve Bloom mountains in what was then the Queen's County (now Co. Laois), hard by the ruins of the ancient monastery of Aghaboe. In his childhood Pat imbibed that love of any intense familiarity with his native district—its natural beauties, its old monuments, and their associated lore—which Irish-speakers characterize by the term *duchas* (doo'-kass), and which even today, after more than 60 years in California, remains imperishable in his memory.

It is also fitting that Pat should have undertaken that task now, for although the Irish have dominated the economic, social, and political life of California perhaps more thoroughly than anywhere else in urban America, during the past 20 or 30 years there have been unmistakable signs that dominion has come to an end, symbolized, for example, by the post-World-War-II flight of San Francisco Irish-Americans from their old neighborhoods in the Mission district to the outlying suburbs, and by the recent ascendancy of urban politicians with decidedly non-Irish names, such as Alioto, Moscone, Feinstein, and Agnos.

In part, it was their conscious desire to preserve Irish society and identity from decline which inspired Pat Dowling and other Irish-Americans in 1973-75 to create the impressive United Irish Cultural Center of San Francisco, along with its 3,000-volume Irish Library to which Pat has devoted the last ten years. Sponsoring college-credit courses in Irish history, literature, and Gaelic, as well as Irish music, dancing, and sports, the Center and its Library have created a veritable renaissance of Irish consciousness among Irish immigrants and their descendants in the San Francisco area. Pat's present book is the culmination of this work, guaranteeing that Irish-Americans will not forget that their careers and even their suburban homes are built upon the successes and often the extensive farms and ranches which early Irish settlers carved out of the northern California wilderness in the middle decades of the 19th century.

Much to his credit, Patrick Dowling is a self-made man and a self-made historian. Like most Irish immigrants, during his long career in America he became more familiar with the shovel, the butcher's knife, the grocer's ledger, and the realtor's property lists than with either the pen or the Ph.D. programs which train today's professional historians. Although always deeply interested in history and literature, until recently Pat could spare little time from his successful businesses to study and write about his people's past.

Nevertheless, Pat's thoroughly-researched and well-written book on the Irish in California corroborates and fleshes out many of the findings of other writers—not just of early amateur historians such as the Rev. Hugh Quigley, who eulogized the accomplishments of *The Irish Race in California* (1878), but also of recent, professional scholars such as James P. Walsh and Robert A. Burchell. In their respective books and articles, Walsh and Burchell have demonstrated that Irish immigrants to California fared on average much better than did those Irish who remained in eastern states such as Massachusetts and New York, much better even than the Irish who settled in Midwestern states such as Illinois and Wisconsin.

In eastern cities Irish immigrants—usually poor and unskilled—were obliged to compete for the lowest-paid and most dangerous jobs at the bottom of American urban society. Living in crowded, disease-ridden cellars, shanties, and tenement slums, the Irish in cities such as Boston encountered a firmly-entrenched Yankee Protestant upper- and middle-class whose members regarded the largely Catholic newcomers with resentment and prejudice which sometimes, as in the 1850s, flared into open hostility and violence. By contrast, when the first waves of Irish immigrants arrived in California the Gold Rush was just underway, San Francisco and Los Angeles were sleepy Mexican pueblos, and the Irish were able to rise in wealth, social status, and political power along with the booming communities which they inhabited and soon dominated by force of numbers, energy, and talent. In short, the American western frontier provided the Irish with a much more open and fluid environment than did the nation's eastern states, and the Irish were quick to take advantage of their unparalleled opportunities.

Although Pat Dowling's book substantiates recent historical scholarship on the California Irish, the story he tells is much more personal and thus much more interesting and appealing to the general reader. Thankfully absent from Pat's book are the cold statistical tables and graceless sociological jargon which burden works by most recent social historians, myself included. Instead, Dowling, as the modern *seanachai,* relates a series of fascinating accounts of the colorful lives of many Irishmen and Irishwomen, representing every county in Ireland, who settled in early California.

For example, in Dowling's pages the reader will probably learn for the first time of Patrick Clark, an evicted tenant from Co. Meath, who pushed and pulled a handcart filled with his worldly possessions all the way from Kansas City to the Sierra Nevada mountains in order to join the Gold Rush; of William Shannon from Ballina, Co. Mayo, whose oratory helped persuade California's first state constitutional convention to bar human slavery from the Pacific shores; of exiled Irish rebel Thomas Henry Dowling, who came to California in search of freedom and land, found both, and then ironically was stripped of his estate by that very United States government whose protection he had sought; of Daniel O'Connell from Co. Clare, grand-nephew of his famous namesake and displaced Gaelic poet who composed popular operas for his adopted city and cofounded San Francisco's famed Bohemian Club; of James Concannon, a barefoot Irish-speaker from the rocky Aran Islands off the Galway coast, who established the successful California winery which bears his name; of John Downey, a small farmer's son from Roscommon, who arrived in California with only $10 but became governor of the state at age 32 and went on to become Los Angeles' first great land developer; of Martin Murphy, illiterate patriarch of a Co. Wexford clan which once owned more land in North America than any other family, and whose golden wedding anniversary in San Jose was celebrated with the largest and most lavish feast in American history.

To be sure, the Irish immigrant lives which Pat Dowling describes in his book are, with few exceptions, unqualified success stories, and for the sake of perspective we must remember that even in California the Irish experience was not always idyllic. Protestant Californians often resented Irish Catholic immigrants, all the more so because there were fewer barriers than in the east to curb the latter's ambitions. In addition, most of the highly successful Irish immigrants whom Pat Dowling chronicles were not penniless, unskilled laborers when they began their California careers, but instead arrived already possessing degrees of capital, education, business experience, and marketable skills which far exceeded those of ordinary Irish settlers. The great majority of Irish immigrants, even of those who managed to pay or work their way to California, possessed fewer advantages and usually achieved less spectacular success.

What made California unique was the rapid rise of a large and influential Irish-American upper- and middle class, but many Irish immigrants remained in the ranks of skilled and unskilled workers and they often suffered in competition with imported Chinese laborers and during economic depressions as in 1873-77. A few even felt like "exiles" in America, and, like the Kerry-born western miner, James Moriarty, sometimes they lamented, "Alas that I ever came to this land and that I left my beloved Ireland behind."

In fact, however, Moriarty eventually found a decently paying job, a wife, and contentment in California, and most Irish immigrants—for example, in San Francisco—assuaged feelings of homesickness through the companionship they found in Mission District neighborhoods, parish churches, labor unions, and specifically Irish societies such as the Ancient Order of Hibernians, the Gaelic Athletic Association, and the numerous country clubs whose attrition in recent decades gave rise to the need for the new United Irish Cultural Center. Most important, even if California sometimes proved to be less than the fabulous "golden land" prophesied by Oisin, most Irishmen and Irishwomen clearly recognized that the economic opportunities it offered them and, especially, to their children far exceeded those available in the Irish countryside and towns from whence they had emigrated. "(Y)ou need not wright to me abought going back" to Ireland, declared one Irish Californian, James Sinclair, to his relatives in Ulster; "I will not go back that country wood not do with me now I stead to long in it...(for) from the first day I landed in California my pocket never wanted money (but) when I was in Ireland I could not say that any day." Although most immigrants did not reject Ireland as strongly as did Sinclair, they were satisfied with the bargain they had made.

Thus, in the last analysis Patrick Dowling is right, and although the Irish immigrants his book described were perhaps exceptionally successful and colorful, the Irish experience in California was generally much more favorable than in either America's eastern cities or in contemporary Ireland. Certainly Pat's own long life perfectly exemplifies the dominant theme of immigrant success. The youngest son of an Irish farmer who died when Pat was but three years old, he arrived in San Francisco on the eve of the Great Depression, aged 21, with merely the clothes on his back and some change in his pocket. When he began his American career, California contained merely five million inhabitants, and many of the great cities which today sprawl across the landscape were then only crossroad market centers. However, Pat's fortunes rose in tandem with the mushrooming growth of his adopted state, and he progressed steadily from day laborer on the railroads, to delivery boy, to butcher, supermarket manager, grocery store proprietor, real estate broker, and finally to honored community leader and historian of his people's receding heritage.

Certainly for Patrick Dowling, California has been "the golden land," and consequently his heart blends equal measures of love for

Ireland and for his adopted home. "California has been good to me," he writes, "and naturally I have tried to reciprocate." Likewise, Patrick Dowling has been good for California, and San Francisco's United Irish Cultural Center, its unique Irish Library, and finally, this remarkable book testify eloquently to the success of Pat's efforts and to the strength of his character and vision.

* Associate Professor of History, University of Missouri, author of *Emigrants and Exiles: Ireland and the Irish Exodus to North America* (New York: Oxford University Press, 1985).

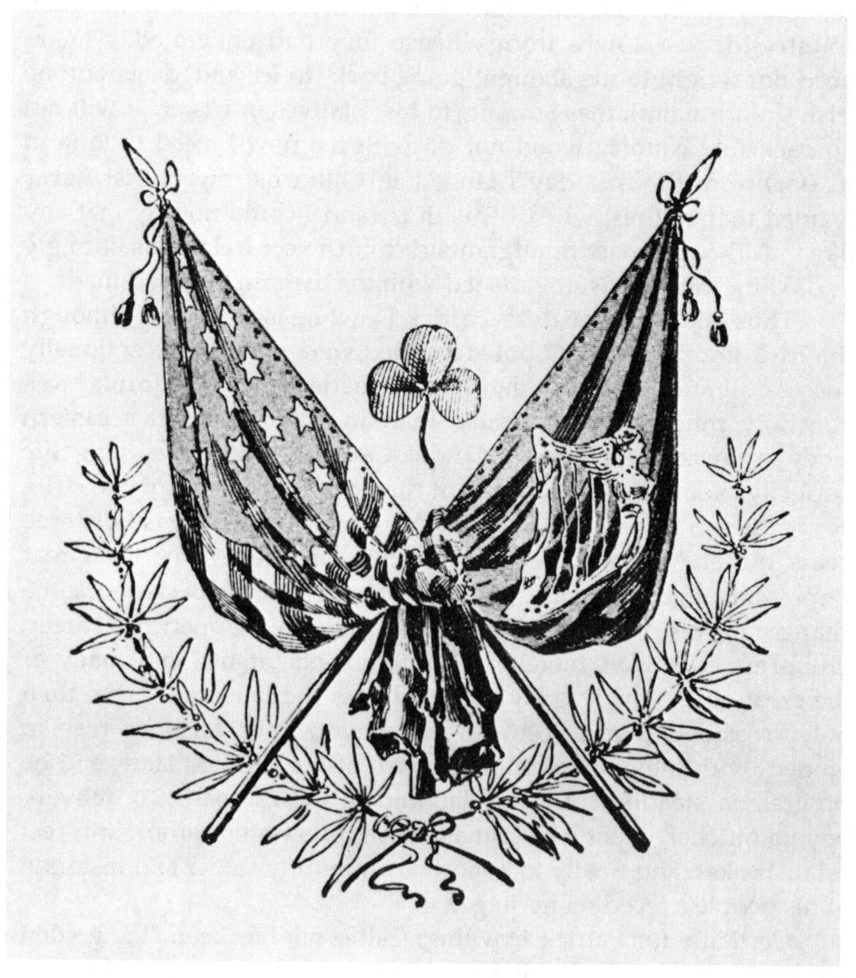

Ireland's 32 Counties

Ireland: Historic Place-names

MAP
OF
THE STATE OF
CALIFORNIA
SHOWING
COUNTY LINES, COUNTY SEATS
AND
RAILROADS.
1892.
B.M. LELONG, SECRETARY
AND CHIEF HORTICULTURAL OFFICER.
CRESCENT CITY
DEL NORTE
KLAMATH RIV.
YREKA
SISKIYOU
MODOC
PIT RIV.
ALTURAS
EUREKA
HUMBOLDT
TRINITY
WEAVERVILLE
SHASTA
REDDING
LASSEN
SUSANVILLE
RED BLUFF
TEHAMA
PLUMAS
QUINCY
GLENN
BUTTE
WILLOWS
OROVILLE
UKIAH
MENDOCINO
COLUSA
SIERRA
DOWNIEVILLE
YUBA
SUTTER
NEVADA
NEVADA CITY
LAKE
YOLO
WOODLAND
PLACER
AUBURN
EL DORADO
PLACERVILLE
SONOMA
NAPA
NAPA CITY
SOLANO
SACRAMENTO
AMADOR
JACKSON
ALPINE
MARIN
SAN RAFAEL
SAN FRANCISCO
CONTRA COSTA
SAN JOAQUIN
SAN ANDREAS
CALAVERAS
SONORA
BRIDGEPORT
MONO
REDWOOD CITY
SAN MATEO
ALAMEDA
TUOLUMNE
MODESTO
STANISLAUS
SAN JOSE
SANTA CLARA
MARIPOSA
SANTA CRUZ
MERCED
FRESNO RIV.
FRESNO
PACIFIC
HOLLISTER
SAN BENITO
SALINAS
MONTEREY
INDEPENDENCE
INYO
TULARE
VISALIA
SAN LUIS OBISPO
KERN
BAKERSFIELD
SANTA BARBARA
VENTURA
LOS ANGELES
MOJAVE
SAN BERNARDINO
OCEAN
ORANGE
SAN DIEGO
SAN FILIPE CR.
CARRIZO CR.
N. N.W. N.E. W. E. S.W. S.E. S.
SCALE
50 MILES
100 MILES

California's Counties Historic Place-names

San Francisco Bay Area

Marin County: Little Ireland

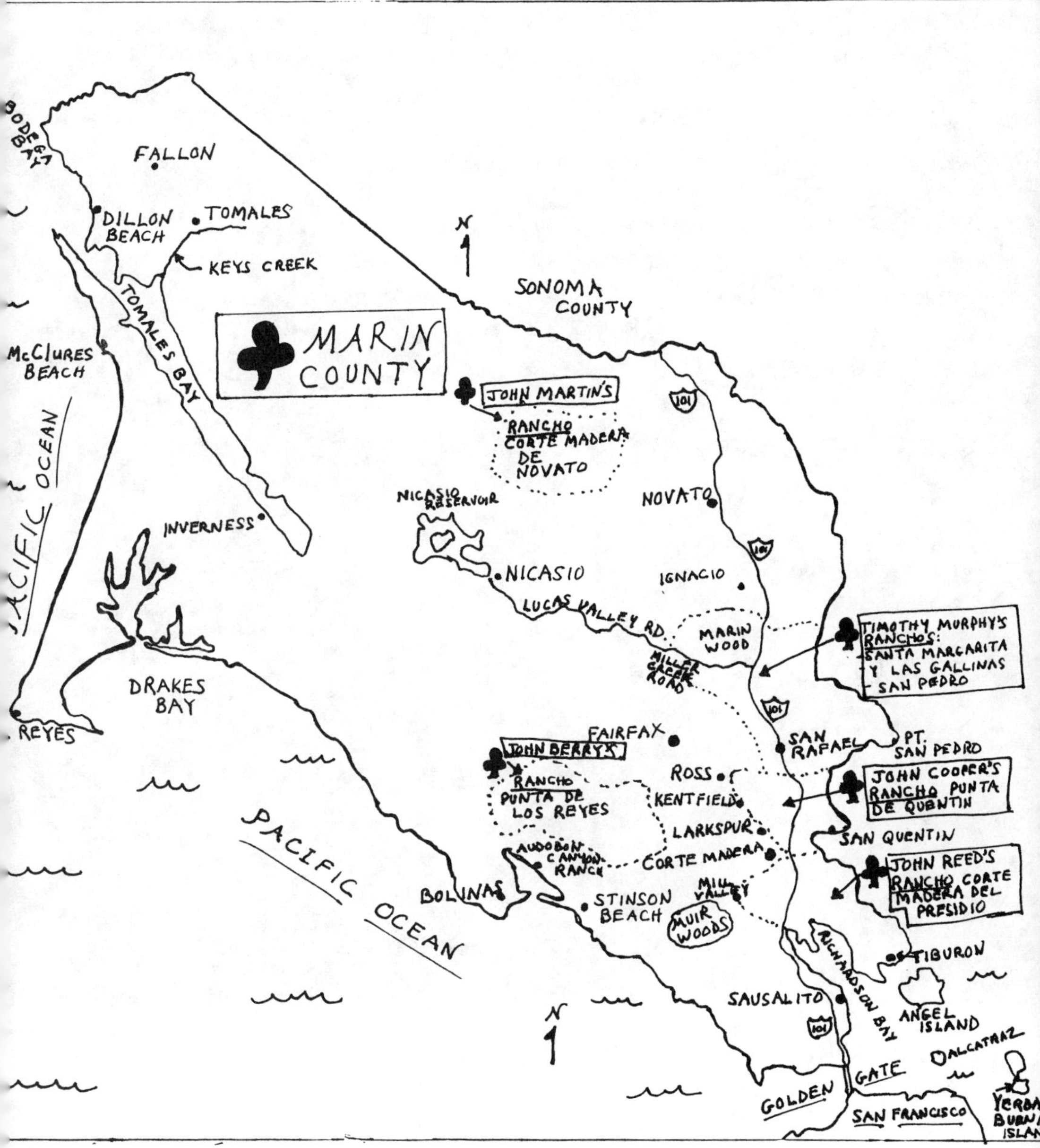

Stained glass window depicting the wandering bard Oisin and the fairy maiden Niamh with the utopia of Tir-na-Nog in the background.
[St. Patrick's Church, San Francisco]

1

The Prophecy of Oisin: California as Utopian Dream

In Irish myth, Oisin or Ossian (*Ush-een'*) is the prophet who poetically conjured up a paradise-land of dreams fulfilled, an Eden hidden away in the far West that would one day come alive for millions of Irish in California. *Tir-na-nog,* Oisin's fabled "Land of Youth," became a real Irish utopia in the Golden Land of California. Indeed, the 1980 U.S. census reveals that California boasts the largest population of Irish ancestry (3,725,925) of any state in the Union.

The warrior-bard Oisin (along with his father Finn and his son Oscar) is celebrated in the Fenian cycle of myths about third-century A.D. Celtic Ireland. Oisin took his own name from the same word root as the place-name Ossory. And Ossory is located in the fertile southeastern heartland of Ireland (around Co. Laois) and is itself an enchanted region, fabled to be Ireland's most ancient kingdom.

Oisin, then, belongs to the storied land and heritage of ancient Ossory (*Uisge Rioghad*), the Celtic Mesopotamia that lies at the confluence of the three free-flowing rivers: the Barrow, the Nore, and the Suir. All three had their sources in ancient and spirit-haunted *Slieve Bladhma* (Slieve Bloom Mountains), which the poet O'Hern describes as "the mountain of most beauteous rivers." In bardic lore the three rivers are the daughters of the giantess Bladhma, who was named to honor the birth of King Conn of the Hundred Battles. This landscape, symbolic of our human Self, is Oisin's Land," who, say legendary annals, lived in a castle in the shadow of the glens beneath the majestic and Olympus-like Mount *Arderin* ("Erin's Height").

Oisin, a symbolic image of our human heroic Self, stood majestic, clothed in crimson robes with lacings of purple and gold. His cohorts were famed Coalte and Conan, but none possessed the magic power of this Great One. He had only to cast a breath over the land, and immediately snow melted, earth grew warm, green shrubs and exotic flowers sprang forth, the wolves played with the lambs, doves cooed, birds sang, and peace reigned throughout the land.

Remains of the ancient monastery of Aghaboe in Ossory.

Chapter 1: *The Prophecy of Oisin*

Ossory, that evocative, primordial kingdom of Celtic Ireland, is the birthplace and cradle of Irish folklore. From Ossory sprang forth a cycle of legends, myths, and poetry that spread throughout all Ireland and Gaelic Scotland. Ossory truly is a land where landscapes harbor historical memories and where exotic place-names preserve something magical of the glory of a proud heritage and the grandeur of an ancient tongue: *Aghaboe, Roscomroe, Mondrehid, Clonoghil, Boheraphuca, Coolnagour, Coolnafin, Glenconra, Glenkitt, Glenall, Glenamoon, Knockannagad, Knockanina, Keeloge, Gortlusky, Garranbawn, Gortnaglogh, Rosnado, and Rosnacreena.*

According to Keating's *History of Ireland* and the translations of Dr. O'Donovan, Aengus Ostiraige (Ossory) founded the Ancient Kingdom in the reign of Elim MacGory, Monarch of Ireland, in the first century A.D. This ancient territory gave birth to Finn, Oisin, Oscar, and the *Fianna*, legendary warriors and hunters of the hills.

It was in this storied land of Ossory that Saint Cirian, first-born of Ireland's saints, laid the foundation of the Gaelic Bethlehem and planted the cross of Christianity in Irish soil long before the coming of Saint Patrick. Saint Columkille of Iona also shared a special affection for the Kingdom of Ossory, where he took rest on his way to the mainland of Europe. In gratitude, he blessed its inhabitants:

My blessings then on Ossory's men
And on her children fair and bright
My blessings on her soil and silt
For Ossory's men obey my word.

It was in this ancient kingdom that the Irish 'Pony Express' was inaugurated when a *garranbawn* (grey horse) carried the mail between Aghaboe in Ossory and Monahincha in Munster day after day, without a guide or protector. However, when the mailbag was robbed, old Dobbin was dismissed and his place taken by a monk from Aghaboe. All went well until one day the monk sat by the roadside and fell asleep. When he awoke, a thief had absconded with the pouch of letters. The old monk was so incensed that he left a malediction on the community that old-timers said the locals were wary of for generations thereafter.

Oisin and the Utopian Land of Youth: Tir-na-nog

The names of the mountains evoke exploits in the lives of Oisin and the hunters and warriors who were the mythical *Fianna* of Ireland:

Three heroes, we, at the hunting,
The chase on the slope of Slieve Gua,
Started a stag from the oak-wood
That was pearly with fresh morning dew—

His like for height and for antlers
On the height of Slieve Gua never was
In all the days of my hunting—
A lithe stag eating young grass!

We loosed them, the dogs for that stag,
We raced on to pierce him and slay
But the stag held on and ahead
Till he reached Slieve Magh, its green brae.

T'was there he fell to our spears
Oisin, I, and Caolte were there—
In all the Fian there were not
Three heroes as good as we were!

Niamh's Portrait of Tir-na-nog

On a misty morning, when the *Fianna* with Finn and Oisin gathered together on the shores of Loch Lein listening to the baying of the hounds and the sweet-sounding notes of the hunters' horns, and began to set off to the hunt, they saw coming toward them from the west a beautiful young woman, riding on a fast, slender white horse. She was dressed in the garb of a queen, with a golden crown on her head. Her eyes shone as clear blue as the dew on the grass. Her skin was whiter than the swan of the lough (lake) and her cheeks redder than a rose, with a gold ring hanging from every lock of her auburn hair. She came to where Finn was standing and spoke with a gentle voice, "It is long, my journey was, King of the *Fianna*, and now at last I found thee." And Finn asked who was she and what was her country and the cause of her coming.

> My name is Niamh of the Golden Head, daughter of the King of *Tir-na-nog*, and I have given all my love to your own son, Oisin. Wilt thou go with me, Oisin, to my father's land? It is the country that is the most delightful of all under the sun, the trees are stooping down with fruit and with leaves and with blossom. Honey and wine are plentiful, and everything the eye has ever seen. No wasting will ever come on you. Neither pain nor sickness knows the dweller there. You will get feasts, and playing and drinking, with sweet music on the strings. You will have a hundred horses, the quickest in battle, with a hundred swords and a hundred willing hounds. You will get the royal crown of the King of the Young that he never gave to anyone. A hundred glad young maidens, their voices more charming than the music of the bards, will be at your call and a hundred armed men waiting on you. Come with me to the Country of the Young!

Oisin and Niamh in Tir-na-nog

When Oisin heard all that she was saying, there was not a fiber of his body that was not in love with the beautiful Niamh. When her magic words ceased, he took her in his arms and mounted the tall white steed, and down the forest glade they swept and vanished from sight beneath the light of the silvery moon.

For long indeed it was that Oisin sojourned with the lovely princess in the Kingdom of Youth, the most delightful country of all. But having seen all the wonders of *Tir-na-nog* with mortal eyes, Oisin longed to return to his own country and relate the tale with mortal lips. Finn, his aged father, was already laid away on the hillside, and the friends Oisin had known in his youthful days were now old and worn. He alone had not wasted because he had lived in the land of the ever-young, where none grow old or weary.

Fearing the fate that awaited his people, Oisin called them all together and revealed to them all what would come to pass. He prophesied as follows:

> You will suffer cold and hunger. Fear will haunt you and persecution shall be your lot. You will be cast out in the heat of the day and the darkness of night. Your bed will oft be the roadside. Alas, a sad and sorrowful fate awaits

you in your childhood homeland. *You will be forced to abandon your native soil in weeping and mourning, perhaps never to return. But take heart. You will one day reach the Promised Land, far away in the West*:

It's a *Land of Youth*, of love and truth,
A land from sorrow free
It lies far off in the Golden West
On the rim of the Azure Sea.
Ye shall reach the strand
Of that sunny land
From hate and torture free
And ever more, that verdant shore,
Your happy home shall be.

The West is far, far away, but do not be discouraged. You will cross vast plains, deep valleys, ford brimming rivers and towering mountains, to find your true home in the western land of eternal spring and perpetual sunshine. You will have many signs and wonders to guide you. A bright, golden sun will gradually disappear from your view over the Western Land, a mighty ocean of azure blue will appear in its wake, crowned by a mantle of fleecy white as it pounds relentlessly against the shore.

Go ye to the loftiest mound, there you will observe a huge chasm in the earth, gorged by the awesome power of this mighty water as it races inwards spreading its arms like a giant of the forest. A gentle moon will light your path to the sheltered cove beneath. Rest ye there till dawn of day. Arise with the eastern sun, and behold before thine eyes *Tir-na-nog*, the Promised Land.

This Golden Paradise will be your inheritance. *Your offspring will be many*, and you shall bring joy and glory to all your people.

Oisin prophesied of the Irish: "Your offspring will be many" in the golden paradise of Tir-na-nog. [Eamon de Valera unveiling statue of Robert Emmet at Golden Gate Park, San Francisco, July 20, 1919.]

Early Irish Settlers in the Western El Dorado

Many long years passed after Oisin's predictions before wandering Gaels reached their Land of Youth. The first Irishman of record to arrive in California was Joseph O'Cain, who came ashore at Santa Barbara in 1795. O'Cain was reputed to be not only the first Irishman, but indeed the first foreigner (*el extranjero*) who sought permission to stay. O'Cain came aboard an English ship which put in for supplies following a hazardous voyage across the Pacific. When he beheld the grandeur of the Spanish pueblo, no farther would he go. The scenic beauty, delightful climate, the hospitality of the people, and the charming grace of the lovely *senoritas* proved a strong attraction for this latterday Irish Oisin, and he vowed to forsake the bounding main and give up friends and country to spend his life in this delightful land of promise.

Although the Spanish conquistadors were a hospitable people, the authorities were cautious of strangers in their midst. Yet the dashing Irish sailor O'Cain was received with open arms and his petition for permission to stay was graciously endorsed by the Commandante of the Presidio of Santa Barbara. The Commandante wrote a letter to Governor Diego de Norica describing O'Cain as a skillful pilot of good parentage, now residing in the city of Boston. It noted that the "said Englishman was a native of Ireland." This letter and others pertaining to the Irish presence in early California are preserved in the Spanish archives in Mexico City.

Unfortunately, O'Cain's request to remain in Santa Barbara was eventually denied, and he was put aboard a ship destined for San Blas in Lower California. In later years it was said that he plied the West Coast as far north as Alaska in his own vessel. Whatever became of this Irish mariner, the first of his people to set foot in California, remains a mystery. He left as he came and vanished in the silence of the sea.

How Santa Barbara got its name is as legendary and romantic as the prophecy of Oisin. Saint Barbara was once a pagan noblewoman, a beautiful princess who suffered martyrdom for her Christian faith at the behest of her outraged father. Born to riches in Heliopolis (the Egyptian *City of the Sun*), her august faith and fame spread far and wide, reverberating in the hallowed halls of the crusading Franciscan Fathers in far-off California. It is symbolically fitting that this earthly paradise, as O'Cain described it, would henceforth bear the name of Saint Barbara, one of the most beautiful and popular saints of Christendom.

In the year 1814, some nineteen years after O'Cain's arrival in Santa Barbara, came the next Irish Oisin, John Mulligan, who landed in Monterey, the colonial capital of Spanish California. Mulligan, a weaver by trade, was a native of County Down. He, too, was hospitably welcomed by the Franciscan Fathers, and reciprocated in kind by teaching the resident Indians the art of weaving. Mulligan's name appears in the old Spanish records as *Juan Mulligan*. He was undoubtedly the first of his race to settle in the new country, and there is much evidence that he was the first non-Spanish foreigner to make his home in sunny California.

Oisin and St. Patrick on Tir-na-nog

Thousands of Irishmen, and Irishwomen too, were to follow in the footsteps of the pioneers, O'Cain and Mulligan. By land and sea, the Irish came to set their roots in the Golden Land. "*Your offspring will be many,*" Oisin had prophesied. Oisin's prophecy has been fulfilled. The Irish have found their Promised Land in California.

The ancient annals speak of symbolic encounters when Patrick and Oisin crossed paths—but never swords—as they traversed the Green Isle. Patrick the Christian felt honor-bound to render to Oisin the old pagan things that were Oisin's, while reserving for himself the new things that were God's. Oisin had outlived the rest of the mythical race of *Fianna* to meet and converse with Saint Patrick:

Patrick:

O noble Oisin, son of the King
Whose deeds men sing this day in song!
Thy grief abate and to us relate
By what strange fate thou hast lived so long.

Oisin:

O Patrick, here's the tale for thee,
Though sad to me, its memories old
T'was after *Gabra—I mind me well,
The field where fell my Oscar bold.

Patrick:

O, vain old Oisin, dwell no more
On the deeds of yore in the *Fian* ranks
How did'st, thou, go to *Tir-na-nog*
Come let me know and I'll owe much thanks.

Oisin:

We turned away as I truly said
And our horses' head we gave to the West
When Lo; the deep sea opened before
While behind us bore the billows that
pressed.

No sooner had I touched the ground
Than with a bound my steed took fright
Away, away to the West we rushed
Whilst all stood hushed at such strange
sight.

O Patrick, now the tale thou hast
As each thing passed, indeed, in truth
My going away, my lengthened stay
And return for aye from the 'Land of Youth.'

[* The battle of Gabra (*circa* 284 A.D.) was a turning point in ancient Irish history, where Finn's warriors were soundly defeated.]

The Irish Tir-na-nog in California

The mythical pagan prophet Oisin symbolizes the pre-Christian Celtic longings of our deep human Self for a 'paradise regained' of unlimited life in a Land of Youth (*Tir-na-nog*). Christian and post-Christian poets (see the mystical W.B. Yeat's *Wanderings of Oisin*) in their writings dramatically contrive a meeting and cultural confrontation between the old magic, pagan vision of Oisin and the later Christian spirituality symbolized by the legendary St. Patrick.

In California, San Francisco's architecture keeps alive Oisin's and St. Patrick's quest for a Land of Youth and Eden of immortality. Oisin is today artistically enshrined along with the Christian legends, Patrick, Bridget, and Columkille, and a host of other Irish saints in an artful, symbolic sequence within the lofty battlements of old St. Patrick's Church, an historic landmark in downtown San Francisco.

St. Patrick's Church, near Muscone Center, is a veritable Irish cultural museum, a symbolic summary of Irish immigrant history in California. Here the Irish national colors of green, white, and gold sparkle in rich marble work. Here Christian and Pagan Ireland harmoniously live together in the art of the Church. Thirty-two of the Church's larger stained glass window—16 on each side—depict a parade of the early Irish saints, honoring the patron saints of Ireland's 32 counties. In the window above the Church's main altar St. Patrick takes pride of place among his peers, the four evangelists: Matthew, Mark, Luke, and John. In one of the upper clerestory windows of St. Patrick's Church, we can also gaze on a multicolored jewel fashioned of Tiffany glass: a celestial window which portrays Oisin and the pagan island as the Christian Patrick found it. Window No. 6 depicts Oisin with Niamh in *Tir-na-nog*. Father John Rogers, the inspired builder of the present church and pastor of St. Patrick's from 1905 to 1935, so loved the old pagan myth of Oisin that he also named a men's shelter after *Tir-na-Nog*. In a profound sense, the utopian Land of Youth, long dreamed of by the Irish, has taken root in California:

> The feast shall cloy not, nor the chase shall tire,
> Nor music cease forever through the hall
> The gold and jewels of the Land of Youth
> Outshine all splendors ever dreamed by man.

Symbolically, the Oisin and the Niamh living in each of our hearts have returned to *Tir-na-nog*, the Golden Land of California, to dwell forever among countrymen and countrywomen from Erin.

Oisin and Niamh in Tir-na-nog (a painting by J.H.F. Bacon).

John Daly, rags-to-riches founder of Daly City and prototype of the self-confident Irish who found success in California. [Courtesy of John Sullivan, Librarian of Daly City Public Library.]

2

The Irish in California: A Panorama of Irish Dreams

The story of the Irish in California is indeed a magical tale, the most captivating and triumphant chronicle in the long history of the wandering Gael, either at home or in exile. Truly, the saga of every facet of Irish participation in the Golden State reveals an Irish success story unequaled anywhere else on our globe.

California as the Irish El Dorado

Like *Tir-na-nog,* California's mythical expectations and enchanting beauty have often fired the imagination of writers, poets, and Bohemians alike, conjuring up romantic vistas:

A verdant land of winding vales
  Bright streams and verdant plains
Where summer all the livelong year
  In changeless splendor reigns.
With the green of woven meadows
  And the hills of golden chains
The light of leaping rivers
  And the flash of poppied plains
It lies not east or west

But like a flag unfurled
Where the hand of God has hung it
Down the center of the world.

Rich cornucopia of agricultural California. [Courtesy of the Greater Stockton Chamber of Commerce.]

With a lavish hand, Mother Nature laid out California as a fitting stage for the human drama—tragedy, comedy, romance and epic—that was to unfold. Majestic Sierra mountains overlooked a panorama of farmlands, rivers, and bays rich in minerals, flora and fauna, and unfettered human talent.

The hush of grassy meadows helped smooth the constant din of the miner's pick, while the clatter of the stagecoach harmonized with the thud of horses' hoofs. California has always been a romantic stage. There were Spanish dons and graceful *senoritas,* Indian dancers, and brown-robed Franciscans, Spanish guitarists and Irish fiddlers, miners and ministers, merchants and gamblers. The haunting melody of the Indian love call blended with the distant wail of the prowling coyote.

California has always been a land of enchantment, from horizon to horizon. Nowhere on God's green earth could such a vigorous and romantic people as the Irish find a more suitable rebirth. The Irish are a persecuted race that has inspired such noble bards as Thomas Moore, Clarence Mangan, and Patrick Kavanaugh; eloquent statesmen like Edmund Burke, Daniel O'Connell, and Charles Stewart Parnell; and renowned patriots such as Wolfe Tone, Robert Emmet, and Patrick Pearse. The latent talents of an imaginative race that had been suppressed for far too long would burst forth when the Irish reached the Golden Land of *El Dorado*. Here the Irish had indeed reached their promised land, as was eloquently voiced in an address by California Senator David Broderick on the occasion of the admission of Kansas as a state in that decisive year, 1861:

> I represent a state where labor is honorable, where the judge has left his bench, the master his books, the cobbler his last, for the opportunity of delving into the earth, where no station or position in life is so high that its occupant is not proud to boast that he has worked with his hands. There is no state in the union, no place on earth where men are honored and so well rewarded for their toil.

A Primer on Irish History: "A Most Distressful Nation"

In order to comprehend the Irish achievements in California, let's briefly turn back the pages of history to the troubled Ireland of the twelfth century.

The English centuries-long conquest of Ireland (the Anglo-Norman Invasion)—and thus Ireland's purgatory—began in the year 1169. In a recent BBC television series, the historian Robert Kee, pointing to the Tower of London, declared, "That's where Ireland's troubles began." England's imperialism accelerated when the land-grabs or "Plantation" began in 1549-53 with the confiscation of King's County and Queen's County (Offaly & Laois), over which she ruled for over three more agonizing centuries. The rightful owners of the land were evicted, replaced by lowland Scots and English settlers. The plantation of Munster in 1586-92 and of Ulster in 1608-10 followed. The natives rose in revolt, but their efforts went for naught. Whatever hopes they nurtured were dashed by their disastrous defeat at Kinsale in the year 1601:

Already the Curse is upon her
  And strangers her valleys profane
They came to divide and dishonor
  And tyrants they long shall remain.

In 1649, Oliver Cromwell landed in Ireland, with a well equipped army—to 'finish the job.' As historian Dr. Kevin Starr relates: "Most ferociously, the ambition of the dictator Oliver Cromwell was nothing less than the total destruction of the Irish race by vandalism and genocide." Under Cromwell, the English subjugated the native population during a period of unrelenting persecution. Cromwell laid siege to the town of Drogheda in County Louth and put the entire population to the sword, as a warning to any resisters. He marched south to Wexford repeating the slaughter, and from there to other parts of Ireland that showed any signs of resistance. Again and again, the native Irish fought back, but were ruthlessly crushed at the Battle of the Boyne in 1690.

Shortly afterwards, the passing of the long-lasting anti-Irish-Catholic Penal Laws in 1695 decimated any illusions the natives harbored of a better tomorrow. The poet Davis lamented:

O weep those days, those penal days
When Ireland hopelessly complained
O weep those days, those penal days
When godless persecution reigned.

Henceforth, the British Penal Laws weighed heavily upon the Gaelic Irish, who were forbidden to own land, speak their native language, or practice the religion of their choice. This nightmarish period is best described in the words of the renowned writer, Sean O'Faolain, whose forebears experienced firsthand the unmerciful Saxon and his hirelings:

> They had no land, for they were allowed by law to own none. No schools, for they were allowed by law to possess none. They had no church and no clergy. They had, in a word, nothing, with but one exception: a strong faith. Nothing of a past, a present, or a future. No parliament, no vote, no leader, and no hope.

The British banished Ireland's priests and desecrated her churches, burned the schools, and hanged the schoolmasters whenever they could hunt them down. This totalitarian policy of cultural genocide forced the native Irish to improvise to preserve their heritage. Clandestine masses were said, and the Irish set up their own schools, which became known as the "hedge schools," conducted in the utmost secrecy. Woe betide the teacher who ran the risk of being hanged if caught in the act.

The Irish Exodus to America

These intolerable ordeals brought about the first mass emigration from Ireland to Colonial America in the latter part of the 17th and the early part of the 18th century. These Irish outcasts were destined to play a major role in early America. Present-day historians who have made a more thorough study of the American Revolution would no doubt agree that this first mass Irish emigration had a far greater impact on American history than the more highly touted exodus during the Famine years of the 1850s.

No more authentic proof exists of the presence of large numbers of Irish immigrants in Colonial America before the Revolution than the address of the Continental Congress to the people of Ireland on July 28, 1775. The Congress gratefully acknowledged the many thousands from Ireland who had already found in the colonies: "Hospitality, peace, and affluence, and become united to us by all the ties of consanguinity, mutual interest and affection." Likewise, the muster rolls of the Colonial and Revolutionary armies document the numbers of Irishmen who took part in the armed conflict. Most historians agree that the Irish formed at least one-third of Washington's army. George Washington Parke Custis, adopted son of George Washington, wrote: "In the War of Independence, Ireland furnished 100 men for every single man furnished by any other nation: let America bear eternal gratitude to Irishmen."

More than 1500 Irish officers, with names ranging from Armstrong to Walsh, served in the Revolutionary War. The list includes over 300 *Mc's* and nigh on 100 *O's*. John Hancock, the very first to sign the Declaration of Independence, credits Peter McLouth (an Irish schoolmaster banished during the enforcement of the Penal Laws) for Hancock's own excellent penmanship and learning. Such banished Irish schoolmasters became the first teachers in the

American colonies. Many of these Irish educators became the target of the loyalists for their role in fostering the revolution. One such example was John Sullivan, who taught school for more than forty years in New Hampshire. Sullivan was a true patriot. When the war broke out, he turned in his books, joined the revolution, and became Colonel of the First New Hampshire Regiment.

Irish emigration continued after the American Revolution, but at a reduced level until the Famine years (1846-1851), when it reached a torrential spate. Quoting an early historian:

> They were the outcasts of a teeming shore, illiterate, starving peasants, with little worldly possessions save the rags on their backs. When they sighted the green fields and woods of Staten Island, "America!" they shouted, "America!" Some knelt and kissed the ground.

The Irish emigrants to America were an agrarian people fated to become urban inhabitants, an agonizing readjustment. They were 'free,' no doubt, at least from fear of persecution; yet little could they foresee the long and uncertain road that lay ahead. Most were compelled by circumstances to remain where they landed, seeking shelter in the overcrowded and unhealthy tenements of New York, Boston, and Philadelphia, where they lived, worked, and (most often) died. Ireland sent more of its population to America than to any other nation, shifting the balance of Irish influence to the United States, where it remains to this day. According to the 1980 U.S. census, there are more Irish in the United States (43 million) than in the rest of the world combined. When the Irish arrived, many suffered brutal hardships in their struggle for survival. They were forced to take the most menial jobs at the lowest wages. Often they were the object of ridicule and discrimination, and on the East coast it was many years before the Irish managed to escape from the ghettos and join the mainstream of the American success story.

California as a Haven for the Irish

But once arrived in California, the Irish found life radically different from their earlier experiences on the Eastern seaboard, where they had endured harassment and insults because of their adherence to Catholicism in a predominantly Puritan society. As the Catholic *San Francisco Monitor* rejoiced in the Gold Rush days:

> Our countrymen need not fear that they will have to encounter the prejudices against their race or religion, that are such drawbacks to their settlement in many parts of the Eastern States. Irishmen have made themselves a position here fully equal to any other nationality in our cosmopolitan population, and newcomers of the same race will find no prejudice to bar their advancement, unless what any fault of their own may raise against individuals. Catholicity, too, has stuck as firm a root in California as in any part of the U.S., not excepting Maryland and Louisiana; and as probably over a third if not a full half of the population of our state belongs to her fold. Catholics need not fear the loss of their faith for want of churches and Catholic associations even in the more thinly settled districts.

Their religion actually proved to be an asset the moment the Irish crossed the threshold of the Golden Land. Already a strong Catholic conscience had been established by the Spanish conquistadors. The soldier guardians were led by the kindhearted Franciscans, who generously shared their resources with their Irish Catholic brethren. The Cross, set in the California earth by the *padres*, would be more firmly rooted by the coming of the Gael, who had borne it aloft amid trial and tribulation for more than 1500 years.

Then, again, California was a world all its own. It was a nation apart, where an open society flourished. It harbored no established norm nor catered to any privileged class. It offered an environment where all could compete on an equal basis. As an Eastern journalist on his first assignment in California observed: "It's doubtful that there ever was, nor is there now, or perhaps in the future will there be, any place like California on this globe."

Since time immemorial, men have dreamed that somewhere beyond were the 'Lost Horizons' of a land fairer and friendlier than their own. California's *Shrangri-la* lured more than its share of these dreamers, and many of these lost the desire to return to Ireland after they had sojourned on its sunny shores. The charm of California is no fit of imagination. It is as real as the early morning sunburst blazing over the horizon or the starry skies of the summer night.

California is a land of the artist delight or explorer's adventure, ringed by towering mountains, majestic forests, roaring rivers, sparkling lakes, and endless fruited plains.

California's hospitable environment was partly due to the Spanish pastoral influence, the old Christian principle that the land belonged to the people, and therefore should not be offered for sale but granted free-and-clear to the inhabitants. In the case of California, the Spanish seemed to be over-generous, doling out land grants in excess of the 60,000 acres. A number of lucky early Irish settlers were recipients of this Spanish generosity and Christian fellowship. A case in point is that of an Irishman named John Reed, Marin County's first non-Spanish settler, who in later years married Senorita Hilarita Sanchez the daughter of the Presidio Commandante Don Jose Sanchez and acquired land in the amount of 7,845 acres both before and after his marriage. These grants, as prescribed in the Treaty of Guadalupe Hidalgo (1848), were generally adhered to during the Hispano-Mexican-American regime.

A strong bond of mutual trust developed between the Spanish community and these early Irish settlers, largely because of their shared religion. Dr. John Flannery, in his study of *The Irish Texans*, alludes to the fact that the Mexican authorities had two basic requirements for settling in Texas: that they must be Irish and Catholic. However, no doubt the more heterogeneous makeup of California would have rendered such a test inadvisable. The fair sex, too, a scarce commodity in those days, played an important role in integrating the two communities. Many Irishmen married Hispanic women, and perhaps this arrangement made it easier for them to acquire land. In any case, it does appear that the Irish were indeed "*Los Favoritos*."

The Irish in America helped to plant the tree of state and nourished it with their blood, yet it was not until they settled in the Golden Land that they could equitably rest beneath its shade and reach out and pick the fruit thereof.

The California Irish held a distinct advantage over the Irish who settled on the East coast, since they arrived almost on top, as it were, and were not compelled to barter for the most menial jobs at the lowest wages. Almost overnight, the Irish swept into leadership, as planners, builders, merchants, and financiers. Ordinary laborers swiftly advanced to foremen; the more ambitious became leading merchants; and former Irish saloonkeepers became kings of industry, banking, and commerce.

Perhaps for the first time, nothing blocked their path. Success was within the grasp of every Irishman of ability. They set out for the gold fields like a conquering army, their beards grew long and their brawny arms turned brown in the California sun. They built cabins beneath the hills, and their gold pokes were soon bulging with the precious dust. When day was done, they gathered round a log fire, sang the songs of their native land, and nostalgically related the stories of bygone days when it was mandatory to post a sentry to watch for the approaching Redcoats.

In 1848, an American relief ship arrived in Famine Ireland, bringing wheat and cornmeal for the starving populace. This gesture played no small part in convincing the Irish that America was the place to go if one could only get there. The same relief ship also conveyed the news of the gold strike, which the Irish hailed as a sign from on high, like the manna that fell from heaven to feed the Israelites in the desert.

Actually, a sizable number of famine survivors did find their way to the California gold fields, firmly convinced that the supply of gold was unlimited and easy to come by. Fascinating stories in the diary of a ship's captain bring this era to life. He relates the story of an Irishman who booked passage on a brig sailing around the Horn, fully convinced that he would reach his destination in a matter of weeks. In speaking with other passengers, he was utterly dismayed when he learned the voyage could take months. He approached the captain and blurted out, "Sir, there is so much gold in California, and there are so many people going there, that by the time I reach the mines, gold will be so easy to come by that it won't be worth anything!"

The rise of the Irish in California went hand in hand with the amazing development of the state itself. In his book, *The Irish in America* (1868), John Francis Maguire stated: "There is not a state in the union in which the Irish have taken deeper and stronger root or thrived more successfully than California." Many were men of education and good character who would be assets to any nation: the Reeds and O'Tooles of Dublin, the Murphys and Millers of Wexford, the Roaches and O'Sullivans of Cork, the O'Farrells and McCoppins of Longford, the Phelans and Dowlings of Leix, the Dens of

Waterford, the Jordans of Mayo, Burkes of Galway, O'Connells of Kerry, the Hayes of Limerick, the Sweeneys of Tyrconnell (Donegal), and the Casserlys of Mullingar (Co. Westmeath), to name a few.

The Irish Dream Realized

The first known Irishmen to penetrate the wilderness were trappers and hunters who cleared the trails and became guides and peacemakers among the Indians. One of these stalwarts was Captain Jedediah Smith from King's (Offaly) County, chief trader with the American Fur Company. Smith braved the formidable Sierra Nevada Mountains and led the first party of white men overland to California. Tom Fitzpatrick, dubbed the pioneer "Pathfinder from County Cavan," discovered the South Pass, a more direct route over the mountains and guided General John Bidwell and his men in their exploration of the new American territory. There were many Irishmen too in the John C. Fremont expedition who fell in love with the open territory and resolved to make California their future home.

California was a land of peaceful solitude when Timothy (*Don Timoteo*) Murphy arrived by way of Peru in 1829. A picturesque wilderness as nature had intended, a broad expanse of undulating plains neither mapped or fenced, enhanced by rolling hills dotted with live oak, pine, and birch and sheltered by ageless redwood forests. *Don Timoteo* was truly "a man to match my mountains" as the saying goes. A commanding figure in any gathering, he stood 6 feet-7 inches tall, and weighed almost 300 pounds, with brown hair, ruddy complexion, and an aquiline Irish nose. In the ensuing years Murphy was appointed Indian agent, elected Alcalde of San Rafael, and received a three-league land grant from Governor Micheltorena.

The great majority of Irish immigrants were born and reared on the land. During the English conquest, they were dispossessed; but, not surprisingly, many of them returned to farming when they settled in California. Practically all of the area skirting the San Francisco North Bay, from Sausalito to Point San Pedro, was owned at one time by three Irishmen: John Reed, Jasper O'Farrell, and Don Timoteo Murphy.

To explain why so many wandering Gaels were captivated by the magic of sunny California would be a legend in itself. The story of Thomas Hope, who was born in Ireland in the year 1820, is a case in point. At the age of 25, he set out to see the world as a deck hand aboard an English ship. On the return voyage from the Orient, his brig sailed into Santa Barbara harbor in 1849. Enamored by the sun-latticed serenity of the fertile valleys and sloping hills, he jumped ship and headed for the hinterland where he was destined to spend the remainder of his life. In the placid surroundings, he got off to a prosperous start by raising sheep on the vast territory, a part of which was occupied by the Cienequitas Indians. A somewhat similar arrangement that of sharing undeveloped territory and bog lands for grazing was not unusual to in remote areas of rural Ireland. In time, young Hope acquired title to a portion of the far-flung Cienequitas Rancho and named it Hope Ranch. He constructed a substantial dwelling to house his growing family which is still in use. Having lived a long and fruitful existence he departed this life in his beloved Santa Barbara in the year 1887.

Irish-born Matthew (*Don Mateo*) Keller (1811?-81) was a gifted musician who spent some years in a Mexican seminary and arrived in the Los Angeles area in 1850. Keller perceived a possible fortune in the rich valley sheltered by the Santa Monica Mountains, planted the first grapevines in the area, and established a thriving winery, the first in the southland. His wines became celebrated in both California and on the east coast. He bought the Malibu Soquel Rancho 13,000 acres (for ten cents per acre!) and became one of the most successful land barons in southern California.

Mountain Charley, Patrick O'Daley, and the Tormey Brothers

Charles McKernan was a true pioneer in every sense of the word. A native of County Leitrim, the Lakeland of Ireland, he came directly to California in 1848. He was a true frontiersman in name and nature, and he headed for the hills where he engaged in mining for a brief period. Later he took to game hunting and trapping. McKernan acquired the nickname of "Mountain Charley" as owner of a large tract of land on the slope of the Santa Cruz Mountains. An accomplished equestrian, he herded his flocks on horseback and occasionally did battle with the local Indians, who took delight in stampeding his herds. At other times he was attacked by wild animals when hunger drove them out of the hills in search of food.

In one adventure, McKernan was cornered by a ferocious grizzly bear. From this encounter he lost part of his skull and almost his life. He had at hand only a single-barrel shotgun; with this he fired at the encroaching animal, but this served only to further enrage the onrushing beast. Before Charley could reload, the bear was on top of him and crunched part of his scull between his teeth. Luckily a companion arrived in the nick of time and shot the bear. The doctor who attended him gave the mountain man up for dead; but fortunately he survived, minus part of his forehead and with his bright blue Irish eyes distorted. However, despite the foregoing calamity, McKernan survived and purchased a 200-acre ranch which he farmed successfully. Eventually he became a man of considerable wealth, and the owner of an elegant mansion in San Jose where he raised a large family and lived until his death.

In California's Lake County, the name of O'Daly was revered. Patrick and Mary O'Hara O'Daly were the first farmers in the area. They bought land and became the proprietors of the largest stock ranch in that county. They specialized in hog raising, a product much in demand in the booming city of San Francisco. O'Daly's pork and bacon became a household word: their motto was, "High on the hog with O'Daly." One of their sons took up farming on his own and had three hundred acres in the fertile valley of Yokohl set to wheat and barley.

The Tormey brothers, John and Patrick, from County Westmeath, were two of the most successful farmers of that early period. They owned considerable acreage in Sonoma, Napa, and Contra Costa Counties. John was born in 1825, and settled for a brief period in Peoria, Illinois before moving on to California with his sister, her husband Peter Fagan, and a cousin. They braved the frontier in two ox-wagons and arrived safely in the fall of 1850. John owned 3000 acres in Sunol in Napa County, where he took up farming and stock raising. He bought an additional 2000 acres from the Martinez heirs of the Pinole Grant in Contra Costa County.

Patrick, the other Tormey brother, was born in 1840 and came to San Francisco by way of Panama in 1858. He herded cattle for his brother and acquired land of his own in Sonoma County where he farmed for four years. In a joint venture, the brothers bought an additional 7000 acres from another section of the Pinole Rancho fronting three miles on San Pablo Bay.

Patrick Tormey, successful pioneer farmer and politician.

Irish-born Dr. Richard Den, the first foreign physician in California.
[Courtesy of the California Historical Society.]

John was elected to the Board of Supervisors of Contra Costa County in 1866 and served until his death in 1877. He married Anna Waterhouse, a native of Missouri, and together they raised a family of nine children. John was buried in Martinez Cemetery in the family plot on a hilltop overlooking the Straits of Carquinez. The grave site is marked by a graceful monument of solemn beauty and excellent workmanship. Few men of the period had as many close friends, and the throngs at his funeral bear this out. A train of carriages numbering over 120 accompanied his remains over seven miles of dusty roads to Martinez Cemetery.

Patrick Tormey took the seat made vacant by the death of his brother, a position he then occupied for a period of nine years. He married Mary Mathews, a native of Boston, who bore him three children.

The Irish in Politics

The achievements of the Irish in California politics matched their success in other endeavors. Since the beginning, California favored the Irish with high state and federal offices, two generations in advance of their Irish counterparts on the East coast. When John Downey was elected governor of California at the age of 32, he became the first Irish-born executive of any state in the Union. In the burgeoning city of San Francisco, public office proved more readily accessible to Irish-born and first-generation Irish Americans than in other American cities. The election of Frank McCoppin from County Longford as Mayor of San Francisco in 1867 predated the election of Hugh O'Brien as Mayor of Boston by some 17 years.

David Broderick (1820-1859), frustrated in his attempt to gain a foothold in the political arena in New York City, departed for San Francisco in 1849. New York had taught him political organization, and he quickly identified with the ambitions and needs of the Irish-Americans. He galloped into leadership and was elected to the state Senate a little over a year after his arrival. Broderick served as President of that body in 1851. By 1857 he had satisfied his burning ambition to become a United States Senator.

Broderick was born in Washington, D.C. in 1820 and moved to New York with his family, where he received his primary education. His father, Thomas, was an Irish stonemason who put the finishing touches on the cornices that adorn the Senate Chamber in our nation's Capitol. During Broderick's term as U.S. Senator (1857-59), he would point with pride to the handiwork of his departed father.

Broderick tragically died in a duel to California Justice Terry. Later, a more astute politician, Irish-born John Conness, was chosen U.S. Senator from California (1863-69). When Conness completed his term in 1869, another Irishman, scholarly Eugene Casserly (1820-1883), was the unanimous choice of the California electorate.

Casserly was born in the year 1820 in Mullingar, County Westmeath, a town famed in song and story. His father, an Irish patriot named Patrick Sarsfield Casserly, took part in the ill-fated rebellion of 1798. Consequently he forfeited all his holdings, but managed somehow to escape with his life. He was a man imbued with a burning love of freedom, and he sought refuge in America a nation synonymous with liberty and justice. With his wife and young family, he made good his escape, settling in New York City. Upon his arrival, Casserly gave vent to his feelings by heading for the nearest courthouse to declare his intention of becoming an American citizen. Mr. Casserly, a scholar in every sense of the word, endowed his adopted city with an unmatched record in the field of classical education. He pioneered the first Chrestomathy Institute in New York City, which was the envy of the entire nation. In the meantime, he coached his son Eugene in his study of Latin and Greek. Like father, like son: Eugene mastered the classics and competently assisted his illustrious father in the preparation of the Jacob's *Greek Reader*. Young Casserly next took up the study of law and passed New York City bar exams at the age of 24. But he set aside his law practice to try his hand as an expert free-lance newspaper columnist. He contributed articles to New York, Boston, and Washington newspapers and gained enough experience to enable him to assume the prestigious position as Editor of the *Freeman's Journal*. In due course, he wrote for the famous *Democratic Review* published by Henry Langley, who migrated to California and compiled the original issues of the *San Francisco Directory*. Eugene Casserly was appointed Chief Attorney of New York City at the age of 27, the youngest man ever to hold such an honorable position.

When the gold fever struck, Casserly journeyed to California, arriving in August of 1850. By 1851, he had founded the *Pacific Balance*, a daily newspaper, under the name of Casserly & Co. On May 1 of that same year, the legislature appointed him State Printer.

Next, in 1869, he was elected to the United States Senate, a position he held until 1873, when he resigned from office and returned to San Francisco to resume his law practice.

In 1854, Casserly married the sister of John T. Doyle, a distinguished lawyer whose name is synonymous with such important California litigation as the Pious Fund case. Doyle also became the founding president of the California Historical Society.

Casserly died in San Francisco on June 14, 1883, leaving his widow and son John, an attorney and member of the Board of Education. As proof of the high esteem in which he was held during his life, Eugene Casserly was honored by being chosen to deliver the eulogy in San Francisco that commemorated the passing of the illustrious statesman Daniel Webster in 1852.

Joseph Gorman, who came to California in 1868 and established his home in San Francisco, left no doubt about an Irishman's adroitness in the political arena. As he related to the press: "The political Irishman is always a power among his associates. The Irishman who is not a politician has not yet been discovered." In his bid for State office, he gave his age as 35 and his birthplace as "the loveliest Island in the World." In this, his first venture in politics, he was elected State Senator and served with distinction during the second State Constitutional Assembly in 1878-79. (The first State Constitution had met 30 years earlier in 1849.)

Literary Men

James Sullivan, a native of County Cork immigrated to America in 1841 and settled in New York City. At the outbreak of the Mexican-American War, he volunteered for duty with the First New York Regiment. The Company set out on the long journey around Cape Horn in 1846 and arrived at their destination in California in 1847. When hostilities ceased in 1848, Sullivan was mustered out of service with other members of his Company in the Western Command headquarters in Old Monterey. Following his discharge, Sullivan set out immediately for the mines with a number of his Army buddies. The intrepid soldiers of fortune apparently wasted no time in staking their claims. The so-called Sullivan party is famous in mining lore as the founders of historic Mokelumne. Following a stint in the mines, the Corkman disposed of his claim and became a reporter for the *Sonoma Herald* newspaper. In partnership with a local Judge named Walter Murray, he purchased the popular journal outright. In 1854, Sullivan purchased Judge Murray's interest in the publication and became its sole owner. This was at a time when the *Herald* was classed as one of the best journals in California.

Cornelius Mahoney, a native of County Dublin, came to California by way of Peru. His father was an organizer of the 1848 Irish rebellion and had suffered imprisonment. Somehow he managed to elude his captors and escaped to America with a wife and family in tow. Cornelius was evidently a well educated young man and found immediate employment as a correspondent for the San Francisco *Call*. Some years later he quit the *Call* to work for the *Evening Post*, where he was advanced to the editorial staff. Eventually Mahoney become one of California's leading newspaper editors.

James McClatchy was another Irish immigrant who came to California to seek his fortune in the gold fields. But he abandoned prospecting in exchange for a career in journalism, which culminated in his founding of the *Sacramento Bee* newspaper in 1857. Newsprint proved to be an even more lucrative and indeed a more long-lived money machine than any gold mine. With the addition of the *Fresno Bee*, the *Modesto Bee*, the *Hollister Free Lance*, and the *Gilroy Dispatch* in California; the *Tacoma News-Tribune*, and the *Tri-City Herald* in Washington; and the Anchorage *Daily News* in Alaska, plus several non-daily publications. The McClatchy newspaper chain became one of the most successful, if not the most profitable, enterprises of its kind in the history of the American West. And now, for "The Rest of the Story," as Paul Harvey says. Young McClatchy, on his way to California in 1848, survived an unforgettable hair-raising experience. He arrived at Mazatlan on the Mexican peninsula, following a hazardous journey around the Cape of Good Hope. After a brief stopover in the port to replenish the vessel's larder, the battered sailing rig set out on the last leg of the journey to California. Fate, however, intervened as it sometimes does: a storm arose and the helpless craft was shipwrecked off the coast of southern California. The lucky survivors made their way to the barren foothills. And there they nearly perished for lack of food and water. However,a dog standing guard over his master's corpse helped save their lives. The half-starved animal led them to a nearby canyon where he abruptly hesitated to begin vigorously pawing the earth. The shipwrecked party quickly dug deeper and found a gurgling spring sufficient not only to cool their thirst for the moment but enough to last them for several days. Encouraged by their good fortune, the party pressed on until they made contact with local farmers and sheep herders, who most generously took care of their immediate needs. After recuperating, they trudged for miles overland to their intended destination of San Francisco. With barely the rags on their backs and no shoes on their feet, they arrived in San Jose, then the state capital. Already, a goodly number of Irish lived in San Jose, including its most prominent citizen Martin Murphy, who housed and fed the survivors, and sent them on their way with renewed energy and in high spirits.

John O'Sullivan was one of a family of several brothers who achieved renown in English literature. His brother Richard edited the *Nation,* an influential Dublin journal. John immigrated to California and became editor of the *Monitor,* which served as the official voice of the Catholic Diocese of San Francisco.

In 1849, John Nugent established the *Daily Herald* newspaper, which gave the Irish a strong voice from that day forward. Nugent expounded on the noble qualities of the Gael, and at every opportunity he pilloried British atrocities in Ireland. The Irish in California garnered an enviable position on the American scene, with such leading newspapers as the *Irish News,* Mooney's *California Express, The Sacramento Bee, The Daily Herald, San Francisco Monitor, Sonoma Herald,* and the *San Francisco Examiner* to extol their good deeds and publicize their accomplishments.

Architects and Builders

Smith O'Brien, an architect by profession, was born in Cork City and came directly to San Francisco. He found immediate employment in his chosen field and put his expertise to good use in designing the Monadnock Building, the Humboldt Bank, and the Rialto. Eventually he established an architectural firm of his own that was credited with such ornate structures as the Hamman Baths, the Youth Directory, the Rucker-Fuller Building on Mission Street, and other imposing structures.

James Flood, born in New York of Irish parents, was one of the four Bonanza Kings of the Comstock Lode. He invested his new-found wealth in San Francisco real estate, where he began his rise to fame and fortune as a saloonkeeper. His brownstone mansion (now the Pacific Union) on Nob Hill—which affords a panoramic view of the city and the bay—and the landmark Flood Building on Market Street stand as memorials to the onetime bartender.

Medical Profession

Dr. Richard Den was the first foreign-born physician to practice medicine in California. A native of Kilkenny, Dr. Den received his diploma from the Royal College of Physicians and Surgeons in Dublin in 1842. Like many a young medic of that period he longed for adventure before settling down to practice. He therefore set out from London to Melbourne, Australia by way of India. On arriving in Sydney, he learned that his ship's itinerary was altered and that the next port of call would be Mazatlan in Mexico. This drastic geographical detour did not deter him in the least. When the good ship arrived in Santa Barbara, California, he was surprised to learn that his older brother, Nicholas, was already in residence. The freewheeling young Doctor forfeited his berth on the ship in order to join his brother. Once Doctor Den's presence became known, he was invited to Los Angeles to set up practice in that city which was desperately in need of a qualified physician. In addition to his regular practice, he performed a number of emergency operations which endeared him to the entire populace. Reference is made to Doctor Den's medical proficiency in the historical archives of Los Angeles County:

> It is of record that Doctor Richard Den, in obedience to the laws of Mexico relating to foreigners, did present his Diploma as Physician and Surgeon to the Government of the Country March 14, 1844, and that he received a special license to practice from said government.

Doctor Den also served with distinction as chief surgeon of the Mexican Army during the Mexican-American conflict in 1846, and in addition treated wounded American soldiers at the request of Captain Gillespie, an American Army officer. When Thomas Larkin, the U.S. Consul at Monterey was taken prisoner by the Mexicans and placed in confinement in Los Angeles, it was Dr. Den who attended to his medical needs.

The good doctor was not only highly respected during his active practice but was also remembered with affection for many years thereafter by the residents of Los Angeles and the immediate vicinity. Doctor Den was conspicuous among his peers: he made his rounds on horseback on a coal-black charger, and was himself dressed in black, with a black felt hat covering his bushy snow-white hair. The historian William H. Davis (*75 Years in California*) speaks of the doctor, known affectionately as *Don Ricardo,* as a man of learning, honor, and distinction, and a credit to his profession.

Nicholas Den, Richard's older brother, practiced medicine at various times in and around Santa Barbara, but the lure of gold and ranching was all too tantalizing to set aside. He acquired so much land that at one time he owned in excess of 70,000 acres. On these holdings, he grazed as many as 10,000 head of cattle, making him one of the wealthiest land and cattle barons in southern California. Nicholas Den is better known for his contribution to California Catholicism by associating with the state's first bishop, Garcia Diego, when it was under Spanish rule. Den was the first non-Spanish settler and the first of his race to "pick up the Cross" and reinforce the pillars of a decaying church. Through Doctor Den's intercession, Santa Barbara was chosen as the episcopal see of California. He too was most instrumental in seeing that the California Missions, which were confiscated by the Mexican authorities, were returned to their rightful owners, the Franciscan Fathers. In local lore, Nicholas Den is best remembered as the Good Samaritan who harbored Edward McGowan, a fugitive from the marauding San Francisco Vigilantes. As a mark of gratitude, McGowan dedicated his book, *A Narrative of Edward McGowan,* to the charitable medic who bravely sheltered him from the infuriated mob. (For a more complete account of the life and times of Doctor Nicholas Den, see Davis' *75 Years in California* or the book by Den's daughter Katherine, *Swinging the Censer.*)

Another Irish-born physician, Doctor William Kelly, settled in Angels Camp in the Gold Country to take up mining, but when the cholera epidemic broke out, he discarded his mining gear and became the town's first practicing physician. Doctor Kelly was never known to submit a bill; he trusted each would pay when he could afford it. His practice thrived, but evidently not enough of his patients paid up to provide him with a livelihood. He was unable to meet his everyday expenses and decided to put an advertisement in the local journal, hoping for a favorable response to his plea. It read as follows:

> All persons having themselves indebted to the undersigned, please call and settle a portion of your indebtedness as I am very much in need of money.
>
> (signed) William Kelly, M.D.
>
> [P.S.: this writer could find no reference as to the results of this generous man's appeal.]

Other Irish in California

John Daly

John Daly, the founding Father of Daly City, was the marvel of early California pioneers. At the age of thirteen he set out from Boston with his mother on the treacherous sea journey to California by way of Panama. When they reached the isthmus at Chagres, they were put on board a mule train that wended its slow way through the jungle to reach the western terminus at Panama City. The boy's mother, fatigued from the long journey and overcome with the heat, contracted the dreaded yellow fever and died on the way. All alone and lonely, the lad continued on his journey to California. The arduous trip would challenge the most seasoned traveler, but for a boy of thirteen, it seemed nigh impossible.

The old, creaky ships plying the route from the Straits of Magellan at the tip of South America and on to San Francisco were often unseaworthy, manned by drunken sailors or common laborers pressed into service. Pathetic tales relate that quite often the shabby crafts fell victims to the stormy Pacific or capsized on the rocky coast.

Young Daly was fortunate, however, when he was taken in tow by the Good Samaritan ship captain who shepherded him for the remainder of the journey. Following his safe arrival, John supported himself by doing chores for local dairymen in northern San Mateo county, which was then farm land. Evidently, John was mature for his age, and he undertook the job of transporting the mail from Millbrae to Belmont, a distance of some six miles. Eventually he quit his job as mail carrier to take up work on a dairy ranch in the vicinity of Pilarcitos Lake, below the present Skyline Boulevard that skirts the Pacific Ocean. Within a few short years he had saved enough money to strike out on his own in the dairy business. It was then he purchased the landmark Holenworth Ranch in what is now the City of Colma. He renamed it San Mateo Dairy. Young Daly did a thriving business for many years in dairy farming and produce, which were in great demand because of the influx of new settlers. He employed a number of workers, mostly young single men who lived on the ranch in Colma, in addition to a number of draymen who distributed the farm produce throughout the booming city of San Francisco.

In later years, Daly opened a quarry in nearby hills, the first enterprise of its kind in San Mateo County.

His scanty education did not hold Daly back. With ease, he could accurately figure the acreage of land and the condition of soil, while professional men poured over calculations for hours on end to find the same answers. His daughter related, among other anecdotes of his generosity, how he never refused to lend a helping hand to those in need, and that he built a cabin on the farm, installed a cook stove, a bed, a table and chairs, so that the destitute would have a place to stay and cook themselves a meal. The wonder of it was that none of the nomads were ever known to have abused the privilege or took advantage of Daly's homespun hospitality.

Newly arrived Irish immigrants found ready employment with John Daly, and this fostered an Irish settlement on the sloping terrain in the area of what is today Daly City. The extant records of San Mateo County list the names of these early Irish farmhands and laborers: Michael O'Riley, John Brooks and his brother Patrick, James Casey, Michael Fahy, Dennis Murphy, and Patrick Flannery, to name just a few of the Celts.

The Irish felt quite at home in their new environment where they outnumbered all other nationalities. The average Irish home was the center of life in the manner of the 'old sod,' filled with mirth and the art of lively conversation. Every Irish gathering had its musicians, songsters, and *seanachai* (storytellers) who performed just for the joy of it. One exemplar comes to mind, Robert Thornton, an

Irish fiddler of note and a lifelong friend of to John Daly, was a fixture at most every *'Ceili'* dance.

In pioneer days the San Francisco Irish predominated in such areas as Southpark, Rincon Hill, Happy Valley (site of the Palace Hotel), and the Inner Mission, where they engaged in small-scale farming. Here, too, potatoes were the main crop along with cabbage, carrots, and onions, as it had for decades in their native land. A special variety of seed potatoes, said to be immune to the 'blight,' was imported from the State of Oregon and these proved very suitable to the San Francisco soil and climate. As the city grew and developed the Irish found more lucrative employment in other fields and farming fell to the lot of the next immigrant group, the Italians. The Italians were quite adept in both farming and gardening, and were still growing potatoes and vegetables in the Sunset and Westlake districts when this writer arrived in San Francisco in 1927.

For well over half a century, a narrow two-lane road leading over Daly Hill (as it was originally called) was the only way out of the city by road or railroad. When the late night Market Street Railway's 'Owl Car' left the depot at Fifth and Mission Streets on its last run to San Mateo, it stopped briefly at Daly City as the Conductor bellowed out "Top of the Hill, Daly City: All aboard for Lomita Park, San Bruno, Milbrae, Burlingame, and San Mateo!" Today, few, if any, of the thousands of motorists passing through Daly City, on their way to the Peninsula are aware of the immigrant Irish orphan who founded this up-and-coming city that bears his name.

Jeremiah Casey exemplifies the creative capabilities of Irish men and women in an open society that provides equal opportunity for all. Casey was born in Macroom, County Cork in November, 1848, the same year that gold was discovered in California. His parents were Patrick and Margie Buckley Casey. Patrick took part in the Irish rebellion of that same year, 1848, which ended in defeat. Undaunted by the setback, he returned home, attended to the farm, raised a lively family, and lived to the ripe old age of 93. Jeremiah worked with his dad on the family farm for a number of years until he decided to emigrate to America. At the age of 25, he set out for California to seek his fortune. Casey first went to Yolo County in the north, where he worked as a day laborer and farm hand during the summer and fall and for the Southern Pacific Railroad in the winter.

He saved his earnings and invested them in a saloon in the town of Port Costa on San Francisco Bay. In later years he built a hotel and bought a local brewery, which he operated successfully for several years. In 1890, Casey married Mary Boyle from his native County Cork, and she bore him four children: Mary, Patrick, Margaret and Jeremiah. The mother died young, leaving Jeremiah with the sole care of the young family. Despite the heavy burden, he found time to participate in local politics and in due time was appointed Justice of the Peace for Contra Costa County.

Casey's apparent lack of education instilled in him its central importance, and as time went on he became an ardent advocate of schooling. He pioneered the first school in Port Costa, and served as a member of its Board of Trustees. His many contributions became legend and resulted in his election to the Board of Supervisors of Contra Costa County, where he served until his death at the age of 76.

William Young

By coincidence, William Young, like Casey, was born in County Cork and made his way to California in 1879. As an apprenticed seaman Young miraculously survived a stormy voyage around Cape Horn on his way to San Francisco. His first job was as a deck hand on a ship that hauled grain up and down the West Coast from Port Costa terminal on San Francisco Bay. He too fell in love with the place and in time became superintendent of the Herriman & Mills Stevedore Company. He returned to Ireland in 1889 to fetch his sweetheart, Sarah Jacobs, a native of County Carlow. They were married shortly after his arrival in the bride's hometown of Carlow and returned together to California as man and wife. William was said to be one of the most ambitious young men to settle in Contra Costa County. He studied law and served as judge of Port Costa for a period of eight years. William and Sarah Young were the parents of five equally ambitious children.

John Nichol was one of the founding fathers of the city of Richmond, the hub of oil refining on San Francisco Bay. John was a native of County Antrim, born to Hugh and Mary Aiken Nicolin in 1822. At the age of twenty-seven he immigrated to New York City and worked as a day laborer. In 1853, he married Agnes Hodge, also a native of Ireland, who accompanied him to California in the following year. They took up residence in Alameda County, where John worked on a nearby farm. In 1857, they moved to Contra Costa County, and bought 200 acres of land which was a part of the San Pablo Rancho. Sometime later they purchased an additional 400 acres nearby. The Nichol's raised a family of nine children: John, Janetta, Marie, Ruth, Joseph, Agnes, Lulu, Hester, and Willie. John brought his mother from Ireland and she lived with the family until her death at the age of 90. Mr. Nichol initiated the building of the first school in Richmond and generously donated the timber grown on his land for its construction. He also purchased land in Oakland and erected a number of buildings called the Nichol Block. His holdings included 900 acres in San Buenaventura (Ventura County) in southern California. John Nichol's successful rise from rags to riches is typical of the many Irishmen who found health and wealth in abundance in the Golden Land of California.

Patrick Fleming

Irishman Patrick Fleming was born in Co. Kildare in 1831. After the death of his father, he accompanied his mother to America to settle in Boston for a brief period with relatives. Soon they journeyed on to California. They voyaged around the Horn to San Francisco, at the behest of an older married sister, the wife of Captain Bloomington. For unknown reasons, their stay in San Francisco was brief. They relocated across the Bay to Contra Costa County and built a home in an area then called Potrero Gap.

In later years, Patrick nostalgically and ruefully recalled that he could, in the early years, have acquired all of Point Richmond for the princely sum of $200. But then he foresaw little or no prospects in that rocky mound. He had thought it more prudent to put his savings in a tin can which he buried on the ranch, for safe keeping, only to have it rooted up out of the ground by his hogs.

Fleming married an Irish-born lass by the name of Bridget Brannon, a childhood sweetheart and neighbor from County Kildare. Miss Brannon accompanied the Flemings to Boston and remained there until Patrick earned enough money to pay her passage to California. They settled down to married life on the East Bay ranch where ten children were born to them. Patrick next brought his mother over from Ireland. The mother lived to an advanced age with the family on the farm, and she enjoyed many happy years surrounded by her brood of grandchildren.

In addition to providing for his large family, Mr. Fleming contributed generously to his church, civic, and charitable functions. When someone broached the idea of building a church in nearby San Pablo, Fleming advanced the first $20 to get the project started. When the church, named in honor of to St. Paul, was completed, Patrick became one of its most dedicated parishioners. The story goes that Mr. Fleming took up the collection every Sunday without fail for nigh on fifty years. Like his mother, he too lived to a ripe old age and worked every day on the farm until the weight of his years forced him to retire. Patrick Fleming was a legend in his time, an octogenarian who basked in the friendship and neighborliness of the old settlers and pioneers of Contra Costa County.

John O'Brien

Honest John O'Brien, jack-of-all-trades and master of many, was born in County Roscommon on January 6, 1822. At the age of 14, he emigrated with his parents to New York City. In 1843, his family settled on the western frontier in the state of Missouri, where John at the age of twenty-one engaged in farming for five years. In the Gold Rush year of 1849, O'Brien joined a band of thirty equally ambitious souls and set out across the prairies in a train of ten wagons California-bound. The party arrived without mishap in Sacramento on July 20th of that same year. John sold his horses and wagons and headed off for the gold fields, but instead of mining he purchased farm land for the purpose of stock raising, and he thus became a successful cattle jobber in the Irish fashion. He made the rounds, stopping at other ranches where he bargained for livestock, as was the custom in Ireland, and resold them at a profit.

O'Brien often visited the Hudspeth Ranch, one of the largest in Sonoma County, since it was there he did most of his livestock buying. Neighbors recalled seeing him at the break of dawn on the road driving a herd of cattle bound for Sacramento where he was assured of a ready market. On occasion he prospected for gold at the Trinity mines and others along the Klamath River in the summer months. When the snow fell in the high mountains, he returned to Sacramento to enjoy a brief rest and conjure up the next adventure.

In later years, he removed to Santa Clara County where he also engaged in farming and stock raising. This latest venture, however successful it proved to be, was but another charmed step on life's road in the challenging career of John O'Brien.

"Nothing ventured, nothing gained" was O'Brien's motto. His next project was in the art of brick-making. Undaunted by his complete lack of knowledge in the art, he opened a brick factory in San Jose and offered top quality bricks at $50 a thousand. Talk of the "luck of the Irish"! Who came along to the rescue but Money Bags himself, James Lick, the proprietor of the fabulous Lick House and Gardens in San Francisco. Among Lick's many undertaking's was the construction of famous Lick Observatory on Mount Hamilton (1888), which still bears his name. O'Brien, struck up a hard bargain and sold the brick factory, lock, stock, and barrel, to Mr. Lick for $50,000, almost double its original cost.

John O'Brien, the versatile farmer, trader, and brick maker, etc.

O'Brien was on the road again, this time back to his old haunts in Missouri, where he had farmed years earlier and where livestock was more plentiful and cheaper. While there, he purchased herds of cattle, hired local farm hands, and drove them all the way to California.

After he had acquired considerable acreage in Contra Costa County in the area of the present city of Antioch, he took up farming and stock raising on an even larger scale. On July 29, 1861, John married Mary Howard, who bore him two children, Philip and Carrie. This Irishman was always congenial in manner and firm, but honest, in his dealings. It was said that no man did more to foster the interests of Contra Costa County than honest John O'Brien.

Success of the San Francisco Irish

The general assumption that most of the Irish immigrants of the mid-19th century (the famine immigrants) ended up in the ghettos of America's eastern cities proved inconclusive. In fact, San Francisco's openheartedness paved the way for one of the most successful and prosperous Irish communities in America. The free flow of Irish immigration went unhampered by any official restriction (unlike the regrettable cases of New York, Boston, and Philadelphia), and it grew at a phenomenal rate. As one Irishman exclamed, arriving by ship in San Francisco was a pleasure to be cherished.

By 1870, San Francisco's population approached 100,000, of which the Irish comprised not less than one-third. And the Irish were the first national group to boast of a banking institution all their own, when the Hibernia Savings and Loan opened in 1859. Within ten years, the bank's deposits reached the $10 million mark. The bank encouraged Irish home ownership by providing its clients with loans well below the going rate. (A.P. Giannini, founding father of the Bank of Italy which became known as the Bank of America, followed suit half-a-century later by catering to newly-settled Italian immigrants.) As a result, one Irishman in every three living in San Francisco owned real estate by the year 1870, a prosperous record unmatched anywhere in America. Even more significant, the Hibernia Bank made it possible for the more ambitious to engage in business and industry on a grand scale. The *San Francisco Directory* listings of that period bear witness to Irish participation in business and industry. In 1875, the Irish burghers included:

- Dry goods: J.J. O'Brien & Co. (largest on the Pacific coast), Murphy Grant & Co., McCain & McClure, Keane & Connor, Kennedy & Brennan, Kavanaugh & Co.
- Wholesale grocers: O'Connor Bros., O'Brien & Tierney, Callinan & Co., McMullen & Co., and Foley & Jones.
- Wholesale butchers: Dunphy & Co., Donnelly & Dunne, Kelley & Dooley, Regan & O'Neill.
- Wholesale druggists: McBoyle & Co., McDonnell & Co.

Hibernian Brewery's smokestack dominated San Francisco's landscape, with hundreds of Irish saloons and barkeeps to dispense the foaming brew. (2000 'liquor establishments' existed in 1878.)

- Stonecutters and marble works: Lucas & Co., Donohue & Brennan, Hanna & Co., P.D. Mullaney.
- Carriage-makers: Tierney & Sons, O'Brien & Sons, P.W. Cummins.
- Blacksmiths: Jim Doran, John Grace, James McCarthy, John Casey, Dick Healy, Tim Ford, Joe Farrell, Martin O'Dea, Nick Morrissey McDevitt Bros.
- Bookstores: Michael Flood, John O'Connor, Mrs. Ryan, Sweeney, Geraghty, Dwyer, McArdle.
- Physicians: P.M. O'Brien, Callaghan, Blake, McCarthy, O'Neill, Gibbins, Sullivan.
- Tailors: Thomas O'Dowd, O'Connor & Kelleher.
- The Irish undertakers, as always had the final say: J.C. O'Connor & Co., McGinn, McAvoy & Co., and Carew & English. For an additional fee, they would include a pouch of clay shipped direct from the old

sod so that the departed could rest for
evermore in Irish soil.

* * * *

This is but the briefest summary of the Irish experience and their monumental contribution to California, their adopted state. Men and women, the fairest and best, found opportunity, contentment, and security in a land specially blessed by the hand of the Creator. No wonder so many Irish-Americans in California could echo the words of this delightful old poem:

Of old she called with her lips of song
 She called with her breath of musk
From peaks where the sunlight lingers long
 From the vales in the purple dusk.
With cheeks of olive and eyes of night
 They laughed in her glad caress
And she gave them her land of living light
 For their wandering feet to press.
Yet oft in the light of the mellow moon
 From the jaspered heavens hung
Mid the tinkle of soft Castilian tunes
 And the bells of the mission rung.
Again she called and from far away
 Over desert and mountain keep
In the lands where the windswept prairies lay
 In the ice-clashed torrents sleep.
They came, and she dowered them with spendthrift hands
 The hopes of their wildest dreams
And she flung at their feet the golden sands
 That slept in her shining streams—
Saxon and Teuton and Celt that trod
 The path of her treasured springs
With shown of silver their feet she shod
 And clothed them in the robes of kings.
And so from her heart's unwearied love
 Rings her voice with its olden thrill
From the seas below and the skies above
 She is calling—calling still.

Since time immemorial, the Irish had dreamed along with Oisin of the Promised Land, a magical *Tir-na-nog* at the end of the rainbow.

Strangers in a strange land, the Irish achieved a success story in California that is unparalleled by Irish exiles in any other land. Their bones now lie far away from the hallowed tombs of Old Ireland. Yet the "New Ireland" of California everywhere bears evidence to posterity of their enduring accomplishments. Here, their footprints have left many tracks of the genius and tradition of this noble race. Their veneration for the Old Sod, from which many were unwilling exiles, shall endure and do them honor in the Golden Land.

Colonel Stephen W. Kearny wrested California for the United States in 1846 during the bloody Battle of San Pasqual, part of the Mexican-American War. [Courtesy of the California State Library.]

3

Founders of a State: Irish Architects of the California Constitution

They came, the founders of a state,
The men with spirit brave and free,
Who matched the magic word of fate
And shaped their own high destiny.

The Irish in Spanish California

Although California was discovered by Cabrillo in 1542, two centuries elapsed before the Spanish conquistadors mobilized their energies to colonize the new territory. During this Spanish colonial era, it was stalwart men of the Irish race in the service of Spain who helped take possession of California and save it from foreign intrusion. The historical question is: who were these Irish pioneers and why were they destined to play such a pivotal role on this western fringe of the New World?

The background for this Irish involvement was the British wars of conquest, the broken Treaty of Limerick (1691), and the exodus of the cream of Irish youth to (some 11,000 families) to Europe, Whole Irish regiments of Sarsfield's Army, dubbed in the histories as "the Flight of the Wild Geese," became expatriate exiles in Europe.

The Irishman John Mitchel, the indomitable Fenian rebel, noted: "Most of the choicest intellect and energy of the Irish race were now to be looked for at the courts of Versailles, Madrid, and Vienna." For many generations henceforward, Irish soldiers of rank and nobility fought under the standard of Spain. Once chiefs in their own land, they became the equals of the proudest nobles of Castile. The hybrid Irish-Spanish names that crop up in the Spanish archives (for example, "*O'Donaju*" for O'Donahue) amusingly tell a tale of Irish influence. Among these Hispanic Irish were Commandante O'Donnell (Henry John O'Donnell), who left Ireland following the Battle of the Boyne in 1690, then joined the Army of Spain, and eventually rose through the ranks to become Field Marshal. No new expeditions by land or sea to explore the new territory of California were resumed until the year 1769. Until then, California was viewed by the Spanish authorities as little more than a romantic name in a far-off land. Now, suddenly, Spain awoke to the strategic reality of the legendary island paradise by the sunset shores.

However, it remained for Count De Lacy, the Spanish ambassador to Russia at St. Petersburg, to engineer a serious movement to secure and populate *Alta California*. De Lacy, it was, who kept the King advised of Russia's rival preparations to colonize America's West coast. The Spanish expedition of 1769 came about—as reported in the old annals of Spain and in the Republic of Mexico—in large measure because of Count De Lacy's diplomatic warnings to the Spanish court.

Generalissimo Alesandro O'Reilly (an Irishman born in Dublin in 1725) was the leading military expert in Spain at the time, and he wielded enough power to put teeth into Spain's colonization effort. O'Reilly, it should be noted, was a trusted friend of the then Spanish Viceroy, Bucareli. For a number of years, Bucareli, and O'Reilly kept in constant communication about the affairs of New Spain, as California was then called. Much of their correspondence focused on monitoring the Russian inroads in California. O'Reilly was given the nod to become the Viceroy of New Spain, with the full confidence of Bucareli, who was about to retire. Fate, however, intervened when the Spanish army suffered a crushing defeat by

Moroccan forces. O'Reilly's military reputation ebbed as a result, and he lost his opportunity to become Viceroy. Yet O'Reilly's influence was such that when he urged De Anza's promotion, De Anza was advanced to Lieutenant Colonel and led the momentous Juan Baptista De Anza expedition overland to California in 1775.

During this same period, Irish legions in the service of Spain were conspicuous for their loyalty and bravery. These Irish legionnaires included outstanding leaders such as General Hugo O'Connor, who was assigned to Mexico and given exclusive jurisdiction over its Presidio. O'Connor's forces ranged over a far-reaching territory and helped to advance the western frontier and raise the standard of Spain. In recognition of his accomplishments, O'Connor was made Viceroy of a vast inland region of central México.

Another outstanding Irish leader on the Spanish stage was Lieutenant General Juan O'Donoju (O'Donahue), who served for a period as Minister of War. O'Donoju was an outstanding proponent of Spanish authority, which he helped establish on the western frontier. His ambition resulted in his appointment as a Regent of the Mexican state. During this period, there were over 60 Viceroys of old Spain, and Juan O'Donoju had the distinction of being the last. In 1821, the expatriate Irishman was finally laid to rest in the Cathedral of Mexico City with full military honors.

This survey is the briefest sample of the many men of Gaelic and Norman-Irish birthright, eminent figures among the Castilians, who participated in the epic adventure of taking possession of California for Spain. Carrying this little-known story one step farther, it was the unconscious wish and destiny of the Irish-Spaniards to help keep California out of the hands of other Europeans. Their efforts allowed California later to be readily assimilated intact as an integral part of the United States.

The Irish and the Making of American California

Another Celtic vanguard, led by Stephen Kearny, General Bennet Riley, Philip A. Roach, William Shannon, and John Ross Browne, were Argonauts and trekkers who set the cornerstone of American authority in the new state. These Irishmen were men of character, ability, and experience, who made their entrance on the California scene in its hour of destiny. Their every act had a profound impact on the State's formative years and laid the foundation stone that paved the way during California's rapid ascent to greatness.

The military and political intrigues that transformed California from a Mexican possession to an American state, though complex, involved three major steps. The first and instigating event was the colorful and romantic "Bear Flag Revolt" of 1846. In that year American settlers fomented an armed uprising and sought to make California a territory independent of Mexico and part of the Union. The second major step towards an American California was the aftermath of the Mexican War of 1846-48. According to the terms of the Treaty of Guadalupe Hidalgo, California formally became an American territory for a purchase price of $15,000,000. Originally, this Territory also included Arizona, New Mexico, Nevada, and Utah. The climactic step which brought California into the Union was part of the rambunctious Gold Rush era. In 1850, the mineral riches of California won it statehood, and thereby united a diverse population of Spanish, Mexican, American, and other immigrant peoples, most notably the Irish.

Stephen Kearny

One notable son of Irish ancestry who played a remarkable role in securing California for the United States was Stephen Watts Kearny (1794-1848). Kearny was a career soldier and military leader, strong of will and as courageous in battle as his ancestors, who rose through the U.S. Army's ranks to become a Major General. The Kearnys (the name was originally *O'Catharnaigh,* sometimes pronounced O'Carney) were centered in the plains of Meath, a royal province of ancient Ireland. The Kearnys' valor is manifest in their coat of arms, which displays three charging lions to the fore and a dagger held at the ready in a gauntleted hand.

By the power vested in him by the United States government, Kearny secured the newly-acquired territory (that included California) and established civil government in accordance with the U.S. Constitution. In 1846, his command, the Army of the West, was headquartered by the Missouri River. From there his troops marched the enormous distances through the continental heartland to the Pacific, a feat that almost eclipsed Sherman's march through Georgia during the Civil War. Kearny and his men braved the parched New Mexico desert and arrived at the old colonial capital of Santa Fe, where Kearny raised the Stars and Stripes and laid the groundwork for civil rule.

Continuing on to San Pasqual in California, Kearny's American troops faced strong Mexican resistance. In a fierce battle (Dec. 6, 1846), Kearny lost 21 men since his small force was far outnumbered. Afterwards, his troops fought at San Gabriel (Jan. 8, 1847), where the Mexican garrison was strongly fortified. With the timely arrival of a detachment of Marines stationed nearby, the Americans routed the Mexicans, who fled into the hills. From San Gabriel, General Kearny and his men marched on to the administrative center of Monterey, where he assumed the role of Military Governor of California, the first under American rule. For several months, Kearny continued to serve in this capacity until he securely established American authority. Then, with his primary objective now completed, Kearny handed the gavel of authority over to yet another Irishman, General Bennet Riley. One of San Francisco's oldest thoroughfares, Kearny Street, perpetuates Stephen Kearny's memory.

Bennet Riley

Kearny's successor, General Bennet Riley (1787-1853) assumed responsibility in his dual capacity of military and civilian Governor of California from April 12, 1849 to December 20, 1849. He, too, was at first well-received by the people, and was particularly appreciated for his honesty and strict adherence to military duty. However, in civilian matters Riley met with opposition when he was confronted with the task of setting up a civil government to satisfy the needs of people of diverse backgrounds. Seasoned Californians wished to establish a separate nation; colonial-minded Yankees, desired to be annexed to the new American Republic; for their part, the Spanish and Mexican *Californios* seemed content with any government, so long as they could revert to the pastoral tranquility which they had long enjoyed before the arrival of the *gringos*.

Riley, the soldier-Governor, issued a proclamation calling a convention to draft a Constitution in order to meet the diverse needs of the new state. On October 13, 1849, the delegates assembled in the historic Colton Hall in Monterey, the old Spanish colonial capital of *Alta California*. It was a romantically picturesque gathering of representative men, colorful Spanish dons and gaily attired westerners, sun-browned miners, and bearded *rancheros*, doctors, merchants, and bankers, all in their prime of life. The convention boasted men who would stand out in any gathering. Assembled there were: the affable General Mario S. Vallejo, said to be the most handsome man of the period; the patriarch of the Mother Lode, Captain John Augustus Sutter; Thomas O. Larkin, American Consul and a native of historic Charlestown, Massachusetts; Commandante P.N. de la Guerra Santa Barbara; and the youthful but shrewd *abagado* (lawyer) from County Mayo, William Shannon.

The convention hall measured 65 feet long by 25 feet wide. A railing across the middle separated 48 delegates from the spectators. Two American flags and a portrait of George Washington served as the principal adornments. Belying the rough-and-ready period, the proceedings were conducted in a very dignified manner, with strict observance of parliamentary procedure.

General Bennet Riley, U.S. military and civilian Governor of California.
[Courtesy of the California State Library.]

Philip A. Roach

An added problem for California's first Constitutional Convention was the formidable language barrier in communicating between English-speaking and Spanish-speaking populations. However, fortune came to General Riley's assistance in the person of a skilled Irish linguist named Philip Augustine Roach, who had been born in Fermoy, County Cork, in 1820. Roach had immigrated to New York with his parents, and eventually arrived at Monterey in the Gold Rush month of July, 1849. He was already a seasoned diplomat and a gifted orator, fluent in the Spanish tongue. Roach had previously served as American Vice Consul in Le Havre, France and as Consul General in Lisbon, Portugal. In Monterey, Roach realized the urgency of Governor Riley's difficulty and offered his services forthwith as mediator.

When California's Constitutional Convention was called to order, Captain Robert Semple, the impresario from 'Old Kentuck' and a leader in both reputation and stature (he stood over seven feet tall!) was elected chairman. Captain William Marcy became secretary, and William Shannon was named chairman of the Rules Committee. By sheer coincidence, at this same time, though miles apart, some of the nation's most brilliant orators and legislators, including Henry Clay, John C. Calhoun, and Daniel Webster confronted each other in Congress debating the issue of slavery. America was then equally balanced between fifteen free and fifteen slave states; therefore, all American eyes were turned toward California, whose decision on slavery could tip the nation's balance, either way!

In this watershed moment of our nation's history, the California Constitutional Assembly was fortunate in having in its midst the youthful and brilliant diplomat, Philip A. Roach. When the original draft of the California Constitution was drawn up, the President of the Assembly called on Roach to present it to the delegates. He addressed the gathering in both English and Spanish, explaining in careful, deliberate detail every proposal outlined therein. His elucidation of the proposed document, drafted in harmony with the basic laws of the United States concerning personal and property rights, was so convincing that it was approved almost unanimously.

Though not a delegate, Roach proved to be one of the most influential participants in this historic deliberation. He made such an impression on the delegates and the local residents that they offered him any office within their jurisdiction, but Roach declined. Ignoring his reluctance, they elected him *Alcalde* (Mayor) of the old colonial Capital, which he graciously accepted upon his return from a trip to San Francisco.

Upon ratification of the Constitution (Nov. 13, 1849), Governor Riley resigned, and pious Peter Burnett became the first Governor of California under American rule. Monterey, the old colonial Spanish-Mexican stronghold, became an American city. Philip Roach now had the dual honor of being Monterey's last Alcalde as well as its first Mayor under American rule. In 1851, Roach was elected to represent the counties of Monterey and Santa Cruz in the California State Senate. The following year, he showed his devotion to equal rights by introducing a bill that would enable married women to conduct business on their own, as if they remained single. The bill passed both houses of the legislature and became law in 1852.

Adding to Roach's *cursus honorum,* President Pierce appointed him to the post of United States Appraiser for the district of San Francisco, in which position he served from 1853 to 1861. In 1857, Roach became Director of the Society of California Pioneers, and became its President in 1861. He carried out his final civic duties as Public Administrator of San Francisco, a position he held from 1883 until he retired from public life in 1887.

It seems incredible that so little has been written about a man like Roach who stood out among his contemporaries and gave of himself magnanimously to his State, especially in its formative years. To compensate for this oversight among the historians, we will draw a more comprehensive portrait of Roach's life and labors in a later chapter.

William Shannon

When the California Constitutional Convention was called to order in 1849, some 48 delegates represented the various districts throughout the state. In their midst was a young Irishman named William Shannon, newly elected mayor of Coloma, the miners' delegate. At age 27, he was perhaps the youngest representative in attendance, yet he also proved to be one of the most influential and informative.

Shannon was born in the west of Ireland, in Ballina, County Mayo, to Robert and Anne Kerr Shannon in the year 1821. The family immigrated to America and settled in the town of Bath in New York State, near the Pennsylvania border. Proving himself a brilliant student, Shannon was admitted to the New York State bar at the age of 24. At the outbreak of the Mexican War in 1846, he volunteered for duty with an American regiment commanded by Colonel Stevenson. Upon completing his basic training, Shannon was appointed Captain of Company 1 and assigned to duty in California.

Patriotism was a noble virtue in that era, and Capt. Shannon's legion was given a rousing sendoff. Company 1 sailed aboard the brig *Susan Drew* round the Horn in October 1846, and arrived in San Francisco five months later. The regiment was soon transferred to Monterey and briefly billeted in the old Presidio. They named their headquarters Camp Kearny in honor of General Kearny. While in Monterey, they assisted Walter Colton, the Navy Chaplain (for whom historic Colton Hall was named) to build a schoolhouse which remained in continuous use for nearly half-a-century.

Ballina, Co. Mayo, the birthplace of William Shannon

Under the young Captain Shannon's command, Company 1 was assigned to duty in San Diego. The regiment traveled by ship to the port of San Pedro and marched the rest of the way overland to their destination. During the company's stay in San Diego, Shannon was appointed Collector of the Port, in addition to his military duties. When hostilities between Mexico and the U.S. ceased in the fall of 1848, Shannon's company was mustered out. Since the Army in those days made no provision for return transportation, every man was on his own!

Shannon in the Gold Country

A born adventurer, Shannon foresaw the unlimited possibilities in trade and merchandising made possible by the onrushing hordes of gold-crazed prospectors converging on California's mining country. In preparation for this golden opportunity, Shannon purchased the best horses and wagons, engaged a number of his former soldiers and dispatched them forthwith to Coloma, the hub of the mining country, to await his arrival. In the meantime, Shannon and his former company commander, a fellow Irishman named Lieutenant McGee, set out on separate mission to Monterey.

At the Port of Monterey, Shannon rented a seaworthy schooner, loaded it with provisions, and set out for Coloma to join his caravan. To minimize the cost of transportation, a number of paying passengers were assigned berths on the ship.

On his arrival in the bustling mining center, Shannon joined in partnership with a man named Charles Cady and together they established a supply center and trading post. This trading venture proved to be even more lucrative than digging for gold in the hills. Within a brief period the partners accumulated a substantial bankroll which was put to good use in the interest of the developing community.

In 1849, William Shannon, erstwhile army captain, was elected to the honorable position as *Alcalde* (Mayor) of Coloma.

It is a matter of history that the dynamic young Irishman organized the first patriotic observance of American Independence in the Mother Lode country on July 4, 1849. A stately pine tree was selected in the nearby forest, felled, and set up in the town center. At sunrise on that memorable day, the stars and stripes were hoisted and the celebration began. As soon as the word spread, people from miles around set aside their cares and converged upon the brash *pueblo*. In the manner of Irish hospitality and homespun generosity, the youthful leader provided vituals and drink for all at his expense. That first rip-roaring celebration of Independence Day in Coloma, California was a topic of conversation for days and weeks on end and lingered long in the hearts and minds and in the abodes of the old pioneers. Such celebrations have made the name of California synonymous with adventure.

A Delegate to the State Convention

The merchants and miners of Coloma unanimously chose Mayor Shannon to represent them at the upcoming Constitutional Convention in Monterey. Shannon proved a most worthy choice. With the officers elected, the most important item on the agenda was the election of the decisive Rules Committee, the guardian of parliamentary procedure. Various names were proposed, and the Committee was elected by popular choice. The Committee in turn elected its chairman, his Honor, William Shannon, Mayor of Coloma. The Irishman was a heroic figure, endowed with the energy and the candor of youth. Shannon stood out conspicuously from his more elderly peers, and he was always a power to be reckoned with whenever the inherent rights of freemen were challenged.

As mentioned above, during this critical pre-Civil War era, the question of slavery was the most controversial issue facing a nation composed of fifteen free states and an equal number of slave states. California's constitutional decision could tip the scales either way. Shannon was wholeheartedly committed to California's joining the Union as a free state. However, his proslavery opposition was equally determined.

During the protracted slavery debates, which grew heated and rancorous, Shannon bided his time until all others, pro and con, had their say. He then dramatically strode forward and, like a latter-day Patrick Henry, submitted his antislavery resolution, "Neither slavery nor involuntary servitude, unless for the punishment of crime, shall ever be tolerated in this State."

The slavery advocates were stunned. Shannon's timely presentation of the antislavery resolution and its forceful content offered little opportunity for rebuttal. The secretary called for a vote on the resolution, and it was adopted by a sizable majority.

Shannon's wishes to refrain from any further political involvement and seek a more relaxed lifestyle were dismissed. Despite his every objection, his name was put forward in the State election of 1850, and Shannon was returned to office by an overwhelming majority of votes. Tragically, Shannon was stricken with cholera during the epidemic and passed away before the opening session. His death at the age of 28 saddened the hearts of the Mother Lode communities. Their youthful mentor was gone, and no one of equal caliber to take his place. Casting aside fear of the raging pestilence, Shannon's many long-standing admirers and new-found friends turned out en masse to bid their idol farewell. Governor John Bigler rode at the head of the funeral procession.

Despite his premature death, Shannon set a record of achievement as a lawyer, army captain, collector of customs, merchant, mayor, and architect of the California Constitution, that was unmatched by others who reached more advanced years.

Shannon's words during the inauguration of the California State Constitution in 1849, spoken some fourteen years before Lincoln's Gettysburg address—"Neither slavery nor involuntary servitude, unless for the punishment of crime, shall ever be permitted in this State"—stand as a memorial to his sense of justice and an inspiration of the oppressed in every land.

One of Shannon's army comrades penned this final epitaph on the hillside grave: "Peace to the ashes of the noble and generous Captain. Green the turf that covers his breast."

John Ross Browne, the Convention Reporter

John Ross Browne (1821-1875) was born in a section of old Dublin called "Beggar's Bush." His father, Thomas Browne, was Editor of the Dublin *Comet* during this precarious period in Irish history. The Irish Parliament had been abruptly dissolved, leaving the destitute natives at the mercy of their unfeeling English adversaries. Among other things the British parliament imposed a tax upon the Gaelic Irish of ten percent to support an alien clergy and religious belief. In his brilliant journal, the elder Browne lambasted this outrageous act imposed on a helpless peoples. As a result of his outspoken criticism, Mr. Browne was apprehended, fined, and thrown into prison. Upon his release, all of his holdings were confiscated, and in desperation he gathered together his young family. They were not heard from again until they surfaced in America. John, our subject, was only 11 years old when the Browne family first settled in Louisville, Kentucky. A brilliant student, John completed his formal education in that city and found immediate employment as a roving reporter for a Louisville newspaper.

From Louisville Browne removed to Washington, the political pulse of the nation. With his keen political savvy, he found ready acceptance in the Capital's social circles, which in turn led to his appointment as a Senate reporter. His access to the leading political power brokers was enhanced by his marriage to the Lucy Mitchell, the charming daughter of a prominent Washington physician. Shortly thereafter, he was appointed secretary to Robert Walker, Secretary of the Treasury, a position he held until 1848.

John Ross Browne, Irish-born reporter at the first California State Convention. [Courtesy of the California State Library.]

Browne's influence in the Capital, and the onset of the Gold Rush in California, won him an appointment as Revenue Agent on the Pacific Coast. He sailed through the Golden Gate in 1849, and soon thereafter was appointed Postal Inspector for the San Francisco district, with jurisdiction all the way to Monterey. By an amazing coincidence, he arrived in the latter city not long after General Riley's appointment as Military Governor. Riley already had set in motion plans for the State Constitutional Convention and, on learning of Browne's background, appointed him Reporter when the assembly convened.

Dr. Robert Semple, the President-elect of the Convention, appointed Captain William Marcy, an officer in Stevenson's regiment, as Secretary. Captain Marcy may have thought of his appointment as just an honorary sinecure, for he made no attempt to record the proceedings, but merely relaxed and enjoyed the debates without taking an active role. If it had not been for the Dubliner, John Ross Browne, the story of California's beginnings under American rule would have passed unrecorded and thus denied to posterity.

Written in both English and Spanish, Browne's reports of the Convention were entitled "Records of Debates of the Constitutional Convention" and bore the signature of J. Ross Browne. For his work he was paid $10,000, a considerable sum in those days. A leading jurist of the period acknowledged him with this tribute: "The State of California is indebted to J. Ross Browne for such a valuable report of the proceedings." A later work of Browne's, *Muleback to the Convention*, reflects the colorful pioneering atmosphere of this historic assembly.

Following the Convention, Browne completed his assignment as Postal Inspector and returned to Washington. He was granted a belated vacation and set out on a tour of Europe with his wife and family. Upon his return to the Capital, he was appointed Ambassador to China by President Johnson. The assignment proved not to his liking. He resigned and returned to his beloved California. He retired to a life of writing in the East Bay hills where he built a home overlooking San Francisco Bay and the Golden Gate.

Browne's literary work covered a broad spectrum of people and places: *Confessions of a Quack* reflected his apathy as a medical student; and *Apache Country, The Land of Thor, Adventures in California and Washoe,* and *Yusef* were all tales of his many wanderings. He contributed articles to *Harper's* and other national publications. His temperament was restless and romantic, but he could skillfully interweave somber narrative with disarming humor.

In his day, Browne ranked with writers Bret Harte and Mark Twain. He often sketched a truer picture of California life than any of his contemporaries. However, like so many other Irish, Browne's merits went until historian Richard Dillon acknowledged Browne's contributions as an author, diplomat, and pioneer Californian.

The foregoing are but a few of those early Irish pioneers, noble sons of the Gael, who arrived in California when it was a little more than a sparsely populated wilderness. These Irish Americans resembled the Irish monks of another era who trekked to Europe in time to stem the advance of the Dark Ages. Our latter-day courageous Irish Oisins arrived in California in her moments of travail and helped her blaze a secure path for future greatness.

Colton Hall, where the California Constitutional Convention met in 1849. [Courtesy of the Monterey Historical Society.]

John Gately Downey, Civil War Governor of California and the founder of Downey City. [Courtesy of Elena Quinn and City of Downey.]

4

John Gately Downey: Irish-Born Governor Of California

John Downey's life (1827-1894) was the epitome of Irish super-achievers in early California. Downey arrived on the scene in 1849, a barefoot lad with ten dollars in his pocket, barely enough to pay his coach fare to the gold mines. He overcame this wretched beginning; he persevered and rose to become Governor of the Golden State (1860-1862) at the youthful age of 32, a record as yet unbroken.

Although a Democrat Civil War Governor, Downey judiciously supported Abraham Lincoln (a Republican). He maintained California's allegiance to the Union in the face of hostility from secessionists and Confederate sympathizers. Out of office, Downey pioneered the first massive land development in early California, the forerunner of the more touted contemporary projects for which California is world-famous. In partnership with a McFarland, Downey opened the first pharmacy in Los Angeles. His pathbreaking efforts also helped to establish the banking system in Southern California. Downey foresaw the unlimited possibilities of developing Los Angeles when it was little more than a mud-walled

Mexican *pueblo*. The Downey block in the heart of this bustling metropolis stands as a living memorial to the penniless immigrant from old Erin. As proof of his many and varied contributions, Downey's name heads the list of California entrepreneurs in *The Chronicle of the Kings*, edited by archivist H.H. Bancroft.

What were Downey's main achievements? During the Civil War, Governor Downey guided the State when many states were seceding from the Union. His leadership in the strategic office of Governor helped change California's and the nation's history. Although a Democrat, he loyally sided with Abraham Lincoln and the Union. In addition, Downey vetoed a scheme to deprive the City of San Francisco the full use of its magnificent harbor. During his administration, he also had designed and laid out the foundation for the California State Capitol. In public life, Downey demonstrated honesty, integrity, and the courage of his convictions by upholding the law of the land. In private life, he was equally renowned for kindness and generosity.

Birthplace of John Downey at Castlesampson, Co. Roscommon. [Courtesy of Margaret O'Keeffe Umanzio.]

Chapter 4: *John Gately Downey*

Governor Downey and his wife were the youngest couple to grace the Sacramento Executive Mansion. Downey was only 32 at the time of his inauguration, and his wife, Maria Guirado Downey, became first lady at the tender age of 21. In addition, Downey is distinguished as being the seventh Governor of California and the first of foreign birth. His career spanned a period of some 40 years from his arrival in the State at the age of 22. He began work in California as a miner, became a successful merchant, land developer, banker, builder, city founder, philanthropist, and ultimately chief executive of his adopted State.

John Gately Downey was born in Ireland in the townland of Castlesampson, County Roscommon, on June 24, 1827. He was the son of Denis and Bridget Gately Downey. His birthplace, Roscommon (*Ros Coman,* the wood of Coman), was so named in honor of Bishop Coman, the saintly Abbot of Clonmacnoise, one of Ireland's most hallowed shrines, founded by Saint Kieran in the year 545 A.D. The Downey family's Irish homestead was built with stones retrieved from an old Norman castle in his grandfather's time, which may have accounted for the name of *Castle*-sampson itself. The locality is comprised of small farms which have become somewhat less productive over the years through soil depletion and over-cultivation. Hard times, emigration, and flight from the land have severely dwindled the native population.

Castlesampson lies west of the River Shannon, about six miles northwest of the town of Athlone, renowned as the birthplace of the beloved Irish songster, John McCormack. This picturesque territory gave birth to other Irish patriots, scholars, and artists. These have included the immortal Percy French, whose songs, "The Mountains of Mourne" and "Come Back Paddy Riley to Ballyjamesduff" are as popular today as when they were first composed. Other celebrated natives have included Douglas Hyde, founder of the Gaelic League and first President of the Irish Republic, and the popular Hollywood actress of yesteryear, Maureen O'Sullivan.

When interviewed in later years, Downey hinted at the hardships of life in the Irish countryside in those earlier times: "I did all kinds of work as a boy, and that experience made me satisfied at all times and with whatever I got to eat, and wherever I went." His hard circumstances were typical of a time when many a laborer worked from dawn to dusk, year in and year out, merely for his bed and keep, with an occasional bonus of a suit of clothes and a pair of hobnailed boots.

When Downey immigrated to America, he first settled in Maryland, where he lived with two half-sisters and attended a Latin school. In true Irish family tradition, the two young ladies induced John to come to America and make his home with them. Being well established as the proprietors of Saint Mary's Female Institute in Maryland, the sisters valued a good education. Accordingly, they enrolled John in the prestigious Latin school nearby. Since those simple days did not require a college education to work in a licensed pharmacy, a youth could quickly enter the profession. Through diligent study, hard work, and dedication, John became a full-fledged journeyman pharmacist within three years.

He realized that Washington, D.C., the heart of the nation, provided the best opportunity, so he took leave of his affectionate hosts and set out alone for the Capital. He found immediate employment in Washington at a local pharmacy, where he rigorously worked to become a qualified pharmacist. From Washington, Downey moved on to Vicksburg, Mississippi, to take up a position as journeyman pharmacist in a drug and stationery store. The following year he entered into partnership with a man name John Darling in Cincinnati, where he remained until 1849, when he set out for California during the frenzy of the Gold Rush.

California Bound

Downey planned his route to California differently from most others: by way of New Orleans, Louisiana, across the Gulf of Mexico to the Isthmus of Panama, and from there to California by ship. The delay his party encountered in crossing the Isthmus prevented him from making connections at the western end as planned. As a result, he was compelled to spend several weeks in Panama waiting for a ship to take him north to San Francisco. The trip consumed 87 days from the time of his departure in Cincinnati until the old four-masted brig arrived in the bay city. On arriving in California, Downey immediately set out for the mines with only ten dollars in his pocket. To pay his fare to Grass Valley, he was forced to sell his only valued possession, a gold watch. From there, he hiked all the way to the diggings and took up prospecting in high spirits. To his dismay, however, Downey soon discovered that gold was not so easy to come by as he had been led to believe. His frustration in his efforts to locate a productive vein in the diggings forced him to return to Sacramento. In dire straits, he sought work on the docks in order to pay his return fare to San Francisco.

Other less ambitious youths might have been discouraged, but not John Downey. The hardships of his youth and the desire to make it on his own had toughened him. A story in one of the San Francisco newspapers caught Downey's attention. The article contained a brief description of a consignment of drugs and related items from New York, sitting on the open dock at San Pedro, awaiting a buyer. Without a moment's hesitation, John set out for Los Angeles, a distance of over four hundred miles, no mean adventure in the time of the horse-and-wagon. Lacking the necessary funds he sought out a partner to share in the purchase. By a stroke of luck he encountered a man named McFarland, a well-heeled prospector, who had just arrived from Tennessee. McFarland, no slouch himself, who knew a good thing when he saw it, joined in partnership with Downey and together they purchased the complete shipment at a fraction of its cost. With the proceeds from the waterfront purchase, and the contents of an old trunk stuffed with pharmaceutical products that Downey had acquired during his sojourn in Washington, Vicksburg, and Cincinnati, they opened a pharmacy, the first ever in the city of Los Angeles. Their shop was the only source of medical supplies between San Diego in the southland and the booming city of San Francisco.

In pioneer days, when medicines were for the most part purveyed by prescription only, operating a pharmacy was quite a chore So-called over-the-counter drugs had not become a way of life yet. The two pioneer pharmacists came to be highly esteemed in southern California, and particularly in Los Angeles, the names Doctors Downey and McFarland became household words. It's of little wonder, that the firm, devoid of any competition, amassed a considerable fortune within a period of a some three years.

Downey's first business venture was brilliantly successful, but his consuming interest was in the land. At the first opportunity he disposed of his interest in the pharmacy and invested the proceeds in the broad Nietos Valley, an area of unspoiled beauty and good soil south of Los Angeles.

In 1851, some two years after his arrival in California, Downey became an American citizen and from that day on he gave freely of his time and talent for the good of his adopted State. At his own expense he published and distributed a quarterly bulletin extolling California's many attractions and unlimited opportunities.

Two years later, at the age of twenty-seven, John fell in love with a native belle, Senorita Maria Guidaro, a young lady of great beauty and charm. The attractive young couple were united in marriage in the year 1853 in the old adobe-walled chapel of Mission Dolores in San Francisco. In keeping with the California Spanish tradition the wedding celebration spanned several days. The Downeys enjoyed an ideal marriage, which lasted for more than thirty years, until Mrs. Downey's tragic death in a railway accident in the Tehachapi Mountains north of Los Angeles. The Governor himself was seriously injured in the collision, which hindered him for the remainder of his life.

Downey the Politician

Though he strove to stay clear of political involvement, Downey's name was put forward as a candidate for Lieutenant Governor in 1859. At the time, California was mostly cow country, a land apart, and the whipping boy of a more sophisticated eastern society, who dubbed it the Wild West. Politically, however, the timing was just right for a prospective Irish candidate in a State where the Irish already outnumbered all other national groups, and where their favored party, the Democrats, was in a position of power. The Irish vote was courted by everyone seeking political office, and a candidate bearing an Irish name had a distinct advantage. Milton Latham, an astute politician and candidate for Governor in 1860, was well aware of this ethnic political imbalance when he chose Irish-born John Downey as his running mate. The importance of having an Irishman on the ticket was evident in an article which made the headlines in the *Sacramento Bee*: "Downey was selected for the purpose of offsetting among the Irish voters, the selection of John Conness on the other side." The hotly contested election with two well-known Irishmen in opposing political camps appeared to be a tossup. When all of the votes were tabulated, however, the Latham-Downey ticket was declared the winner by an overwhelming majority. The vote tally read as follows:

Latham-Downey:	44,023
Curry-Conness:	24,180
Leland Stanford ticket:	8,466

Latham was inaugurated as California's sixth Governor, with John Downey as Lieutenant Governor. But Latham held office only from January 9-14, 1860. For ambitious politicians, election to state office was the first step on the way to higher national office. Governor-elect Latham was no exception. The untimely death of California Senator David Broderick in late 1859 (he lost his life in a duel on the shores of Lake Merced, San Francisco) made it possible for Latham to be elected to Broderick's vacancy. This game of musical chairs saw John Downey, the Lieutenant Governor, move up the ladder to become Governor. When sworn in, Downey became the seventh Governor of California, the first of Irish birth. In fact, Downey was the first Irish-born Governor of any state in the Union.

Governor Downey was a man of imposing stature and presence. His powerful jaw and deep-set hazel eyes made him a charismatic figure in political gatherings and civic functions. His inaugural address struck the note of a poised, veteran statesman. He clearly articulated his policies regarding California and demanded strict accountability of everyone in a position of authority. To all department heads he issued guidelines pinpointing their duties and responsibilities: meticulous accounts were to be kept of all expenditures; and costs were to be held within the limits of state revenues. He vowed that his administration would stay firmly in the path of integrity and provide equal opportunity for every citizen.

California's financial crisis, when Downey took over, challenged all his ingenuity. The State's deficit put California in the red to the tune of more than $4,000,000, the legacy of political corruption and uncontrolled spending during the previous Weller administration. "Much money has been spent and but little to show for it: no State Building, no Universities, and a poor system of transportation," he commented. During his first year as Governor, Downey reversed pork-barrel politics and profligate expenditures; he set the state on the high road to fiscal sanity. In his first annual report, Governor Downey could even boast that in one year the State had accumulated a surplus of more than $5,000; that interest on State bonds had been paid in full; and that money had been set aside for their orderly redemption. Downey was an ultra-conservative in financial matters. He waged an unrelenting campaign against waste of public funds and extravagance and duplication of civic effort. He made good on his fiscal promises when he became Governor by keeping expenditures in tune with revenues, and he saw to it that state employees in positions of trust did likewise. When his term ended (1862), Downey turned the state over to Governor Leland Stanford in healthy financial condition. He then returned to Southern California to initiate his pet project, the development of the Santa Gertrudis Rancho that he had acquired in 1859.

Downey Vetoes the Bulkhead Bill

During his term as Governor, a notorious political scheme known as the "Bulkhead Act" (1860), designed to create a gigantic monopoly on the San Francisco waterfront, was well on the way to becoming law. The bill had been approved by both houses of the state legislature and awaited only the Governor's signature. This power play was concocted by two wealthy land promoters from Southern California, the lawyer John Felton, and the physician Levi Parsons. If enacted, the bill would have allowed the developers to construct a seawall, with piers and docks, along the San Francisco waterfront, with the added right to collect dockage fees from incoming and outgoing ships. The citizens of San Francisco were outraged at the prospect of losing their most prized resource, the only natural harbor and shipping port in Northern California. Tempers and polemics flared when the full impact of the waterfront legislation was sensationalized in the local press. The bizarre legislation would have worked a disastrous effect on San Francisco and its environs. The proposed bill confronted the youthful Governor with a formidable challenge. Downey temporarily set aside lesser matters to scuttle the pending legislation. He made a painstaking review of every aspect of the bill, including recorded testimony and the plan of design. Predictably, but unsuccessfully, partisans in the dispute pressured and cajoled the Governor. Downey's non-noncommittal response was that he would faithfully attend to his duty. When the moment for his decision came, the Governor calmly vetoed the bill.

Downey next issued a carefully worded statement in support of his action:

> After giving the Bill the most careful consideration in all its details, I am led to the irresistible conclusion that its provisions are not only in conflict with the Constitution and principles of natural justice, the measure as a whole is calculated to work irreparable injury to our Commerce, internal and external of which San Francisco is and must forever remain, the Metropolis.

The citizens of San Francisco greeted the Governor's veto decision with jubilation. It was a time for celebration, in typical Western style. Business came to a standstill; all cares were temporarily set aside; and crowds gathered on the streets in festive spirit. Friends embraced and newcomers looked on in wonderment. Banners waved, church bells rang out, and horns blew in an uproarious celebration. The Governor himself arrived to a hero's ovation. The joyful crowd stood shoulder to shoulder to catch a glimpse of their hero as the torch-lit procession, led by a brass band, wound its way up Market Street. The jubilee continued throughout the night, to the lyrics of "Auld Lang Syne" and "For he's a jolly good fellow!" and "We won't go home until morning...."

San Franciscans' love of parades can be traced partially to this spontaneous cavalcade and mirthful reception that honored Governor Downey over a century ago. San Francisco newspapers of the day were enthusiastic in their editorial kudos about the Governor himself and more especially for his part in putting to rest the notorious waterfront scam. The San Francisco *Bulletin* eulogy was even more extravagant, dubbing the Governor the Andrew Jackson of California:

> A great power is gone; he has vetoed the most gigantic scheme ever presented to a Governor in America; a great power that was organized by the cohesion of corruption is stricken down.

The San Francisco Board of Supervisors meeting in special session adopted the following resolution:

> Governor Downey, by his firm action and fearless conduct, officially displayed during the last session of the Legislature, in opposition to acts of that body detrimental

to the rights and interests of our City, has merited the approbation and gratitude of the people of San Francisco.

In the aftermath of the bill's defeat, a serious altercation took place in San Francisco between partisans of the opposing sides. The Governor was confronted by Henry Cobb and John Middleton, the leading proponents of the Bulkhead scheme. In the ensuing argument, Downey referred to Middleton as a "Bulkheader." Middleton retorted, accusing the Governor of being drunk or in a daze. Evidently Downey's Irish got the better of him, and he floored Middleton with a blow to the jaw. Miles Sweeny, one of the founders of the Hibernia Bank and a close friend of Downey, hauled Middleton aside and cautioned him, "You shan't strike the Governor, damn you!" The police arrived in the nick of time and carted both Middleton and Sweeny off to jail. The Governor, tired and worn, but still in high spirits, enjoyed a well-earned rest. The disappointed conspirators dropped from sight and the heartened citizens returned to work, grateful of their victory.

Downey as Civil War Governor

The State of California and America as a whole owe a debt of gratitude to Governor John Downey, the Democrat who loyally supported Abraham Lincoln, a Republican, throughout the Civil War. During the nation's most critical hour, when the states were debating secession or Union, Downey's conciliatory posture should inspire all Americans. He surprised and dismayed his political cronies by holding California fast to the Union.

At this period, California was bitterly divided on the issue of slavery, and political power for the most part was in the hands of southern sympathizers. What alternative history would we have witnessed if Milton Latham, a rabid southern sympathizer and Lincoln antagonist, had become California's Governor instead of Downey? As a lifelong Democrat, Downey was, in fact, opposed to some of the policies of Lincoln's Administration, yet he felt duty-bound to support the President's efforts to preserve the Union. To every request from either the President himself or his Secretary of War, the Governor's response was quick and supportive. Downey's support of the war effort and his loyalty to the President as

Commander-in-Chief are clearly evident in his letter to Lincoln on the subject of supplying California volunteers to the Union Army:

> Dear Mr. President:
>
> The first requisition made upon this State for six thousand and five hundred volunteers has been filled and the command given to Colonel Carleton. It was indicated by the War Department that it was your desire that this office should have the command. I cheerfully complied as I have every confidence in his experience, patriotism and gallantry.
>
> Yours sincerely,
> John G. Downey
> Governor of California

Downey's letter of August 28, 1861, addressed to General Sumner, Commander of the Pacific Division, also evidences his loyalty: "Enlisting is going on rapidly, and the fife and drums are heard in every village. I had repeatedly assured you that none other than those loyal to the General Government will be offered clearing commissions of the State."

California was spared the bloody strife of the Civil War within its own borders primarily because of Governor Downey's timely action in unreservedly placing California on the side of the Union. But that was only part of the story. Without California in its camp, it would have been impossible for the Union Army to police and defend the vast territory west of the Mississippi River. Downey's patriotism was never that of a flag-waver or firebrand zealot. His character was realistic: a hard-working administrator who cared little for dramatics. His low-keyed personality may have been the reason that his countless contributions to the state and the nation have been largely overlooked.

Downey's Vision of California's Potential

California's phenomenal growth and development owed much to the Governor's farsighted policies. His enthusiasm spurred Downey to envision the possibility of extending the State's eastern boundaries. The text of his proposal to the State legislature reveals his economic savvy: "This would embrace the Silver Region of Nevada and Utah, add to our material wealth, and bring within the jurisdiction of our own State thousands of citizens whose interests, sympathy and attachments are purely Californian."

With his roots in the land, Downey early on perceived agriculture's vital role in developing the State. He endorsed State support of agricultural societies to foster interest in farm policies and encourage financial subsidies to stimulate the cultivation of flax, cotton, and corn. He also played a role in the birth of a vibrant wine industry. Downey was an enthusiastic supporter of Agoston Haraszthy (1812-69), the adventurous Hungarian immigrant who was chiefly responsible for the early development of California viticulture. In association with other winelovers, Downey financed Haraszthy's trip to Europe to procure the choicest vines that would be suitable to the soil and climate of northern California. Haraszthy's trip resulted in his influential report, entitled *Grape Culture, Wines and Wine-Making; with Notes upon Agriculture and Horticulture* (1862).

Downey clearly foresaw the United States as a leading power in the Pacific Basin and advocated a strong national Navy to protect trade and commerce. He vigorously endorsed a national railroad, linking east and west, that would enable the state to exploit its geographical advantages in both transport and trade with the Orient.

The State Capitol: a Downey Project

It was during Governor Downey's administration that a permanent site for the State Capitol in Sacramento was selected. At the Governor's behest, a bill providing for the purchase of four square blocks of land and an appropriation of $500,000 was introduced. After fierce debate, the bill was approved by both houses of the legislature. The law, when passed, bore Downey's signature as Governor. The laying of the Capitol's cornerstone on May 15, 1861 marks a memorable turning point in the history of California. It signalled the moment when the State was beginning to assess her potential for future greatness. In his farewell message to the Legislature in January 1862, Downey could speak with justifiable pride of a truly successful administration: "The record of this past year is replete with the most gratifying evidence of prosperity and of social and material progress."

John Downey (second from left) at cornerstone ceremony for the State Capitol in 1861. [Courtesy of Elena Quinn and City of Downey.]

Downey in The Chronicle of The Kings

In light of his many achievements and noteworthy contributions to his adopted State, it is little wonder that Downey's name heads *The Chronicle of the Kings*, edited by H.H. Bancroft, the renowned curator and pioneer founder of the Bancroft Library of the University of California at Berkeley, who was most lavish in his praise of the former Governor. Bancroft's biography of the former Governor details Downey's illustrious Irish ancestors and roots and gives an account of his early life and struggle to acquire an education, his journey to California, Downey's personal story of that first pharmacy in Los Angeles, the various land purchases and development undertakings, banking and building enterprises, together with his oil and water explorations. When Bancroft's biography was submitted to Downey for approval, he felt flattered by the contents. *The Chronicle of the Kings* was published in 1892, two years before Downey's death; the Governor's life story, which appears in Chapter 4 of Bancroft's second volume, should be of vital interest to students of both California and Irish history.

Downey's Love of the Old Sod

Throughout all those tumultuous California years, John Downey never lost touch with his family in Ireland. In later years, he visited the old homestead at least once. Brian Cunniffe, correspondent for the *Roscommon Herald*, reports that Governor Downey even returned to his native parish to erect a headstone over the grave of his deceased father, Dennis.

The Downeys of Castlesampson

John Downey's mother, Bridget Gately, bore her first husband, John Martin, two daughters, Mary and Winifred. The daughters immigrated to America and settled in Maryland. Following her husband's death at an early age, Bridget married Dennis Downey. The Downey's had four children: John (the Governor), Patrick, Eleanor, and Annie. All the children immigrated to America and eventually settled in California. Patrick died young, a bachelor. Eleanor married Walter Harvey, and they had two children, Mary and J. Downey Harvey.

Following Martin's death some years later, his wife Eleanor married Edward Martin, an officer in the Hibernia Bank of San Francisco. John Downey died in 1894 without children, and his nephew J. Downey Harvey inherited his estate. Annie married Peter Donoghue, a pioneer San Francisco industrialist. Her name is memorialized in the city of Anaheim (or "Annie's home"), site of the world-renowned Disneyland. Eleanor Martin lived out a long and eventful life, dying at the age of 102. One of the oldest and most dedicated members of the California Historical Society, Eleanor was a living witness to the Industrial Revolution, a century of transition from the covered wagon to the airplane, together with major developments in transportation and communication along the way: the Pony Express, the railroad, telegraph, telephone, and radio.

Downey's Pioneer California Land Development Project

As we have remarked, Downey's term as Governor (1860-1862) could boast of several solid accomplishments for the future growth of California: the state was in sound financial health, secession was no longer at issue, and California was steadfast within the Union. In his final act as Governor, Downey passed on the reins of authority to the Governor-elect Leland Stanford.

Ex-Governor Downey then returned to Southern California to continue the healthy growth of the state's economy by initiating the land development of the Santa Gertrudes Rancho. At this period, the area was still virgin country, adorned by a sea of yellow mustard, the landscape interlaced with tall grass and colorful wildflowers. This first large land subdivision proved providential as a lure to populating California.

Downey's promise of cheap land attracted thousands of families, and the vast majority of new arrivals were landless, uprooted Southerners whose property had been destroyed during the Civil War. These adventurers had traveled west to begin a new life. The newcomers included a substantial number of farmers or potential farmers. Their settling in California during that turbulent period achieved a stabilizing effect.

When Downey's land advertisement appeared in the Los Angeles newspaper in 1866, it sparked almost as much excitement as the discovery of gold some eight years earlier. Imagine the joyful hope and dreams aroused among would-be farmers on reading Downey's advertisement:

FOR SALE
20,000 ACRES OF
CHOICE AGRICULTURE LAND
WITH WATER FOR IRRIGATION

Situated in the Valley of the San Gabriel River, sixteen miles from the Port of San Pedro. The above land will be sold in lots to suit purchasers from 50 acres upwards on long terms of credit at $10.00 PER ACRE with ten per cent per annum interest. The best land for homesteads and vineyards in this section of the state. One tenth to one fifth of the purchase money will be required in cash according to location.

John G. Downey
Los Angeles
Nov., 1866

Thomas Jefferson's democratic dream of America as an ever-expanding frontier providing land, bread, and work for all was fully realized in Downey's massive land development project. The sensational story of land in abundance at ten dollars an acre was played up in all the nation's press, and John Downey's name became a household word throughout America. Within a period of three years, the promise of land lured over 100,000 people into the state in search of their own homesteads.

James Burke, the First Grantee

Among the new arrivals was an Irish-American named James Burke, a descendant of a pioneer Irish family who settled in the State of Virginia before the American Revolution. Like thousands of his countrymen, Burke's grandfather (also named James) fought in both the Revolutionary War and the War of 1812. Despite bone-shattering wounds, the old soldier lived to the age of 113. James the younger delighted in recalling how, as a lad, he witnessed the nostalgic reunion of President Andrew Jackson and the old veteran at Jackson's Hermitage in Nashville, Tennessee. The name James Burke heads the list of grantees in that momentous year of 1886, the year of the great divide. As a matter of record, the historic document bears the signature of the ex-Governor Downey. Title to the five hundred acre parcel was conveyed to James Burke upon receipt of the sum of two hundred and fifty dollars. There was earnest speculation at the time as to why the Virginia native got first choice: whether it was (as some suggested) by reason of his family's patriotic record, or (more likely) because he was Irish like John Downey himself.

The First Bank in the City of Los Angeles

Downey appreciated the fact that a developing economy needed financing. He set his sights on establishing a local banking system that would enable enterprising merchants and farmers to acquire capital at reasonable rates and thereby help to curb the usury of private lenders. The newly arrived farmers and artisans had plenty of know-how, but lacked financing. The most vexing problem, however, was that most California wealth was concentrated in the northern part of the state. How to get the northern capitalists to loosen the purse strings was a perplexing matter. This problem did not dampen the spirits of Downey or his associates. Soon a committee of the leading citizens of Los Angeles was formed with the ex-Governor as their spokesman. This southern California delegation, imbued with the importance of their mission, set out for San Francisco in high spirits. Downey's presence ushered in a pleasant interlude for the Golden Gate city, where he was held in the highest esteem for his opposition to the notorious Bulkhead Act, which would have ruined the great seaport of San Francisco.

During the lengthy negotiations, Downey made the acquaintance of Alvinza J. Hayward, one of the most influential bankers in northern California. Hayward was impressed by Downey's sincerity and enthusiasm and determined to accompany the southern delegation on their return journey to assess the matter first-hand. Eventually Hayward believed in the feasibility of Downey's banking proposal and suggested that they enter into a partnership. With a capital of $100,000, the partners opened the first bank in the City of Los Angeles (Hayward & Co) in 1868. So successful was the venture that a year later Downey and the enterprising Isaia W. Hellman formed another partnership which gave rise to the Farmers and Merchants Bank. These two venerable financial institutions pioneered by John Downey provided most of the funding for the economic development of Los Angeles and the surrounding area until the dawn of the twentieth century.

Founding Father of Los Angeles

When Downey's banking business was on firm foundations, the elated entrepreneur sought a suitable location for developing a retail trading center and produce mart. His original project consisted of a row of two-story buildings on Main Street adjacent to the newly established Bank of Los Angeles (Hayward & Co.)for the convenience of merchants, traders, and customers alike. Los Angeles, today the epitome of open-air markets, supermarkets, and shopping centers, owes the origin of its ambience to the barn-style open-front shops pioneered by John Downey over a century ago.

A Railroad to Los Angeles

The year 1869 saw the last spike struck for the historic transcontinental railroad. It snaked across America to its westernmost depot in Sacramento. But southern California, five hundred miles farther south and a potential colossus of wealth and influence, remained isolated, with transportation limited to horse and buggy. With economic power concentrated in the hands of the so-called Big Four of the Southern Pacific Railroad (Huntington, Stanford, Hopkins, and Crocker), hopes for extending the line to Los Angeles were dismal indeed. Even worse, Southern Pacific had introduced a bill in Congress that would permit them to bypass Los Angeles by running the railroad through the Mojave Desert and on to Arizona by way of San Bernardino. But the Railroad Barons underestimated the growing power of the Los Angeles business community and its intrepid spokesman, ex-Governor John Downey.

Downey was a relentless foe of every monopoly, and he was not about to let the dream of southern California's future be dominated by any one industry. His economic vision and blueprint were for a broad-based economy that embraced every region of the State. His vision was shared and supported by the now-flourishing Los Angeles community and its influential boosters, such as Isaia Hellman, his banking partner, and by Francis Temple and William Workman, proprietors of the Workman Bank. The economic future of southern California, centered in Los Angeles, required rail transportation to link it up to the market place. But the uncertainty over whether the railroad would ever reach Los Angeles kept the business community in anxiety. Downey himself, however, was not discouraged: "We built the present railroad," he said, "and we can build another!" Downey organized a committee of local businessmen in May 1872, with himself as chairman, for the avowed purpose of bringing the railroad to Los Angeles. Downey's committee decided to make a firm offer, based on the Los Angeles county's assessed valuation, in order to invite the participation of the railroad magnates. Downey and one of his associates traveled to San Francisco to negotiate with Leland Stanford, spokesman for the Big Four.

The meetings were drawn out for weeks with little progress. Stanford, a northerner at heart, could see no future in the southern region, but only parched desert and cow country. Sarcastically, he suggested that the cows could be driven to the proposed railroad depot at San Bernardino. Downey refused to allow his Irish temper to interfere with the more important business at hand. At every opportunity, he reasserted the unlimited potential of southern California, which the railroad could rightly advance by linking the region to the nation's markets. Stanford and Downey were both successful businessmen, and Downey knew the language Stanford understood. True enough, they were both shrewd bargainers; and Downey, the more polished diplomat, had something up his sleeve if all else failed. In dealing with Leland Stanford, he knew only too well that money talked and business was business. As the appointed representative of the Los Angeles, he informed Mr. Stanford that he would personally recommend to the voters of Los Angeles that they hand over their investment in the Los Angeles-San Pedro line to the Southern Pacific in exchange for a written guarantee that the railroad would pass through Los Angeles. Downey also stipulated that within fifteen months following such approval, the Southern Pacific would construct 25 miles of railroad track north from Los Angeles and 25 miles eastward toward San Bernardino. Surprisingly Stanford offered no rebuttal and assented to the proposals rather gracefully. Downey and his associates returned to Los Angeles bringing with them the historic agreement which was destined to alter the source of southern California history for years to come.

A City Named Downey

The history of Downey, the city, is a monument to the character of the man himself, John Gately Downey, the penniless Irish immigrant whose foresight and initiative were so remarkably evident. The City of Downey was at the hub of the unique system of land division that Downey had pioneered. This first aggressive land development system was the catalyst that sparked the phenomenal growth of southern California. As a general rule, most inland

American communities owe their origins to the coming of the railroad, but this did not hold true in the case of the progressive City of Downey. In fact, the Downey Land Association was founded in 1873 in anticipation of the coming of the railroad. The original tract comprised 196 acres with an assessed valuation of $330. The principal parties involved were John Downey and Martin Crawford, a native of North Carolina.

At that same time the ex-Governor was involved in other projects, and the task of building the proposed new city fell to his energetic associate Mr. Crawford. Neither Crawford or Downey were speculators in any sense of the word; their primary goal was a stable community that would foster homesteading and cooperation. Downey himself tried in every way to discourage any potential landsharks and get-rich-quick opportunists from settling in the new community. While Downey was preoccupied with grandiose Los Angeles civic developments such as water supply and efficient transportation, his partner Crawford guided the development of Downey City.

Crawford, by all accounts, used his commission wisely and in good taste. In due course he helped plan the lay out of streets and utilities to make way for the construction of homes and business. He personally supervised the laying of rails to connect with the incoming Los Angeles-Anaheim Railroad and built a depot which in later years was appropriately named Downey. Impressed by Crawford's accomplishments in his absence, Downey proposed naming the town Crawfordville. But Crawford was a man who shunned the limelight, declined the honor, and insisted it be named Downey City, to the delight of local inhabitants. Eventually, the word "City" was dropped and the town is remembered today simply as Downey. Within a short period the new city boasted among other things a hotel, three schools, two churches, and its first newspaper, the *Downey Courier*.

There was much more to the city of Downey, however, than the name itself implies. Situated in the fertile Los Nietos Valley, the Eden of southern California, it was the epitome of the best that the state had to offer. In addition to banking, building, and land development the ex-Governor pioneered and fostered the orange industry for which the State became famous.

The City of Downey during John Downey's lifetime. [Courtesy of Elena Quinn and The City of Downey.]

Downey, the enterpriser, had again chosen well. The rich virgin soil and climate was favorable to almost any crop, be it wheat or barley, beans or potatoes, cotton or corn, lemon, or lime, figs, dates or grapes. In the year 1875, with land selling for as little as $75 an acre, Los Nietos Valley (Downey's Domain) produced over half of the agricultural products grown in Los Angeles County

As an example, a forty-acre farm yielded 56,720 pounds of castor beans, which fetched a sizable profit on the San Francisco market. That same year, it was noted one acre produced twenty tons of onions, and another acre twenty-five bushels of corn. A partial list of farm products and merchandise shipped from Downey Station in March of 1876, read as follows: 800,000 pounds of grain, 16,000 pounds of meal, 8,000 pounds of potatoes, 68,000 pounds of timber, and 7,000 pounds of merchandise, for a total of 899,000 pounds.

Assessing Downey's Contributions to California

At the time that John Downey took over the reins of State government back in 1860, it was a most crucial moment in California's history, a time when many states were deciding between secession or for the Union. Into this political inferno, young John Downey moved with composure and confidence far beyond his years.

Downey was undoubtedly a man with the courage of his convictions and the fearlessness to carry them forward. A concise article in the *Trinity Journal* of the Mother Lode during his term of office tells how he was regarded:

> California has reason to be proud of the man now filling the Executive chair.
>
> Through all the conflict of public opinion, through all the conflict of public influence of sectional political organizations, through the spirit of partisan feeling, and against the money, power and pressures at the Capital, for the passage of fraudulent schemes of legislation, he stood bold and firm, like a skilled mariner guiding the helm of the ship of State.
>
> His record will be a moving power in the hearts of the people, and a monument to the man who has on every occasion rebuked the importunities of political tricksters and self-constituted Party leaders and who dared to do right in the honest discharge of his duties.

Braving anger from his own political associates and standing tall despite derision from Southern sympathizers, Downey held the State firmly in the Union. This, along with his other achievements, he accomplished without fanfare or dramatics. As a result, his great contributions to the State and Nation have been largely overlooked.

His memory is today still perpetuated in the State Capitol which he mightily helped to create. Traces of his legacy are also found on a hilly street named Downey in San Francisco, and in the city of Downey which bears his name. His death in Los Angeles in 1894 was mourned not only by those who knew him personally, but by men and woman throughout California whose lives he had enriched. The name of John Gately Downey will be forever linked with the progressive state of California, whose ardent champion he always was. An Irishman by birth and an American by adoption, Downey was every inch a noble soul whose like may not be seen again.

Maria Guirado Downey, California's First Lady, 1860-62. [Courtesy of Elena Quinn and City of Downey.]

John Conness as a California state legislator from the gold-rich county of El Dorado (1854-58 and 1860-62). [Courtesy of the Society of California Pioneers.]

5

Senator John Conness: Confidant of President Lincoln

The life of John Conness (1821-1909) epitomizes the dramatic rags-to-riches saga of how numerous Irish immigrants rose to fame, fortune, and even national influence.

Throughout the turbulent era from the California Gold Rush through the Civil War, Conness forged an adventurous career. He was a versatile businessman and a California 49er whose Midas touch struck it rich in the Gold Rush bonanza. He also wielded power as an influential political figure: first as a state legislator, then as California Senator on the national scene. But Conness' chief claim to fame was as President Lincoln's wartime confidant. Conness' heroic efforts delivered desperately needed California gold into the war coffers of the Union cause and thereby changed the fortunes of United States history.

What was the golden thread that unified Conness' life and vision? This Irishman combined a statesman's insight with a shrewd businessman's savvy. He has a remarkable grasp of the political and economic potential of developing the resources, commerce, and transportation of California and the West. Conness foresaw the importance of a transportation system linking East and West. In addition, several farsighted public policies were largely his own brain children: conservation efforts to preserve natural resources, building a transcontinental railroad, and establishing the wilderness preserves of Yosemite and Yellowstone Parks.

Nature fashioned Irish-born John Conness to be a leader in anything that enlisted his noble heart and energies. A man who could neither be cajoled nor brow-beaten, Conness served his state and nation with honor and loyalty. Conness had a step as steady as time and he displayed a lust for adventure as keen as life itself. He rose above his limited education and left an impressive legacy of devotion to America and its ideals of freedom and democracy.

Yet despite these weighty contributions, Conness' name is rarely mentioned in our history books. Historians for the most part have not come to grips with the full impact of his leadership. This historical silence was decried by E.N. Morgan, managing editor of the *Pittsburg Union*, following the death of John Conness in 1909:

> I was a neighbor of John Conness for thirty years or more and was for many years of the time a close friend. The scant notice given him in the press does not do justice to a self-made and remarkable man; one as honest and upright as ever lived, and a man to whom fear, physical or moral, was absolutely unknown.

During the challenging years of the Civil War, Conness—California's Irish-born legislator—was one of President Lincoln's most trusted advisors. Conness dedicated himself to preserving the Union above all other interests. His rise to political leadership came at a time when the California legislature was composed of a majority of Union Democrats and a minority of Republicans. He stood forth as the leader and spokesman of both parties on the issue of preserving the Union. When the California Republicans proposed a coalition of Union supporters, Conness took the first step and won over hundreds of Democrats whose interests lay in the welfare of the Nation as a whole. Long before he became a United States Senator Conness' uncompromising opposition to the secessionists attracted the attention of President Lincoln. Conness was unequivocal in his pro-Union stance:

> I will not associate, nor shall I knowingly associate with men who are secessionists, disunionists or traitors, nor will

> I advise others to do so. Treason is as foul a crime as it was in the time of Benedict Arnold, any opposition to our present nationality is treasonable, pending a war, and ought to be punished by banishment from the State or incarceration in prison.

Conness underlined the same patriotic spirit:

> My opinions do not grow out of the influence of my neighbors, but are the result of my love of country and my estimate of its value. Upon the terms of Union I can have political association, and upon no other. I care not whether my associates come from one party or the other as long as they are true on one vital point. With me the Union is above all parties. I have but one desire, which is, that this government may be more firmly established in the fear and love of our people, that its prosperity may be continued, and that it may be securely transmitted to our posterity to the remotest ages.

Early Life and Times

John Conness was a native of Abbey, County Galway. Born on September 20, 1821, he was the youngest son of 14 children born to Walter and Mary Williams Conness. The Connesses (*O'Connise*) were of a distinguished family with roots west of the River Shannon, where several families of the name are still to be found. The elder Conness was esteemed as a man of principle and honest endeavor and a stalwart enthusiast of all things for the good of his embattled countrymen. Such noble qualities, however, counted for little in an impoverished nation where the natives were demeaned in every possible manner and had to struggle day in and day out to eke out a bare existence.

Shortly before his death, John Conness recounted how he ran away from home at the age of 14 and made his way across the Atlantic to New York City. Fortunately, his father, as an educated gentleman, had provided young Conness with a sound basic education and a positive philosophy that stood him in good stead in the New World. All went well for the youthful exile from the very moment he landed in America. His teacher in New York City was none other than William A. Walker, a brilliant educator who in later years became a U.S. Congressman. Mr. Walker set high standards for his students, who included the notables Edward Cooper and Abraham Hewitt (of the Cooper-Hewitt controlling firm), and also John Stewart, who became a banker and Assistant U.S. Treasurer. Professor Walker's two-year course was Conness' only formal schooling before entering business. However, the youth had a keen and retentive mind and made a little education go a long way.

At 17, Conness left school to become an apprentice piano-maker. He quickly became a skilled master craftsman, and at 21 rose to factory foreman. 1n 1909, an interviewer of the octogenarian noted that a quaint piano with candle brackets, which Conness had made in his youth, adorned the drawing room of his home in Mattapan, Massachusetts. Conness worked continuously at the pianoforte trade until the year 1849, when he ventured West to pursue a more lucrative career in gold mining.

John Conness' birthplace in Abbey, County Galway. [Courtesy of Joseph and Claire Fahy.]

Upon arriving in California, Conness settled in the Gold Country of El Dorado County and took up prospecting in the hills. This also proved to be a successful venture, and within a brief time he was able to sell his claims at a hefty profit. He then judiciously invested the windfall in nearby Georgetown, where he became a leading merchant and community leader.

The historic old settlement of Georgetown, located majestically in northern California on the twin forks of the American River, owed much of its early vitality and development to early pioneers like John Conness. The Georgetown area diggings proved so fabulously wealthy that the newcomers were limited to claims as small as 15 feet along the river. The old mining camp was originally called Growlersburg after the huge nuggets that were pried from the hills and "growled" as they rolled in the miners' pans. The early prospectors cherished their town as the pride of the mountains and changed the name to the more respectable Georgetown.

By 1854, the population of Georgetown exceeded 3,000. It took the lead in business and industry in that part of California, and developed the first up-to-date water system in the mining region. It also housed the first telegraph system, linking Georgetown and Coloma, where gold was first discovered by James Marshall in 1848. It was from mineral-rich Georgetown that John Conness was sent to the California legislature in 1853 (eventually being reelected three times) and later to the U.S. Senate in 1863. Unlike many other Mother Lode towns and mining camps that have lapsed into disrepair, Georgetown has preserved much of its nostalgic grandeur. A number of buildings constructed during the Gold Rush are still in use, reverently maintained in their pristine state. With the coming of modern roads, Georgetown became the gateway to a scenic region stretching all the way to the pine forests and Lake Tahoe. In more recent times, the area has become a mecca for tourists, artists, and Gold Rush aficionados and historians.

In 1853, within four years following his arrival in California, Conness was elected by the citizens of El Dorado County as their representative in the California legislature. He served in the 4th and 5th sessions in 1854-1858. In 1860 he sought office again and once again served two terms in the 11th and 12th sessions.

Conness consistently supported David Broderick during the struggle for political power between William Gwin and Broderick.

In this power struggle, he became a political pro and a fearsome opponent. Early on, he displayed his talent as an investigator and was adept at digging up the facts and exposing cons and schemes. It became second nature to consult Senator Conness before introducing any loosely-drawn legislative proposals. His star shone even more brightly in 1859 when he was nominated for Lieutenant Governor of California. However, the Democratic party was in disarray at that time, and the split ticket led to the Democrats' defeat. The contestants in that election included: Milton Latham for Governor and John Downey for Lieutenant Governor on the Lecompton or Southern Democratic ticket; the anti-Lecompton ticket consisted of John Curry for Governor and Conness for Lieutenant Governor. Latham-Downey wound up polling 44,023 votes, Curry-Conness 24,180, and Leland Stanford (the Republican candidate) 8,466. But after a brief time in office, Governor Latham resigned to become U.S. Senator; Downey was then installed as Governor.

Conness' Bid for the Governorship

The California Democrats were still at odds when Conness ran for Governor in November 1861. The Union Democrats nominated him with Richard Irwin as his running mate. The rival Breckinridge faction of the Democratic party put up John McConnell for Governor and Jasper O'Farrell for Lieutenant Governor. Leland Stanford, who made a poor showing in the previous election, was again the nominee of the Republican party, with John Chellis as his running mate. Despite the split in the Democratic party, the Civil War, and various other factors, the Republican Leland Stanford polled fewer votes than the other two combined but swept the election because of the Democratic party schism. The election results were as follows:

Stanford	50,036
Conness	30,944
McConnell	32,751

For their loss, the Democrats had no one to blame but themselves, since they previously had won every election for Governor since California became a state (except for the time when the ill-conceived American Know-Nothing Party's nominee was elected in 1856). It was commonly conceded on both sides that John

Conness was the most knowledgeable politician on the scene. Had the Democrats united behind him, he would most assuredly have been elected. Contributing to Conness' defeat was the divided Irish vote—the most powerful bloc at the time—which was split down the middle, with Conness on one ticket and Jasper O'Farrell, a prominent San Franciscan, on the other.

With Abraham Lincoln as President, and a bitter Civil War now raging that could determine the fate of the Union, 1861 was a Republican year. The war climate too was a decisive factor in the election for the governorship of California. Democrats by the hundreds crossed party lines to vote the Republican ticket, which helped the candidacy of Leland Stanford, the party's nominee.

The Broderick Connection

John Conness became a close personal friend of the pro-Union U.S. Senator David Broderick, who was killed in 1859 in a duel with a Confederate sympathizer, State Chief Justice David S. Terry. Broderick, in fact, tragically died in Conness' arms. (Terry himself was eventually (1890) to be shot himself in a restaurant by a security officer assigned to protect Chief Justice Stephen J. Field. Field had rendered a decision that had angered the hot-tempered Terry, who thereupon had sworn vengeance against the Justice.)

The Broderick tragedy had tremendous repercussions not only in California, but throughout the nation and gained particular attention in the halls of Congress. Conness and Broderick had teamed up in support of the Union and the abolition of slavery. This position angered Southern supporters and proslavery factions. Broderick's death also sent a shock wave through northern California, second only to the later assassination of Abraham Lincoln in arousing sympathy for the Union cause. Colonel E.D. Baker, who some say exploited the death of Broderick, held his audience spellbound by his eulogy of Broderick, rising to this histrionic peroration:

> But the last word must be spoken, and the imperious mandate of death must be fulfilled. Thus, O brave heart: we bear thee to thy equal grave. As in life, no other voice among us so rang its trumpet blast upon the ear of freemen, so in death its echoes will reverberate amid our

> mountains and valleys, until truth and valor cease to appeal to the human heart.

The sobering effect of Broderick's grave on Lone Mountain in San Francisco played no small part in Abraham Lincoln's reelection to the presidency in 1864. Just as men and nations revere the name of Irish patriot Robert Emmet as a symbol of freedom, in like manner Senator Broderick served as a symbol of loyalty to the United States during the Civil War. The very mention of Broderick's name had a sobering effect on the anti-Union proslavery advocates. Following Broderick's demise, the mantle of the Union supporters was passed on to John Conness, who bore it proudly in the halls of Congress in support of President Lincoln and the preservation of the Union.

U.S. Senator, 1863-69

Before a distinguished audience assembled in Washington, newly-elected U.S. Senator John Conness presented President Abraham Lincoln with a polished cane of California live oak. On the handle was a gold plate inscribed, "Broderick to Conness," with a newer plate "Conness to the President" attached thereto. Conness then told the President that this symbolic cane was being offered in admiration for his issuing the Emancipation Proclamation and for resolutely maintaining it as a public law. Conness went on to praise Lincoln as "a great leader in the civilization of the world." The *Washington Chronicle* picked up the story and described the presentation ceremony: "An Interesting Ceremony: The Late Senator Broderick's Cane Presented to President Lincoln by Senator Conness." The story went on to describe how the President accepted the cane "with emotion," and that he considered it a high honor, especially since his act had merited the posthumous approval of the great man, David C. Broderick.

With the Civil War in progress and Abraham Lincoln in the White House, the political tide turned in favor of the Republicans. This pro-Republican sentiment was particularly strong in California, which joined the Union as a free state supporting Lincoln. Conness, an astute politician, was quick to size up this political turnabout. In 1863, he ran for the U.S. Senate as a Union Democrat and was elected. When he took his seat in Congress, he devoted every effort to support measures necessary to maintain the Union. Only when order was restored on the national level at the end of the Civil War, did he give his primary attention to legislation benefiting his home state.

During his six-year term in the Senate, Conness became a power among his peers on the Washington scene. His influence was largely the result of his social qualities, coupled with his vigor of character, which was always spirited and versatile. He served with distinction on the Committees of Finance, Railroads, Post Office and Roads, and as Chairman of the Committee of Mines and Mining. His appointment to this latter post was welcomed by the majority of his peers, as Conness was without doubt the most knowledgeable member in mining matters because of his firsthand experience in the hectic days of the California Gold Rush. The Washington correspondent of the *Saint Louis Democrat* in comparing the two California Senators, McDougall and Conness observed:

> The latter is a man of unusual dignity of deportment and the very opposite of his colleague. Senator Conness is, indeed, an ornament to the State that sent him. It is well known that he was not elected as a Republican, but as a Democrat, so that the Administration had only a right to expect that he would support (the Democratic Party) in its general war policy, but he has worked constantly true as a member of the Union Party, and to-day there is not a more reliable and efficient anti-slavery man than he in the United States Senate. If there were anything to console California for her betrayal by McDougall, it would be the faithful representation by Conness of her interests and principles.

Confidant of Abraham Lincoln

During those turbulent Civil War years, a close personal friendship developed between the California Senator and the President, and become more pronounced with each passing day. In his anecdotal memoirs, *Reminiscences of Lincoln,* Conness brings to light many little-known insights into the character of Abraham Lincoln. Of particular interest is the often misquoted account of Abraham Lincoln, that he "split rails" [working on the railroad]. That myth originated in the enthusiasm of Lincoln's followers and over the years passed into the realm of accepted fact. In a lighter moment when chatting with Conness, the President revealed how the story got started and why he had decided to let it pass.

He told Conness that he never had "split a rail," and he went on to describe being taken aback when, following his nomination for President, people came to congratulate him, bringing on their shoulders the 'rails' he had split. Since it was incorrect, his first impulse was to correct it. On second thought, here were many of his followers taking their own way of expressing their elation at the event of his nomination.

Not wishing to dampen the ardor of his supporters who had worked so hard during the campaign, he decided to let it go. Conness was deeply touched by the humility of the President and his concern for people's feelings on such a trivial matter in such precarious times. However, since Conness was now made aware of the true story, he felt conscience-bound to pass the facts on to posterity with the following notation:

> Though his humble beginning gave ample room for this story, and though it seems to have contributed to the simplicity of life rather than otherwise, as I am asked to write of him, whom the Nation reveres and loves, it must be done as he revealed it himself to me.

Whenever President Lincoln was about to make a political appointment, he leaned heavily for advice on Senator Conness. On one occasion, as soon as the Senator walked into the President's office, he inquired if Conness knew Captain Maltby, who was then living in California. "He is visiting here and his wife is with him," Lincoln said. Conness replied that he had heard that the Captain was in Washington. The President appeared to be very concerned about the plight of Maltby and went on to relate the circumstances in which he first met the Captain and his wife.

Lincoln confided that when he first came to Springfield, (where he was unknown and a carpetbag contained all he owned in the world and he needed friends), the Maltbys had generously taken him into their modest home and cared for him. During his stay with them, the Maltbys encouraged Mr. Lincoln to post his shingle and solicit prospective clients for his law practice. He had known the Maltbys at the time of the Black Hawk War and declared that no one ever treated him more kindly. Now, he'd risen in the world while the Maltbys were still poor and the Captain was in need of some place to make a living. The President turned to Senator Conness and said, "Senator, Maltby wants to be Superintendent of the Mint in San Francisco, but he is hardly equal to that. I want to find some place for him, and into which he will fit, and I know nothing about those things."

Conness scratched his forehead for a moment and replied:

> There is a place, Superintendent of Indian Affairs in California, where the incumbent should be superseded for cause; and the place is simply a great farm, where the government supplies the means of carrying it on; there is a good supply of Indian labor, and making it produce and accounting for the products are the duties principally.

The President appeared relieved, a soft smile crossed his brow and in measured tone replied, "Maltby is the man for this place." He looked outwardly pleased in being able to serve an old friend and good man.

John Conness relates in his own words the mutual bond between himself and Abraham Lincoln: "Having had the closest relationship with Mr. Lincoln for some years while I was Senator, many of his humorous anecdotes became known to me." One particular incident concerned the relationship between the President and his trusted Secretary of the Treasury, Salmon P. Chase (whose image appears on U.S. $10,000 bills). Conness felt a moral obligation to set the record straight, since he was a personal witness who had sat through the sometimes heated discussions in the President's office.

The year was 1864, nearing the end of the President's first term in office, and by common consent Lincoln was an odds-on favorite for reelection because of the truism, "It is not well to swap horses in the middle of the stream." Lincoln was willing to be a candidate because he felt that he could best deal with the issue, raised by the Democratic party, namely, that the war was a failure and that a Democratic candidate should take over. To make matters worse, Chase, who had been Lincoln's trusted Secretary of the Treasury, was also a candidate for President.

Their rival candidacies naturally led to a strained relationship between the two men, who until then had been supportive of each other during Lincoln's first term in office. Supporters of the President and Mr. Chase, each in turn made statements derogatory of the other, which only threw added fuel onto the political fire. Chase had tendered his resignation to Mr. Lincoln at different times, but the President merely set the matter aside. Chase's latest letter of resignation, however, was presented with a tone of some irritation, and as such the President accepted it. The resignation took the Senate by surprise, where nothing was known of the sudden turn of events until that body received a letter from Lincoln, nominating Governor David Todd of Ohio for the position of Secretary of the Treasury.

The Senate went into executive session, and referred the nomination to its Finance Committee, who in turn called on the President in a body. The Committee convened in the executive mansion to present their case. Lincoln at once relieved the tension by stating he had just received a dispatch from Governor Todd declining the office. The President then spoke about the difficulties that had come between him and his Secretary, which he attributed to the improper conduct of Chase's political friends, and saying that of course Mr. Chase had a right to be a candidate; but that such a state of feeling had developed that it was unpleasant for them to meet each other; and now he had accepted Mr. Chase's resignation. In a more stern tone the President added, "I will no longer continue the association. I am ready and willing to resign the office of President and let you have Mr. Hamlin [Vice President] for your President: but I will no longer endure the state I have been in."

Quoting Senator Conness' memoirs:

> The above were nearly his words spoken with deep seriousness. Through all this interview, and the history of painful relations, there was no word nor thought impugning the motives or purposes of the outgoing Secretary. It was a deeply interesting insight into the character of Abraham Lincoln. The history of this episode in the President's life would be incomplete, and would fail to illustrate the magnificent purity and generosity of his nature, without calling to mind how soon after he was able to appoint Mr. Chase Chief Justice of the Supreme Court.

Conness went on to relate that the President performed a great act in this appointment, and one of which few men are capable. Senator Conness, who was present during the proceedings, was deeply touched by Lincoln's sublimity in putting principle above any personal advantage or consideration, and he concluded:

> It is a vain proceeding to try to correct a popular error which has universal acceptance. I suppose one might as well attempt to storm the tide of an established theology among its cohorts; yet it is due to truth to state it, as we have it from its fountains.

The progress of the war had not been going too well and public morale was at a low ebb. Even some of the members of the President's Cabinet expressed moments of doubt. But Senator Conness never wavered in his loyalty and support of the President in the prosecution of the war and the preservation of the Union. With each passing day he grew to idolize Abraham Lincoln, and it appears the admiration was mutual. Conness lived within walking distance of the White House and made himself available 24 hours a day during this stressful period. As evidence of this, the day Lincoln was assassinated in Ford's Theater, Conness and Senator Sumner were socializing in Conness' residence when a young man pounded on the door and screamed that Lincoln had been murdered. They dashed over to the theater, and both men were horrified when they caught sight of the President gasping for life. "How could this have happened to such a great man?" was the question on everyone's lips.

Lincoln's Spokesman in California

During Lincoln's second presidential campaign, Conness was his personal choice to address a mass meeting of Union supporters convening in San Francisco an October 18, 1864. The meeting which brought together one the largest political gatherings in northern California up to that time was held in the historic Platt's Hall at Bush and Montgomery Streets. Mr. Conness spoke as follows:

> Mr. Chairman, ladies and fellow citizens of San Francisco: the mightiest stake is at issue, the greatest contest is being waged that was ever known in America. Heretofore for generations past, since our country began, all questions, no

> matter how important their character were determined by popular voice. We are now to determine by popular voice the great question of who shall be the chief magistrate of this nation and for four years to come; and by and by, in addition to that we are to determine whether or not as the United States of America shall be considered, and be in fact, the home of the oppressed of every nation, this home, the secure home of Liberty.
>
> While this civil contest is going on at this time, war, deadly and horrible war is carried on upon the fields of this country, a war in which the lands and homes of the country are laid waste and her sons are slaughtered by hundreds of thousands. We thus have a double contest inaugurated against us—one of the most important civil contests and one of the most terrible and sanguinary conflicts that the world ever saw. Who is it that is responsible for this double contest? Who is it that has evoked this terrible war, and has brought it upon us? In part this is the theme of our discussion tonight. I submit to you now to this audience, to you, fellow citizens. To every man in the land who has a spark of reason and a particle of justice in his composition. I submit to all this question whether there was cause for this terrible war; whether we might have gone on as we had gone on since the nation began its existence, submitting every question to popular arbitration and in that respect commanding the admiration of all the nations of Europe.
>
> Until this war began, no matter how fierce our contests were, no matter how strong and deep our convictions were, when the majority decided, the great body of the people acquiesced. Then we were the admiration of the civilized world. Now we have almost become its sport. I say we have come together in part, to discuss tonight, and determine as to who are responsible for this terrible change, and to shape our actions accordingly.

Conness then described the sequence of tragic events that brought about the conflict, placing the blame on those most responsible who could have done so much to avoid it:

San Francisco's Platt's Hall, where in 1864 Conness eloquently pleaded for California's remaining loyal to the Union. [Courtesy of San Francisco Archives Collection in the San Francisco Public Library.]

Let me tell you, my fellow citizens, a fact that is not generally and popularly known...that when Mr. Lincoln took the office of President in 1864, the education of every court in Europe, aye and South America that was of the slightest political consequence was complete, having being carried on and completed by American ministers. They had been taught by those same ministers that our country and government was at an end. 'Shame!' It is a shame, and damning proof of treason early hatched, and thus attempted, in the most...despicable manner to be launched against a generous and magnanimous people.

This fact, fellow citizens, accounts for a most remarkable circumstance—a circumstance entirely new in the history of the intercourse of nations; namely, the immediate recognition of belligerent powers in this bastard Confederacy. It had no sooner sprung into existence than

> the powerful nations of the earth recognized them as our equals, admitted their pirate ships into their ports and gave their representatives audiences. This circumstance is accounted for, by the facts I have stated to you—that they have been told, and educated to believe by the ministers of our country, that our nation was at an end; and so they have hurried up to divide the garments of Christ among them. They desired to make an early association with the Southern Confederacy. They clamored and strove, each with the other, for early treaties and bargains, by which they could gain advantage, and they were unwilling to listen to the declaration of our government that we could maintain it intact.

Having related these setbacks to the Union cause, Conness then described what had been accomplished to preserve the Union under Lincoln's leadership. Like his mentor, Conness was also a powerful advocate of the abolition of slavery:

> They say that the war has been reduced to a contest for the abolition of slavery. Oh, Great God, shall it be said, can it be maintained to-day eighty years after the organization of the Republic, after eighty years of teaching? First by the fathers, and then by every good and great man along the line to the present period, that to tell the world we will rise and remove the damning stain is a crime.
>
> Ignorant and untaught men sometimes imagine that if Negroes got their freedom, that is, if they have a right to themselves, and to the profits of their labor, that they the working men—will be encroached upon. Do they not know, that they never can be elevated, that they can never rise, that capital has its foot and its heels upon labor, as long as such a mill stone weight as slavery hangs around the neck of labor. If there be one class who, above another, ought to sing paeans to the rising star of liberty in the land, it is the men who toil and sweat in daily labor.
>
> I don't know, fellow citizens, that I should close this brief and somewhat irregular address without alluding, and I hope you will pardon me for it, to the little intimations made by some of your papers that the enlightened, honest

> and patriotic man who stands at the head of the government and myself in my humble capacity have disagreements.
>
> Why fellow citizens, I have stood day by day and night by night giving all that I had and all that I could think and feel to build him up and to make him stronger. How ridiculous now that any man should be found professing to be a Union man who shall talk about this man or that who reaches a high public station, and has one spark of light that fits him for it, as thinking of mere groveling conditions, and not giving himself, whatever there is of him, be it little or much to the great cause of American liberty. The President with me never sinks the President in the Senator, and it is not necessary for me to say to those who know me that to him the Senator is never, has never been and never will be sunk in the President. We each, in our share, stand by each other through this great conflict. We stand by you, the great Union people, and you stand by us. In that, like the Union, I trust and religiously believe, we will be one and indivisible.

Conness concluded his speech by eulogizing the great men whom the President had chosen to defend and preserve the Union, men like Secretary of State William Seward and Edwin Stanton, among others; and he concluded:

> But thank God again, the Republic will live.
> It lives in the hearts, in the minds, in the courage, and in the virtue of the people. We are told there is one glory of the sun, and another glory of the stars. Let it be ours, fellow patriots and citizens, that the Republic shall live in glory, represented by the national starry ensign, the signal of hope, the light of the world, and the security of liberty for mankind.

After a brief stay in California, while he renewed his ties with old friends and constituents, Conness returned to Washington to attend to the affairs of state in the nation's Senate. Already the rigorous campaign of '64 for the Presidency was in full swing. It was the time when the Democrats, Confederate sympathizers, states-rights extremists, and avowed secessionists and others were raising a chorus of blaming the war and its consequences on President Lincoln and his administration. For example, when the Democratic convention met in Chicago, New York's Governor Seymour took the gavel, and amid loud applause declared: "If the administration can't save the Union, we can! Mr. Lincoln values many things above the Union; we put it first of all. He thinks a proclamation worth more than peace; we think the blood of our people more precious than the edict of the President."

Senator Conness' rebuttal left the Democrats speechless:

> They call themselves Democrats! Now what is Democracy? Is it not that scheme of government which proposes to confer rights alike upon you and me? Is it not that scheme of government that proposes the greatest extent of civil rights to mankind consistent with civil order? The men who are now haranguing the multitudes and calling themselves Democrats, did not admit then that those original secessionists were Democrats. Nay! They were opposed at that time to being known themselves as Democrats.

Lincoln's Second Term

On the eve of the 1864 election, on November 8, John Hay wrote in his diary, "I have nothing to say till the day after tomorrow. God save the Republic!" A day of wind and rain and an atmosphere of fate was over. The national electors, designated in the first three words of the Constitution, "We the People," had spoken; and the nation had said "Yes" to Abraham Lincoln.

Of all the great men like Seward, Stanton, Wells, Blair, and Usher who surrounded Abraham Lincoln, none was more elated than California's Senator John Conness. *The London Times*, acutely aware of Conness' influence and the importance of the Irish vote, noted:

> It may probably be that we are safer in the hands of Mr. Lincoln that we should be in the hands of anyone else. As regards foreign states, ourselves in particular, we may reasonably believe that he has sown his wild oats: he has gone through the course of defying and insulting England which is the traditional way of obtaining the Irish vote, and

> may we not unreasonably hope that he is unlikely to repeat the experiment.

General Grant assumed command of all Union forces in 1864 and vigorously carried the war to the Confederacy. General Sherman marched through Georgia, took Atlanta by force of arms, and laid siege to Savannah. Grant next took Richmond, and shortly thereafter the Confederates under General Robert E. Lee surrendered on April 9, 1865. The war which had pitted brother against brother was over, but the scars would take many years to heal.

Abraham Lincoln's plans to abolish slavery throughout the land, and to restore the South to an honored position in the Union, were shattered by the assassin's bullet five days later, on April 14. Outside the President's immediate family and close friends, no man was more distraught than his companion and faithful friend, John Conness. The great man he sought to emulate was gone, and no one could take his place. However, it was only when the Senator Conness was chosen as a pallbearer, that the nation became aware of the intimate relationship that existed between the California Senator and the martyred President.

Reminiscing on Lincoln's funeral in later life, Conness recalled seeing the hushed and stunned multitudes on the streets of Washington, down which he and the other pallbearers helped carry the body of the President:

> The city was full of soldiers and they were a pretty orderly set as those things go. I remember after the assassination of the President, there was a general consternation among the public men at the time. No one knew who was to be the next. They all took precautions, because they thought it was their duty to the country.

Conness hesitated a moment and then added, "No, the precautions were dictated by private cowardice, I say."

Abraham Lincoln's death was a formidable setback to Conness, who had acquired the status of a leading statesman under his administration and was the President's choice for Secretary of the Interior for his second term. Conness was widely recognized as being one of the most savvy legislators on the Washington scene, and was viewed by some as the President's most informed consultant. Conness' unswerving loyalty to Abraham Lincoln (both to the man and his philosophy) made him one of the most conspicuous legislators in the U.S. Congress.

Little is known of Conness' association with Lincoln's successor, President Johnson, apart from his duties in the Senate. Conness, however, was still a power on the national scene. When a Senate bill to readmit the States of North Carolina, South Carolina, Louisiana, Georgia, and Alabama to the Union was under consideration, Johnson chose Conness to speak on behalf of his administration in the hopes of restoring those states to their rightful place in the Union. Conness' address was judged to be one of the most eloquent deliveries in the Senate chamber during the Johnson administration.

A Gentleman Farmer in Massachusetts

By 1869 Conness had served out his Senate term and reluctantly, yet gracefully, he set aside his political career. That same year he married Mary Russell Davis, a native of Greenfield, Massachusetts, and took up farming in the Boston suburbs. The estate Conness acquired in Mattapan was set in the middle of beautiful landscaped grounds with an imposing Victorian home at its focal point. There, free from business cares and political controversies, Conness raised a family and kept aloof from public life except for occasional socializing with local citizens.

A picture of the Connesses' farmhouse—with his neighbors and himself engaged in haymaking the old-fashioned way—adorns the front cover of a booklet published by the Boston Corporation in 1976. Conness remained in continuous occupancy and farmed the land until his death in 1909. Part of the original Mattapan ranch forms the site of a modern hospital, an affiliate of the Boston State Hospital system.

In an interview given in his home in Mattapan shortly before his death at the age of 87, Conness had much to think and talk about as he strolled leisurely along his sunny garden paths. He reminisced about his early days in New York when he made pianos and taught others the craft, and then went home at night to his bachelor quarters to cook his oatmeal and chops and feed his prize canaries. Then he recalled his adventures on the prairies as he struggled westward with the weary 49ers, who risked life and limb in pursuit of the Mother Lode. Conness then reminisced about his vicissitudes in mining, merchandising, and politics in California, and the stormy sessions of the U.S. Senate during the Civil War. He had witnessed the drama of some of the most stirring events in our nation's history. Now nearing the end of his life, Conness was still an impressive figure as he strolled through his garden while being interviewed.

Speaking of his adventures in the gold fields, Conness confided:

> No. I did not go to California by sea, nor did I navigate in a prairie schooner. There were all sorts of ways of getting there. I remember some went down to the West Indies and up the Gulf, hoping to get there across Texas and Arizona. I went by land, horseback and tramping; and it took a long time.

He was asked, "What kind of men were those adventurers?" He replied in his eloquent style:

> A good set; they were darling men. Many of them came from good families, and not a few of them were men of considerable property. There were adventurers, of course; we were all adventurers. But as far as roughness was concerned, it was a pretty orderly crowd. Mark Twain (and Conness flushed rather wrathfully) has grossly exaggerated that side of it.

How about Bret Harte and his stories of the mining camps and the 49ers?

> He is different, while just as amusing. He sticks a great deal closer to the facts. In general, I think his pictures of California life can be depended upon. They are too florid, of course, but that is the business of the storyteller, and that may be forgiven him. I have enjoyed reading his sketches of Western life very much, largely because they are relatively free from this fault of exaggeration.
>
> But I wish to repeat my objection that the men of '49 were a rough set. For that kind of place and time, and considering the circumstances of their coming out, they were as sober a set of men as ever got together. When I got there the big end of the population was in San Francisco, and what is now Oakland. By that time they were finding great

quantities of gold in the mountains, but not so much in the plains, though these were being worked. Also we got together a short time after our arrival and made provisions for the preservation of law and order.

Father of Yosemite National Park

Conness' career as a U.S. Senator is worthy of the Nation's highest honors. But, in addition, his contribution to the aspiring young state of California deserves equal praise. He was a practicing conservationist, long before the word acquired its modern meaning. It was Conness who introduced a bill in the Senate turning Yosemite Valley and the Mariposa Forest over to California for a state park. He guided the bill through the legislative process to become law on June 30, 1864. Francis Farquhar, the California mountain historian, recalls the naming of a mountain peak for Senator John Conness.

Mount Conness in Yosemite National Park, stands majestic in the high Sierra Range, when one views it looking north from the high plateau of Tuolomne Meadows. Although not as spectacular as the great Half Dome towering over the Valley, stately Mount Conness manages to dominate the landscape for miles around. Clarence King, the first director appointed to head the U.S. Geological Survey, in referring to the mountain said that because of its "firm peak with titan strength and brow so square and solid it seemed altogether natural we should have named it for California statesman, John Conness."

A feature story appearing in the *Sacramento Bee* on March 27, 1931, paid tribute to California's departed Senator on the occasion of the naming of Mount Conness. It drew particular attention to a picture of the Yosemite peak, a striking photograph entitled "Mount Conness" which was presented to the Senator's youngest son, Leland Stanford Conness. On the occasion of the presentation, Horace M. Albricht, Director of the National Park Service, paid a glowing tribute to Senator Conness for his foresight in preserving the splendor of Yosemite as a public park for all future generations to enjoy. The mountain was christened by Clarence King, Director of the U.S. Geological Survey, who credited Conness with carrying through the bill that organized the first geological survey in California.

A Born Leader

A leading newspaper described John Conness as a "Master of parliamentary tactics, assiduous, untiring, vigilant, pertinacious—neither to be bullied, cajoled, placated or persuaded, and his headstrong determination to have no will but his own never bent to accommodation."

During his term in the California legislature, Conness drew the wrath of marauding vigilantes. If these self-appointed law-and-order proponents harbored any illusion of Conness as a week-kneed, indifferent politician, they were soon sobered. A full-blooded Irishman, with the courage of his convictions, was not a man about to be bluffed. The gun-toting gang of vigilantes threatened him with vengeance if he attempted to curb them. Conness took up the challenge and was prepared for any contingency, with the guns on his desk in typical western style. With fierce determination, he proclaimed that he was "ready to begin business" whenever the vigilantes were. The "business" was never begun. The fearless Irish legislator had called their bluff.

The many occasions that Senator Conness spent in the company of Abraham Lincoln had a profound influence on the Californian. He was particularly impressed by the President's desire never to hold a grudge in the aftermath of political confrontation. Lincoln's principle of forgiveness Conness applied with the deepest understanding in his own dealing with Leland Stanford. Though he had lost to Stanford in his bid for Governor, he offered the hand of friendship to his erstwhile opponent, and even named one of his own sons Leland Stanford Conness after his political rival.

Conness memorable address at Platt's Hall in San Francisco drew immeasurable richness from Lincoln's own Gettysburg Address. Conness' words echoed Lincoln's convictions about freedom and justice for all. The Washington correspondent of the *Sacramento Bee* thus summarized Conness friendship with Lincoln:

> Mr. Conness became his fast friend and a confidential adviser of President Lincoln, conferred with him freely upon the policies of the Pacific Coast, the strength of the union sentiment there, and especially in regard to the support of the administration in the extreme war measures which might be inaugurated or become necessary. He was also consulted by members of the Cabinet and others in the

confidence of the Executive Department on all matters and questions of the hour.

How California Gold Helped Save the Union

During the Civil War the federal government desperately needed gold to support the bales of paper money 'greenbacks' that were being printed to finance the war effort. The gold was shipped from California by way of Panama, across the Isthmus by horse and cart, then reloaded and sent along to the East Coast ports. Confederate spies quickly discovered the route over which the Union gold was transported and they began plotting to intercept it. Senator Conness got wind of British-Confederate collusion: he discovered that Confederate cruisers were being outfitted at British docks in China in order to intercept the Union gold ships in the Pacific.

Senator Conness was agitated when word reached him of this Confederate plot. He lost no time in contacting Gideon Welles, Secretary of the Navy, to impress upon Welles the urgency of the situation in the hopes that the Navy would provide an escort for the ships and their precious cargo. The Secretary, by all accounts a pompous, self-centered bureaucrat, paid but scant attention to the Senator, whom he considered but an upstart Westerner and dismissed Conness forthwith. This brushoff did not deter Mr. Conness: he well knew the gravity and urgency of the gold situation question; it was a serious matter.

Having been denied a hearing by the Secretary, Conness dashed out of Mr. Welles' office and went directly to President Lincoln to repeat word for word what he had told Secretary Welles. Years later, in a postwar address, Conness described his conversation with the President: "Mr. President, I did not come to complain about the heads of your departments, but there is one with whom I cannot do any business; the Secretary of the Navy." After giving the matter some serious thought, President Lincoln turned to Conness and said, "Well there is one live man in the Navy Department. Do you know Mr. Fox? Well, suppose I give you a note to Fox."

Senator Conness thanked the President, took the note, and then hastened out the door as if every moment counted. Admiral Fox, proved to be a gentlemanly official who had taken the lead in organizing a professional U.S. Navy at the behest of the President himself. Unlike Mr. Welles, the Admiral listened with rapt attention to every word as if it were coming from the Commander-in-Chief. The Admiral's reply was brief and to the point: "It is a serious matter and will be attended to in like manner. It's a problem that calls for secrecy at every level, this you well understand." Admiral Fox thanked Senator Conness and sent him on his way. The rest is history. The Confederate plot to seize the California gold was nullified thanks to the vigilance and timely action of Senator John Conness.

By 1863, the Civil War had reached a stalemate with neither side possessing the capability of overcoming the other. In fact, the odds appeared to favor the Confederates. Economics plays a major role in the fortunes of war. Armies march to victory on their stomachs, whereas starving patriots simply fall by the wayside. With sufficient California gold in the Union coffers to bolster a sagging economy, the tide was gradually turning in favor of the Union cause. Farmers, gunsmiths, harness makers, and other merchants were demanding payment for their goods and services in hard currency which the Administration was now in a position to honor. Military victory was within the reach of the party which controlled the purse strings.

Enhanced by a stable currency, the Union Administration was now in a position to provide both guns and butter to help prosecute the war. This economic upswing spelled the beginning of the end for the Confederacy. History was determined by a secured supply of gold from California to the Union cause. The facts in this little-known episode are not disputed: it was the sagacious Senator John Conness more than any other politician, whose unwavering commitment helped save California for the Union. Conness, as Abraham Lincoln's right hand during the Civil War, played a hero's role in preserving the Union itself.

Conness' Political Reputation

An article which graced the pages of the old *San Francisco Call* in 1863 bears evidence of Conness political astuteness:

> Our old partner John Conness received the nomination for U.S. Senator from the Abolition Caucus on Monday night

> and on Tuesday in joint convention was elected, the Abolitionists to a man voting for him.
>
> John is a professional politician, has an intimate thirst for office, and has pursued it, not always successfully with a step as steady as time and an appetite as keen as death. John possesses in an eminent degree, subtlety, energy and gift of speech of a peculiar order, which captivates the timid and imposes on the unreflecting. He is temperate, industrious and persevering, and in point of ability is superior to either of his formidable competitors, though this is a questionable compliment.
>
> He has a happy faculty of detecting the weak points of his opponents and concealing his own. Some Republicans pretend to be indignant at his election; they have no reason to be. The party which elected Lincoln to the Presidency cannot consistently complain of the election of ordinary men to subordinate positions. Conness is infinitely better qualified to discharge the duties of Senator, than Lincoln those of the President.

Conness was aided and abetted by other distinguished legislators such as Senators Charles Sumner and Henry Wilson, both of the whom like John himself were most instrumental in the affirmation of the Constitutional Amendment for the abolition of slavery. Conness outlived every Senator who supported and voted for that historic measure. He, too, was the first Chairman of any Congressional committee to appoint a black man, a Mr. Harrison, as a clerk on the Committee on Mines and Mining.

Although Conness was a patriotic American, he never forgot old Erin, the land of his birth, nor did he ever lose interest in the struggle for the rights of his countrymen. Throughout his life he had a soft spot in his heart for everything Irish, in time of need he was a cheerful giver. In the troublesome times of the Land League agitation he forwarded his personal check for $100 to the appointed committee, a practice which he continued for a number of years. John was a long-time friend and cohort of the poet John Boyle O'Reilly whom he met in Boston, and the two men spent much time in each other's company in their declining years. Speaking of his friend, Conness said, "There was a man, it would be well for all Irishmen in America to study and emulate."

Conness' Legislative Vision

There are many examples of Senator Conness' prescience in legislative matters and worthwhile causes during his term in office which bear repeating. It was Conness who first proposed setting aside Yellowstone Park, one of the great scenic wonders of America, as a public reservation. He made several visits to the wilderness at his own expense and to Yellowstone to assess its awesome grandeur. He presented his findings to Congress and outlined his recommendations long before a chartered expedition made a survey and filed its report.

Conness was the first to broach the idea of a transcontinental railway, a proposal which was ridiculed by some of his peers as an impossible dream. John, however, had the last laugh at the historic occasion of the so-called *Driving the Golden Spike* at Promontory, Utah in 1869, when he played a major role as an honorary participant.

Thus, the building of the Continental railway was the brainchild of Irish-born John Conness. This monumental communications link, uniting east and west, was, without doubt one of the most important developments in the history of America. Thomas Hill's painting commemorating this historic event once hung in the California State Capitol. (A key to the portraits of the illustrious participants identifies the likeness of Senator Conness as No. 4 in the first row.)

A grateful nation likewise gave expression to its feelings by naming a locomotive in honor of Conness. The historic railroad engine was emblazoned with the name of John Conness, the father of the Transcontinental Railroad.

Conness' Last Years

When Conness left the Senate to take up farming near Boston, his home was the scene of many reunions of old political cronies, longtime friends of Abraham Lincoln, and men of influence on the national scene. The esteem in which Conness was held is borne out in correspondence from Chester A. Arthur, the 21st President of the

Gold Spike ceremony at Promontory, Utah in 1869. Conness is the fourth figure from the left. [Courtesy of the Conness family.]

Union-Pacific railroad engine named "CONNESS" to honor his role in the transcontinental railroad. [Courtesy of the Conness family.]

United States, such as a letter dated February 9, 1882, and addressed to the Honorable John Conness, Dorchester, Massachusetts.

A word on Conness' appearance: Of average height and build, he was said to be one of the handsomest men in the U.S. Senate, as an early portrait would also indicate. Even In his twilight years he stood tall and erect, the epitome of a gentleman farmer who had enjoyed a long and fruitful life. when he posed for a picture at the age of 84.

Conness' declining years were spent in quiet repose at his home in Mattapan, where he passed away on January 9, 1909 at the age of 87. His remains were interred in Cedar Grove Cemetery in South Dorchester, a suburb of Boston.

In Search of Conness' Family and Children

The California senator was survived by his wife of some forty years, the former Mary Russell Davis of Greenfield Massachusetts, two sons and one daughter. One son, Leland Stanford Conness evidently acquired many of the prodigious qualities of his illustrious father and as such became a leader on the national scene. Leland was the driving force of the Democratic Party in 1914, being the campaign manager for Woodrow Wilson who was elected to the high office as the 28th President of the United States.

According to an article which appeared in the *Boston Globe* on April 9, 1942, when Leland passed away, he also was interred in Cedar Grove Cemetery in the family plot. The obituary listed two surviving sons, John and Dudley, both living in California.

The question remained for the present author, *where* in California were the surviving Conness children living?

The search to locate either of the two surviving Conness sons was for me a long and frustrating one, which led from California to Washington, D.C., and from there to New York and Boston and back again. At this point the thought occurred to me to search the local telephone directories for the name Conness. I looked in the current San Francisco directory hoping to find someone by that name, but found none.

Going on a hunch, I picked up the Oakland City directory, and oddly enough I spied the name of one Dudley Conness. On the spur of the moment I picked up the receiver and dialed the telephone number, and waited breathlessly for a response. A lady answered in

Mattapan, John Conness' retirement farm and estate outside Boston from 1868-1909. [Courtesy of the Conness Family.]

Picture of Conness and his wife in old age at Mattapan. [Courtesy of the Conness Family.]

a very restrained voice, which I immediately concluded as being that of a woman of advanced years. "Am I speaking to Mrs. Dudley Conness?" I inquired. "Yes, this is Mrs. Conness," came the reply. In the course of our conversation, I asked about her husband, Dudley, who she said had passed away years ago. She informed me that her late husband's brother John had also passed away but that his widow was hale and hearty and living in San Bruno, south of San Francisco. She volunteered, "I have her telephone number if you would like to give her a call; I know she would be most anxious to speak with you, and besides she is more up on the story than myself."

Shortly afterwards, I spoke at some length with Mrs. John Conness, whose maiden name was May Fitzgerald, a proud native of San Francisco. Mrs. Conness invited me to her home to discuss this matter further. To my delight, I learned that she was well informed about the life and times of Senator John Conness and had many important documents in her possession.

Connie (as she was known to her friends), I discovered, had more than a passing interest in the late senator. She had already taken sharp issue with perpetrators of the *Lincoln Conspiracy* (a book and later a movie) who had fabricated a blatant distortion of President Lincoln's assassination, a theory that allegedly implicated the late Senator Conness. When she learned of my interest in Conness, she gave her permission to reproduce any document or family portrait that would assist in putting together the true story of her late husband's illustrious grandfather, John Conness.

As previously mentioned, Senator Conness was interred in the family plot in Cedar Grove Cemetery in Dorchester. His son, Leland Stanford Conness, passed away on April 8, and was, as we know, also buried in the Cedar Grove family plot, leaving as survivors: his wife, Rosalie Thornton Conness, a brother Irwin of Syracuse, Wyoming, and a sister Mrs. Harkinson of Babylon, Long Island. Also listed in the *Boston Globe* obituary of April 9, 1942, were two sons of Leland Conness by a former marriage, both of whom were living in California. My research, as sketched out above, revealed that both of those men, John and Dudley Conness, had already passed away. This information was provided by May Fitzgerald Conness.

Conness' Stature as a Man

In summation, the career of the Honorable John Conness, adventurer, statesman, man of affairs, and friend of prominent men, spanned a period of nearly three score and ten years. He initiated his career as a mere boy at the age of 17 as an apprenticed piano maker, and at the age of 20 he rose to become foreman of the factory. He dared the treacherous journey to California in order to dig for gold, and became a successful merchant in Georgetown, the pride of the mountains. Conness served two terms in the California State legislature and ran unsuccessfully at different times for both Lieutenant Governor and Governor of California. In the perilous times of the Civil War, he represented his beloved state both with honor and distinction in the United States Senate.

Picture of the aging Conness. [Courtesy of the Conness Family.]

The youthful Senator Conness was reputed to be one of the most sincere, knowledgeable, and patriotic men in the Senate, admired by friend and opponent alike. Conness rubbed shoulders with the great and near-great and broke bread with President Lincoln, the noblest of them all. Conness had much to do with the growth and development of his adopted state and helped keep her borders and her honor intact before the nation. An avowed abolitionist and foe of secession, Conness fought many heated battles to save the Union. He left a moral and political legacy of achievement in trying times and proved by his actions that he was every inch a man of principle, and one of the best informed and patriotic immigrants to ever grace the American scene.

Martin Murphy, Jr., founder of Sunnyvale. This land baron owned more land than in all of his native County Wexford. [Courtesy of the Martin Murphy, Jr. Museum in Sunnyvale, California.]

6

Martin Murphy: High King Of Early California

The influence of Martin Murphy, Jr. (1807-1884), his wife Mary Bolger Murphy, and of their descendants was monumental for early California history. According to historians, anything of importance that transpired in California during its formative period involved the Murphys.

One wonderfully colorful testament to Murphy's success and influence was the 1881 extravaganza celebration of the Murphys' Golden Wedding Anniversary. This elaborate party, with its dazzling display of wealth, victuals, and entertainment, came from the lavish hand of Martin Murphy, the Irish-born land baron who acquired more arable land in California than existed in all of County Wexford, his birthplace.

An inventory of the Murphy land holdings in Acres:

SANTA CLARA CO.:	
Bay View Rancho Acres	5,000
The Milpitas Rancho	800
La Purissima Rancho	5,000

SAN LOUIS OBISPO CO.:	
Santa Margarita Rancho	17,000
The Assuncion Rancho	39,000
SANTA BARBARA CO.:	
Point Conception	12,000
COMBINED TOTAL:	78,800

There was much to celebrate, and celebrate they did in the grand Murphy manner. The trials and tribulations of bygone years were but a memory as they celebrated fifty years of happy married life surrounded by family and friends. The Golden Wedding anniversary of Martin, Jr. and Mary Bolger Murphy (said to be the grandest party ever staged in California) took place about a century ago, but its memory survives in the legends of this pioneer Wexford family that founded the Silicon Valley city of Sunnyvale.

Preliminary arrangements for the gala celebration were planned well in advance in order to provide for everyone's comfort and enjoyment. To make sure than none would be slighted, the Murphys sent invitations to everyone in California through the medium of the *San Jose Mercury News*, a leading newspaper of that period. To suggestions which came from the family about sending special invitations, the old pioneer replied, "Don't talk to me about cards of invitation! All our friends, my wife's and mine, and all your friends, are welcome!" Murphy added that he "did not expect to celebrate but one golden wedding," and he added that he neither could nor would undertake to discriminate or select among his friends, old and new, throughout the county and state. No presents would be expected or accepted.

California's Grandest Party

During the three-day celebration which began on July 18, 1881, some 50,000 people converged on the Murphy Bay View Ranch on the sun-drenched plains of Santa Clara County. The scene was idyllic and spectacular. Murphy's home was poetically described by Charles South "as a white ship in a golden sea of grain" since Murphy's extensive wheat fields stretched from San Francisco

A romanticized scene of Murphy's Bay View Ranch in 1876, five years before Martin and Mary's golden wedding anniversary. [Courtesy of the California Department of Parks and Recreation.]

Bay to the far-off coastal mountains. El Camino Real (The Highway of the King), which skirted the Murphy homestead, was jammed with conveyances of every description, from farm drays to gaily decorated coaches, followed by equestrians arrayed in western attire and hundreds of others on foot, all in a mood to serenade California's most beloved pioneer couple Martin Jr. and Mary (Bolger) Murphy.

The San Jose city merchants proclaimed a holiday. The Board of Supervisors followed suit and postponed its calendar during the festivities. A Superior Court trial already underway was adjourned and the presiding judge escorted the jury, plaintiffs, defendants, witnesses, and counsel to the Murphy party. The gaily decorated railroad depot (Murphy Station) was the focal point for even greater numbers who came on special trains chartered for the occasion. Marching bands attired in colorful regalia were on hand to serenade the arriving guests and to escort them to the Murphy ranch. The whole affair was a colossal undertaking, but the Murphys, who had methodically planned the event, took it all in stride.

A Barbecue for Thousands

Joaquin Argues, Murphy's, son-in-law, took charge of the intricate planning for the three-day celebration, ably assisted by other members of the Murphy family. Wining and dining a gathering almost equal to the adult population of the San Francisco Bay area at the time required the skills of a master of the culinary arts. The Herculean task was placed in the capable hands of Captain Isaac Branham, a past master in the art of gastronomy, who journeyed from Los Angeles at the behest of the Murphy family. Captain Branham was portrayed by one newspaper as being "without equal in California, having superintended the principal barbecues of Southern California ever since the art had become a feature at large gatherings, both social and political, in that good-living part of the state." The article added: "He is as he should be, well-larded in person and rosy cheeked. His movements too are deliberate, for it's no moment's work nor child's play to properly barbecue a beef."

To make way for such a titanic barbecue, a trench measuring 114 feet in length by four feet wide and four feet deep, was excavated. Seven wagonloads of wood were heaped onto the fire which was ignited the previous night and fueled steadily until six in the morning. Into the roaring holocaust descended 7 steers, 14 sheep, and 10 pigs. As a special culinary treat for the more fastidious, seven steer heads were prepared and cooked to perfection by the Maestro himself. With no effort spared to satisfy every taste, there was a plentiful supply of cooked hams, 500 roast chickens, 150 turkeys, hors d'oeuvres, bologna, and cheese. Bread by the wagonload, and salad by the bushel. Fifty barrels of beer, 500 gallons of coffee, hogsheads of punch and lemonade, and a lavish supply of French, Spanish, and California wines to wash it all down.

The ornamentation for the grandiose celebration was in keeping with all aspects of the Murphy wedding-anniversary celebration. Murphy's oak grove stood out in magic splendor, illuminated by torches and Chinese lanterns. A stuffed bear—a symbol of the '49ers—stood guard at one end of an elaborately decorated table that was reserved for the honored couple. Overhead hung a magnificent floral piece made of exotic flowers and ferns and fashioned in the shape of a wedding bell, a gift from the Murphys' daughter, Mrs. Richard Carroll. One reporter observed: "The main body of the giant bell was of white flowers resembling tulips, on one side in crimson buds, were the figures enclosed in a wreath date line 1831, on the reverse in simple style the figures 1881." Alongside the jubilarians' table stood a huge confection of sugar and nuts, representing a pavilion, seven feet high and with a figure of a bride and groom in candywork on top.

Seating was informal, in keeping with the Murphy tradition. At the hour of 12:30 on the first day of the party the assembled guests were instructed to seat themselves at tables spread out under the oak trees. Eight hundred or more were served at each sitting, with enough victuals in readiness to feed 10,000 hungry revelers.

The jubilarians, Martin and Mary Murphy, were serenaded at their home on the ranch and escorted to the bridal table to the tune of "Haste to the Wedding" by the gaily attired Parkmans' eighteen-piece band. All eyes were centered on the feted couple as cheer after cheer echoed through the woodlands. Throughout the evening, plaques and testimonials were presented to the honored couple, followed by many impromptu toasts from intimate friends and well-wishers from among the boisterous gathering.

Prominent among the speakers who paid tribute to Martin and Mary Murphy were several California pioneers and long-time friends: the industrialist Colonel Peter Donahue, U.S. Senator William Gwin, James Phelan, Philip A. Roach, and Judge Ryland of San Jose. General Patrick W. Murphy, a son of the jubilant couple, accepted the gratuities on behalf of the Murphy family.

The elaborate dancing pavilion, adorned with gingerbread edgings, was constructed under the direction of John Gash, one of the leading architects of the day. The huge dance hall, that measured 8,000 square feet, was bathed in soft lighting and skillfully adorned with floral bunting. Its seating could easily accommodate 1000 spectators at a time. A raised platform was erected at one end to accommodate the musicians.

In keeping with the Spanish *fiesta* tradition of early California, the festivities spanned three consecutive days without letup. The near-exhausted revelers occasionally napped under the spreading oaks or stretched out on the new-mown hay and resumed dancing when partly refreshed. The more sophisticated young ladies set aside their usual dignity, kicked up their heels, and danced the more stalwart young men under the table. Not to be outdone, old grey-haired fathers flipped heel and toe, to and fro, and swung their partners in a manner reminiscent of their youthful days.

The gala affair was also a time for romance, and many a fair maiden was said to have pledged her troth at the Murphy wedding anniversary. One visiting journalist noted, "A pleasant freedom from all restraint was noticeable." The bountiful libations played no small part in the overzealous bash. The well-lubricated participants must have suffered a mammoth hangover following the Murphy bonanza on July 19, 1881.

Bancroft reflected on this upbeat historic event in his *Chronicle of the Builders*:

> Far into the night, the multitude lingered among the illuminated groves, for the scene was of surpassing loveliness that has never before or since been witnessed in California, and one that will be long remembered.

The San Francisco *Examiner* volunteered its own rating by describing the celebration as "a feast that has never been equaled in point of stupendous liberality and profusion on this Coast."

The Murphys of Wexford

Martin Murphy, Jr., the oldest of six children, was born in the townland of Ballynamough, adjacent to the old City of Wexford, on November 9, 1807. His parents were Martin and Mary Foley Murphy. Martin, Sr. was born and reared in that same house, where he lived until circumstances forced his immigration to Canada. Besides Martin, Jr. (the subject of our narrative), the Murphys had five other children: James, Bernard, Margaret, Mary, and Johanna.

To comprehend the plight of the Murphys and other Irish families, one must appreciate the British oppression that provoked the unsuccessful Irish rebellion of 1798. The Penal Laws gruesome edicts that had been perpetrated against a helpless people were now even more rigidly enforced. The totalitarian Laws denied the Catholics the right to participate in politics, to attend schools, or to practice the religion of their choice. The British Parliament tried to convert the Irish to Protestantism by controlling education. Catholics resented this denial of their cherished faith and refused to enroll their children in state-appointed schools.

Things went from bad to worse. In 1800, the English Parliament passed the "Act Of Union," forcibly amalgamating England and Ireland into one Nation. The law altered the course of Irish history for generations, and was savagely enforced by well-equipped English troops dispatched to Ireland. Conditions were so intolerable for the Catholic Irish that their only alternative was to live in degradation or to emigrate. The Murphys of Wexford and thousands like them chose the second course and fled their native land on a one-way ticket.

The Murphys in America

Martin Murphy, Sr., accompanied by his wife and four of their children, set out for America in 1820 and arrived at the port of Quebec, Canada in that same year. Martin, Jr. and his sister Margaret stayed behind to look after the Murphy interests in County Wexford. The Murphy family worked out the plans, agreeing that Martin Jr. would work the farm until he could find a buyer and when the transaction was completed, Martin Jr. and his sister were to leave for Canada at the first opportunity. These plans did not materialize for some six years. When the sale of the Murphys' holdings was finally consummated, Murphy Jr. and his sister set out for Canada to join their parents, who had settled in the suburbs of Quebec, Canada.

An Irish settlement developed in Frampton, outside the city of Quebec, where the Wexford Murphys settled. A bit of old Erin came alive for the transplanted Gaels at the Murphy ranch, where the door was always open and a hearty welcome awaited every newly arrived Irishman. The familiar sounds of melodeon, the fiddle, and the flute that flooded the Irish countryside on a Sunday afternoon, rang out from the open door of the Murphys' Canadian home to welcome all newcomers.

The close family relationship that existed between the Murphys and the Bolgers in County Wexford was rekindled when both families resettled in the new world. In due course this neighborliness led to a romance between Martin Murphy, Jr. and Mary Bolger. A search through the Canadian records reveals the young couple were united in marriage at the French cathedral in Quebec on July 18, 1831.

The Murphys in Canada

The newlyweds settled down to married life in Quebec, where Martin found employment. Six children were born during their stay in Canada: James, Martin III, Patrick, Bernard, Mary, and Nellie. The growing family prospered in Quebec until an outbreak of cholera ravaged the city and took the lives of the two youngest children, Mary and Nellie. Fearing the worst, the grief-stricken family fled the city of Quebec in haste and took refuge in Frampton, where the elder Murphys lived. The area was sparsely populated, with plenty of land available for newcomers. Martin, Jr. purchased several hundred acres, mostly forest, adjacent to his father's property. The land was dry and mostly hilly, and the task of clearing it was formidable. The Irish, accustomed to the water-logged lowlands, heathery moors, and unproductive peat bogs in their homeland, preferred the higher ground for farming. Their French counterparts invariably chose the lowlands. To their dismay, the Irish soon discovered that unlike Ireland the higher ground was generally poor and unproductive while the bottom land was for the greater part rich and fertile.

Canada proved disappointing, too, for other reasons. Although the Irish merged agreeably with the French settlers, the union of Upper and Lower Canada did little to enhance either the social or economic conditions, for the time being at least. A powerful, wealthy pro-British element in Upper Canada took full advantage of the merger to enhance their influence in Lower Canada, and lavished their favors on the English settlers. The economic depression of 1837 also inflamed the ill feeling that existed between rival factions which eventually led to open revolt.

In contrast to these disturbing conditions existing in Canada at the time, there were encouraging reports from south of the border. There the political climate was more stable and ample opportunity existed to acquire land on the expanding Western frontier. The harsh climate, hot summers, and freezing winters had always discouraged the Murphys and other Irish immigrants from settling permanently in Canada.

The Murphys Immigrate to the United States

After deep soul-searching, the Murphys, led by the indomitable patriarch Martin, Sr., set out for the United States and settled in Missouri. They chose the fertile region east of the Missouri River where land was cheap and plentiful, adjacent to the present city of Saint Joseph. The senior Murphys settled in Holt County. Martin, Jr. purchased a 320 acre parcel nearby, at the confluence of the Platte and Missouri Rivers. Missouri, like Canada, had its drawbacks. On the plus side of the ledger, the soil was rich and productive, enhanced by a plentiful supply of water and adequate transportation by river boat. On the negative side, the air in this low-lying region was infested with malaria, which posed an immediate threat to the growing Murphy family. Martin Murphy Senior's wife, Mary and Martin Junior's youngest daughter, Ann Elizabeth were among its many victims.

Father Christian Hoecken, a frontier missionary who came to minister to the grieving family, did much to encourage the Murphys to vacate the malaria-infested region and seek a more favorable climate. He related the attractions of California: he was personally familiar with this Eden: a land rich in natural beauty and productive abundance and blessed with a salubrious climate, an earthly paradise by the shores of the Pacific, where Catholicism was the favored religion. This religious openness surely appealed to the family, who were chafing at the lack of Catholic religious facilities in their section of Missouri. Father Hoecken's story was so persuasive that the Murphys decided to resettle in California.

California-Bound

In the spring of 1844, the Murphys sold their holdings in Missouri and made plans for the precarious overland journey to California. To insure the success of this prodigious undertaking, the Murphys left nothing to chance. They purchased the strongest wagons, sturdiest horses, and healthiest oxen that money could buy. Foodstuffs, cooking utensils, clothing, medicines, and other necessary items also consisted of the best quality.

Elisha Stevens (1804?-84), a canny mountaineer, was chosen as guide to lead the way to California. The Murphy-Stevens party, as it was called, numbered 51 people who braved the wilderness in 13 covered wagons and reached their destination without loss of a single life. Actually their numbers increased because of the birth of two children during the westward journey. The exuberant party was given a rousing sendoff on that memorable day, May 9, 1844, as they crossed the Missouri River and headed out into the open prairie. The Murphys, who initiated the adventure, outnumbered all the other participants: Martin Murphy, Sr. and his sons, Martin, Jr., Daniel, Bernard, James, and John; his daughters, Mary, Margaret and Ellen; and finally Murphy's son-in-law, James Miller, along with James' son William and his three daughters. Martin, Jr.'s family included his wife Mary Bolger Murphy and their sons James, Martin III, Patrick W., and Bernard.

The Murphy party arrived at Council Bluffs, Iowa, where they were joined by another wagon train bound for Oregon. Following a cordial rendezvous, the two groups set out for Fort Laramie, along the Old Emigrant Trail to the forlorn plains of old Wyoming. During their stopover in Laramie, while the families rested, the men fed the animals, lubricated the wagons, and made ready for the next move. The leaders traded several fatigued horses for more sturdy Indian ponies, making friends with the natives in the process.

A Birth on the Trail

The parties planned their next encampment at historic Independence Rock, near the Sweetwater River, where they camped for a few days. During their stay, a hunting party went in search of wild buffaloes to replenish their depleted meat supply. While the men were away, a baby girl was born to Mary Murphy Miller, the wife of William Miller. The Miller baby, the first born to a white woman on the westward trek, was appropriately christened Ellen Independence Miller.

Without mishap, the combined wagon trains eventually reached Fort Hall, where they parted company. The Murphy party, the larger of the two, changed direction and set out on the remainder of the journey to California as the others waved good-bye and headed for their destination in Oregon.

The California-bound Murphy party followed the winding Humboldt River for days until the trail vanished, leaving them precariously stranded. Had it not been for a frizzy-faced old Piute Indian, who miraculously appeared out of nowhere and offered to act as their guide, the Murphy party might well have perished. In keeping with his promise, the Indian led them through the parched wilderness until they sighted a gushing stream which has been known ever since as the Truckee River. The Murphys nicknamed their faithful guide "Truckee" because of his resemblance to a French-Indian they once knew in Canada. The name stuck, and to this day both the town and the river bear the name of the old Piute Indian who played such a vital part in the Murphy legend in early California.

Echoes of the Donner Party

With a superhuman effort, the first of the Murphy wagons scaled the eastern slopes of the Sierra Mountains and reached the summit at Donner Lake. Snow piled mountains-high confronted them in every direction. The leaders decided to set camp near the lake and await the coming of spring. The rough-hewn cabins built by the Murphys in 1844 were used to good advantage by the ill-fated Donner Party which came that way five years later in 1849.

To relieve the snow-bound pioneers, a scouting party led by the younger Murphys, John and Daniel, set out across the snow-covered

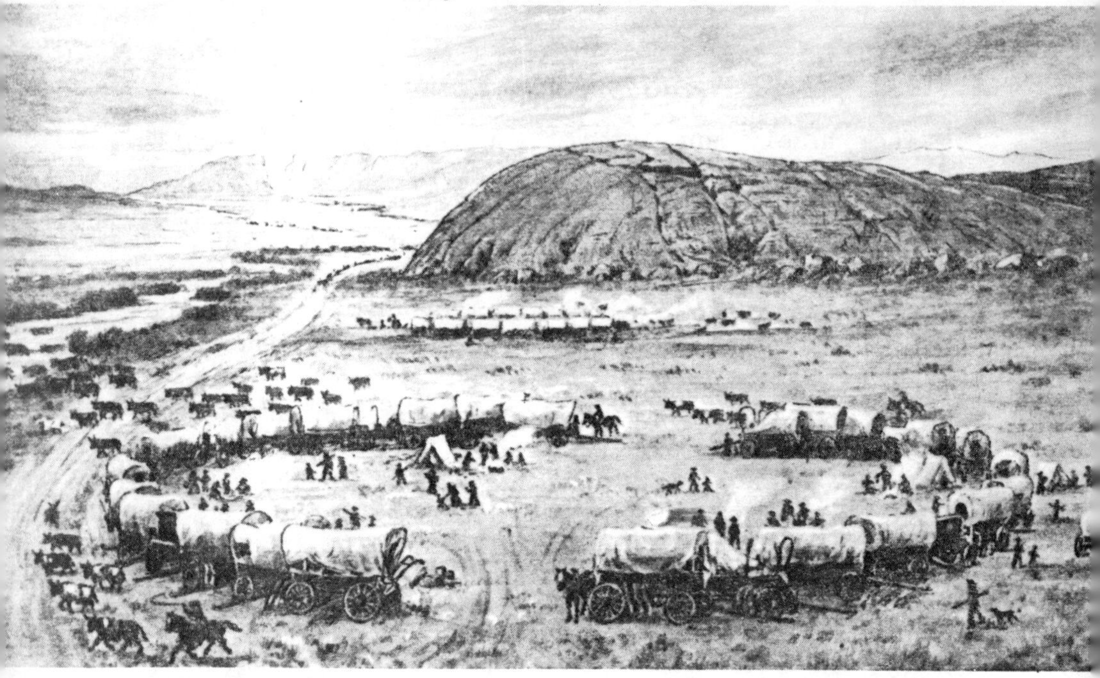

Independence Rock, Wyoming on the Oregon Trail. Here in 1844 Ellen "Independence" Miller was born to Mary Murphy Miller, daughter of Martin Murphy, Sr. [Courtesy of Murphy Museum in Sunnyvale, California.]

Martin Murphy, Sr., father of the Santa Clara land baron.

mountains to the nearest trading post at Fort Sutter in search of food and other necessities. When they finally reached their destination, they learned to their dismay that Spanish California was on the verge of civil war: the opposing parties were the Alvarado-Castro faction vying for power with the Pio Pico-Carillo forces. Pico, a former governor, whose personal interests were primarily based in Southern California, wanted the state capital moved from Monterey to Los Angeles. General Castro, a more affable leader, commanded a much larger following, especially in the northern half of the state.

The unsettled strife spelled more trouble for the Murphy scouts, whose principal mission was to procure food for their half-starved families stranded in the icy heights of the Sierra Mountains. Their pathetic pleas for help went for naught. The Californians were preoccupied with their own problems, and all other considerations took second place. The Castroites struck a hard bargain: cast your lot with us first, and in return we guarantee that your demands will be fulfilled.

The Murphys, too, were no pushovers when it came to bargaining. Besides the promise of the basic provisions for the relief of their starving families in the mountains, the Murphys extracted an agreement enabling them to acquire land as if they were Mexican citizens after the cessation of hostilities. History records that both parties honored their commitments.

The Murphys rode out with the Californians matter-of-factly on their way to Southern California to put down the so-called Pio Pico revolt. As to how little or much actual combat ensued, no one knows for sure. One incident bears mention, however: John Murphy who was only nineteen at the time, was captured and held prisoner for several days. The revolt eventually petered out and young Murphy was released, unharmed.

On the return journey, the Murphys stopped off in Monterey to ensure that the Californians would fulfill their part of the agreement. It was a happy ending for both parties: California was at peace and the Murphy party headed back to the mountains bringing desperately needed supplies for the starving families. Soon the hitherto snow-bound party moved on and set up camp on the Yuba River. Their stay was marked by the second memorable event on their journey to California. A baby girl was born to the wife of Martin Murphy Jr., and she was appropriately named Elizabeth

"Yuba" Murphy. Elizabeth was the first child born of pioneer immigrant parents in California.

The Murphy relief party returned barely in the nick of time to forestall death from exposure and starvation. There was much to reminisce and celebrate when the party was reunited for the first time since their arrival at Donner Lake the previous winter.

With the coming of spring and a warm sun in March 1845, the party broke camp and prepared to leave on the last leg of the journey to Sutter's Fort. The first obstacle they encountered was the Yuba River, usually a placid stream, but the melting snow had transformed it into a raging torrent. For the older members, crossing the river presented no great problem, but for a mother with a baby in her arms, it was a formidable. To insure their safety during the crossing, Martin, Jr. tied the baby to the pommel of the saddle so that his wife would have both hands free against any mishap.

Sure enough, the unexpected happened; the horse stumbled and all three were thrown into the raging current. Luckily, however, the animal regained its footing and made it safely to the other side with both mother and child. The baby, Elizabeth Yuba Murphy, in later years married William Taaffe, a prosperous wholesale merchant in San Francisco, and lived out her life in the Bay Area.

The Murphys Arrive at Sutter's Fort

The arrival of the Murphy-Stevens party at Fort Sutter in March 1845, was heralded with much fanfare. Theirs was the first wagon train to cross the plains, forge the raging rivers, scale the high mountains, and make it all the way to California without loss of life or limb. It was a feat that made history and captured the attention of California historian, H.H. Bancroft, who noted: "The Murphy-Stevens party were the first to open up a wagon trail to California, their route being mainly traversed by the Union Pacific Railroad in later years. They were also the first to cross the Sierra by way of the Truckee and Bear Rivers."

The Murphys were warmly welcomed by John Sutter, the Swiss pioneer founder of New Helvetia, the town we now call Sacramento. There is every indication Martin Murphy, Jr. was one of his most trusted associates and collaborators in the development. The reasons for this trust on Sutter's part are obvious. The Murphys had proved their worth in helping to put down a revolt which Sutter also opposed. Besides, they were already men of substance, with a record of achievement as farmers in both Canada and Missouri, frontiersmen, and intrepid trail blazers.

The Murphy rendezvous at Sutter's Fort was the first reunion of the entire party since they left Missouri as a group in the spring of 1844. They last met as a unit in October of that same year, when they set camp in the snow-covered mountains at Donner Lake. As the old Pioneer Martin, Sr., now in his sixtieth year, remarked, "It's a time to celebrate our safe arrival and to count our many blessings."

Martin Murphy, Jr. purchased as his first property two square leagues (a league is in the neighborhood of nine square miles) of land on the Consumnes River, some 17 miles from his friend John Sutter. Murphy, who was an experienced farmer, planted mostly wheat, which he marketed at the Fort Sutter trading post. It proved a profitable business, enabling him to make additional land purchases in that area. The Murphy Ranch developed into a social center where family, friends, visitors, and newly-arrived Irish immigrants sojourned on weekends.

The Murphy Schoolhouse

Martin Murphy is credited establishing of the first school in Sacramento, which was then known as the "Embarcadero." Classes were first held in a building on the Murphy Ranch where his children received their first instructions. The first teacher was a roving Irish schoolmaster named Patrick O'Brien, a throwback to the hedge school in Ireland's penal days.

All went well at the Murphy Ranch schoolhouse for Mr. O'Brien until the arrival of General Sherman, who took O'Brien into custody as an army deserter. His incarceration, however, was short-lived, partly because of Murphy's influence and the fact that O'Brien was the only qualified teacher to be had in the vast territory. O'Brien was elated by the recognition of his importance in the educational world, arrived unannounced at the Murphy Ranch, and proceeded to take up where he had left off.

The Murphys displayed the true pioneer spirit that paved the way for the occupation of California. They came to establish permanent homes and to share a living partnership with a land so richly endowed. Luckily, they arrived in California when it was still under Mexican jurisdiction and when land grants were more readily available than when the state was under Spanish rule.

Martin Murphy, Sr. chose to settle in the more fertile Santa Clara Valley, where he acquired the vast Aquede La Cocho Rancho. After taking possession, he made many improvements, which included the construction of a fine adobe residence in keeping with Spanish-California tradition. The old pioneer named it San Martin, which would have greatly pleased the saintly missionary, Junipera Serra. The Murphy home became something of a latter-day Hospitality House, a place where all were welcome regardless of their station in life. Bayard Taylor, the roving journalist, relates his impression of the old pioneer and his family, where no stranger was left waiting outside the Murphy door.

Murphy prospered, surrounded by his children. He lived in patriarchal abundance, with his flocks and herds, his lands, and his numerous household. As mentioned , the Murphy home was a stopover for all travellers on the highway, for Murphy was known for hospitality cordially extended to wayfarers.

General Sherman, for one, made it a point to stop at Murphy's place anytime he passed that way. He knew that he could always count upon a delightful evening at the Murphys' Ranch. The indomitable patriarch of the Wexford Murphys made San Martin his home from the time of his arrival in California in 1845 until his death in 1865 in his eightieth year.

Martin, Jr. farmed the Consumnes River Ranch until 1849, when he moved to Santa Clara, which according to his father was a healthier location. He hired local Indians for the most part and taught them the basic principles of farming: how to cultivate the soil and plant the seed. Most of the work in the early stages was done by hand.

According to local diaries, the first wheat crop grown on the Murphy Ranch in New Helvetia was harvested with old-fashioned scythes and reaping hooks. Another account mentions the first threshing bee, and how Martin Murphy improvised a method of extracting the grain from the straw by having his horses stomp the sheaves. It was a far-cry from the massive harvesting combines that delight the eye as they sweep across the California heartland today. John Sutter tells of a delivery of eleven wagonloads of wheat from the Murphy Ranch in the year 1847. Another account notes

Murphy's 39 visits to Sutter's Fort, bringing with him horses and cattle to be offered for sale.

The writer Bayard Taylor relates an interesting anecdote on the time he sought refuge at the Murphy Ranch during a severe rainstorm, where he was greeted by Mrs. Murphy with typical Irish hospitality:

> Martin Murphy, I found, was a son of the old gentleman whose hospitalities I had shared in the valley of San Jose. He had been living for years on the river, and his three sturdy sons could ride and throw a lariat equal to any Californian. There were Indian boys belonging to the house, one of them, a stolid, shock headed urchin, as grave as if he were born to be a 'medicine man,' did all the household duties with precision and steadiness.

The Bear Flag Revolt

Whether by fate or coincidence, the Murphys were at the forefront of many unheralded events before California's becoming a part of the United States. One of these was the historic (if not bizarre) Bear Flag Revolt in 1846. Whenever there is a confrontation of this sort, the Irish are usually involved. This time around, however, Martin Murphy acted the part of the peacemaker. Over the years there have been many conflicting accounts written about the Bear Flag conflict, but all are in agreement that the conflict was initiated at the Murphy Ranch. This first overt act by the Americans against Mexican rule marked a turning point, but was overshadowed by the outbreak of the Mexican War.

Despite its apparent insignificance, the Bear Flag Revolt forms an integral part of California history and heritage. According to Bancroft's *History of California*, Lieutenant Francisco Arce and his men were driving 125 horses from the parched foothills to greener pastures in the San Joaquin Valley. The Mexicans stopped at the ranch overnight and stabled their horses in the Murphy corral. During their stay a party of Americans, led by General John Fremont and Captain Merritt, surprised the Mexicans and made off with the horses. These Americans then captured Sonoma, raising the "Bear Flag" as a sign of Independence. Martin Murphy, by now a man of means, came to the rescue of the Mexicans providing a horse for each of the men in order to maintain the cordial relations that existed between the Mexican authorities and the settlers.

From Rover to Land Baron

Martin Murphy's rise from an obscure wheat farmer to a man of wealth and influence can be traced to his Consumnes Rancho in New Helvetia, which he acquired shortly after his arrival from Missouri. His profits from wheat alone was astronomical, not to mention the income he derived from flocks and herds. The timing was right on target. The discovery of gold in 1848 brought people by the thousands in search of fortune. The prices of every commodity, including land, skyrocketed. The old saying that "The man who sells at a profit never goes broke" must have appealed to Martin Murphy. He realized a profit substantial enough as to make him a rich man for life. According to a family diary, Murphy retained the family residence plus 160 acres which he disposed of some years later.

Martin Murphy, Jr. Relocates to Santa Clara County

Paternal guidance had a tremendous influence on the close-knit Murphy clan. It induced Martin, Jr. to follow his aging father to Santa Clara County. The opportunity to acquire Pastoria de la Borregas (Sheep Pasture) Rancho came about in an unusual way, according to a family diary. It appears that Murphy had a trading post on his land supplying horses, cattle, and tools to the settlers. On one occasion, Murphy made a trip to San Jose to buy cattle to resell or trade to the miners. Unable to agree on a price, Murphy offered to buy the ranch instead, which he did, at a price of $12,000 for more than 4,000 acres. The land originally belonged to Governor Alvarado, who possessed it until 1842. The deed, however, was signed by Mariana Castro, who evidently had acquired it in the meantime. Title was confirmed by the U.S. Land Commission in 1855, when Murphy changed the name to Bay View Ranch.

The Murphy Home in Sunnyvale

Martin Murphy did all things well. This included the construction of the family residence on his Bay View Ranch in Sunnyvale, which was occupied continuously by the family until

1953. The home was not of the usual adobe construction, but rather, a substantial wood-frame building, the first of its kind in Santa Clara County. Milled to his specifications in Maine and transported all the way around Cape Horn in sailing ships, the building was fastened together by wooden pegs and secured by rawhide thongs in the absence of nails, a scarce commodity in that early period. The house was meticulously maintained by many generations of the Murphys and remained in good living condition for more than a century. It was a two-story dwelling planned for both convenience and privacy, with a spacious central hallway running from front to back with doors leading to an enclosed garden. A winding stairway led to the upper floor with its spacious bedrooms, closets and baths.

When the house was completed in 1851, the lower reaches of the San Francisco Bay were in full view of the Murphy dwelling. Many an evening after dinner, family and friends seated themselves on the open portico to watch the continuous parade of boats plying the Bay. To quote a local gazette of that period: "Set in a large oak grove with a view of the bay, the Murphy home, Bay View Ranch, became a social and political center for the Santa Clara Valley." The spacious home was adorned with family portraits, done in oil by various artists, including several generations of the Wexford Murphys in both Ireland and America.

To this house at regular intervals walked the priests of Santa Clara Mission to celebrate Mass. A room with an a consecrated altar stone was set apart for this purpose, and here marriage and christening services took place as well.

The inherent desire for both religious and educational fulfillment for their children was of prime importance in every part of Martin Murphy's life. It induced the Murphys to vacate Missouri and resettle in Spanish California, a Catholic country. To an even greater degree Murphy realized a lifelong dream of both religious and educational advantages when he settled within walking distance of Santa Clara Mission. There a vanguard of Jesuits had already been stationed the year previous. Even more encouraging news was in the making: Joseph Sodoc Alemany was appointed the first bishop of California in 1850, the year Martin Murphy, Jr. settled in Santa Clara. The newly-appointed bishop made his headquarters in the former colonial capital of old Monterey. The Murphy home became something of a halfway house, a stopping place for the bishop on his visitations throughout his far-flung diocese. On special occasions, he celebrated mass in a room set aside for that purpose which in time became known as the "Bishop's room." One such visit is recorded in the church annals of December 15, 1863, "Visited Murphy home where I blessed Church under title Saint Patrick." Other visits were noted in the register in 1862 and 1868. From all indications, the good Bishop was having his difficulties with the English language.

The friendship that developed between Martin Murphy and Bishop Alemany bore fruit in the advancement of Catholicism in California during the different stages of the states development. One example of this teamwork comes to light in the refurbishing of the Santa Clara Mission in 1851, which had lapsed into decay following the secularization of the Missions by the Mexican Government.

Murphy was a man of deep humility and avoided any references to his charity or to any of his generous contributions to the church. It was only in later years that a family member alluded to his late father's benevolence to churches up and down the California coast.

Founding Father of Santa Clara University

Martin Murphy's unstinting interest in education was inspired by his apparent lack of it. The Penal Laws had prohibited Irish Catholics from enrollment in state-sponsored schools. In order to make amends for this deficiency, one of his very first acts when the Murphy family acquired a home in New Helvetia in 1845 was to hire a qualified teacher to instruct his children.

One of Murphy's more notable philanthropies was to help establish Santa Clara College in 1851. He was its generous and leading contributor. According to William McQuaid, one of H.H. Bancroft's literary associates, the Murphy boys were also the first to enroll when the College opened its doors:

> The Murphy children were the first who attended Santa Clara College, of which their father Martin Murphy was de facto founder. Before this schooling, the boys had a private tutor in residence whom they took along with them and who became a part of the teaching faculty.

From this grass-roots beginning developed one of the most renowned institutions of higher learning in northern California, better known in our time as the University of Santa Clara.

Beyond these accomplishments, Murphy was the primary mover in the establishment of the Notre Dame Academy, a school for girls in nearby San Jose. When Sisters Loyola and Marie Catherine first arrived in California from their western headquarters in Oregon to await the arrival of the other members of their community, they were guests for a brief period at the Murphy residence in Sunnyvale. San Jose was an inconsequential Mexican pueblo until the year 1849, when it suddenly loomed into prominence as the capital of the new-born state. It was at the Murphy Ranch that the Sisters first met Bishop Alemany, who prevailed on them to open a convent in California. The Sisters were heartened by the many offers of cooperation and financial assistance from the newly arrived settlers, whose primary concern was to promote both educational and religious facilities. They were also encouraged by the news that a boys College was being planned by the Jesuits in nearby Santa Clara.

Notre Dame Academy is a name revered in California Catholic annals. It opened its doors for enrollment in the fall of 1851. Murphy's daughter was the first of more than one hundred young ladies to seek admittance. This came as no surprise when it became known that it was her benevolent father who had donated the site for the new school. For over seventy years, the Sisters of Notre Dame provided a classical education for thousands of young women in the growing city of San Jose and the surrounding area. In 1924, the Order acquired the coveted Ralston Estate in Belmont on the San Francisco peninsula and changed the name to the "College of Notre Dame."

California Land Baron

As a pioneer farmer and land owner, Martin Murphy was decisively influential in developing agriculture in early California. There are countless examples of his foresight and ingenuity in wheat growing, stock raising, viticulture, and mechanized farming. As the state's pioneer wheat-growing farmer, he initiated a research study that led to the development of a superior type of grain that could be stored for long periods of time without decay or loss of potency.

When this hybrid crop was marketed it fetched a price of $1.80 a hundredweight, compared with the standard variety that sold for $1.30 a hundred. According to an 1874 San Jose city directory, Martin Murphy planted 172,573 acres in wheat which netted 1,578,843 bushels. He planted the first orchards that grew so profusely in the virgin soil as to transform the broad valley into a veritable garden of Eden in the blossoming season. Neighborliness was a way of life in those early years. Why not have an old-fashioned picnic, some would suggest, and share nature's paradise with the less fortunate city dwellers? People began by inviting friends to see the blossoms. Most of those who came had never seen anything like that before. Every spring brought bigger crowds, which gave birth to California's most spectacular outdoor celebration, the "Blossom Festival."

Murphy was heartened by the unprecedented growth of the citrus industry which he pioneered. He envisioned even greater possibilities in viticulture, which was most suitable to the state's rich soil and warm climate. Over one million of the choicest grape vines were imported from Europe as a starter, which were supplemented by other varieties as the need arose. According to Santa Clara County records, the annual yield for the area tallied 2,500,000 bottles of wine. California's world-renowned wineries, and one of the state's most lucrative enterprises, owe their beginnings for the most part to the original vines rooted on Martin Murphy's land well over a century ago.

In that same period, he introduced a new breed of cattle more suitable to the states warm climate and dry terrain. This well-bred herd thrived on the rolling hills and grassy ravines the year round with a minimum of care. He imported the first Norman horses all the way from his ancient homeland in County Wexford. At various times he travelled to the East coast to buy the most up-to-date farm tools, which he shipped out to California by way of Panama.

Murphy, San Jose's Pioneer Builder & Benefactor

Although his interest in farming outran every other consideration, Martin Murphy was the first to broach the idea of an inner-city marketing center for the exchange of goods and services. San Jose, a Mexican pueblo of little note, became the State capital following the California Constitutional Convention in 1849

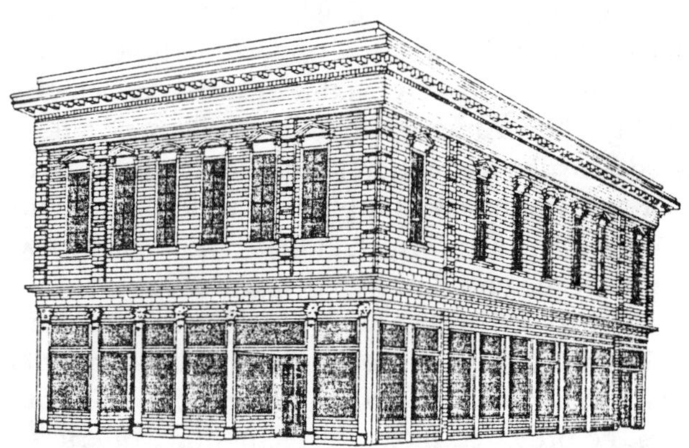

San Jose's Murphy Building, built in the 1860s and used for commerce, courthouse, and post office. [Courtesy of Murphy Museum in Sunnyvale.]

Looking north onto the 100 block of Sunnyvale's South Murphy Avenue in the early 1900s. [Courtesy of Murphy Museum in Sunnyvale, California.]

Although the area had little to offer prospective investors at that time, Murphy shrewdly perceived its potential with the advent of modern transportation. It was the opportune time to acquire land when the vast majority were forsaking it in the hopes of striking it rich in the gold fields. Although there was plenty of land to be had, what attracted Murphy's attention to that particular location was the assurance of an abundant supply of water from the nearby Guadalupe River. The area, which at that time was but a wildflower wilderness, is now the nostalgic hub of Old San Jose.

In this his first urban venture, Murphy constructed a row of commercial buildings with office space and living quarters on the upper floors. When the newly organized city council lacked a meeting place, he provided them with temporary quarters while the terms and conditions of a rental agreement could be negotiated. The City Fathers agreed to take a five-year lease with the provision that Murphy refurbish the building in a manner becoming such an august body.

When California became a state in 1850, the first Supreme Court under American jurisdiction convened in a large hall in one of Murphy's San Jose buildings at Market and Eldorado Streets.

Although he was a lifelong member of the Democratic party, Murphy never sought political office during his career. Still, his advice was constantly solicited in matters of public policy. He cast his vote for the first time as an American citizen in the year 1850. In the registry of voters his name is listed as "Irish" and "Farmer." His two sons Patrick W., born in 1838, and Bernard D., born in 1841, were both active in politics for many years. Patrick represented the three counties of Ventura, Santa Barbara, and San Louis Obispo from 1865 to 1868 and was reelected to the same position in 1877. Bernard represented Santa Clara County in the Assembly from 1868 until his election to the State Senate in 1877. The following year he was elected Mayor of San Jose.

Kings and High Kings

An unnamed California journalist, somewhat enamored of Irish history, noted: "The Murphys ruled like ancient Irish Kings over much of California for well over half a century." Though his wording is extravagant, there was much truth in the statement. The Murphy kingdom extended all the way from the Santa Susanna

Mountain Range north of Los Angeles to the city of San Francisco, where Martin was listed as owning property in excess of $100,000, a considerable sum in that early period. The above holdings were exclusive of the original 12,000 acre ranch in the Sacramento Valley, one-half of which they still retain.

According to the terms of Martin Murphy's will, the properties were to be divided equally among his surviving children. To avoid the expense of probate and partition, he made a joint deed of trust for the holding of each heir's property until his death, when the surviving joint trustee became the sole owner.

With an eye to the future, Murphy, the old pioneer, took a keen interest in state transportation. With the coming of the Transcontinental railroad, which was completed in 1869, California was no longer isolated. Shortly thereafter, the San Francisco-San Jose Railroad Company was formed for the purpose of building a railroad on the San Francisco peninsula. When the good news got around, Martin Murphy deeded the company a right-of-way through his Bay View Ranch. As an added gesture of goodwill, he donated the land on which he constructed a depot at his own expense. Over the years a thriving community developed near the depot, which became known as the Murphy Station.

Money Lender and Philanthropist

One example of Murphy's share-the-wealth philosophy came to light when he began making loans to Santa Clara County settlers with interest far below prevailing rates and with payment terms to suit each borrower. From 1851 to 1857 inclusive, he charged one-and-a-half percent on loans of $25,000 or more, with comparable rates on lesser amounts. Evidently he was influenced by his father, Martin, Sr., who charged no interest on loans when he settled San Martin in 1849.

While Martin, Jr. will be long remembered for his many and varied contributions to California, his wife Mary was also well-known for her generous and sympathetic nature. On one particular occasion when her husband was attempting to evict squatters from his land, Mary took care of the intruders' families. Mary's benevolence evidently shamed the squatters into vacating the Murphy property, something which the courts had attempted without success.

The Society of California Pioneers was founded in 1850 as an exclusive association admitting only those who arrived in California on or before midnight of December 31, 1849. Martin Murphy was admitted as a member in 1853, along with his wife, Mary. When James, Bernard, Daniel T., John M., and James T. Murphy joined a year later, the Murphys outnumbered all of the other families listed in the organization's archives.

The End of an Era

Murphy's health began to fail in 1882, when he suffered his first heart attack. He never fully recuperated from this setback. He continued to live at his Bay View Ranch until 1883, when he removed to San Jose on the advice of his physician. On October 20, 1884, he passed away at the age of 77, surrounded by his loving wife and family.

Funeral services were conducted at Saint Joseph's, the mother church of San Jose, which was filled to capacity on the solemn occasion. Archbishop Alemany, his lifelong friend and confidant, celebrated a solemn Requiem Mass and imparted the final blessing. Father John Prendergast, Vicar General of the diocese, gave an eloquent account of the life and times of Martin Murphy and the legacy he had bequeathed to future generations. It was a sobering day of mourning for the residents of Santa Clara County, many of whom were close friends of the deceased.

People came from throughout California to pay their respects to a man some had never met but all had grown to love and admire. Flags were lowered to half staff, State and City governments set aside their calendars, and business houses closed shop for the day.

A long line of carriages, followed by mourners on horseback and foot, accompanied the remains all the way from Saint Joseph's Church to Santa Clara cemetery, a distance of more than five miles. When the funeral reached the Convent of Notre Dame, an honor guard of Sisters and students lined the streets to pay a final tribute to their mentor and patron of the pioneer academy.

The *San Jose Mercury* expressed the sentiments of the saddened community in the aftermath of the burial:

> Seldom has an event transpired within the City's history that has caused so general a feeling of sadness and regret

> as the death of Martin Murphy. This was testified to by the large number who visited the home of the bereaved family. Many were comparative strangers who, actuated by a knowledge of the good deeds of Martin Murphy, desired to look for the last time on a face they had learned to love.

The San Francisco *Call* added its tribute in an article dated October 21, 1884, entitled "Death of a Well-Known Pioneer and Millionaire":

> Martin Murphy, foremost of pioneers and widely known for his wealth and generous hospitality, died of heart disease about 3 o'clock yesterday morning (Oct. 20) at his residence in San Jose. The life of Martin Murphy is worthy of study in these days of shifting occupations and gambling speculations.

The mantle of the Murphy clan fell to his son Bernard, who became the family spokesman and heir apparent to the Bay View Ranch. Following the dictates of his father, Bernard devoted his best efforts to preserving the family homestead in Sunnyvale and the pastoral grandeur of Santa Clara Valley, the epitome of early California.

With the constant influx of new settlers and the predictable increase in the price of land, the rich plains were no longer best suited to for diversified farming or stock raising. The vast wheat fields gave way to more profitable orchards and vineyards. Despite the clamor for land division by prospectors who struck it rich in the gold mines, the Murphys hung onto the ranch until 1953, when the City of Sunnyvale acquired the property for public use.

Nothing remains of the Murphy residence, once the social center of Santa Clara County and a haven of Irish hospitality. The only reminder of its former glory is a commemorative bronze plaque, with the inscription: "*California Historic Landmark, No. 644.*" The plaque was erected on May 22, 1960, by the State Park Commission at the behest of the Sunnyvale Historical Society and the City of Sunnyvale.

In order to make amends for this apparent lack of appropriate emphasis on the Murphy family's contributions to California, the Sunnyvale Historical Society, in cooperation with the City of

Sunnyvale and other civic-minded enthusiasts, staged a centennial commemoration of the Murphy Golden Wedding celebration in 1981. It was a Trojan effort in every respect, well planned, lavishly funded, and well-publicized. With names like Dianne McKenna (Mayor of Sunnyvale), Pat Malone (President of the Sunnyvale Historical Society), Noreen Moran, Sherri McLoughlin, Paul Taylor, and Sheila Kelleher, leading the way, the twentieth-century revelers set out to revive the Murphy memory. A long weekend celebration was planned, just as it was in 1881, with special trains bringing guests from all over northern California. The festivities began with a parade of covered wagons that had previously crossed the Sierra Mountains following the route blazed by the Murphy wagons in 1844. They were followed by vintage automobiles, old fire engines, horses and buggies, and strollers in period costumes. Barbecue tables were set up with seating for 1,000 at a time, as it was 100 years ago. High-stepping Irish dancers dressed in authentic Gaelic costumes added a twentieth-century touch. It was a stupendous affair; however, it lacked the old-time flavor and the more relaxed atmosphere of the Murphy era.

The Murphy Historical Legacy

Family names connected with the Murphy clan still dot the streets of Sunnyvale, California. Murphy Avenue was named for Martin Murphy, Jr., its most revered citizen. Carroll Avenue was named for Richard Carroll, Mary Ann Murphy's husband; Taaffe Avenue for William Taaffe, Elizabeth Murphy's husband; Bernardo Avenue for Bernard Murphy, and Arques Avenue for Joaquin Arques, Helen Murphy's husband.

The Murphy historical legacy is impressive. Even a partial list of the Murphy contributions to California history would have to include the following:

- The first to cross the Sierra by the Donner Pass.
- The first whites to gaze on Lake Tahoe.
- The first immigrant group to bring wagons over the mountains to California.

* The first successful wheat farmers in the Sacramento Valley.
* The first to import American cattle and Norman horses.
* The first frame house in Santa Clara County.
* The first orchards in the Santa Clara Valley.
* The first brick buildings in San Jose.
* The first school in Sacramento County, conducted in the Murphy home.
* The first child (Elizabeth Yuba Murphy) born of pioneer immigrants in California.

A perpetual memorial to the indomitable pioneer stands on the banks of the Consumnes River, the site of the original Murphy Ranch in Sacramento: California Landmark No 680. It was approved by the State Historical Landmarks Commission in May 1959 at the behest of the Sacramento Historical Society and the University of the Pacific History Foundation. The plaque, dedicated October 17, 1959, reads as follows:

> This is the site of the beginning of the conquest of California by the United States. On June 10, 1846, American settlers led by Ezekiel Merritt overpowered the soldiers under Lieutenant Francisco Acre and took their Mexican army from the corral of the Murphy Ranch on the north bank of the Consumnes River.

This story is confirmed by historians H.H. Bancroft and R.D. Hunt. The Murphy Ranch saw the first skirmish between the Americans and Mexicans for the control of California. It was a brief encounter, but its significance cannot be ignored in either American or California history. The episode, ruthless though it was, was typical of the pioneer spirit that steered California into the union.

The many dramatic events in the life and times of Martin and Mary Murphy are now but a memory. A golden era vanished when the last of the tired, happy revelers at the Murphy's golden wedding anniversary bid good-bye as they made their way out through the Murphys' garden gate and into history, nearly a hundred years ago.

James Phelan, Sr., the tycoon in the prime of his life. [Courtesy of the Bancroft Library, University of California at Berkeley.]

7

James Phelan: Patriarch of the 49er Pioneers

Irish-born James Phelan, Sr. (1821-1892) is best remembered as a dynamic entrepreneur in early California and as the father of his statesman-son, James Duval Phelan (1861-1930). The father's creative spirit stimulated fantastic growth throughout the state and around the world. But the Phelan name is especially linked with the adventurous metropolis of San Francisco. Here, James, Sr. revealed himself as one of the city's earliest practical utopians. Back when Market Street—today San Francisco's main thoroughfare—was only a modest horse trail winding through bleak sand hills, Phelan had ambitious plans for the area. Here he purchased land that today is the site of the impressive Phelan Building, a historic landmark in downtown San Francisco. As San Francisco's first modern building (*circa* 1871), the ornate structure quickly became the hub of the far-reaching Phelan empire in California.

Though James Phelan, Sr. won fame and fortune as a merchant, banker and builder, he was best known as a man of honesty and integrity. Phelan's word was impeccable, and he never lent a deaf ear to those less fortunate than himself. Through perseverance and honest endeavor he rose from a five-dollar-a-week grocer's apprentice to become one of the most highly respected businessmen in early California. With unflagging industry and civic pride, this self-made tycoon involved himself in every aspect of the state's development, from the frenzied Gold Rush era beginning in 1849 to the mammoth construction of the Panama Canal.

History and Home of the Phelans

In the year 1821, James Phelan, the son of James and Judith Brophy Phelan, was born in Middlemount, Parish of Aghaboe, Queen's County (Laois or Leix). Aghaboe, the ancestral homeland of the O'Phelans, was the principal city of Ossory in ancient times, as well as the site of the monastery founded by Saint Canice in the sixth century A.D. Aghaboe prided itself as one of the oldest and most revered centers of learning in early Christian Ireland. It was a flourishing community long before either Paris or Berlin were even dots on any map. The monastery at Aghaboe could boast among its alumni a former Abbot named Virgilius, whose labors helped to stem the tide of barbarism that swept through Europe during the Dark Ages. Abbot Virgilius founded the See of Salzburg in Austria and became its first Bishop in 776 A.D. In 1976, the year the youthful United States commemorated its two hundredth birthday, Salzburg Cathedral celebrated its twelve hundredth. In European literary circles, the monk is better known as "Virgilius the Geographer" since he was among the first scholars in western Europe to proclaim openly that the world was round, an idea that drew the wrath of many conservative astronomers of the day. *Lives of the Saints* and other ecclesiastical biographies simply give his hallowed name as "Saint Virgilius."

But let us return to Ossory and the Phelans. According to O'Heerin, the twelfth-century scribe, Ossory was the tribal land of the O'Phelans. The Rev. William Carrigan in his monumental tome, *The History and Antiquities of the Diocese of Ossory,* gives this translation of an ancient Gaelic poem that links the O'Phelans to Ossory:

> In Magh Lacha of the warm-hill slopes
> Is O'Faolain of manly tribes;
> Extensive is the district due to them
> Which the O'Faolains have filled.

Chapter 7: *James Phelan*

When Aghaboe, the seat of the Diocese of Ossory, came under the jurisdiction of the Dominican Order in 1382, Father John Phelan became its first Prior and Pastor. Every attempt to destroy the old monastery failed, and it continued its holy works for centuries. Even following the monastery's desecration at the hands of the British during the Penal times, a hidden Mass Station was erected in the nearby woods, where religious services could be conducted in secret. On one grisly occasion this holy site was the scene of a murder: a priest named Father Phelan was set upon and cut down while celebrating a clandestine Mass. The ruins of the centuries-old Phelan Chapel, so-named to honor this martyred priest, is a grim reminder of Ireland's long history of persecution.

They were a renowned Gaelic clan, the O'Phelans, and had farmed the fertile lands of Upper Ossory, which for centuries has been known as the breadbasket of Ireland. Little wonder that this bountiful territory was the first to be confiscated when the English plantation (foreign colonization) of Ireland was inaugurated in the year 1549. The native Irish—the O'Phelans, O'Dunnes, O'Dempseys, O'Dowlings, O'Dorans, O'Moores, O'Lalors, O'Kellys, the Fitzpatricks, and many other families—fell victim to this plundering scheme. Eventually they were dispossessed of their holdings, which were then handed over to settlers with such unmistakably English and Scottish names as Hamilton, Leslie, Crosby, Watson, Franks, Coote, Graham, Gilbert, and Thompson. Ironically, the O'Phelans themselves, because of their high standing in the community, were granted a dubious privilege: they could remain as servants to the newly settled foreign masters.

The passage of the Act of Union in 1800 led to disbanding the Irish Parliament. Ireland became annexed with, and subservient to, a tyrannical United Kingdom. Earlier, the United Irish rebellion had nearly collapsed with the murder of of capable soldier, Lord Edward Fitzgerald in 1798; the 1803 martyrdom of Irish patriot Robert Emmet meant a leaderless nation could offer little if any resistance. The oppressed Irish had only two bleak alternatives open to them: either to stay put and suffer or to emigrate and take their chances in the new world beyond the western seas.

The Phelans in America

James Phelan, the elder, decided to take his chances. In 1827, he journeyed to America with his three sons, John, James, and Michael, and settled in New York City. (Since there was no mention of the boy's mother in records of this time, we may assume that she had already passed away.) We can also conjecture that James may have been encouraged to immigrate to America by relatives who at settled in New York and who were willing to offer a helping hand.

Apparently the newly-arrived Phelans fared well at first. James, Sr. found employment and enrolled the boys in school. Despite the expense of rearing and educating three growing children, he managed to save sufficient capital to establish a business of his own.

Unfortunately, the Phelan family faced harder times when their business failed. To help the family survive, James, the oldest of the three Phelan boys (and the hero of our story), quit school and found a job; but there was little work to be had for a schoolboy with no particular skills. His only opportunity was an apprenticeship in a nearby grocery store with a beginner's salary of $5.00 a week. Though the wages were meager, the job proved a blessing in disguise, since these early business skills helped pave the way for James' fabulous success as a merchant in later years. Indeed, by 1846, at the age of 25, the former grocery clerk had risen to the status of a leading retailer in the bustling city of Cincinnati, Ohio.

Two years later, gold was discovered in far-off California. The spectacular bonanza was loudly proclaimed in headlines on the front pages of every American newspaper. California gold ignited the imagination of people to an unprecedented money-making opportunity. Unlike thousands of others, Phelan did not impetuously rush westward. He patiently awaited verification of the gold-find story from official sources. However, when he had confirmed the reports, he swiftly took decisive action. He had no interest in the chancy prospects of digging for gold in the hills. Instead, he was a shrewd entrepreneur, and he foresaw the unlimited opportunities for trade and merchandising that would inevitably arise when the hordes of prospectors settled into the new territory.

To fund the long journey and to bankroll his future career in merchandising, James disposed of his holdings in Cincinnati and returned to New York City, where his brother John was a leading wholesale merchant. With the money from the sale of his assets in Cincinnati and from some other interests, he purchased a huge quantity of goods that he foresaw would be in demand in cupboard-bare California. His challenge was how to transport the bulky inventory over thousands of miles, with no guarantee of safe arrival. In order to avoid a total loss from any unforeseen catastrophe, he consigned the goods to three different vessels and dispatched them over different routes. Two tall-masted sailing ships named the *Francis* and the *Fulton*, carrying the bulk of Phelan's merchandise set sail in tandem on the long journey around Cape Horn. The third vessel, appropriately christened the *El Dorado*, came by way of Panama with Phelan himself on board. When the *El Dorado* arrived at Chagres, the merchandise had to be unloaded and transported over land across the peninsula to Panama City on the west side of the isthmus (the Panama Canal, of course, was not built until many years later).

To complicate matters, the ship's crew was stricken with yellow fever, which postponed the unloading of the cargo for three weeks. During the layover, Phelan himself fell victim to the dreaded epidemic. He became so ill in fact that he despaired of ever reaching California. However, with the skillful treatment of the ship's physician, Dr. Carpenter, Phelan's health rallied and he continued the journey.

By then a crowd of several thousand gold seekers had gathered on the waterfront in Panama desperately awaiting passage to California. During the long delay, several of the stranded argonauts died from the devastating disease. Heat prostration and other maladies felled many others. In reckless greed, some gold-mad gamblers fled to the local forests, chopped down trees, and constructed primitive wooden boats that proved to be unseaworthy. One of the makeshift crafts with twenty-eight men on board, set sail for the gold fields never to be heard from again. Two other jerry-rigged boats also set out together only to be shipwrecked on the coast of Mexico. Fortunately, this mishap resulted in no loss of life. The beleaguered passengers continued on foot and luckily made a safe passage overland to their destination in California.

After many weeks of waiting, the brig *Panama* finally arrived in Panama City, to the delight of thousands of frustrated adventurers.

Mr. Stout, the ship's purser, was flabbergasted when he saw that the impatiently awaiting mob was far larger than his ship's capacity. Some would have to be stranded. After some thought, Strout decided that the only fair way to select the passengers was to cast lots, as in biblical times. With a bit of Irish luck, James Phelan drew a steerage ticket which he could have disposed of then and there for several times the price of its face value As it turned out, his good fortune was only beginning. Phelan's merchandise aboard the ship included a quantity of saleratus (baking soda), an essential ingredient which the ship's scullery had in scant supply. When the captain learned of Phelan's baking powder, he purchased the entire lot from Phelan at four dollars a pound, and threw in cabin accommodations as an added bonus.

Phelan Arrives in San Francisco

With Phelan aboard, the *Panama* arrived in San Francisco in August 1849, where his brother Michael welcomed him. From the moment James stepped on California soil, fortune prospered the Phelan brothers. Within months the weary traveler regained his health in the salubrious air for which San Francisco is renowned. Shortly thereafter, the other two ships, laden with Phelan's merchandise, also arrived on the San Francisco waterfront.

James and Michael soon formed a partnership under the name of J. & M. Phelan Company, located on Jackson Street near Montgomery. Consumer demand was so high that they easily disposed of their merchandise for cash at a considerable profit. The markups were spectacular: kegs of nails that cost $3.00 sold for $12.00; iron safes purchased for $100.00 realized as much as $500; wallpaper bought for seven cents a roll retailed for $7.50; and a box of tacks which cost five cents brought in $1.00. With glassware, household goods, and stationery earning similar profits, within a period of some three years the Phelan brothers amassed a fortune of more than $100,000. In 1851, their holdings were assessed at $50,000 for the purpose of taxation, or approximately one fourth of their actual net worth.

Later, the Company moved to Front Street, where they continued in business together until Michael's death in 1858. James, as sole owner, remained active in business as a wholesale merchant on Commerce Street, opposite Pier 17, on the Embarcadero. An advertisement in the San Francisco *Herald* dated April 11, 1859, read as follows:

Brandy and Rum, etc., in Bond or Duty Paid

Alexander Segnette Brandy

Narriot & Co., Fine Cognac

Jamaica Rum and Scotch Whiskey

For Sale in Lots to Suit

3,500 German Demijohns (1/2 to 4 gallons) to arrive shortly

By James D. Phelan
Commerce Street near Battery

One notable illustration of Phelan's business acumen was his savvy investment in oil. When whale oil from the Sandwich Islands (Hawaii) accumulated in warehouses and glutted the market, Phelan bought all he could lay hands on for as little as ten cents a gallon. In due course, after he received a shipment of lamps from his brother John, a wholesale merchant in New York, James resold the undervalued oil for as much as two dollars a gallon and made a respectable profit on the lamps to boot.

In 1850, when the United States government began phasing out its commissary operations at the San Francisco Bay town of Benicia and offered for sale its entire stock of foodstuffs (barrels of beef and pork, dried fruit, and assorted pickles, appraised at $75,000), Phelan made a cash offer and bought the whole lot at less than half the market price. The merchandise was then resold by the Phelan Company in San Francisco and reaped a colossal profit.

Banker and Builder

Phelan with extraordinary prescience envisioned a great city rising out of San Francisco's sand dunes, and systematically prepared for its destiny. When Market Street, which was to become the city's main thoroughfare, was still only rolling sand hills barely noticed on city maps, Phelan purchased land at the intersection of Market and O'Farrell Streets. There he constructed his imposing Phelan building. This was the city's first modern structure, and it pioneered the spectacular growth of San Francisco from a pueblo to a metropolis. The site had once belonged to the eccentric, half-demented Joshua Norton, the self-proclaimed Norton I, Emperor of Mexico and Protector of the United States.

The original Phelan Building, a $500,000 extravaganza, stood out conspicuously among the city's adobes and flimsy wooden shacks. Five million bricks and two million board feet of timber, in addition to impressive quantities of iron and brass, were used in its construction. When completed, Mr. Phelan made the building his headquarters—from which he directed his affluent dynasty with its many tentacles throughout California. This original Phelan building was partly destroyed during the 1906 earthquake and fire, but it was rebuilt by the old pioneers only son, James Duval, who was destined to uphold and perpetuate the Phelan legacy.

The First National Bank in San Francisco, the first gold bank in the State, was another brainchild of the indomitable pioneer James Phelan. Congress had passed a law in 1863 permitting national banks to redeem their notes in greenbacks, which were the only alternative for a government strapped for funds during the costly civil war. When the nation regained its economic equilibrium in 1870, the law was amended, making it mandatory for all members of the federal banking system to redeem their certificates in gold. Phelan was convinced that gold redemption would consolidate and modernize the state's banking system. He boldly acted on his conviction and inaugurated plans which led to the establishment of the First National Gold Bank of California with a capital of $1,000,000. Leaving nothing to chance, Phelan journeyed to Washington to deliver in person the necessary documents and security bonds as required by law to complete the transaction. Little wonder that the bank's progenitor, James Phelan, was unanimously elected as its first President. Within a brief period of twelve years after its opening, the bank paid out $2,000,000 in dividends, a record in those pioneer days. The unprecedented opulence and growth of Phelan's gold bank focused the eyes of the nation on California and set in motion a western trend that has prevailed to this very day.

The Phelan Building erected in 1881-82 on Market Street in San Francisco. [Courtesy of Bancroft Library, University of California, Berkeley.]

Phelan in San Jose

In the year 1880, Phelan purchased the Martin Estate which stands on the site of present-day Old San Jose. Two years later he erected a substantial block of buildings at the intersection of First and Eldorado Streets, some of which are still standing. The historic structures were christened: Phelan Hall, in honor of his only son James Duval; the Alice Building for his daughter Alice (Mrs. Frank Sullivan); and the Louise Building for his daughter Mary Louise. Dubbed the "Garden City," San Jose owes much of its early development to the two purposeful Irish pioneers: James Phelan and Martin Murphy, whose life story is related another chapter. Even the enterprising Phelan could not have dreamed from this humble beginning that San Jose would become the hub of one of the most technologically advanced regions in modern America.

Building the Panama Canal

At the age of 61, when most men would be planning to retire and seek a quieter life, Phelan was about to embark on one of the most challenging adventures of his entire business career: as an sparkplug in the building of the Panama Canal. The Canal was to alter the course of history and set in motion the expansion of American power and influence on a global basis. This enormous project consumed the energies of over four decades from its inception in the 1870s to its completion in 1914.

In this monumental endeavor, the American Contracting and Dredging Company, founded by James Phelan and the Slaven brothers (Moses and Henry), played a major role. However, resembling the dauntless Henry Ford, who set out to put the nation on wheels despite his lack of mechanical know-how, neither Phelan nor the Slavens knew anything about building a canal. But this inexperience failed to dampen their enthusiasm.

The company's initial design for the dredging machine was based on a model that proved successful in dredging California's San Joaquin River to prevent flooding in the rainy season. During a visit to one of his holdings in central California, Phelan witnessed firsthand this monstrous contraption in action and speculated that a similar machine with even more power could dredge the proposed canal. Phelan's improved model, a monolithic excavator costing

$125,000 surpassed anything previously designed in either Europe or America. The giant powerhouse, measuring 100 feet in length and 30 feet in width, was capable of moving 3,000 cubic feet of earth a day.

These all-powerful excavators were manufactured in Philadelphia and floated down the Atlantic all the way to the construction site at Panama. From a distance they resembled huge storage tanks creeping through the churning waves. In operation an endless chain of iron buckets revolved in a continuous pattern like an old fashioned mill wheel. These machines were manned by specially trained operators with a backup of 500 brawny laborers. The "Earth-Gobblers," as they were dubbed, ran day and night, belching smoke through their stacks that blackened the skies for miles around. Despite the enormous expense involved, the company showed a substantial profit, which enabled them to pay a dividend of $388 a share to the investors in 1885, the first year of its operation.

Phelan Solves the Wheat Surplus Crisis

By the year 1865, California's agricultural production had reached such unprecedented levels that wheat glutted the market. What was once a sun-drenched wilderness carpeted with yellow mustard, wild flowers, and dense shrubbery had given way to a vast sea of waving grain. The overabundance of wheat with no means of adequate storage robbed many a pioneer farmer of sleep. No one could find a solution to the problem, which worried not only the farmers but also the general community. With time running out and no answer in sight, the old pro, James Phelan, was summoned once again to save the day, and in short order, he fulfilled his crucial mission.

Calling together the growers and the shipper companies, he advanced his simple plan, "Why not ship the surplus to the British Isles, like we do with other goods?" This proved to be an ideal solution, helping not only the farmers to sell their surplus wheat, but enriching the shippers and the entire state in the bargain.

Phelan Takes a Wife

Six years following his arrival in San Francisco, James set out for New York to bring back Alice Kelly, his childhood sweetheart, as his bride. Alice's parents, Jeremiah and Jane (Mulhall) Kelly, were born in Stradbally, Queens County Laois a short distance from Middlemount, the birthplace of her husband-to-be. The O'Kellys, one of the seven septs of ancient *Laoghise*, were of pure Gaelic stock and had crossed swords with invaders and their hirelings on numerous occasions. Their descendants served with distinction in the armies of France and Spain, and these relocated Irish became known as the Wild Geese. The Stradbally branch of the O'Kellys retained the cross of Saint Louis that was bestowed on them during the French wars.

This grand reunion of the Phelans and the O'Kellys in New York City, however, was cut short upon receipt of a communique from James' brother Michael in San Francisco. Michael, it appears, had made an imprudent judgment which might eventually put the Phelan Company in jeopardy. This crisis required James' immediate departure to San Francisco, leaving his fiance waiting. But soon, Alice set sail to San Francisco, chaperoned by General Joseph Lane, a long-time family friend.

Alice's arrival in San Francisco was heralded by the press. She received a warm welcome from Phelan's many friends and business associates and the well-established Irish community. The distinguished young couple were united in marriage in 1859 at Saint Mary's Cathedral by California's first bishop, Joseph Sodoc Alemany.

Following a brief honeymoon, the newlyweds settled down to married life in San Francisco in the Phelan Villa near the Old Spanish Mission Dolores (*circa* 1776). By all accounts it was a happy marriage and a happy home in the Irish family tradition. Two girls and a boy came from this union. The Phelan home was a substantial dwelling for that period. It was nestled among oaks in the sheltered valley, an imposing structure in contrast to he adobes and wooden shacks in the nearby foothills. It resembled a Garden of Eden, landscaped with fruit trees, flowering shrubs, and bright roses, according to a letter from James D. to his father, written in 1884:

> The garden is in high bloom and the trees are bent down with fruit. Lush berries are in the mood to match colors with the flushed roses and the wandering nasturtiums have gone over the wall and appear to be heading west like the pioneers of your day.

Alice Phelan, wife of James Phelan.

Phelan's Country Residence

Besides Phelan's San Francisco home, the family maintained a hideaway, named Phelan Park, south of the city in the Santa Cruz Mountains. This rustic hacienda perched atop a high cliff commanded a panoramic view of Monterey Bay and the horizon of the Pacific Ocean. The environment was ideal for a man with little interest in rubbing shoulders with high society, preferring to spend his leisure time with family and friends.

Phelan's San Francisco home in the Mission Dolores area.

During these years, James developed a special affection for the friendly inhabitants of nearby Santa Cruz. As a devoutly religious man, he believed in sharing the good life with those less fortunate than himself. Imitating the Good Samaritan, he consistently provided food for twelve of the most needful residents of Santa Cruz, in honor of the twelve apostles.

In 1890, after Phelan turned 69, his health began to fail. This turn prompted him to move to Harbor Springs in Lake County to recuperate. However, the weeks at the resort failed to restore his health, and he eventually returned to the family residence in San Francisco, where he lived until his death two years later. On Christmas Eve in the year 1892, the old patriarch passed away surrounded by his devoted wife Alice and their three children.

In the usual Irish tradition of that period, the Phelan wake was held in the family home. A single white carnation adorned the casket, one olive branch hovered over the bier, a tall crucifix stood above his head, and a sheaf of wheat bound together by a purple ribbon lay at his feet. Men and women from all walks of life came to pay their respects, bowed their heads in silent prayer, and bid farewell to their kindly benefactor.

Funeral services with requiem high Mass were conducted at San Francisco's Saint Mary's Cathedral on California Street, where James and Alice had been married 33 years before. The Cathedral was packed, with a huge overflow lining the streets outside. A long line of carriages draped in mourning, followed by many others on foot and horseback, accompanied the remains to San Francisco's Calvary Cemetery on Lone Mountain: business associates in striped pants and long tails, Spanish dons in their bright regalia, ladies in black, brawny miners in crimson trousers and mountain jackets, and ordinary citizens from every walk of life.

Pallbearers and honorary pallbearers included old pioneers, captains of industry, government leaders, literary greats and longtime friends: James Fair (one of the four Bonanza mining kings), Judge William Wallace, Thomas Coleman, Doctor Gregory Phelan (a distant relative and leading California educator), S.W. Halliday, Joseph Eastland, Samuel Murphy, C.S. Murphy, and William Tisdale, to name a few. The remains were placed in the Donahue family vault in Calvary Cemetery. Some years later when burials within city limits were discontinued, the remains were re-interred in Holy Cross Cemetery in Colma, south of San Francisco.

Letters and telegrams bearing condolences poured into the Phelan residence, including the following one from ex-Governor Downey:

Office of the Downey Block
Los Angeles, California
December 26, 1892

Dear James,

I learned with deep regret of the death of your great Father. He was a good husband, a good father and a true friend and adviser. Receive and accept my condolences.

Your Friend,
John Downey

Last Will and Testament

"As man lives, so shall he die," or so it has been said; and this was particularly true in the case of James Phelan, who planned for death in the same methodical manner that had characterized his life. The first name mentioned in his will was his wife, Alice (who continued to live in the Phelan residence near Mission Dolores), followed by their three children, James D., Mary Louise (Mollie), and Alice (Mrs. Frank Sullivan). Then came a long list of relatives and intimate friends, to whom he bequeathed specific amounts, followed by bequests to schools, churches, and charitable institutions in America and Ireland. Among these was the parish of Aghaboe, where James himself was born, along with an additional bequest for the pastor, Father O'Keefe, to divide among the poor. Phelan also contributed a substantial amount for the Presentation Convent in Stradbally (the ancestral home of the O'Kellys, forbears of his wife Alice) for upkeep and improvement. Of a more intimate nature is Mr. Phelan's beautiful stained glass window in Clough Chapel, where generations of the Phelan's knelt in worship.

Phelan Family Archives

While written accounts of early Irish pioneers who came to California before and during the Gold Rush era are hard to come by, James Phelan is the exception. A goodly number of important papers, family correspondence, and other written accounts of the O'Phelans of Ossory and California have been preserved for posterity, most voluminously in the archives of the Society of California Pioneers (of which James was a life member), and in the Bancroft Library at the University of California at Berkeley. These records have proved invaluable to this writer, in piecing together the story of such a prodigious figure, one whom pessimists and prophets of doom would do well to emulate.

The correspondence between the Phelans in Ireland and the James Phelan family in San Francisco sheds instructive light upon family relationships, and also informs us of the harsh conditions prevailing in Ireland at that time. Of particular interest is a letter from one Maggie Quinn, who styles herself "a loving cousin" and whose appreciation knew no bounds after she had received from the Phelans a check for $100 (a considerable sum a century ago):

> Lisdowney
> Queens County
> September 6, 1886
>
> My dear Mrs. Phelan,
>
> Your very dear and most loving letter and cheque for $100 came to hand this morning. I received it all myself alright for which, dear Mrs. Phelan, I return you and dear Mr. Phelan my most grateful thanks. Really I cannot find words at the present moment to explain to you how thankful I am to you and Mr. Phelan for your kindness to me. You have acted both as a father and mother to me. Now, dear Mr. Phelan, when I am settled down in Co. Wicklow, which I will be—Please God—as soon as I receive the duplicate from you.
>
> You may rest assured you will hear from me frequently. I hope and trust that when you and my dear cousin come to Ireland, and which I hope you will shortly; you will be happy coming to see all your poor dear cousins, Maggie and her new home. Now, dear Mrs. Phelan, I am delighted to hear that Mr. Phelan's health is improving and also to hear he intended coming to Ireland soon. I hope and trust I will have the pleasure of seeing him soon. Dear Mrs. Phelan, please give my best wishes to Mr. Phelan when next you write to him and, also, to Jimmy and Millie and Mr. Sullivan and Barbie. My brothers, William and Michael, send their love to all and wishes to be remembered to all their dear cousins.

Dear Mrs. Phelan, I will bid you a fond loving good-bye. Hope to hear from you soon and I expect to hear from you soon and I expect to have a lot of news to you in my next letter. Good-bye, dear Mrs. Phelan, for the present.

Your fond and loving cousin,

Maggie Quinn

A more pathetic appeal came in a letter from a Mrs. Fannie Phelan, whose late husband John, it seems, was a cousin of James Phelan:

Ballyhenode
Ballacolla
Queens County
October 4, 1893

Dear Sir:

I applied for a portion of Mr. Phelan's money that he was so kind to leave to the poor of the Parish, but the most of it was given out before I applied, so all I would get would be one pound. But I will leave it up to your generosity to help me to live. I am sixty years of age and had to work out in the fields to this day and badly able to do it. I could not afford to pay anyone so I had to do it by myself.

My husband, James Phelan being a second cousin to the late Mr. Phelan. He lived on three acres of your Father's land in a poor little cabin by the side of the road, so I am still there. When Mr. Phelan came to Ireland, he was kind enough to give me a little help at the time. Mr. Phelan sent his photograph to Father Phelan and said he would come again. I went to his likeness and thought I would see him again in Ireland, but it was not to be. Trusting again in your generosity, I will not trouble you only that I am aged and struggling for a living, so I hope Sir you will excuse me.

I am respectfully,

Fannie Phelan.

P.S. I will remember the late Mr. Phelan in my prayers

There's a familiar saying about the Irish, "You can take the man out of the country, but you can't take the country out of the man." This axiom governed James Phelan, who in spite of having spent all of his adult life in America, cherished a nostalgic love for Ireland, which he often expressed. His loyalty to Ireland was typically shown when a delegation representing evicted Irish tenants arrived in San Francisco. He received them with open arms and stressed that they were not strangers in a strange land, but rather at home among their own. He also initiated a fund on their behalf, to which he generously contributed.

Retracing Phelan's Footsteps

In order to ascertain the Irish roots of James Phelan firsthand and (hopefully) to locate his birthplace, this writer visited with longtime residents in the ancient parish of Aghaboe. My first contact was with a farmer named John Delaney, the present owner of the house and small farm by the side of the road (mentioned in Fannie Phelan's letter). Mr. Delaney's son led me down the road to a field, in the corner of which stood what remained of the house which John and Fannie once called home. It was quite evident to any one familiar with farming that it would be nigh impossible to make a living on this miniature holding, and that Fannie was in dire need when she applied to the San Francisco Phelan's for assistance.

I was encouraged by my good fortune and set out with renewed enthusiasm to locate the James Phelan homestead in the adjacent townland of Middlemount. It was a "soft day," as they say in Ireland, plenty of moisture in the fields and more in waiting from the dark clouds looming overhead. The gloomy atmosphere was magically transformed by the warmth of local farmers who are always agreeable for a chat or to relate an amusing anecdote at the spur of the moment. With a tumbler of Irish whiskey set before me: "You'll be having a little drop won't you?" I replied in the affirmative: "Never take a shingle off the roof," as they say in America. A "little sup never hurt anyone," came the reply. "Me Father before me and his father before him, never refused a wee drop when the occasion arose, and lived to a good age, both of them."

As the libation mellowed our minds, the conversation soon took a more intimate tone. "How are things in America?" he enquired. "No need to ask, it's such a great country." Why me Father told me that one of the family went to Philadelphia years ago and became one of the greatest men in America." "Ah, we don't have much here in poor ould Ireland, but thank Jesus and his blessed Mother for what we have." In Ireland patience is a virtue, and it takes a bit of time to get around to the question at hand. When I prepared to leave, those in-the-know directed me to a delapidated farmhouse which had been converted into a cattle barn.

When I stuck my head in the door, it seemed as if the animals sensed my mission: they arose as if on cue and ambled out the door one by one, leaving me alone. What I beheld was the usual three-room dwelling with a kitchen and two rooms on either side. The only amenities, if one could call them such, were an open fireplace and stone floor. According to local legend, this abandoned farm house was the birthplace of James Phelan, the lucky lad who rose to fame and fortune in the golden land of California. During my sojourn in the area, I learned that James had visited the old family homestead back in 1886, and had been planning a return visit sometime before to his death in 1892.

The Phelan Legacy in California & James Duval Phelan

Phelan's contributions to California are memorialized in the landmark Phelan Building, a symbol of the fantastic transformation of San Francisco from pueblo to metropolis, and an inspiration which launched San Francisco's rising star among the world's great cities. The family mantle was passed down to his son James Duval Phelan (1861-1930), who bore it even more flamboyantly for 40 years. As an only son born to wealth, culturally sophisticated James the younger felt secure in his birthright. In addition to the family fortune, he inherited some of his father's foresight and assertiveness, which inspired his city adornment campaign in the late 1890s. His sincere appreciation of all things bright and beautiful fed his desire to make San Francisco the world's most attractive city. In his dreams, he foresaw his native city, with its unlimited potential and ideal location, as the city of the future—the "Paris of the West."

Certificate from the Society of California Pioneers honoring James Phelan's arrival in California in August 1849. [Courtesy of Bancroft Library, University of California at Berkeley.]

Elected as a reform Mayor of San Francisco in 1897 (and later elected as California State Senator), James Duval Phelan worked tirelessly to achieve those lofty ideals. As past president both of the prestigious San Francisco Art Commission and of the Bohemian Club, his competence lent greater force to his "City Beautiful" movement. What San Francisco needed, Phelan observed, were parks and playgrounds, spacious plazas, great monuments, ornate homes and stately public buildings, to match the best in Athens, Paris, or the nation's capital. James' progressive vision inspired the inauguration of San Francisco's elaborate Midwinter Fair in 1895, as well as the landmark de Young Museum, named after M.H. de Young, who was the proprietor of the *San Francisco Chronicle.*

In 1912, James D. built Villa Montalvo at Saratoga as another expression of his gracious personality and sophisticated life style, a country estate with every possible amenity. He wanted to share Montalvo with like-minded company while basking in California's perpetual sunshine. Neither Jefferson's Monticello in Virginia nor Jackson's Hermitage in Tennessee could compare with Phelan's hideaway in Saratoga. The Mediterranean villa's sheltered foothills provide an unobstructed view of the shimmering wheat fields, sprawling orchards, and flowering trees of the Santa Clara Valley. At sun-latticed Montalvo, James entertained on an extravagant scale, far beyond that of any of his contemporaries. The names of the great and near-great adorn the pages of the artistic guest book: Alfred E. Smith, John McCormack, John Barrymore, Gertrude Atherton, Franklin D. Roosevelt, Helen Wills, and Knute Rockne.

James Phelan's Other Children and Grandchildren

Alice Phelan, the oldest daughter of James, Sr., married Frank Sullivan, whose pioneer father John Sullivan came to California with the Murphy-Miller party in 1844. Their marriage united two of the most prominent Irish families of early California, the Phelans and Sullivans. The Frank Sullivans had two children, a son Noel and a daughter, Ada. Noel became one of the most noted philanthropists of the period and contributed generously to the Catholic Church in California and elsewhere.

One of Noel's pet projects was the Carmelite Monastery Library in Oakville, which houses a priceless collection of rare books and other items. In 1975, at the behest of this writer, the Superior, Father

Edward, donated this treasured collection of books to the newly constructed Irish Cultural Center Library in San Francisco to insure their availability at all times, and to a wider public. As we left the monastery grounds with our valuable cargo, the curator, an aged monk, bid us a tearful good-bye.

Ada Sullivan entered the Carmelite Monastery in San Jose, where she remained for the rest of her long and productive life. She took her vows in the Carmelite Order, one the strictest in the church, as Sister Agnes of Jesus. For one born of wealth, Ada's was the complete sacrifice, giving not only of herself in body and soul but her inheritance (said to be in the millions) as well, a fortune which she bequeathed to the Carmelite Order in America and Europe.

California's Benefactor: James Phelan

California has had its share of great men and women, long gone and mostly forgotten, but the legacy of the Phelans and their contributions to the American West, and California in particular, are truly unforgettable. After the old pioneer's death in 1892, California's leading historian and biographer H.H. Bancroft paid James Phelan, Sr. a brief but all-encompassing tribute: "By all who knew him, he was acknowledged as one to whom the State was most indebted for its early prosperity." An anonymous admirer also captured the essence of Phelan's character in a few words:

> He fought life's battle and won; others sang his praises; the work he set out to do has been done, and he died at his appointed time in full honor and glory.

Michael Cahalan, immigrant Irish rebel and pioneer San Jose farmer. [Courtesy of Don Cahalan.]

8

Mike Cahalan: San Jose's Pioneer Farmer

It's a long way from Tipperary, where Mike Cahalan (1790-1874) first saw the light of day, to his adopted home in the sun-drenched plains of California. Between the two lands spanned a life that would bear witness to a period of spectacular change and conflict. Cahalan, the scion of a long line of Tipperary farmers, fled to the New World in 1820, to escape persecution as a defender of Robert Emmet's earlier Irish rebellion. Moving westward with his ever-increasing family, from Nova Scotia to Boston to Illinois and Iowa, 40 years sped by before Cahalan found his final heart's desire, on golden lands in what is now the center of the Garden City, San Jose. But this is getting ahead of our story.

The Cahalans, like the Mahers, Gleasons, Ryans, Kennedys, and other Gaelic families, had farmed the land for centuries. The Tipperary "Golden Vale," a land as rich as a plow ever turned or a cow ever relished, stretches as far as the eye can see, from Slievenamon (the Hill of Reverence) to the Towering Galtees where sun and shade play over lordly heights. It is an enchanted land that has cradled many literary giants. Tipperary-born Charles Joseph Kickham was the bold Fenian rebel, famous for his novel, *Knocknagow*, but even more beloved for his nostalgic ballad, "Patrick

Sheehan." Another son of Tipperary, Geoffrey Keating, preserved the romantic past and grandeur of Erin in his epical *General History of Ireland*. Tipperary was also the cradle of fearless patriots like James Stephens and Michael Doheny, and it boasts of being the ancestral home of the eloquent martyr-rebel, Robert Emmet.

Tipperary also treasures its sainted, venerable status in Irish Catholic history. Even before the coming of Saint Patrick, Saint Kieran had planted the cross of Christianity and preached the Gospel from the hilltops of Tipperary. Kieran rested from his missionary labors in Dunkerrin (Fort Kieran), a coach stop in ancient times on the sacred, magical route from historic Tara to Cashel of the Kings. In this, the storied land of "Knocknagow," heartland of poets and patriots, young Mike Cahalan grew to manhood. Mike was a fiery rebel like his ancestors, a thorn in the side of the local Constabulary, He often incurred the wrath of the English conquerors.

Cromwell's Legacy to Mike Cahalan's Tipperary

Following his surrender at Yorktown to the American rebels in 1781, Lord Cornwallis set sail for England, crushed and humiliated. To counteract the nationalistic ambitions of Ireland and to bolster his morale, the British assigned Cornwallis to duty in England's first subjugated colony. Cornwallis was informed by the British Home Office that his defeat in the American colonies could be attributed in large part to Irish immigrants. His new Irish post would provide him with an opportunity to even the score. The Irish themselves knew only too well what to expect from their terrifying experience in the aftermath of their defeat in the 1798 rebellion. The wholesale butchering of the survivors and the mass murder of men, women, and children was fresh in their memory. Such mindless savagery was followed by the introduction of the "gibbet" and the "pitch cap," methods of excruciating torture designed to force the helpless Irish victim to submit and inform on his comrades. The "gibbet" was made in the shape of a cross, upon which the prisoner was tied and whipped unmercifully. If the unfortunate victim continued to resist, his head would then be clamped with a "cap" smeared inside with burning pitch. If he tried to tear it off, his hair and scalp came off with it, ending his hellish interrogation with merciful death.

Young Mike took to the hills, well aware of the consequences of being apprehended. Under cover of darkness he traveled to the

Michael Cahalan's Irish birthplace at Terryglass in County Tipperary.

Napoleon Tower on the River Shannon, scene of Mike Cahalan's escape from the British constabularies.

town of Banagher, where he hoped to make his escape across the Shannon River. West of the Shannon, where the hated conqueror dared not intrude, Cahalan would find safety among his own. However, he was forced to change his plans when he spotted the military watchtowers high above the river. These weather-beaten walls embodied oppression as they glistened menacingly in the fading twilight. These fortresses, commonly known as Napoleon Towers, had been erected to secure control over the waterway.

The British warlords of the period were paranoid in their fear that the French were about to invade Ireland, with the support of the Roman Pontiff, and join forces with the Irish rebels to drive England out of Ireland. Recent disturbances made the threat seem real enough; after all, had not the French, with full support of the Irish immigrants, joined forces with the American revolutionaries and succeeded in driving the British out of their own colonies?

Young Mike, now a hunted rebel, realized that the Banagher Bridge on the River Shannon was under constant surveillance by the Constabulary. He decided to make his escape further down the river to a place called Baleera. This more secluded area, blanketed by dense forest all the way to the river's edge, provided excellent cover for an escapee. At this point the free-flowing Shannon veers sharply, as its pace is slowed by the curved embankment. From here Mike crossed over and made his way to safety among his compatriots on the Connaught side of the river. His flight and later escape to America is alluded to in an 1870 letter written by his brother Patrick, who lived in a town called Eglish, a short distance from the Cahalan ancestral home in Terryglass: "I cannot help thinking of all you went through since you left Dramina to Banagher to Baleera, thence to America."

Safe in Connaught

The province of Connaught was peopled by escapees and their descendants who had survived Ireland's seventeenth-century Cromwellian persecution. They had chosen the second option in the bitter slogan, "To hell or to Connaught." But to complicate matters, Mike, then in his thirties, had a wife, Frances, and an infant son, Christy. The family moved farther west and gradually vanished into the "Hidden Ireland" portrayed in the writings of Daniel Corkery. Nothing more is known of their whereabouts until they surfaced in

Halifax, Nova Scotia, in 1821. But we can well imagine their long, harrowing voyage aboard a creaking old sailing vessel at the mercy of the stormy Atlantic, made all the more uncertain because by now a second child was on the way. No doubt the young couple's hearts leaped with joy when they caught the sight of the bustling Canadian port of Halifax shimmering in the western sun. It was the custom in those trying days for recently-settled immigrants (who had themselves survived the treacherous voyage) to gather on the dock to welcome the half-starved and exhausted passengers. A large Irish community had settled in Halifax. Many of these Irish refugees had also fled their persecuted homeland under similar circumstances. Mike and his family were welcomed with open arms.

To the vast majority of Irish immigrants of that period, Halifax was only a temporary first port in a storm. Like the Cahalans, many viewed this English colony with cautious optimism, since the Union Jack fluttered ominously overhead and the long arm of the British Constabulary was a constant threat. The British knew only too well that the seeds of rebellion had been nurtured in the American colonies by Irish immigrants, and were on guard not to make the same mistake in Canada.

When the Cahalans arrived in Canada, Halifax was prospering in the middle of a building boom: the original hastily-constructed wooden shacks (a constant fire hazard) were being replaced by solid stone houses. Most of the Irish farmers' sons had learned back in poverty-stricken Ireland to do a bit of handy work on the side in order to supplement their livelihood. The transplanted Irish craftsmen could design a sturdy arch construction in which the keystone formed a gravity bond without the aid of mortar, making the building almost indestructible. Experienced in the trade, Mike found employment as a stonemason immediately upon his arrival in Halifax.

The couple's second child, a daughter by the name of Catherine, was born soon after their arrival, and later another son was born. But, as we have noted, since many Irish settlers had fled their native land in fear of persecution, torture, or the hangman's noose, they were never quite at ease under the Union Jack. Many of the Irish moved on and crossed the American border to complete freedom under the Stars and Stripes during this unsettled period; the Cahalans were part of this exodus.

When Mrs. Cahalan had regained her strength after the birth of Edward, their third child, the family made their way to the booming city of Boston. It was akin to a family reunion for the Cahalans, in a city that boasted a large Irish population that included many who had fled their native soil to escape persecution. During his stay in Boston, Mike worked at his profession as a stonemason and helped to build a number of the city's elegant structures. Some of his buildings still stand. He also helped align the foundation of the Bunker Hill monument. He later referred with pride to his part in setting the cornerstone. Although the Cahalan name was not listed among the war heroes memorialized on that monument, a full roster of the daring Minute Men would include a litany of Irish patriots, such as the Carrolls, Connors, Collins, Fays, Farleys, and Foleys, McCarthys, McBrides, and McGuires, O'Briens, O'Dunnes, O'Tools, and a company of other Celts.

During their stay in Boston, three more children (Mike, Jr., Mary Jane, and Julia) were born to the Cahalan clan. But in 1832, the family was overcome with grief when Mike's wife, Frances Maher Cahalan, died at a tragically young age. The widower Mike realized that he would be unable to rear such a large family by himself, and took Honora O'Brien as his second wife. Honora bore Mike two more children before the family left Boston.

Though evidently faring well, Mike was never fully at ease in the city; his heart was set on the land. For quite some time, he had been corresponding with an uncle, Pat Hogan, in Galena, Illinois. There was the attractive prospect of acquiring some farmland in that area. There was also considerable lead mining in Galena. As a result, a great many Irishmen, out of place in the crowded eastern cities, moved to Galena to find employment and clean air.

From Boston to Galena, Illinois

Galena was over a thousand miles distant from Boston. It must have taken heroic courage for Mike and his brood to pull up stakes and head out across an uncharted territory. No doubt he was encouraged to set out when he received a hundred dollar bonus, a considerable sum on those days, from his employer as a reward for faithful service. The Cahalans had spent fourteen years in Boston, but the lure of the land strongly beckoned the Cahalan family.

The Cahalans packed all of their belongings on a large wagon with a two-horse hitch and set out on the long journey westward. The trek lasted nearly a year before they reached their destination in Galena, Illinois. Their route took them from Boston to Albany, in New York State, then on across the lowlands by way of Syracuse to the city of Buffalo. From Buffalo they followed along an unpaved road paralleling the present New York State Throughway, and thence in a southwesterly direction bordering the Great Lakes, to Chicago. Along the way the Cahalans stopped over at various places where Mike found work at his trade as a stonemason, while his wife and children recuperated from their travels.

When the travellers finally reached Galena, a pleasant town in the northwest corner of Illinois near the Mississippi River, they were greeted with open arms by Pat Hogan, who had been anxiously awaiting their coming. The Cahalan clan found the country of Illinois to resemble their Irish homeland, an area rich in farming and stock raising. Galena's flourishing lead mines also offered employment with good wages for the more ambitious. It was a welcome change from their cramped lifestyle in crowded Boston. Bustling Galena was also experiencing rapid land development and a building boom. The timing was opportune for the Cahalans with three hardy lads, Christy, Edward, and Michael of working age. Yet despite their apparent good fortune, old Mike did not acquire land in the Galena area as he had planned. The Cahalans, seasoned adventurers, took their misfortune in stride and soon moved on to Bellevue, Iowa, across the Mississippi River.

Once the Cahalans settled in Iowa, their fortunes rapidly improved. The older Cahalan boys found work, and their father bought land. Now becoming for the first time landowners in the New World, the Cahalan family prospered.

Bellevue was a busy town close to Dubuque, a hub of boating activity on the mighty Mississippi. The family increased during their stay in Iowa, where Elizabeth, Nellie, and Francis were born: the census of 1850 listed Mike as having eight children. (His second wife, "Onny," died in 1847.) The 1850 count of Mike's household listed daughter Catherine's three children. Catherine died young and left these in the care of their grandfather. Winny (Winifred), a daughter of Mike's brother, John, was also listed in the census.

The family prospered in Bellevue. Christy, the eldest son, advanced to chief mate on a Mississippi steamboat, and Edward also worked as a river pilot. Young Mike (Michael M.) worked on the land with his father, during their stay in Iowa, and again when the family settled in California. The elder Mike was by now a full-fledged American citizen, having acquired his certificate in 1839. He was proud of his growing family, and well aware of their good fortune in a land endowed with the blessings of freedom and opportunity, which were denied him in his Irish homeland. Mike ,the old warrior, stood proudly before the bench in the Davis County Circuit Court on the 24th day of October, 1839, flanked by his two witnesses, Michael Murphy and Hugh Boyd. His blue Irish eyes sparkled as he read the document, word for word: "Michael Cahalan be henceforth admitted to all and singular rights, privileges and immunities of a naturalized citizen of the United States of America." The trials and tribulations of bygone days were but a memory as the Cahalan clan took time out to count their many blessings and to revel in their good fortune.

The Cahalans, California-Bound

There is every reason to believe that the family intended to stay put in Iowa, with their future prospects looking bright. Mike, Sr. had acquired farm land (his lifelong ambition) for the very first time in America, with the possibility of further enlarging his holdings, as circumstances permitted. This was not to be, however. When word of the discovery of gold in California came the Cahalans, like most others, felt compelled to change their plans to take full advantage of fortune. Christy, always the leader and initiator, was the first to go and took young Mike along with him. In the company of other argonauts, the two boys left Bellevue, Iowa in the spring of 1850 and headed west along the trail from Council Bluffs, Iowa through southern Idaho, along Sublette's and Hudspeth's Trails, and arrived safely in California in September of that same year.

The Cahalan brothers, descendants of hardy stock, stout of heart and keen of mind, were a match for the most ambitious gold diggers. Hard work and perseverance was the name of the prospecting game. They were in the midst of a determined band of adventurers of many nationalities and stations in life, including (in addition to their own countrymen) Chileans, Peruvians, Germans (referred to as "Dutchies" or Dutchmen), Australian convicts, Mexican *caballeros*, farmers and frontiersmen, New Englanders, and native Indians. These were joined by soldiers A.W.O.L. from their command and by sailors who had abandoned ships. All were obsessed by the magic word, "gold!"

To say that the stout-hearted Cahalans struck it rich would be an understatement: within one year they were able to buy land in the fertile plains of Santa Clara, which had been opened up to Americans after California became a state. Christy Cahalan had set his sights on the political arena and was elected State Senator from Nevada County less than two years after his arrival. It is little wonder, then, that any thoughts of returning to Iowa were scrapped as Christy and Mike pooled their resources and prepared to bring the whole family out to California.

The Cahalans' earlier cross-country trek from Boston to Galena, Illinois was a remarkable achievement, a journey of more than a thousand miles, much of it over dirt roads, cow paths, and swampy ravines. But from Bellevue on the Mississippi to the gold fields in California, a distance of more than seventeen hundred miles, presented an even more formidable challenge. Mike Sr. was now over 60 (which was an advanced age in those days), and the prospect of such a journey through dangerous Indian territory, across the sunbaked prairie and the treacherous snow-covered mountains, would frighten men half his age. In order to convince their aging father of the unlimited opportunities in California and to help sell off the family holdings in Iowa and prepare for the long and difficult journey, the brothers decided that it would be diplomatic for young Mike to go on a mission of persuasion to the family homestead in Bellevue, Illinois.

Young Mike set out from the mines in Nevada City to Bellevue in the fall of 1851. His route took him down the coast by ship to Panama, overland across the Isthmus, and sailing across the Gulf of Mexico to New Orleans. From there on upriver it was like a pleasure trip to be on the Mississippi, where Mike's brother Edward was still working as a river pilot.

There was much for young and old Mike to talk about when the prodigal son returned to Bellevue. Even though young Mike gave a glowing account of how he and Christy had struck it rich in the gold fields and already had acquired rich land in the very heart of

California, it must have taken great powers of persuasion for his father to abandon the land he had bought such a short time before. But it seems that the lad's description of the Golden West was too much to resist. Furthermore, old Mike would make any sacrifice to reunite his growing family, be it in Iowa or faraway California.

Any misgivings about this long and hazardous journey were somewhat allayed by the fact that Christy and Mike Jr. had made the trip the year before without mishap. When Mike Sr. finally became convinced of the opportunities awaiting in California, the old patriarch began disposing of his Iowa holdings. The sale was completed a month before the family's trek to California. [This sale was recorded in a Jackson County, Iowa deed dated February 6, 1852, a copy of which has been provided to the author by Edward Cahalan Steffani, a great-grandson of old Mike].

The caravan that included Mike and his seven children left for California in March of 1852, with young Mike as guide, and they arrived in the gold fields in the fall of that same year. This daring adventure and the route that the Cahalans took was later related by Ellen, one of Mike's daughters, to Edward Steffani (her grandson, who is today a resident of Los Gatos, not many miles from the site of the former family ranch in what is now the city of San Jose). The Cahalans followed much the same route as young Mike and Christy had blazed the year before: from Bellevue across Iowa to Council Bluffs, then along the Platte River and on to Fort Kearney, where the route joined the Oregon Trail coming from Independence, Missouri. They next continued along the Mormon Trail following the Platte to Scott's Bluff and Fort Laramie, crossing over the river at Caspar, Wyoming and on to Independence Rock, a national landmark.

There the road turned west to the Continental Divide (the eastern base of the South Pass), which became the route of the Western Pacific Railway in later years. The party then changed course, veering south of the Sublette's cutoff and on to Salt Lake City. Here they once again changed direction, turning northwest to reach another landmark, the "city of rocks," thence down the sloping hills to the base of the Humboldt River, and across the California state line at Truckee Lake, coming out of the hills above the present town of Marysville. (They purposely avoided the Donner Summit to the north, which had been the scene of tragedy for the ill-fated Donner Party just two years earlier.)

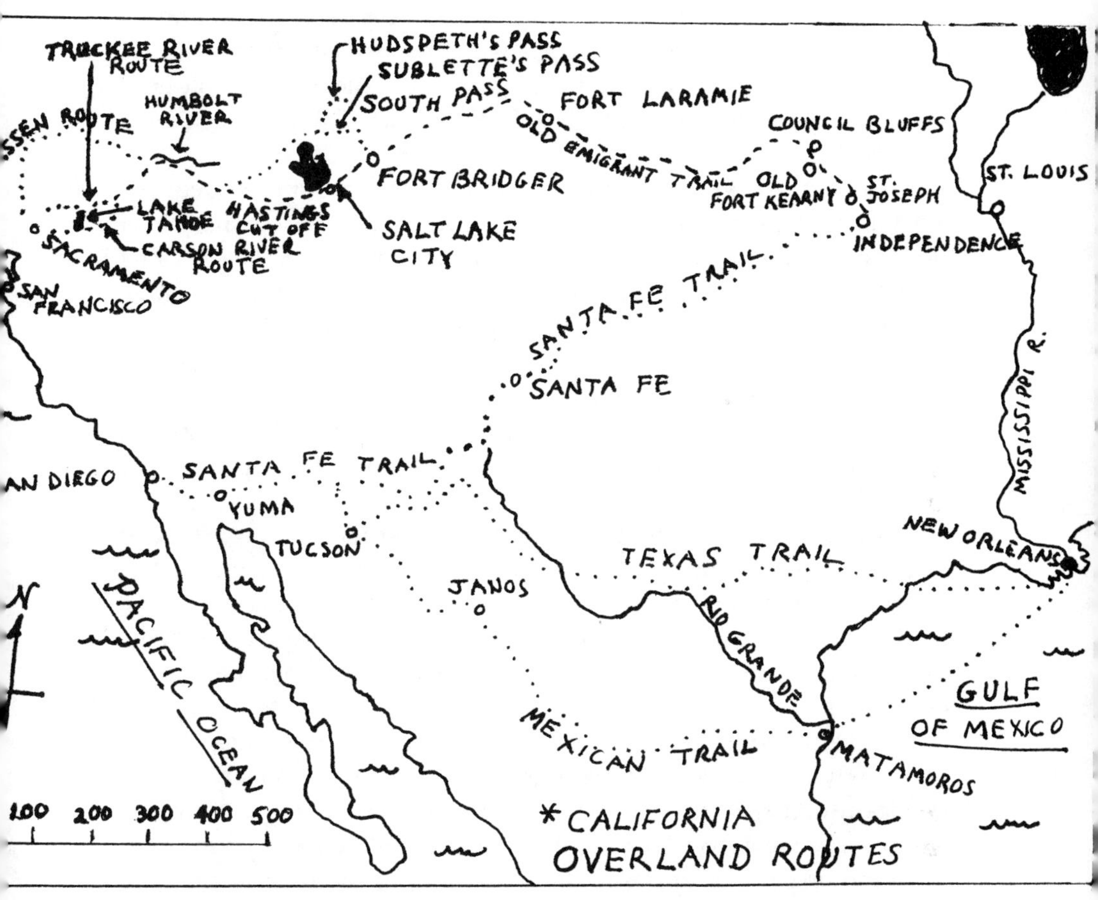

Route taken by the Cahalans on their 2000 mile trek to Hangtown (Placerville), California. [Courtesy of Ed Steffani, Los Gatos, California.]

The Cahalans arrived in Nevada City in August 1852, where they were greeted by the eldest son, Christy. Thanks to "the luck of the Irish," the family arrived safely, with no mishaps everyone in good health. On many occasions throughout his life, Mike, the old pioneer, had expressed strong religious convictions, but perhaps none more so than on this occasion, as he knelt with his family, like ancient pilgrims, in prayer and thanksgiving for their safe arrival.

After a brief rest in Nevada City, the family set out again down the foothills and across the flatlands skirting San Francisco Bay onward to San Jose. No doubt the old pioneer's heart raced with joy as he beheld this vast Eden of virgin soil, more fertile than any he had ever set foot upon. He now owned more than eight hundred acres in the Santa Theresa Rancho, part of an ancient Spanish land grant that became available to new settlers when California achieved statehood.

The temperature at this time was hovering around 90 degrees, but this heat proved no deterrent to Mike as he tackled the job of clearing the land with the gusto of a man of lighter years. The flatlands within his holdings were dotted with live oak, red birch, and madrone, as well as a scattering of sycamore and redwoods. The foothills abounded in wild life: grizzly bear, coyote, wildcat, and mountain lion, ever ready to challenge all intruders; numerous herds of deer still roamed the hillsides. Such was the virgin land with its flora and fauna when the Cahalans first settled in the valley in the year 1852.

The Franciscan Missions, which had earlier been confiscated and secularized during the Mexican regime, were at long last returned to the care of the mission *padres*. The Santa Clara Mission and trading post a few miles to the north was bustling with activity. This allowed the Cahalans to buy horses, farm tools, and other necessities.

Mike Sr. soon found his own pot of gold in the wheat fields. The newly-arrived settlers were growing tired of the steady diet of Mexican food (*frijoles* or beans, and cornmeal cakes) and hankered after good wheat bread. It seems ironic that while most young men were moving in the opposite direction in a frantic rush to the gold diggings, both the Cahalans in San Jose and Martin Murphy in Santa Clara enjoyed a near-monopoly in wheat production for a number of years.

The Cahalans also engaged in dairy farming, taking advantage of the "commons" pasturage in the foothills which were made available for cattle grazing to farmers. They drove their herds to pasture in the mountains when the lowlands became barren of grass during the hot summer months. A vivid account is provided in an 1859 letter from old Mike to his son Edward in Saint Louis: "We have one hundred and forty head of cattle. Mike is away with them in the mountains, when Ellen comes home, her and Fanny goes to help him milk and make butter."

Thus followed many happy years for old Mike and his family. At long last they were in possession of vast amounts of the most fertile land on the planet. The plow broke the soil so easily that within a few short years the whole area was carpeted with waving grain and fields of hay. Eventually, the timber on the land became another source of income when William York began the manufacturing of curly redwood dressing tables, high-posted bedsteads, and chairs.

The atmosphere of those happy, prosperous years comes to life in old Mike's letter to Edward in Saint Louis, dated March 31, 1859:

> My dear son:
>
> I have received your kind and affectionate letter on the 21st, dated February 20th by overland mail. Yes, with that loving gratitude I embraced that homage from your good children sending kisses to grandpa. When I rec'd that beautiful case of likenesses, I kissed them all. And indeed my first was the children, then your wife and lastly yourself. Your wife and children I never seen, but O happy would I feel to see them and have the consolation to look at them. A kiss then would be more comfort than to hold up that and look at the appearance of those that could not reach out their gentle little hands and smiling lips and countenance. Your loving wife would say, My dear Edward, this is your father. The children clinging round me. O this is my grandfather. Until then I must be contented with the hope of those long expectations to embrace one another with love and fondness that I cannot express, but still in hopes it will not be 7 years or 1/2 or 1/4.
>
> You perceive and recollect yesterday 7 years we started for California from Pleasant Creek, 30th March 1852, on the 25th of the same month, you recollect, I met you at Duck Creek coming out from Bellevue to see us. You turned back with me as the rest of the family was coming after me. Julia and T. Sullivan was married that day. I can't ever forget that days meeting until I meet your family again, as I had the pleasure that day of shaking hands with your first wife, and, I shall never forget the kiss she impressed on my cheek on the beach when ye were going aboard the

steam boat at Bellevue that day for St. Louis, may the Lord have mercy on her soul, amen.

In my next letter I will make some inquiries of you of some affairs of [H C]. It will be concerning matters of importance between us.

I expect Christy here in a few weeks. The legislature will adjourn about the middle of April. He is acting a good member of that body. He may remain a few days or weeks then return to the mines. James and George Mitchell formerly from Andrews has a crop on his place. The crops look pretty good here although we have cold harsh wind and a little frost these few days past. [Volunteer] wheat looks very fine. I ploughed and harrowed 80 acres myself this winter with two mares, one of them young Kate, you recollect she raises good stock, also we have now 8 head of horses young and old and 140 head of cattle young and old. Mike is away there at the foot of the mountain with them this 3 weeks. As soon as Ellen comes home, her and Fanny goes to help him to milk and make butter. She went on a visit with Eliza 4 weeks ago when Eliza and her husband was here. They live over 100 miles from here, Merced County. James went for her. I expect them today or tomorrow.

Then I will be alone then until harvest, very disagreeable to me, but it's better do so than to hire and pay $30 or $40 per month. Julia and Family are up in the mountains. They rented their cows to Buron Ballard until fall; then they will I believe come down to their place. Christy and Sullivan has a good prospect of quartz leed ['lead' or vein]. I hope it may turn out well and prove good. Christy has had pretty hard times this 3 or 4 years past, but he will make pretty good this winter. They get $10 per day. I am told the legislature commenced about the first of January.

My loving respects to your wife and children. I love them dearly. Fanny sends her love to you all. None here but her and me; we are well, thank God.

> Hoping you, my son, your wife, and children enjoys good health; and Mary Ann, let me know when you hear from her; I want her to write to me.
>
> Your loving Father,
>
> Michael Cahalan

This letter reflects his sensitive, caring, loving personality and a rare talent for expressing his innermost feelings. No doubt he was quite pleased with the family's prosperity, although at the same time somewhat remorseful about its scattering and his inability to be with all of his kin:

> O happy would I feel to see them and have the consolation to look at them. A kiss then would be more comfort than to hold up that (set of pictures) and look at the appearance of those that could not reach out their gentle little hands and smiling lips and countenance.

His feelings of loneliness are even more evident in his letter of 1864 to Christy, his first-born, by then mining for gold in Durango, Mexico. Christy evidently had not replied to his father's letters (one of which is reproduced below) for some time. In that letter, there is a touch of uneasiness and anxiety: old Mike senses an alienation creeping between them, and expresses concern as to the cause. Mike leaves no doubt of his fatherly love for Christy and other members of the family, and he begs Christy to write a letter, hoping it will give some clue to any misunderstanding between them:

> San Jose
> Jan 31st 1864
>
> My dear Son,
>
> I have been hoping and wishing to receive a letter from you, for a long time, in answer to one or both of two letters I wrote to you since I received your last letter written shortly after Mr. Stapleton leaving there, you know, perfectly well, how glad and happy I would feel to hear from you. You know, also I love you, absent, or present. And not hearing from you but seldom, I am uneasy in

mind. And think and regret, in what manner, it occurred. But withal and through all I never did and never will lessen my love and affection for you. Above any of the Family although it is my duty to love you all. So I do. But them that is worthy of most, I admire and respect them most. And, I firmly believe you are certain of that, and for the love and Esteem you had for me in your early days, in your childhood boyhood, and manhood. You have performed, and acted your part of a loving son, towards his Father.

And now, dear Christy, you will admit that, one letter from you now would bring more Consolation to my mind, than I can Express or tell you, as I am, getting old, thank God for his mercy. And I beg and request of you to write to me, as often as you can, and may God bless you, give you good health and happiness.

This is the driest winter, up to this time, I have ever seen since I came here. We could not plough, but very little about 50 acres. The weather was dry and warm after the first [undecipherable word] every thing dried up, all, or checked it. The ground got dry and hard but to-day its raining a little and has every appearance of a heavy fall of rain God grant it, it is greatly needed.

I had no letter from Saint Louis since last July, that too appears strange to me. They did or used to, write frequently. Edward Mary Ann, or some of them would write. I hope they are all well and nothing wrong with them. I had a letter from E. Kelly [a grandson] about the 15th. He was well. He wrote from Fort Dodge. He is desirous to hear from you. He writes a good letter very well-stated and correct.

If the war still continues, there is not much excitement about it as there was. The news we get to day they are contradicted the next day. Enrolling drafting, is at an end. Mike and James were enrolled, among the number of cousins they could not escape.

I suppose you heard of the grand celebration in San Jose at the first arrival of the Iron horse. It appears great sight to a great many, Indeed it appeared so to me, so long since I seen one. Not since they started from Boston to Lowel [Lowell, Mass.].

There is rushing to the mines from here. Some to Reese River, Washoe others going South. Colorado and other different places. All seem to give rich accounts. John Montgomery is in Bois river Charly on the Colorado. They praise their diggins rich, so, their Father tells me, he is living in San Jose. He quit farming, he has stock on Kings river.

My love and request, I hope you will not long forget, as soon as you receive this. James and family are well. Mike and the girls sends their love to you and feels glad when they hear from you. There is no better girls. They refrain and absent themselves from Balls or Parties.

I still remain your loving father

Mike's Brother Writes from Ireland

The vast difference between California as a land of opportunity for Mike Cahalan and his family, and the desolate Ireland of the Great Famine days which Mike avoided by emigrating, is vividly evident in the letter of 1870, written by Mike's closest brother, Patrick, who remained behind on the farm in Tipperary:

Eglish
December 26th. 1870

My dear Brother,

It is so long since I wrote a line to you that I hardly know what to say, but first I must say that you have no idea of the heartfelt gladness I or we feel when we hear from you. My dear brother, you must be what I always said and do say still, that is, that you were the best (I must put you in the superlative degree) man of the Cahalans (or any other man I knew) at the same time the whole Cahalans were good men. My dear, I do not like to be filling a letter with sorrowing details, yet I cannot help thinking of all you went through since you first left Dramina to Banaher to Baleera thence to America and especially since you landed in Halifax [Nova Scotia] until you settled in San Jose. You may rest assured that my mind's eye is looking at all your difficult enterprises. I hope and I am sure you sincerely thank Almighty God for giving you such powerful nerve and grace to make good use of them.

You said in your last letter to Brother Thomas you expected a long letter from me. Now, my dear Brother, I suppose I need not tell you that I am not able to write an intelligent letter for I am one of those that cannot put any subject upon paper half as well as I could talk about it. However, I will just give you a short account of my career in life since I married.

Well then, I was married the 13th of April '26. I got 50 pounds fortune. I gave 40 to me mother to put up for me. I don't know how that went, but I had no account of it in a short time. You know poor James was fond of money, peace and rest to them all. However, I went on well (you know there was a great drive in us) until the middle of February '39 me wife took fever, and she 7 months in the family way. The child was born at 7 months. He lived 12 hours. Then that time 2 years after she took fever again, and she 7 months the same way, but did not lose the child as before. Out of 6 she had, he—that is, John—is the strongest and biggest man of them. They were all low sized, but strong and hardy men like yourself. John was 13 stone weight when he left for America.

I took the fever meself the second year. The two years sickness cost me 70 pounds. The second year me wife was for 6 months that no kind of food but port wine and sago [an edible starch from the sago palm], a bottle of wine and half a pint of sago every day. Only for poor Doctor Carroll, she never would get over it. I had not a shilling after that ordeal.

Thomas got married in '38. Then we were going to make 3 divides of the 40 acres. I thought 13 acres too little for me and being all well out of the fever I took 21 acres of a nice farm in Eglish. Wheat was 2 pounds a barrel when I took it and for 4 year before it. The first crop of wheat after coming in it was only one pound and some years less for the ten years I had it. He was a tyrant landlord. He broke me out of it then in '51 when I was forced to give it up. I was scarcely able to make up what took my eldest daughter Nelly to America. Then in '52 I had to send me eldest son Mick. Then in '56 I sent me second eldest son Patt. When I had to give up the little farm in '51 I had to go earn 6D a day. That was the highest hire any man would or could get at that time and from '46 to '50 a man would not get one meal in the day for his days work. They were called the famine years for thousands died of hunger.

Mull, the landlord's brother, took me to the county Kildare to mind a place for him. I was there only 14 months when he died. I must give you an incidence of the respect was and is for our family the Cahalans. Me son Patt worked for his steward here in Eglish. The steward sent Patt to England with two horses. He did not know what it cost him but call to me in Kildare and I would go with him to his agent in Dublin. I did and the agent, a Mr. Ducket, I told him my business. He asked me name. I told him. Oh yes, Cahalan, said he. Any money you want you must get for your family was the honestest and most respectable name in the county of Tipperary, for he said he was well acquainted with all Tipperary, though there is not many of them in it now to what was 50 years ago. They have the same respect still, and I hope you won't think it egotism in me to tell you that I and Tom are some of the most respectable of them, though much we came down in the world to what we were. When I was earning my days hire, I had as much respect as if I was in a carriage so far as to have an honest independent principle made.

Then, my dear, when I came back here from Kildare I had no house or place to stop in until Pat Kelly gave me a little cabben to stop in. At the same Nelly sent me 8 pounds and I got two acres of ground. I was able to work then. I straggled [struggled]. The children were growing up. Mr Saunders, the agent of this property, seen John one day he was down. He asked the man he was working with who he was. He told him I want a boy. He has an honest face.

Send him to me. Well he went and when he was about a year with him Pat Kelly that had this place died. His Nicholas took it up. He did not hold it only a year when he gave it up, but when he was about to do so, he said to me: keep that part pointing out what I have. I said I had no means. I met Mr. Saunders one day. He said to me, Cahalan, Kelly is giving up that farm. He has enough without and let you keep part of it that yours the two acres you have. O, no sir, I said. I have no means and what could I do with it. Your son is a good boy and I will assist you. Well, sir, I can't say against.

Mick, Pat, and Nelly sent me the price of a cow. Before that I sold the ass and bought a horse. I bought a cow. Then the boys soon sent price of her then Pat and Mick paid John and James passage in '64. James would not go. He says he can live easier at home. He is teaching school in Rathcabbin about 6 miles from here at about 40 pounds a year. He has 28 pounds from the National Board of Education and the scholars fees with that is something about 40 pounds.

John and Pat are good scholars, although they did not go to school since they were 12 years old. They were all very bright to learn but the youngest son I had Dennis was most singularly bright. I sent him to a model school to Birr, a pupil teacher at only 10 pounds a year. His age could not have any higher. He made such a progress in learning in one year he had 15 pounds the 2nd. year. The 2nd of July he got sick. He got paralyze. I brought him home. He lay prostrate from that date until the 28th of September he departed this life (rest to his soul). If he lived he would be the biggest man of his name. The Doctor that attended him said to me he had the most extraordinary intellect he ever met in any one. Anything he would read or hear once he did not need to hear it or read it second time: he had such powerful memory. The inspector of the school came to see him while he was sick. He said to me if he was 19 years of age he was a scholar good enough to fill a situation worth 400 pounds a year and when he would be 19 years of age he got his sickness and death cost me 30 pounds. The boys sent to me 15 pounds together. Only for them I would not have house or place. I have now two horses and 1 1/2 year colt, two cows and 1 year old heifer and 8 sheep. Still I am as much [?] as Tom but I have better means.

Now, my dear Brother, I have said so much about meself I must say a little about poor Brother Tom. He married in '38. He went on well for 10 or 11 years. Then his wife died and two of the children. He did not marry a second time. He has a sensible good boy of a son and a good sensible good girl of a daughter. When his wife died, he lost a fine mare. The times got so bad he was not able to get another. Then he was not able to hold all the land he had. James kept it and after a short time Sister Bridget was turned off her farm in Ballyquirk. She could get no place and James brought to him. He did not live long after (may the Almighty God have mercy on his soul). Her 28 acres and Tom 12 acres. I can't help saying that he left poor Tom in a very awkward position.

My dear Michael, of all the good acts you ever done the 10 pounds you sent Tom puts a climax to them all. And now, my dear Brother, if possible I entreat of you sent 10 pounds more as soon as possible and that enable him to hold on. Since I got two horses I do send one to plow his stubble. He does all the other work with one horse he has.

Now about uncle Patt's affair, I have not space in this note to state half the particulars, but my son John wrote to me saying that me uncle Pat Hogan left a property worth 10 or 12,000 dollars after him and had no heirs after him to possess it and that of course [we] were the nearest heirs to him a history of the Hogan family. I sent it the first of October last. I got no answer yet. I am expecting a letter every day. I am surprised at what you said that he had a son daughter. It cannot be possible that John would say anything about it if he had. It was (poor, misfortunate) Brother John that rambled through Galena last summer that made it out. My son wrote several letters to Corwith [a prominent Galena resident] about it but could get no satisfactory answers about it and then he went to Galena himself. He says there is no doubt but it can be recovered. The claim is indisputable he says. Corwith is a rich man and can support the law a long time. If they don't settle it without law though for all of you are I will let you know all about it when I get an account from the boys.

I cannot say half of what I would like to say in this letter, but I assure you I will send a more intelligent letter before long, God willing I live. You will wonder I did not say more about Sister Bridget than I said will be a subject in my next.

Now, my dear Brother, I earnestly [?] you will on receipt of this note you write without delay and give me a particular account of all and everything about yourself and all your sons and daughters especially Christy. You remember it was I that went for nurse Flannery the night he was born. When I went to the door the next day to go home she asked was I the boy that went for her. You said, yes. She said this boy is a lucky messenger. She then said, or repeated something in rather a low voice, that I could not understand, but I remember the last words of the sentence was that child will become a great man yet.

My daughter Nelly said in more than one of the letters to me from Galena that some people that was in California knew you that came back to where she lives told her ye were a most respectable family, and especially Christy that he was a first rate man. In my next I will give you an account of all the Griffen family and all enquiring friends. We are all in good health at present as I hope this note will find you all when it reaches you. My wife Mary, James, and Morgan join me in their best respects and love to you all.

I remain, my dear Brother, your loving and affectionate brother. You will address your letter thus,

Patrick Cahalan
Eglish Borrisokane
County Tipperary Ireland
Patrick Cahalan

Final Days of Mike Cahalan

Old Mike was the first known member of the Cahalan clan to come to the New World, and one of the few early pioneers in California of whom we have a detailed account. He was born in Terryglass, County Tipperary, in 1790, and died in San Jose, California, in 1874. He was rather short in stature, but of stout build and limitless energy, which diminished little even in his later years. It was said of him that even at the age of seventy, he could still plough a furrow from the headland to the hills as straight as the Cahalan Avenue that bears his name. There are many lasting memorials to him around San Jose in addition to his namesake thoroughfare, such as a marble altar erected in his name in St. Joseph's Church (the oldest in San Jose), and the Cahalan Shopping Center in more recent times.

Mike Cahalan a man possessed of full faith in his Creator, lived strictly according to the commands of his church, died in its bosom, and reposes in its lore. The strength of those convictions is borne out in the opening paragraph of his final will:

> In the name of the Father, and of the Son, and of the Holy Spirit, I, Michael Cahalan residing in the Co. of Santa Clara, State of California, knowing the uncertainties of life and desire to dispose of my property, do ordain and declare this my last will and testament.

Mike Cahalan of Tipperary died rich, not only in children but in more than 1,000 acres of some of the best land in the Santa Clara Valley. With the passing of time, Mike's lands have undergone a rapid change from pastoral grazing and dairy farming, through conversion to row upon row of fruit trees laden with apricots and plums. These in turn were bulldozed to make room for dense, built-up blocks of business and apartment buildings in what is now the very center of today's San Jose. But though the landscape has undergone a drastic transformation since his days, Mike Cahalan and his fellow immigrants from Ireland to California have left behind them an enduring legacy of hard work, optimism, and love of the land which has contributed much to social and economic progress in the Golden Land.

Dowling family coat of arms, whose Latin motto means: "I overcome with the help of God." No picture survives of Thomas Henry Dowling.

9

Thomas Henry Dowling: Irish Rebel & San Francisco Pioneer Entrepreneur

In the aftermath of the American Civil War, it seemed to many that our hero, the American-born Irishman, Thomas Henry Dowling (1794-1870), was on the verge of becoming a man of fabulous wealth. In a lead article dated June 20, 1868, the *Boston Pilot* summarized the prospects of this California adventurer and Irish patriot who had earlier returned to his ancestral home and fought in Irish uprising at Ballingarry in 1848:

> There is in this city a gentleman from California named Captain Thomas Dowling, who as the owner by purchase in 1849 of the island of Yerba Buena, in front of the city of San Francisco, has the prospect of becoming a millionaire.

The *Pilot* story went on to recount possible legal complications that might threaten Dowling's fortune. In the course of its report, the newspaper traced part of the Dowling's family history:

Mr. Dowling is about fifty years of age, born in Philadelphia, but when four years old was taken back to Ireland by his father, Captain Daniel Dowling, to his native place near Mountrath, Queens County (Laois). His father was a captain and a paymaster in the British army in the rebellion of '98, but becoming a United Irishman, he 'swore in' some of his company, two of whom (of the name of Reilly) were offered their lives, while kneeling on their coffins, to be shot if they would reveal the name of the person who initiated them. They preferred death to dishonor. The Captain was with the rebels at the Battle of Ross. The family, when Captain Tom was about eighteen, a general amnesty and pardon being granted, moved to Rochdale, England where the father died.

Captain Thomas Dowling, following the teaching of his father, went to Ireland in 1848 and was with William Smith O'Brien, Doheny, and others at Ballingarry during the unfortunate fiasco there. He afterwards found the British Island unsafe, if not an uncomfortable place of residence, and came to the asylum of oppressed and persecuted humanity, and in 1849 settled in California, purchasing the right of a (Mr. and Mrs. Gorham H. Nye), acquired in 1835, to the aforesaid island.

The United States took possession of it [Yerba Buena Island] for military purposes, and officers in command there acknowledged that if sold by auction the 140 acres which comprised the island would realize five millions of dollars. The matter is now before the committee on private land claims of both houses of justice and equity be done. Captain Dowling will be the richest man of his name in the world, from Eodah Neadh Dowling, King of Leinster, who died A.D. 241 down to the present time. The descendants of old Cahir Mor (Cahimore) will then have something more substantial than a kingly name to boast of.

It may be proper to state for the benefit of those affectionately disposed towards their rich relations, and can't see any merit on the poor ones, that the Captain married a Miss Singleton in England, who when she died left him one son and two daughters, all hale and hearty. Although "Indiana" owing to accidental circumstances, is

> slightly suspected of being one of his clan, he will relinquish his claim to any interest in the five millions if the Captain will establish, under patriotic circumstances, a college and Irish library and endow a few free academies for the benefit of the rising generation of his countrymen.

A Forgotten History: Dowling & Yerba Buena Island

While the story of the Dowling family is a rich history unto itself, the litigation over Dowling's title to Yerba Buena Island is an especially melodramatic tale of intrigue, politics, red-tape, and deception. Today, as their cars rumble through the tunnel over the Bay, few of the harried commuters fighting traffic across the San Francisco-Oakland Bay Bridge have even an inkling of the colorful history of Tom Dowling's connection with the verdant, wooded, U.S. Navy-run island of Yerba Buena. According to the article, "Three Lonely Graves in Yerba Buena Island" in the *San Francisco Chronicle* of Sunday, February 9, 1896, the ferryboat passengers of 90 years ago were equally unconcerned:

> The transbay traveler may have observed on Yerba Buena Island, in passing on the Oakland Ferry, standing out prominently, a small square of white crowning the very summit of the hill. Any one who may have seen it no doubt wondered for a moment what this small, white thing is, and then straightaway may have forgotten it. Perhaps not a hundred out of the hundreds of thousands that pass and repass have ever had their curiosity whetted sufficiently to inquire as to what that small, white patch is. There are probably not more than a dozen persons who do not reside on the island that know. But there is a history connected with that thing so dimly seen in the distance—a history of a hope and its failure of fruition; the history of a claim that drags a slow and interminable length at Washington. The square of white encloses a grave. Geraniums and sweet mignonette, a few violets and a tangled mass of weeds and grass grow within the enclosure, almost hiding the headstone that marks it. Brush aside the verdure and one reads: 'D.R.A. Dowling, Died A.D. 1860.'

The headstone is for the son of Thomas Henry Dowling, owner of all of Yerba Buena Island from 1849 until the U.S. military forces in San Francisco wrongfully seized it from him in the year 1867.

The Dowling Pedigree

What was the distinguished Irish pedigree of our American-born hero, Thomas Henry Dowling? According to the renowned Irish genealogist, Edward MacLysaght, the Dowlings were of noble birth: one of the seven septs of Laois (Leix or Queen's County). The ancestral homeland of this Gaelic clan lies west of the River Barrow, sheltered by the Slieve Bloom Mountains and referred to on vintage maps as *Fearann N-Dunlaing*, O'Dowling's country. The Dowlings, like the O'Connells, are of pure Melesian stock. O'Dunlaing [Dowling] is one of the oldest Gaelic names recorded in Irish annals, dating from Cahir Mor, King of Ireland in the year 144 A.D., and also including Eodah Neadh Dowling, who reigned as King of Leinster. These illustrious ancestors of Thomas Henry Dowling were rediscovered in later years by Andy Dowling, the "Sage of Clonmeen," the historian and family biographer, who pinpoints the Dowling territory in the parish of Ballyfin which lies between the county towns of Mountrath and Mountmellick in County Laois.

It's a typically tragic Irish story that compelled the forebears of Thomas Henry Dowling to immigrate to America. Following the disastrous defeat of the Irish by the English at the Battle of Kinsale in 1601, the leaders of the Dowling clan were evicted from their holdings and banished to north Kerry on the southwest coast of Ireland. From that branch of the family came the illustrious Bartholomew Dowling, author of the moving poem "The Brigade of Fontenoy." This Dowling immigrated to America and went on to even greater literary heights in his adopted state of California as editor of the San Francisco *Monitor*, the voice of the Catholic Church in California. Other Irish diehards of the Dowling clan heeded the British edict of banishment "to Hell or to Connaught" and remained in Ireland, settling west of the Shannon River in County Galway in the province of Connaught. From this family branch sprung one Patrick Dowling, who himself immigrated to California and served with distinction in helping to revise the State Constitution in 1878. Despite the upheavals and exiles, however, still others of Dowling clan managed somehow to remain in their original homeland of

Queens County (today's Co. Leix). From there, they multiplied and expanded to the surrounding counties of Carlow, Wicklow, and Kildare, where they are numerous today. As memorials to their tenacity and endurance, these Dowlings established many communities with eponymous place-names called "Ballydowling" ("Dowling's Town").

The Dowlings who left Ireland were among the first Irish immigrants to the New World, settling in Georgia and the Carolinas in 1638. Your memorialist can state unequivocally that the Dowling contribution to American Independence and development is an extraordinary one, which would take volumes to relate. Suffice it to say that their solidarity and success are manifest in the large Dowling Family annual reunion which celebrated its fiftieth anniversary in 1980.

Of the many immigrant Dowlings who journeyed to California during the Gold Rush, our subject Thomas Henry Dowling was assuredly the most noteworthy. The circumstances which had originally brought our hero's father, Daniel Dowling, to the New World at the time of the American Revolution were briefly touched on at the beginning of this chapter. Thomas Dowling was born in Philadelphia in 1794. Daniel, the father, and his young four-year old son Thomas Dowling returned to Ireland in time for the outbreak of the 1798 rebellion. Thomas Dowling's return journey to America came as a result of the 1848 disastrous defeat of the Irish rebels at Ballingarry in County Tipperary, in which he played a conspicuous role. The story of Dowling's return to America runs as follows.

Following the capitulation of the Irish rebels at Ballingarry, the British parliament lost no time in legislating the infamous Felony Act which institutionalized Kangaroo courts against the Irish and meted out harsh death sentences. The first to be convicted were the leaders of the uprising: William Smith O'Brien, Thomas Francis Meagher, Terence McManus, and Patrick Donaghue. Their grisly death sentence reads:

> That you be taken hence to the place from whence you came and thence drawn on a hurdle to the place of execution; that each of you be there hanged by the neck until you are dead and that afterwards the head of each of you shall be severed from the body and the body of each

> divided into four quarters to be disposed of as Her Majesty may see fit.

This judicial atrocity ended with a sanctimonious note of British 'piety': "And may Almighty God have mercy on your souls." Fortunately, an outraged public opinion halted the carrying out of the death penalty, and the Irish rebels were transported in chains to the penal colony of Tasmania. That, however, is another story of theatrical escape that needs telling at another time. Our present focus highlights the return of Thomas Dowling to America.

Thomas Henry Dowling in California

Of the many Dowlings who journeyed to California during the Gold Rush, our subject, Thomas Henry Dowling, was assuredly the most noteworthy. As Captain Dowling, he managed to elude his British adversaries after the Battle of Ballingarry in 1848 and make good his escape from Ireland to America, his birthplace. He arrived in San Francisco later that same year following a horrendous journey across the prairies and over the mountains to California. A keen observer in every sense of the word, Dowling was quick to perceive great possibilities in the Island of Yerba Buena, a brush-covered hunk of rocky earth that rose out of the bay and within rowboat distance of the bustling Gold Rush city of San Francisco. Obsessed, no doubt, with the island's strategic position and by the solid stone of which it was composed, Dowling purchased the rocky island from Gorham ("Captain") H. Nye, a navigator who had acquired it from the Mexican Government for services rendered. The document conveying ownership bears the signature of the then acting governor of Alta (Upper) California, Castello Negrate, and reads as follows:

> This is to certify that Gorham H. Nye is the owner of Wood Island, one league east of the Pueblo of Yerba Buena, in the Bay of said Pueblo. This being compensation for transporting the deceased Governor from Monterey to Santa Barbara, and that he is not to be disturbed in possession thereof. [It should be noted that the "Pueblo of Yerba Buena" was then the name for San Francisco itself; and "Wood Island" is now known as Yerba Buena Island.]

Nye's title to the island, as indicated, was granted for services rendered to the Mexican Government. When Governor Figuroa died, his remains were transported on Nye's ship from Monterey, the old Spanish capital of California to Santa Barbara for burial. Nye made "Wood Island" his home for a number of years before selling it to Thomas Henry Dowling. The affirmation of legal ownership, prepared after California became a state, noted that Captain Nye was providing a comfortable living for himself and his family on the island, his pay as a navigator being supplemented by the sale of goats to the Sandwich Islands (Hawaii). Goat meat was a San Francisco delicacy in this early period when beef and mutton were in very scant supply; hence the name "Goat Island," the name reaffirmed by the U.S. Geographic Survey of 1895. (Its earlier name of "Wood Island" was soon forgotten). It was not until the year 1931 that the Island had restored to it, the old Spanish name of Yerba Buena, and that name remains to this day. Of interest to local historians on the value of goats in that period, is a legal announcement that appeared in the *Monterey News* by Nye's tenants just prior to Dowling's purchase of the island:

> Notice is hereby given that the goats in Yerba Buena, or Wood Island, are the property of the undersigned, any encroachment wherefore upon our right, either by shooting or taking away said goats will be considered a robbery and treated as such.
>
> (Signed)
> N. Spear
> J. Fuller"

Dowling proved to be a more enterprising occupant of the island than the first settler, Captain Nye. Dowling cultivated a portion of the island to provide food for his family and his workmen. He also built a substantial home to house his growing family, a windmill for power, a work shop, and a dock for boat building and repairs. Later, he opened a stone quarry and ferried the hard rock across the channel to San Francisco, where it was put to good use building more substantial housing in a city plagued by devastating fires. The influx of new settlers continually increased the demand for food, and Dowling profitably met this demand by establishing a vegetable farm and raised poultry. Through a well-calculated schedule, he returned to the island with groceries and other supplies on the same days he transported poultry and fresh vegetables to market in the City. In the hearings pursuant to Dowling's legal claim to Yerba Buena Island almost two decades later, Captain Robert W. Haley paid tribute to Dowling's industry and dedication and testified that Thomas Dowling had expended at least $200,000 in the way of improvements and beautification of the island.

For almost twenty years, the Dowling's resided on the island undisturbed. For the most part they enjoyed a peaceful and prosperous existence; but on occasion they were beset by claim-jumpers, imposters, desperadoes, and weekend squatters. Unable to keep up with all his enterprises, Thomas found it appropriate to lease the rock quarry. One of the lessees remained in possession of the quarry's boarding house and laid claim to the property. Since there was no statute for eviction in those early years, the adversaries themselves had to resolve the dispute, which in this instance almost provoked a pistol duel. Dowling, never a man to be bluffed or bullied, stood firm; in due course right prevailed over might and the disgruntled tenant took off never to be heard from again.

One of the few pleasures Dowling allowed himself was puffing on his ever-present pipe, a vice he indulged in with the gusto of an Indian chief. Hanging above his bed was this rhyme extolling the virtues of the pipe:

A pipe in the mouth is worth two in the shop,
And those two are worth four in the 'pop.'

Whether they're pawned, in use, or at rest,
The pipes of John Purcell are always the best.

They're cool and they're wholesome, they're pleasant
  and sweet;
In price and in value all pipes they can beat.

With tobacco to fill them, the best that are made
In the shops of John Purcell you'll see them displayed.

Dowling's habit of taking a final "Long Smoke" before bedtime may even have saved his life. When two men claiming to be castaways appeared on the island, Dowling, with typical Irish hospitality, fed them and gave them a room in his house for the night. However, the interlopers had other intentions than reciprocating his kindness, for that very night, as Dowling finished his pipe and was about to retire, he was startled to hear some provocative utterances in his guests' room, followed by short, whiplike cracks which sounded like clicking pistols. The host, a veteran of many such confrontations, calmly and resolutely prepared for the worst, in typical western manner, with guns at the ready. His guests, thinking he was fast asleep by now, tried to bash in the door

Dowling's Yerba Buena Island in 1865. Photo taken from San Francisco, looking east from Montgomery Street. [Courtesy of the San Francisco Archives Collection, the San Francisco Public Library.]

Dowling's Yerba Buena Island, showing lighthouse and dock yards.
[Courtesy of the San Francisco Archives Collection, the San Francisco Public Library.]

Dowling's "Goat Island" with its wharves, stone quarry, and other improvements. [Courtesy of the Society of California Pioneers.]

to his room. Dowling shouted to "get out of the house if you know what's good for you." Down the stairs they scrambled until the reached the hallway where they then turned and started firing into the house. Dowling took up the chase with guns blazing until the culprits disappeared from sight. He bolted the door and barricaded the house to ward off any return of the desperadoes. He then lit his pipe and puffed away while standing watch until daybreak.

Tragedy struck the Dowling family in 1860. One of the boats used for transporting stone to the city broke loose from its moorings in a storm. A son of Dowling was playing on the boat when it suddenly dashed against the rocks and the unfortunate child was swept overboard and was drowned. When the remains were recovered, they were laid to rest on the hilltop under a stone—as described above—on which was engraved:

D.R.A. Dowling

Died in 1860

Romantic History & Yerba Buena

The island of Yerba Buena in time became almost as renowned in its day as the Golden Gate is in ours. As the years passed, with the steady influx of gold-seekers and other adventurers into the Bay Area, the island became both a haven of romance for many young people as well as the site of tragedy for a few. It was here that the young bride of a dashing young Army Engineer learned of her husband's infatuation for another woman; unable to bear the burden of her grief, it was on the island that she brooded and died of a broken heart. The jilted woman was laid to rest on the hill overlooking the Golden Gate, where she had often sat to gaze on the setting sun. Far away from the graves of her own people, there is now no monument to mark her grave, no epitaph to mourn her untimely passing.

Another sad tale of the island centers on the fate of an Italian nobleman, a great favorite of his King, who fled Italy when the Crown fell and the nobleman was swept away by the wings of chance to far-off California. Few men of such sheltered origins have been able to provide for themselves when cast out into a completely alien world. The unfortunate outcast finally found himself in San Francisco surrounded by strangers and with no means of support. He somehow made his way to Dowling's Yerba Buena Island, intending there to end it all. He dug his own grave, and arranged the clay on wooden supports attached to the trigger of his pistol, so that when he fired the pistol, the earth would fall upon him. By this bizarre contraption, he was both killed and buried by his own hand. But the unfortunate suicide did not rest for long in his shallow self-dug grave. Upon discovery, the corpse was dug up, ferried across the channel to San Francisco, and buried in a pauper's grave.

Although communication was rather poor in those days, the story of this tragedy spread, and a second suicide was attempted in the same spot. Comically, the second unfortunate was either too drunk or lazy to dig his own grave. He carefully positioned himself in the open grave while contemplating the final act. But it was not to be, as alcohol defeated his suicidal willpower: he passed out and fell into the pit. His loud snores and groans attracted the attention of some soldiers on patrol, who yanked the dazed would-be suicidal bum out of the hole, disarmed him and chased him back to the city.

To some, the island shining in the Bay was a place of reverence, as witness the case of Edward Lindsey, a man so enchanted with the rock that he chose it as his final resting place. A sea-faring captain at the age of twenty, Lindsey transported the first batch of women convicts to the penal colony in Tasmania. He rode the waves far and wide before settling down in Hobarttown (Hobart), where he engaged in shipbuilding for some years. Lured to California during the Gold Rush, he set sail in his own ship named *Palmyra*, with his wife and six children on board, and arrived in San Francisco on June 4, 1850. On that voyage, he carried a cargo of bricks and timber in the hull. This cargo was put to good use in replacing the flimsy shacks that dotted the hillsides.in the erstwhile Pueblo of San Francisco. Lindsey moored his vessel in an inlet on the city's north bay which was later filled in and became Greenwich Street. The old bark became somewhat of a landmark in the Gold Rush city since it served as the family residence for many years until the good Captain's demise.

Like countless others,Captain Lindsey was fascinated with life in San Francisco. A seaman at heart, his favorite weekend outing was a boating trip to Goat Island accompanied by his family and friends. His oft-repeated wish was that when he died that he be laid to rest on the island; and so it came to be as he requested. Mourners gathered from near and far to pay their respects at his wake, held in his *Palmyra* home anchored in the sheltered lagoon.

No horse-drawn hearse could bear Captain Lindsey's remains to the island. Instead, the coffin was placed in a long flat barge and rowed over the channel by his intimate friends. A procession of boats filled with mourners accompanied the Captain on his final journey to Yerba Buena Island where he was laid to rest as he had desired.

Seasoned mariners tell tales of the strong, choppy current between the City and the Island. One of Dowling's sons, who on occasion acted as courier between the Island and the city transporting supplies for the family and quarry workers, related a harrowing experience which happened when he was but twelve years old:

> One day during a severe winter, we had to go over to the City to get flour. We had to have it and I was the only one who could be spared for the job. Not that there was any doubt about my ability, I was a thorough boatman at nine or ten years of age. A storm had been making things lively for three days. It had subsided for the time and Father thought I could get over and back before it started in again. I got over safely in the Whitehall boat, and purchased a barrel of flour, which I stowed in four rubber bags besides other articles.
>
> I was about to start across again when the storm set in. It blew a fifty knot breeze from the Southeast and I knew I could do nothing. I remained all day waiting a chance to go, and about 10 o'clock at night the rain ceased and a beautiful moon rose through the silver clouds. The wind was still blowing at twenty five miles an hour, and there was a heavy sea running, but I thought I would try to get across. They were waiting, I knew, for the flour. Stepping my little sail enough to start me, but not filling up the spirit, I headed for home. The scene, I can see it now, was magical. The rays in the lumpy water, where my little boat literally leaped from wave to wave, converted it into a sea of fire. The hour and the hazard of the attempt perhaps

> contributed to excite my perspective and imagination, but certainly the weird beauty of that night remains with me still.
>
> But I had no time to dream, I had to attend to business, and very serious business it soon became. When about three hundred and fifty yards off the lighthouse point a squall struck and carried my sail and mast away. I was paralyzed for a moment, but after waiting for the squall to blow over I got out my sculls, and with infinite labor, such it seems to me now incredible, pulled out to our house, entering a guest cove just as I was utterly exhausted. As the boat grounded, twenty five or thirty men walked out in the surf and carried me and the boat ashore. They had been watching for me, afraid of some accident and when I told my story I was the hero of the island.

In 1848 the *pueblo* on the site of present-day San Francisco had fewer than five hundred inhabitants. Three years hence, however, San Francisco was by all accounts a vibrant city, boasting a population of over forty-thousand souls. The quiet, pastoral environment of the Spanish period had passed into history. Newcomers, unaccustomed to the constant din of city life, sought escape in a Sunday outing to Goat Island, which for a brief period was the City's only recreation park. As pleasure seekers and weekend revelers roamed the island with little regard for the residents or their property, Dowling could see that his plantings would be trampled, his barns ravaged, and his animals scattered. He conceived an unorthodox but ingenious way to ward off the intruders: Dowling untethered a bull to roam the Island at will.

The desired effect was achieved when the word of the animal's menacing reputation became known. Such animals usually become mean with age, easily provoked by loud noise, and startled by any movement. However, Dowling's bull, the Guardian of Goat Island, soon became a threat not only to intruders but to the Islands residents as well. The islanders organized a hunting posse to dispatch the troublesome beast. But the party themselves were caught by surprise when the infuriated bull suddenly appeared out of nowhere; they dropped their guns and took refuge in the tall trees. The bull's roar was heard for miles as he tore the ground with front feet and trampled the hunters' guns in the dirt. A back-up party was hastily organized, and these men succeeded in capturing the ferocious beast who had to be destroyed on the spot.

The hair-raising drama was captured for posterity in the following ditty:

On Goat Island's secret shore,
  many is the hour we whiled away,
Listening to the breakers roar,
  which haunted the beach night and day.
When we landed on the Isle,
  Dowling met us with a smile,
And the Bull gave out a roar,
  as we left Goat Island shore.

Dowling's Claim versus the U.S. Government.

The Dowling family remained in possession of the island for a period of some eighteen years until the United States Army moved in and took possession in the year 1867. As it was, President Johnson's attention was diverted to the time consuming business of reconstruction following the Civil War, and paid little heed to such minimal matters. Be that bas it may, this writer is firmly convinced that if Abraham Lincoln had survived as President, he would never, ever, have approved of such a bizarre course and especially where a decent human being and his family were threatened with eviction without previous notice. All the improvements made by the hardy pioneer and his sons were confiscated and all of Dowling's property claims were ignored. The many attempts at the local level to vindicate his rights and preserve his title were to no avail. In desperation Dowling finally took his case to Washington, fully confident that his rights would be restored. His petition was presented to the United States Congress on December 11, 1869, attested to and sealed under oath by one Nicholas Callan, (Notary Public) in and for the City of Washington, District of Columbia:

Claim To The Island Of Yerba Buena

To the Honorable The Congress of the United States:

Your memorialist, Thomas H. Dowling, would respectfully represent unto your honorable body that he is a citizen of the State of California, and had for many years prior to the year 1867 resided on the Island of Yerba Buena; that he does verily believe that he is the rightful owner and possessor of the equitable title to said Island. He claims to have derived his said title as follows:

That as early as the year 1833 one Gorham H. Nye, then a resident of the Department of California, entered upon said Island and took possession thereof, with the intention and purpose of residing thereon. This intention and occupancy of the Island being made known to the then Departmental Governor of California, he caused to be given to said Nye a license or permit to occupy, use, and to cultivate said Island with a view of acquiring a title thereto, under the pre-emption and settlement laws then in force in the then Department of California. Said Island is situated in the Bay of San Francisco, distant about one and one-half miles from the city of San Francisco. It contains about one hundred and forty-four acres. Said Nye continued to reside on said Island from the time he first entered thereon until the 10th day of July, 1849, at which time your memorialist purchased and entered into the possession of said Island under said Nye. The original purchase from Nye having been by verbal agreement, the same was not reduced to writing and recorded until the 23rd of December, 1864. During the whole period of Nye's residence on said Island he used, improved, occupied, and controlled the same, and manifested his possession thereof by all such acts of ownership as usually characterize a notorious occupancy and possession.

Your memorialist would state that he made the purchase of said Island from Nye in the best of faith, honestly believing that he was acquiring a good title to the same. Nye's possession was peaceable, continuous, uninterrupted, and adverse to all the world. It was visible, notorious, and evidenced by improvements of all various kinds. With all these evidences of right, with no one to question the same, your memorialist felt the greatest confidence that he was obtaining a good title. The Mexican government was content to acquiesce in Nye's right from the year 1833 until the result of the war discovered her empire. Nye's right was regularly transmitted to your memorialist, and was acquiesced in by the government of the U. States up to the year 1867, at which time your memorialist was ejected by military force. The possession was continuous and unbroken in Nye and your memorialist from 1833 until 1867, a period of nearly forty years. In the meantime your memorialist, on the faith of his right, proceeded to bestow his labor and expend his money in the erection of such lasting and valuable improvements as he considered would add to the permanent value of the Island. It would be too tedious to enumerate in detail the various improvements which were put upon said Island by both Nye and your memorialist. They consisted of wharfs, houses and all such improvements as were calculated to enhance the value of the property.

He also redeemed from the water at least two-and-a-half acres of land, at the cost of a vast amount of labor and money. While Nye was on the Island, he was engaged in the purchase, sale and shipment of hides from the same; he kept a large number of sheep and goats. He made a harbor for his own vessels engaged in the trade. The Government of the United States, through its officers, Major Tower and Admiral Farragut, recognized your memorialist's right by purchasing rock from him to build Fort Alcatraz, and for the construction of the Navy Yard and dry dock at Mare Island. In addition to the evidences of title thus furnished by the long, continuous, and unbroken possession, the various improvements made, the vast labor and expense incurred, your memorialist encountered multiplied difficulties, trouble, and danger in defending the possession of said island against intruders, interlopers, and pretended claimants. He had to contend against force and violence, often at the peril of his life, and also prosecute and defend many suits in order to protect his Island, as will be seen by the proof. Indeed he could scarcely estimate the amount of money it has cost him to protect and defend his right to the Island. He only knows that to take it away from him now, without compensation, would injure him to the extent of several millions of dollars. He has spent the prime of his life, greatly impaired his health, lost a portion of his family in his efforts to protect and improve the island, and to take it away from him now, without compensation, would leave him in abject poverty, and hopeless pecuniary ruin. He therefore appeals to the representatives of his Government, to which he has always been true and loyal, to mete out to him that measure of relief which is, in equity and good conscience, due to the merits of his claims. He prays your honorable body to examine carefully the evidence and proofs and the law, upon which he relies in support of his claim.

(Signed,) THOMAS. H. DOWLING
City of Washington
District of Columbia, as:

Before me, Nicholas Callan, a notary public, within and for the city and district aforesaid, this 11th day of December, A.D. 1869, personally appeared Thomas H. Dowling, who being duly sworn, deposes and says, that the facts stated in foregoing petition, so far as related from his own personal knowledge, are true, and so far as related upon the information of others, he believes to be true.

(Seal) N. Callan
Notary Public
San Francisco, California.,
October 23, 1863

The claim of Pollack et al. for Yerba Buena Island was defeated mainly, I believe, through the energetic exertions of Mr. Dowling in procuring witnesses and adducing evidence to expose the very well-contrived frauds on which it was based. Mr. Dowling was understood to have been in possession of the Island for a considerable time. The precise nature of the assistance rendered to the District Attorney, and the expenses, if any, incurred by him, are of course better known to those officers than to myself.

I consider that he has rendered an important service to the Government; and as he, unlike other settlers on lands fraudulently claimed under Mexican grants, has derived no personal advantage from his efforts, his claim would seem to be entitled to favorable consideration.

OGDEN HOFFMAN
U.S. District Judge.

Letter of Governor Haight

I concur in the foregoing remarks of Judge Hoffman.

H.H. HAIGHT

The following distinguished citizens, early pioneers and men of note, attested to Dowling's claim by sworn affidavit:

* Ogden Hoffman, U.S. District Judge
* John A. Sutter, founding patriarch of New Helvetia (Sacramento)
* Major Edward McGowan
* Captain Robert Haley, John Tripp, attendant on the Island, and Terivio Tanferana, a resident since 1840.

The validity of Dowling's title to the island is made evident and clear in a letter written to President Andrew Johnson by S.S. Inge, U.S. Attorney for the State of California:

Honorable. Andrew Johnson,
President of the United States, Washington, D.C.
Sir:

Mr. Thomas Dowling will proceed hence to Washington, D.C. to solicit of the Government a recognition of the valuable services rendered by him in defense of Yerba Buena Island against the fraudulent claims which have been asserted thereto. His time, energies, and money have been devoted to this object for the past fifteen years, and after having deferred the claims referred to, he was finally himself turned out of possession by the military authorities, completely impoverished in fortune, and without the slightest recognition or compensation for those fifteen years of devoted services to the Government, without which the Island would in all probability have been confirmed to the grantee under the fraudulent grant derived from Alvarado.

These services were rendered on part when I was the Attorney of the United States, and were continued under my successor until complete success attested their value in the defeat of the fraudulent grant. The records of the United States courts establish conclusively the importance of Mr. Dowling's services, and I have no doubt the distinguished Judge of the United States District Court would cheerfully accord to him all the merit he claims therefore. Mr. Dowling was for many years the sole occupant of the Island, made very valuable improvements thereon, and reclaimed from the tide-water about two and one-half acres of land, which have thereby been added to the area of land. His title to this can hardly be questioned, and yet the military have ejected him from it, or refuse to allow him, as I am informed, quiet possession thereof. Assuming (what is assumed to be true) that Mr. Dowling's money and services defeated the fraudulent grants, and established the Government's title thereto, it seems to follow as an equitable sequence that he should be adequately compensated.

Very respectfully,
S.W. Inge,
Late U.S. D. Atty. for California

The above facts are true, as the claim for the Island was defeated in the United States District court while I was United States District Attorney.

(Signed:) William Blanding
Late U.S. D. Atty. for California

Interest in the Dowling case was augmented following the appearance of John Nye, a son of the original resident and title holder on the Washington scene. His testimony was brief and precise: how his father had acquired title to the property, that the grant was recorded in the Mexican National Records, and the manner in which he deeded his interest to Thomas Henry Dowling. His deposition was signed under oath on December 31, 1870.

In addition to all the improvements he made on the Island, Dowling stated that he had to ward off intruders and defend his rights in court against fraudulent claimers, such as Jose Pollack, John Watson, and others who took their cases before the First District Court in San Francisco, only to have their trumped-up claims denied. Dowling further testified that he had saved no fewer than 39 lives of those caught in the rough currents that prevailed around the island's shores.

Pursuant to the land laws of California, a "deed" is the instrument by which the seller conveys ownership of property to the buyer. The deed is then recorded and henceforth the property bears the name of the purchaser. California was ceded by Mexico in 1848 and became a part of the United States with the completion of the Treaty of Guadeloupe. The treaty specifically provides that land and property rights granted under Mexican Law will be adhered to and upheld by the U.S. Government. In 1850, California was admitted into the Union and the City of San Francisco was incorporated, and reincorporated including the island of Yerba Buena a year later. The United States Land Commission was established in 1855, which gave rise to the "Van Ness" ordinance: an instrument whose avowed purpose was in granting clear title to all duly recognized property owners as if such property, rights had been consummated by "Grant Deed."

The matter of rightful ownership was quite often in dispute during this unsettled period, when California was beset with land grabbers, claim jumpers, and chancers of every hue. As an example the illustrious John A. Sutter was subjected to intruders who roamed his land at will, gorged themselves on his crops, and made off with his fatted bullocks. In like manner Comstock bluffed two unsuspecting Irish miners into giving up their claim which he said belonged to him and from which he reaped a fortune.

The backlog of land claims and counter claims may account for the Washington authorities' delay in approving Dowling's legitimate title to the Island.

However, the facts Dowling and his honorable witnesses presented, proved beyond a shadow of legal doubt that Thomas Dowling had acquired title in lawful manner, which title the United

Sates Government was duly bound to honor according to the terms and conditions of the Guadeloupe Treaty.

In this connection, it should be stated that the original document conveying title to Captain Gorham Nye from the Mexican Government bears the signature of the acting Governor Negate and was recorded in the Mexican Archives on December 23, 1864:

QUIT CLAIM DEED
GORHAM H. NYE
to
THOMAS H. DOWLING

Said Nye does remise, release, and quit claim all his right title and interest in and to all that piece of land known as Yerba Buena Island, in the Bay of San Francisco, about two miles easterly of the Custom House in the City of San Francisco; containing on hundred and sixty acres, more or less.

Acknowledged December 23, 1864, before G.T. Knox, Notary Public, recorded December 23, 1864.

Captain Nye was so perturbed by the manner in which the U.S. Government took possession of the Island and evicted Thomas Dowling without due process of law , that he vowed to see right over might prevail and that justice was done. Leaving no doubt in anyone's mind that Thomas Dowling had purchased the Island in good faith and lawful manner and that he in the same manner had deeded it to him, as added proof he signed a Quit Claim in favor of the above.

It is of particular interest, as previously mentioned, to note that the U.S. Government, through its officers Admiral Farragut and Major Towers, were already aware that Dowling was indeed the rightful owner by their purchase of rock from him on the Island. Payment for the same was authorized by General William T. Sherman, by a check made payable to Thomas Dowling, drawn on the banking house of Lucas, Turner and Co. in San Francisco.

As another example of government injustice, when the Army seized the island, they allowed one of Dowling's tenants to remain in possession after Dowling himself had been evicted.

The 41st Congress (3rd session) convened March 3, 1871, when the claim was ordered to be resubmitted. Dowling's claim had been turned over to the Subcommittee on private land, whose Mr. Mahan submitted a lengthy report which reaffirmed most of the evidence presented during the earlier hearings as outlined in this narrative, with one exception. This single alteration would make it appear that the right of the Federal Government to establish its claim to the Island was reserved by an act dated July 1, 1851, whereas such recourse was not taken until 1866 over a decade later.

No request or demand for governmental possession was made until President Johnson's recommendation of October 1866. Evidently the commanding general at San Francisco considered the recommendation to be a "directive" and issued the following orders:

> (1) the commanding officer of Alcatraz Island will send tomorrow a detachment of one sergeant and ten privates and a commissioned officer under his command to take post at Yerba Buena Island. (2) He will see that they are sent with tents, boards for tent floors, subsistence till the 10th proximo, fuel, garrison and camp equipage and such other articles as may be necessary for the detachment.

Forthwith, the soldiers took possession by force and ordered Dowling off the Island. Apparently all the Army sought was possession, as no fortifications were erected, no batteries of cannon set up, and no garrison established, save the original detachment of an officer, a sergeant, and ten soldiers.

In 1864, Congress enacted a law reaffirming land titles in California which pinpointed the intention of the government.in such matters The law specifically granted all the lands to the City of San Francisco, except for government reservations already set aside. This order contained no reservations whatsoever, and it would have no effect or bearing on any legitimate prior right or claim, whether granted by Spain, Mexico, or the United States. Any deviation from this was contrary to the Act and in violation of the will of Congress. No claim whatsoever had been made by the authorities regarding Yerba Buena prior to 1866; and therefore it appears no legitimate U.S. governmental claim existed prior to that time.

The illegality of the Army seizure of Dowling's island seems readily apparent from all the evidence presented by witnesses who were quite familiar with the story of the island; they concurred that Thomas H. Dowling was indeed the rightful and lawful owner. The same was attested to by prominent men familiar with the case, such as the Governor of California H.H. Haight, U.S. District Judge Ogden Hoffman, S.W. Inge, U.S. District Attorney of California, and a host of others. Furthermore, the evidence underscored the fact that Dowling had good title in accordance with Mexican law when he came into possession by a deed from Gorham H. Nye in 1849. The document bore the signature of Acting Governor Castello Negate, leaving no doubt as to its authenticity. The United States was duly bound to honor all previous Mexican land commitments, under the terms of the Treaty of Guadeloupe.

The question remains: why did the U.S. Government not abide by the said treaty in Dowling's case as they had on numerous others!. There is a familiar saying that hindsight is better than foresight, and no doubt that principle applies to government as well as ordinary citizens. During the years prior to 1866, when the rocky mound of Yerba Buena Island sat forlornly in the churning tide of San Francisco Bay, no government agency showed the slightest interest in it. However, when it became a center of commercial activity with fine buildings and industries, and word spread that Dowling's Island domain was worth millions, everyone including Government agents wanted to get a piece of the action. The authorities were caught napping and had to save face. Someone had to be the goat of Goat Island. In this case it was none other than our subject Thomas Henry Dowling.

Lacking any legal authority, the proponents of military ownership of the island concocted the idea of an order bearing the President's signature as Commander in Chief. In this manner they were assured of possession legally or otherwise. To the Army's disappointment, the order turned out to be only a recommendation. Apparently the President had come up with a clever ploy by passing the buck on to the regional commander stationed in San Francisco. No doubt, up to his neck in the problems of reconstruction and rehabilitation in the aftermath of the Civil War, President Johnson was most anxious to get off the hook in whatever way possible.

The Dowling case dragged its slow, tortuous way through the Congress; but despite all of the testimony, no decision was handed down. Time, quite often plays a major role in such lengthy litigations as it most assuredly did in this particular situation.

Captain Thomas Dowling passed away on June 12, 1871, frustrated in his attempts to regain possession of his island by legal means. He had been worn out by the agonizing hearings that dragged on for five years or more. The *National Republican* noted: "the adjournment of Congress without taking any action on his claim hastened Captain Dowling's death." The Washington *Chronicle* likewise sympathized with the deceased, his reduced circumstances, and his fruitless struggle to obtain what he had considered a just claim.

It was a sad ending for such an industrious man, who forfeited his holdings without recompense to the very government whose obligation it was to honor and protect the property rights of its citizens. Today there is nothing left on Yerba Buena Island to mark the memory of the colorful Irish pioneer, Thomas Henry Dowling, who devoted the best years of his life to protecting and beautifying the shimmering island that stands majestically in San Francisco Bay.

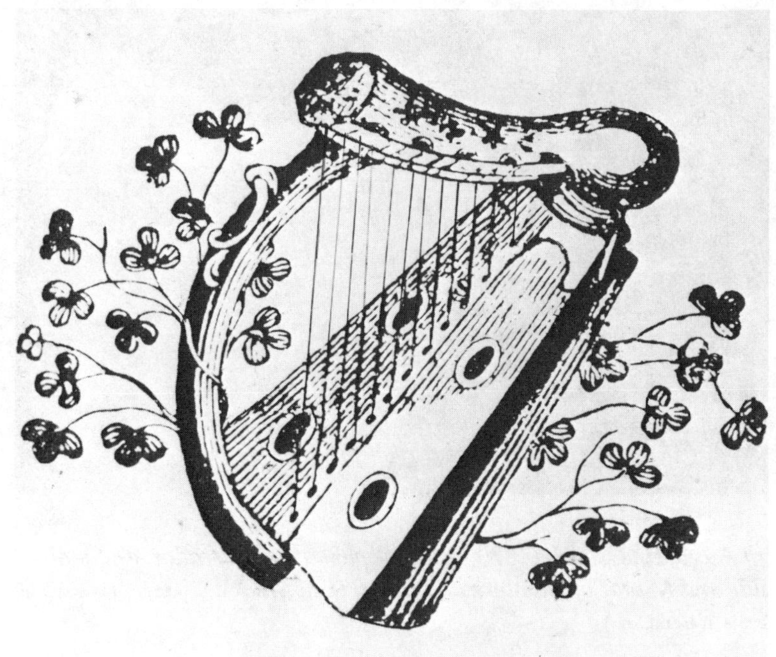

Philip Augustine Roach (1820-1889), diplomat, ambassador, and both Alcalde and Mayor of Monterey. [Courtesy of the Bancroft Library, University of California at Berkeley.]

10

Philip A. Roach: Alcalde, Mayor, & Ambassador

He was Irish-born and a leader and pioneer among pioneers. Philip Roach (1820-1889) played a key role in guiding California from a military-governed territory to a sovereign commonwealth in the Union of States. Roach was to boot an accomplished orator, linguist, and statesman. Few figures in California history have been as dedicated or successful in planting the seeds of patriotism and honest government in the state he grew to love.

The San Francisco Examiner paid this tribute on his death in 1889:

> For over 40 years he was a conspicuous figure in the social and political life of California. There have been few men who have borne so conspicuous a part in the history of California as Philip A. Roach, and no man for whom the people had a more affectionate regard. It was shown so often that whenever his name came up for office, the issue was as good as settled.

Roach was born in Fermoy, *Cpoic Riorear* (Roach's Country) on November 1, 1820. His forbears were of Norman stock who came to Ireland and settled in the sheltered valley of the meandering

Blackwater River. Over the years the Norman Roaches became immersed in the local community and eventually became more Irish than the Irish themselves.

His father died shortly after Philip was born, and we can only imagine the hardships their large family endured without a breadwinner in that troubled period. The widowed mother emigrated with her young family at the first opportunity and settled in New York City. Details are obscure as to how the growing family eked out a living and adjusted to conditions in the New World. Philip's formal education ended when he completed grammar school, which was considered adequate in those days. Also he had the guidance of a good Irish mother, the teaching of Mother Church, plus the advantage of growing up in a strict family-oriented environment in the New York of the 1830s.

New York was already a melting pot of humanity. Poverty was rampant, yet the ambitious could find ample opportunity to improve their station. It was in this bustling society that young Roach developed his philosophy of life, and to which his career in the political and social life of California is inextricably bound.

Upon leaving school at the age of 14, young Roach found work as a clerk in an import house and learned some of the intricacies of foreign trade. He took a keen interest in the countries with which the firm traded and thus gradually acquired a knowledge of French, Spanish, and Portuguese, which helped open a new world of opportunities in later years.

Heading West

At age 24, Roach travelled to visit relatives in Vicksburg, Mississippi where his elder brother James had been elected Mayor. During Philip's stay, the editorship of the *Sentinel* newspaper became vacant when the editor was incapacitated in a duel. Philip assumed this position for a short time. But as his knowledge of foreign languages opened up new career frontiers, he was soon off to Europe, working as a salesman for American cotton. In 1845, he won national recognition when President John Tyler appointed the scholarly young Irishman as American Vice Consul in Le Havre. While serving in this position, he managed to attend a series of seminars dealing with commercial and international law at the University of Paris. In 1846, he returned to the U.S. and was soon appointed as Consul General in Lisbon, Portugal by the new President, James K. Polk. By this time Roach was familiar with most of the modern European languages and proceeded to carry out his assignment with confidence and skill. Apart from the trials of surviving a devastating earthquake which destroyed much of the city, his stay in Lisbon appears to have been relatively uneventful.

In 1849, Philip received a letter from his brother, Thomas, in California, informing him of the gold discovery and urging his coming to the 'land of opportunity.' Thomas, a Captain in Colonel Stevenson's New York Regiment, was assigned to duty in the West. When the Mexican War ended, he was appointed Deputy Collector for the Port of San Francisco. In 1851, Thomas left San Francisco and settled in California's Trinity Bay, Klamath County, and a year later was elected judge, but was drowned in the Klamath River prior to taking the oath of office.

Philip had acted on his brother's advice in 1849 and resigned his Consulship, returning to America in haste. After a brief rest, he left New York on June 30, 1849, and arrived in San Francisco during the first week of August. When the passengers arrived at the Isthmus of Panama, the weather was hot and humid, with torrential rains. When the dreaded Chagres fever broke out and the waiting passengers became panic-stricken, unmindful of his personal safety, Roach took the lead in providing aid and comfort to the sick and dying, being ably assisted by Lieutenant Edward Beale, H. Gray Otis, and others (as later acknowledged by William Neilson, American Consul in Panama).

Roach was disillusioned with what he saw in San Francisco, particularly the overcrowded and unsanitary conditions reminiscent of those in Eastern cities. He quickly made his way to the peace and quiet of the old Capital of Monterey. Here he found a fertile area for his anticipated endeavors. The newly appointed soldier-Governor, an Irishman named Bennet Riley, had issued a proclamation calling for a convention to draft a constitution for the new State. Since there was an urgent need at the convention for a man well-versed in American diplomacy and one fluent in both English and Spanish, Philip Roach found that his own hour of destiny coincided with that of California; and he immediately offered his services to the Governor.

When the convention was called to order, Captain Robert Semple, the impresario from 'Old Kentuck' and a leader in both reputation and stature (he stood over seven feet tall), was elected Chairman. Captain William Marcy was appointed Secretary, and William Shannon was named Chairman of the Rules Committee. By coincidence, at that very moment some of the nation's most brilliant orators and legislators, including Henry Clay, John C. Calhoun, and Daniel Webster, were facing each other in Congress on the momentous issue of slavery. At this time, the states in the Union were equally divided on the slavery question, with 15 free and 15 slave states; and thus all eyes were turned toward California, whose new Constitution could tip the precarious balance.

Roach adroitly addressed the gathering in both English and Spanish, explaining in considerable detail every proposal outlined in the draft Constitution. His explanation and support of the new Constitution, which was drafted in harmony with the basic laws of the Republic, defending personal and property rights, was so convincing that it was approved with virtual unanimity. So impressed were the delegates and local residents with Roach's abilities, that they offered him any office within their jurisdiction. Although he declined this invitation, upon his return from a vacation in San Francisco, he graciously accepted his election as *Alcalde* (Mayor) of the old Capital of Monterey. (Since Monterey, the old colonial Spanish-Mexican stronghold, became an American city after California achieved statehood, Philip Roach had the unique honor of being both its last Alcalde and its first Mayor.)

One of the highlights of Roach's administration in Monterey was a public banquet tendered to the retiring Military Governor, Bennet Riley. The affair was held on July 30, 1850, and Alcalde Roach was toastmaster. The Trustees of Monterey presented Riley with a medal weighing 16 ounces and costing $600, with the arms of Monterey on one side, and on the other the words: "The man who came to do his duty and who accomplished his purpose." Historian Laura Bride Powers remembered the occasion fondly: "Philip A. Roach, a silver-tongued orator and the last *Alcalde,* presided, with profuse libations to cheer them to a proper peroration."

Roach's Courage

An article written in *The Daily Alta California* issue of November 19, 1884, was entitled "Dead Desperadoes, Some Bad Men of California's Early Days: Terrors of the Community. Oregon Ned, Jack Powers and 'Yank' Riley. A Pluck Arrest and a Desperate Escape: Exploits of Belcher Hay." Such a lurid headline illustrates Roach's courage and ability to take stern measures when necessary:

> At that time there lived in a secluded part of the town a widow and her three daughters, good and pretty girls. She had come, with her family, from Lower California, and her husband had been "un soldado del Rey" or soldier of the king of Spain, a position much honored by the native Californians. The widow's home was broken into one night by "Yank Riley," but she and her daughters made such outcry, as soon to bring neighbors to the place, and Riley escaped from the premises, foiled by the desperate resistance of the inmates. Upon application of a native citizen, the next morning, Alcalde Roach issued a warrant for Riley's arrest. He was known to be in his room in the Washington Hotel, and his comrade was with him. When the officer went to arrest him, "Yank" drew his pistol, ordered the officer to leave, and in defiance said, "You and the Alcalde can go to hell."
>
> This was duly reported to the Alcalde, who then expressed his determination that Riley should be taken, alive or dead; that law and order should prevail and protection be assured to all. He called upon General Riley, as the civil force was not sufficient and requested military aid. General Riley promptly replied that the entire force under his command, infantry, cavalry and artillery was at his service, for that or any future occasion. A detail of twelve men was immediately supplied to the Alcalde, and with this force he proceeded himself to the hotel to make the arrest of the contumacious desperado. Six of the soldiers he placed about the hotel; the other six he took with him inside. The landlord was a Frenchman, named de la Haye. He declined to give any information whether Riley was still in his room. He said he never interfered with the coming or going of his lodgers. Alcalde Roach then led the soldiers upstairs into the hall, and knocked at Riley's door.

No response was given. The Alcalde at once in a loud voice, announced his business, and declared if the door was not instantly opened and unless Riley peacefully surrendered, the door would be forced open and himself made prisoner. Desperate as 'Yank' was he felt that it was discretion to comply. The door was instantly opened and Riley surrendered, after shaking his finger in the Alcalde's face, with the threat, "I'll fix you for this!"

His comrade kept quiet. 'Yank' then said they had a good deal of money in the room and begged permission to make disposal of it. A few minutes was granted for this; but instantly the door was closed, the window opened and from it the two leaped onto the balcony, thence upon the shed of the adjoining building, from that over a high adobe wall into the street and got away. The soldiers stationed about the hotel had witnessed the escape; Riley and his comrade saw them and fired upon them with their revolvers. It was now quite dark, and as there were a number of citizens in the street, the soldiers did not return the fire, lest an innocent person might be shot. None of the squad had been hit by the pair. The escape created great excitement in the town. The Californians gathered a large force. Alcalde Roach offered $300 reward for the capture of the fugitives. The next day report came that they had been seen riding at high speed toward San Juan. Immediately, a force of twenty-five mounted men, well armed, started in pursuit. They overtook the pair, and the night following 'Yank' Riley and his friend were brought into Monterey, and committed to prison by the Alcalde. An ample force was ordered from the garrison to guard against another escape. Riley vehemently denounced the Alcalde for putting a 'gentleman' like himself in such a wretched place. The next day the examination was in progress when into the harbor came the steamship from Panama. Among the passengers who came ashore to see the place was Alexander Wells, afterwards Chief Justice of the Supreme Court. Riley offered him $1,000 in gold to defend him. It was declined and Wells came on to San Francisco. Riley was admitted to bail in a heavy sum to await the action of the Grand Jury. The Town Council ordered the reward of $300 which Alcalde Roach had paid to be refunded to him: The firm course pursued by

Alcalde Roach had the effect to clear the place of Riley and other desperate characters.

Roach in Politics

The City of Monterey was incorporated on April 30, 1851. Since he had distinguished himself as *Alcalde,* Roach was elected Mayor under the new law. He was soon elected state Senator representing Monterey and Santa Cruz Counties, and he took up his new duties on January 5, 1852, after retiring as Mayor. It was his first experience in the State Legislature, yet he emerged as one of the most dynamic members of the Senate. On Saint Patrick's Day, 1852, he introduced his progressive 'sole traders bill' and steered it through both houses. This measure permitted married women to engage in business under their own names. Women could sell goods, collect profits, and even sell businesses without the consent of their husbands. Roach's measure is still law in California.

Roach served on a variety of committees: Public Buildings, Commerce and Navigation, State Prisons, Missions, etc. He introduced a bill setting up a commission to examine war claims in Monterey. Through his efforts, the block of land in San Francisco bounded by Washington, Jackson, Battery, and Sansome Streets was set aside for the erection of the Custom House and other public buildings which still stand. On March 4, 1853, President Franklin Pierce appointed Roach U.S. Appraiser for the San Francisco district. Roach then moved to San Francisco, where he served in this capacity for eight years.

Philip Roach pioneered reforms which improved the local prisons and benefitted the working class. In the early 1850s, San Quentin Prison was managed by private contract, which permitted the contracting party to hire out convicts. Roach was strongly opposed to a system which allowed prison labor to compete with free labor. He recommended that the State take over and operate the prison. In recognition of this accomplishment, the Mechanics Institute appointed him an honorary member of their society. At every opportunity he espoused the cause of the working man and his right to earn a decent living wage. At a labor meeting in Oakland, Roach was feted as the enemy of cheap labor.

Senator Roach's hail-fellow-well-met, hearty character is illustrated in the following brief account by B.E. Lloyd:

> Mr. Roach has attained considerable local celebrity by reason of his rollicking good humor and innocent pleasantness, which are perhaps intensified by the venerable appearance his prematurely white locks fix upon him. He is the butt of many a society joke, because he has actually lived and moved among the San Francisco *beau monde* for so many years, without having either got married or lost his heart. He is a confirmed bachelor and at present represents the Democracy of San Francisco in the State Legislature.

No doubt Roach had gained the hearts of San Franciscans as he had won those in Old Monterey. In 1873, not one, but two political groups, the city's "Independent" and Democratic parties, nominated their idol for the State Senate; Roach was elected to this office on October 15, 1873, more than 21 years after he undertook the representation of Monterey and Santa Cruz counties. He brought to the legislature not only two decades of political experience, but also years of living in San Francisco and Monterey which he would draw upon as a great resource in helping shape the destiny of young California.

A Man of Action

During the 1873-74 session, Roach presided as Chairman of the Committee of Navigation, in addition to serving as a member of the Committees on Public Printing, State Prisons, and Military Affairs. During the 1875-76 session, he chaired the Committee on Military Affairs and participated in the Committees on Submerged Lands, Public Printing, Federal Relations, and San Francisco water rates.

A review of the following list of bills that he introduced and guided through both houses of the California Legislature confirms Senator Roach's foresight and tenacity: regulation of public utilities, establishment of San Francisco's own water system, guidelines for the practice of pharmacy, a code for weights and measures, vocational education long before the term was in vogue, and a training ship to be made available for apprentice seamen in San Francisco Bay. This list comprises only a small sample of Roach's legislative achievements.

That Roach was indeed a man of educational vision is borne out by his efforts to establish a trade school as part of the San Francisco public school system. He argued persuasively that the inauguration of such a facility would be of great advantage to the potentially productive youth of the city, and that its economic and humanitarian benefits would amply repay any costs.

Roach was disturbed by the number of wife-beatings in California. To remedy this outrage, he pushed through the legislature a provision giving the courts discretion in ordering corporal punishment for wife-beating husbands. As amended Section 243 of the State Penal Code reads as follows:

> A battery is punishable not exceeding one thousand dollars, or by imprisonment in the county gaol not exceeding six months, or if committed upon a wife of the assailant, it shall be in the discretion of the Court to punish the offender by the infliction of not less than twenty-one lashes on the bare back, to be administered by the Sheriff of the County or any Constable of the Township.

The law was later declared unconstitutional as being cruel and unusual punishment, the clause being deleted entirely in 1881.

Roach was the constant champion of the working class. He opposed the railroads' bringing in large numbers of Chinese as track-layers, which would drive down the wages for local workers. He also led the battle in the State Senate for shorter hours for the railroad workers who were meagerly paid; his efforts finally led to the eight-hour day in California. His primary goal of maintaining an adequate standard of living for the working man is testified to by his statement:

> Every government that has legislated upon the subject of labor, has endeavored to do it with a view to finding employment for its people, and of elevating their character. Any attempt to degrade it, or to deprive honest men of work and food, increases crime, poor houses and prisons, and throws on capital the burden of their support. Our government has attempted to prevent the introduction of paupers and criminals. An American living by the toil of his hands, (if forced to work for very low wages) would exercise a labor as degraded as employed within an

> almshouse. For if we reduce wages to poorhouse rates, it is as degraded as if performed within one of those institutions.

Roach was first and foremost in protecting the rights of California citizens. He often rose to the defense of settlers' rights when they were threatened by land-grabbers, claim jumpers, and speculators in collusion with greedy politicians. In 1873, he pushed through the legislature a bill providing that settlers should have the first option to purchase the sections of land included in surveys of Spanish and Mexican grants, but finally restored to public domain. Furthermore, that the time of application should be extended to one year instead of 60 days, to forestall landsharks from gobbling up all the titles before the settlers became aware of the opportunity.

Roach's dedication to the rights of Californians was especially impressive since it was not confined to male rights. In 1874, he advocated a progressive bill permitting women to hold educational offices, as a follow-up to his 1852 'sole trader' bill which gave women the right to their own earnings. Defending women's rights in another piece of legislation, the educational offices bill, he commented that men on the Board of School Directors (many of whom were of inferior education) had reduced the salaries of female teachers, and added that had there been some intelligent women on the board, such an outrage would not have been attempted.

Roach had the deepest appreciation for his illustrious peers of California's early days. He therefore introduced a petition for the relief of the almost-forgotten patriarch of the Mother Lode, John Augustus Sutter (whose lands had been stolen by squatters), and he sponsored a similar petition for the relief of General Winn, founder of the Native Sons of the Golden West.

Roach's lifelong friendship for an old Spanish Californian, Judge Pablo de la Guerra, was reflected when he obtained an adjournment of the legislature in his memory in 1874. Judge Guerra, a noble Castilian, had been a delegate to the first California Constitutional Convention in 1849, when Roach had served as moderator.

His admiration for Andrew Jackson, the patron soldier and President of the U S., was manifest when he secured unanimous agreement for the following resolution:

> This being the anniversary of one of the most glorious events in American history, to wit, the anniversary of the Battle of New Orleans, I move that, in respect of the day, and the hero who participated in it, that when the Senate adjourns this day, it adjourns in honor of the day.

In 1882, Roach was elected Public Administrator and reelected in 1884, and he continued in that post until the end of 1886, when he retired from public service. He then became administrator of the estate of the Thomas H. Blythe, a wealthy man who died intestate.

Roach's Irishness

Although Roach was truly all-American in every sense of the word, he was also proud of his Irish heritage and spoke out fearlessly on Ireland's behalf whenever the opportunity arose. Incensed by President Arthur's laxity regarding the treaty of 1868 with Britain, which granted full protection to naturalized citizens, Roach spared no effort in publicizing the matter. He wrote to New York's *Irish World*, calling attention to the fact that the British were imprisoning naturalized citizens in Ireland without trial for utterances which any Englishman would have been free to make. He emphasized that the law required the President to take action for the prompt release of any such U.S. citizen unjustly deprived of liberty, and that while Mr. Arthur had been remarkably zealous in insisting on the enforcement of a similar treaty with China, he had taken no action in regard to flagrant violations by Great Britain.

In May of 1883, Roach spoke to a packed house in Union Hall to celebrate the release of Charles Stewart Parnell, the Irish patriot. He predicted that within 30 years the United Kingdom of Great Britain and Ireland would no longer exist, and that Ireland would be a free United Republic.

Roach's integrity and strong convictions are ably expressed by historian Dr. Hugh Quigley, who sought information on the great figures for his history of the California Irish. Though his subject modestly declined to be interviewed, Quigley obtained enough data elsewhere to pen the following sketch:

> Senator Roach is a man of character—a natural born leader of men, and would have made his mark in any community.

> Of fine personal appearance and gentlemanly instincts, he displays marked public spirit and a thoroughly upright and honest heart. His character is agreeably impressive, and he never fails to command respectful attention when he had anything to say. He is like Cato of old, a man of action as well as an elegant orator, and it is in action that his large and generous resources find fitting expression. He is true to his convictions, and from what he conceives to be right he cannot be moved a hair's breadth.

Roach as Newspaperman

Roach's career encompassed far more than politics. Aside from being an accomplished orator, statesman and scholar, he also proved to be an effective journalist. The Civil War created the need for two partisan newspapers in San Francisco. The *Chronicle* was founded as a Republican publication, whereas the *Examiner* stood as a proponent of the Democratic party. Charles Young, Editor of the *Chronicle,* wrote in 1915:

> The most notable journalistic occurrence of the last year of the Civil War was the birth of the only two English morning newspapers that survived the vicissitudes of the intervening fifty years. It was in 1865 that the *San Francisco Chronicle* and *Examiner* made their advent in the field of journalism in this city.

The *Examiner* was founded June 12, 1865, by William Moss, but was almost put out of business shortly thereafter when a mob wrecked the office. Philip Roach and Charles Weller joined in partnership with Moss; when Moss sold his interest to George P. Johnson, Roach, Weller, and Johnson guided the enterprise for 15 years and made it the leading Democratic journal in California. Roach put his prior experience with the Vicksburg *Sentinel* to good use as editorial writer from 1867 to 1874, at which time he became business manager for a number of years. He was ably assisted by such outstanding men as James Coffey, who became editorial writer and later Superior Court Judge of San Francisco; and New Yorker James O'Meara, who in turn became Editor of the *Examiner,* and of the *Argonaut* at a later date.

The partners sold the *Examiner* in 1880, and the retiring proprietors gave a banquet to the employees as a mark of long and faithful service. Roach of course was toastmaster, introducing O'Meara, Coffey and others, and as the golden tenor voice of John Bryant, foreman of the composing room, echoed through the hall.

The policy of the *Examiner* under Roach was always to improve the standard of journalism. The Placerville *Mountain Democrat* echoed the widespread sentiment of those days in their tribute of April 22, 1876:

> To the honor of journalism, we especially congratulate our noble old contemporary, the San Francisco *Examiner,* on having furnished from the ranks of editorial staff two such able, vigilant and faithful champions of honest and just legislation, such splendid examples of the fitness and trustworthiness of journalists as lawmakers, as are Senator Philip A. Roach and Assemblyman J.V. Coffey."

Roach in the San Francisco Community

Somehow, Roach found time in his many careers to become directly involved in the service to his community. He was an active member of the Society of California Pioneers and a Director during 1858-59, Vice President 1859-60, and President in 1861-62. He shared a close affiliation with the leaders of the Native Sons even though his Irish birth made him ineligible for membership in that organization.

Roach was a lifelong adherent to Catholicism and took an active role in the building of San Francisco's new Cathedral to be located on Van Ness, the city's broad central thoroughfare. In November 1887, at the request of the newly appointed Bishop Patrick Riordan, a fair was held at the Mechanics Pavilion on Market Street to raise funds. Roach gave the principal address of the evening (which was later published in a 24-page pamphlet). He concluded his remarks by prophesying:

> We are on the eve of entering the twentieth century. Many in this vast audience will pass many of its decades. It is now distant in time but little over twelve years. To many of us that period will appear less than twelve months did, when we were younger than we are now. Let the grand work of building the new Cathedral, which overlooks the

> placid sea on the shores of which earnest missionaries planted the Cross, go on. Let all vie in zeal in securing its early completion. Every effort is in active operation to make this effort a grand success. The various parishes of the city will be represented in the fair. Many Catholic organizations will take an active part in assisting the good work. United exertions will enable our beloved Archbishop to erect one of the grandest Cathedrals of our country. It will be a structure that, fifty years hence, will be a monument to the piety and zeal of the Catholics of the present time. It will be a temple adequate to the wants of the immense population which in half a century will occupy this peninsula. There is sufficient wealth and liberality among our people to assist our Archbishop in the great work he has undertaken. It behooves us all, to the utmost of our ability, to provide the means of securing, at an early day, the dedication of the new Cathedral to the service of almighty God.

Little did anyone know that this would be Roach's last important public address. On Sunday, April 20, 1889, while he was descending the stairs in his residence on Union Street, he was seized with an attack of vertigo and fell with such force against the banister that it brought on a concussion of the brain. His brother John and his sister Maria heard the crash, but by the time they reached him, he was already unconscious. The best efforts of Doctors Lane and Keeney, two close family friends, were to no avail.

He was given the last rites of the Church and breathed his last on Saturday, April 27. On May 1, the funeral began in old Saint Mary's Cathedral on California Street, where a requiem high mass was celebrated. The church was packed and the mourners overflowed into the streets, the vast majority of which followed the cortege to Calvary Cemetery where his remains were laid to rest.

The pallbearers included Mayor E.B. Pond, Nathaniel Holland, and J.H. Lohse, representing the Society of California Pioneers; his lifelong associate, Judge Coffey; Colonel Martin Murphy, son of the illustrious pioneer Martin Murphy; James Barry, another close friend; Major Jose R. Pico, Judges Wright and Duthill; pioneer James Phelan; and many other eminent Californians.

Of the many tributes paid to his memory, one of the most memorable was offered by Roach's close friend and lifelong associate, James Barry:

> When a good man dies it is not unbecoming in us to mourn. The death of Philip A. Roach leaves a vacancy which it will indeed be difficult to fill. For forty years a resident of this State—during all the time more or less prominently before the public—no man was better known or more dearly loved; nor lives there one among us who will be more sincerely or so universally mourned.
>
> Whenever he appeared at a public meeting one toss of his flowing white hair was the signal for an outburst of enthusiasm which was perfectly irresistible: men, women and children joining in acclamations of delight. While respected by all, it was by the 'common people' he was best beloved, for to them chiefly had he devoted his life. Nature made him a gentleman, and endowed him with a mind broad enough, and a heart big enough, to rise above any narrow part, class or religious prejudice.
> His ambition through life was to do good. He pitied the poor and helped them.... The lame, the halt and the blind, came to him for succor, and departed content, 'with blessings on his kindly head.' His death was worthy of his life. Surrounded by those nearest and dearest to him, who knew and loved him best, he passed away, with a placid smile—at peace with God and the world:
>
> Like one who wraps the drapery of the couch about him,
> And lies down to pleasant dreams.

In retrospect, it is certainly incomprehensible to fathom how a man so highly regarded by his contemporaries, and one who gave so much of himself to his adopted and beloved State in its most crucial times, could be so utterly forgotten by history. Yet we can find consolation in one truth, far more important than mere recognition: while the memory of Philip Roach has faded for the many millions who came after him, Californians still live in a State that has been forever imbued with the vigor and wise guidance of this visionary Irishman.

Kate Kennedy, famous woman teacher and suffragist. [Courtesy of the San Francisco Archives Collection, the San Francisco Public Library.]

11

Kate Kennedy:
Women's Suffragist & Educator

When Kate Kennedy (1827-1890) was born in County Meath, the pride and glory of Ireland's ancient cultural shrine of Tara had long since vanished, and, alas, the half-mythical grandeur of the High King Cormac's days was no more. The harp that once sounded through Tara's halls was only a half-forgotten romantic memory. But Tara's magic continued to inspire. The monstrous *dun* (fort) of Tara was once encircled by nine stout ramparts which the fiercest warriors could not destroy. At an appointed ritual time each year a proclamation was issued inviting the nobles to the great festival in Tara's ornate hall, a feast day unparalleled, the greatest celebration in all the Land. When the great hall of Tara, arrayed in all its splendor, was declared in readiness, the High King of All-Ireland was escorted to his honored place on the golden throne. Seated in position to commemorate the four directions of the cosmos were: the King of Ulster at the High King's right, the King of Munster at his left, the King of Leinster in the forefront and the King of Connaught at his back.

When Tara's assembled guests were seated, they bowed low in unison as if by a silent command. Stillness like the hush of the heathery moors descended on the gathering as if by a weird magic.

The silence was broken by the melodious strains of a thousand harps rising slowly to a crescendo throughout the ancient halls. The light-bearers rose together, the torches were illumined one by one, and soon the huge assembly resembled a burning forest. A trumpet blared as a signal for the noble bards to encircle the banquet table, singing joy and praises in their ancient tongue.

O Tara! Great was its glory. O Tara! Majestic was its inspiring grandeur. But all unmindful of Tara's storied ruins, centuries later Kate Kennedy and her younger sisters playfully skipped over its grassy mounds, stopping now and then to rest on its immortal ramparts. But when a few years had passed and Kate was ready to go to school, Kate's father, Thomas, fired her youthful imagination with the past glories of Tara. In some dim fashion these youthful recollections of Ireland's noble past would live on in Kate's fancy even when she left Ireland for America.

Kate Kennedy was born in the townland of Gaskinstown on the plains of royal Meath, May 31, 1827. She had one older brother and five younger sisters. The Kennedys traced their ancestry back to King Brian Boru and were substantial farmers, but fell on hard times during the period of the Penal Laws and the famine years after 1846.

Kate's early education required a two-mile walk each way over an unpaved road to the nearest school, which was a simple one-room *botan* (cottage) with mud walls, bare earth floor, and thatched roof. The children sat on rough wood benches. It is a wonder the youths learned to read and write so well, for there were not enough textbooks to go around, and their writing tools consisted of discarded roofing slate and a bar of chalk.

Following this rudimentary education, Kate went on to a convent school run by the Sisters of Loretta in the nearby town of Navan. The first two nuns arrived in the town in 1833, following Catholic Emancipation that had been championed by Daniel O'Connell. During the earlier period of the Penal Laws, most Catholic institutions were banned or their properties confiscated; thus the pious sisters had to start the school from scratch. In this convent, amenities for the pupils (as well as the nuns) were spartan, little better than they had been in the one-room country school, for they were housed in an old, dilapidated building with a clay floor and a rough-hewn ceiling. There was no heat except a peat fire in an open hearth, and the hingeless windows offered little ventilation.

Irish birthplace of Kate Kennedy in Gaskinstown, County Meath.
[Courtesy of James Carney of Navan, Co. Meath.]

The initial cost of the convent school was borne by a few well-off farmers and merchants. The operation was kept very inexpensive since the sisters required no salaries, and some of the better-educated townsfolk offered their tutoring services gratis.

Despite these unpromising conditions, Kate acquired a fine education. She learned to speak French, Italian, and Spanish and graduated with honors, first in her class.

The death of Kate's father in 1840 was a tragic blow to the young family, coming just after Kate had finished convent school. Because her father's passing meant there would be no advanced education for the five younger sisters, Kate instructed them herself. She gained practical experience by spending many long hours reading aloud to illiterate older neighbors, who had been deprived of an education because of their religious and national affiliations. Such volunteer work no doubt led her develop the gift of oratory, a resource she would summon most effectively in later years.

At the historic gathering of August 15, 1843, Kate and her brother Patrick were on the sacred hill of Tara to listen in rapt attention to the stirring eloquence of Daniel O'Connell, as he declaimed on favor of Catholic Emancipation and the repeal of the Union of England and Ireland. The Irish came to Tara half-a-million strong from all over the island: long-suffering serfs, hereditary bondsmen ground under the heel of constant oppression. O'Connell implored the vast assemblage to show the world that they were worthy of freedom. Patrick Kennedy was so inspired that he vowed to join the Irish patriots and fight for his downtrodden land. He was denied the opportunity, however, by the collapse of the Young Ireland Rebellion in 1848.

Those troubled years in Ireland were made more tragic by the famine which struck Ireland in 1846. That "most distressful nation" lost more than two million people through starvation, famine-induced disease, and emigration. These agonizing conditions brought Kate, her brother Patrick, and their sister Alice to New York in the year 1849. The girls fared well from the moment they arrived, securing work in an embroidery factory where they employed their earlier skills. In addition, since they were among the very few who could speak both English and French, they frequently worked as interpreters for the many French-speaking working women. To the young Kennedys, America was the promised land; for they saved up enough money from their hard work to bring their mother and younger sisters from Ireland in 1851. Meanwhile Kate studied diligently, aspiring to become a teacher in a public school.

Suddenly, the Kennedys, like so many seekers of that period, were caught up in the Gold Rush frenzy. In 1853, the two younger sisters traveled the immense distance to San Francisco. Kate and the rest of the family joined them in 1856 and lived in a house on Clay Street near the old Plaza. For years thereafter, the Kennedy home was a happy one, full of laughter and Irish hospitality, which were the hallmarks of this closely-knit, well-educated clan.

As a a pioneer herself, Kate proudly witnessed the growth of her adopted city and state and of the public school system with which her name would be for so long associated. San Francisco was the first American city to establish a public school independent of state support. The first school opened in 1848 and was taught by Thomas Douglas, a Yale graduate. The Town Council allotted $400 a year for the school's upkeep. There were only six pupils who paid even the small tuition; other, less fortunate waifs were admitted free. The school's early demise was typical of San Francisco's many ups and downs during the Gold Rush days. For when the cry of "GOLD!" was shouted, the teacher rushed off to the hills along with hordes of prospectors. The next school, taught by a Mr. Patton, opened in 1850 on Washington Street, but its charter was suspended by a new state ordinance in 1857.

When Col. Thomas Nevins became the first Superintendent and proceeded to organize the department, Kate Kennedy received her first teaching assignment (in 1856) in the little town of Suisun in the delta area on the outskirts of San Francisco Bay. Much to her delight, Kate received her first San Francisco appointment in the following year. The wood-frame building, named Happy Valley School, was surrounded by sandhills and stood close to the present site of the Palace Hotel. A pupil who attended the school during Kate's tenure wrote: "I remember looking out the window in Happy Valley School and seeing men carting away the sand piles to fill in the bay."

In 1859, Miss Kennedy was transferred to the Greenwich School. Here she took the examination for principal and passed at the head of the list. In recognition of her abilities, Kate was appointed principal of the North Cosmopolitan Grammar School, which had been created to instruct young people simultaneously in several languages. However, in her new assignment, Kate was paid the same salary as the principal of a lesser primary school; indeed, no woman at that period could be paid a man's wage, despite the fact that Miss Kennedy had been recognized as one of the preeminent teachers in the city. Whereas others may have accepted this salary inequity passively, the indomitable, fearless—and stubborn—Kate Kennedy vowed to bring the the sense of justice she had imbibed near ancient Tara to her new home in the New World.

Kate Kennedy threw herself into the women's struggle for equal pay for equal work, which ended in the year 1874, when Kate finally achieved victory: the state law was passed which reads, "Females employed as teachers in the public schools of this state shall in all cases receive the same compensation as allowed male teachers for like services, when holding the same grade of certificate." The precise and deliberate wording of that legislation suggests that Kate herself had a hand in drafting the final document.

In 1875, An attempt was made by the Department of Education in San Francisco to repeal the measure, but its efforts went for naught Kate Kennedy was without doubt the first woman anywhere in America to receive as a salaried employee equal pay for equal work. It is hardly surprising, then, that when Susan B. Anthony, the matriarch of women's rights, came to San Francisco, her primary goal was to call on Miss Kennedy to congratulate her in person.

Eventually, Kate was able to bring about teachers' permanent tenure of office, which has been a benefit (although not always recognized) for every member of the teaching profession ever since. The law made it illegal to remove a fully accredited teacher without a formal hearing.

From Education to Politics

Miss Kennedy was an accomplished orator, and at public meetings and other gatherings spoke with eloquence and feeling on the issues of women's suffrage, land reform, taxation, proportional representation, and other economic issues. Her dominant efforts were directed toward improving the conditions of working people, and to this goal she contributed both time and talent with tongue and pen. Kate was a protege of Henry George, proponent of the single tax and founder of the California Land Reform League.

Some who suggest that, like Mrs. O'Leary's cow who kicked the lantern that started the conflagration in Chicago, it was Kate Kennedy who kept things hot, pending the arrival of the rabble-rousing Irishman Denis Kearney of the Workingmen's party. The two had much in common, to say the least: a willingness to take the lead in confronting the conservative establishment, whenever it was deemed to be in the interest of the working man.

The long, agonizing struggle for equal rights eventually took its toll. In 1878, Kate's poor health compelled her took a leave of absence and set out on a trip to Europe. She paid a return visit to her native land, and from there to the Continent. Her knowledge of languages powerfully equipped her to examine other educational and economic systems.

On her return she wrote a series of articles directed towards the working man. These set forth her belief that the formation of unions to espouse the rights of the workers was the only practical reform. She vigorously sought to promote Henry George's Single Tax and the Land Reform League. She also threw her hat into the political ring and ran for the office of Superintendent of Public Instruction. However, in those patriarchal days her candidacy for public office was only a gesture to focus attention on women's rights.and related matters. However, she did manage to garner a sizable vote.

The Fight of Her Life

By February 1887, Kate Kennedy was in failing health. She applied for a two-month leave of absence to recuperate, intending to return to finish out the school year. Although she was a successful and popular teacher, her progressive and outspoken views seemed to harden her enemies' resolve to destroy her; and her absence provided the opportunity to strike. On March 16th, the Board of Education transferred her from the North Cosmopolitan School—where she had been principal for almost 20 years—to the little Ocean View School way out in the sticks. At the same time they cut her salary from $175 to $100 a month. The pupils staged a protest when she was removed, but on May 18th she was dismissed altogether, on such flimsy grounds that it was obvious that the Board's chief motivation was both political and sexist.

Although Kate was aging and was in failing health, she remained optimistic and confronted this attack with the same fearless determination that had characterized her entire life. She sued the Board for reinstatement and for her full salary with back-pay from the time of her transfer. For some three years, the tenure case dragged on slowly through the courts. The lower court ruled in her favor, but the Board appealed; and the case was finally settled by the State Supreme Court. Miss Kennedy won! When the case was finally decided in her favor, teachers' tenure was established in clear and precise terms, as follows:

> A teacher of any principal grade, with a proper certificate cannot be placed in a lower grade or dismissed except for misconduct or incompetency.

The Board was ordered to reinstate Kate, and she received back-pay in full in a check for $5,700.75, the largest salary warrant ever

San Francisco Mission District public school named in honor of pioneer educator, Kate Kennedy.

given a teacher up to that time. Teacher tenure was now securely established in California, but the long crusade and ordeal almost killed its proponent. Kate's days were now numbered. Too ill to care for herself, she moved in with her sister in Oakland, where she passed away on March 18, 1890, the day after St. Patrick's Day. Her remains were brought back to San Francisco, the scene of her challenging life. Finally, she was laid to rest among other California pioneers in Laurel Hill Cemetery. (When Laurel Hill was abandoned some 50 years later, her remains were removed to Cypress Lawn Cemetery, outside the city.) Today, a living memorial to this indomitable educator, the Kate Kennedy School, stands in the heart of the city she loved. Her Teacher's Certificate remained fastened to the wall of the school for many years, until it was destroyed by vandals.

True to ancient Ireland's Tara traditions of justice, culture, and patriotism that she had absorbed in her Irish birthplace in County Meath, Kate Kennedy throughout her busy life did battle for those whom she felt had been deprived of a just share of their rightful heritage. Strong of will and stout of heart, Kate heroically devoted her later years to the advancement of humanity and education.

Dan O'Connell, journalist, poet, and Bohemian Master of High Jinks.
[Courtesy of the Bancroft Library, University of California at Berkeley.]

12

Dan O'Connell: Irish Bard & Cofounder of the Bohemian Club

Few men have brought as much Irish wit, style, and character to the West as Dan O'Connell (1849-1899), the mirthful mantle-bearer of the O'Connell clan. This gifted literary Celt was to mark many achievements in California, the most memorable of which might be his "coronation" as the "King of Munster," the mentor of High Jinks for the influential Bohemian Club. Born in the historic town of Ennis in County Clare, son of the distinguished barrister, Charles O'Connell, and grandnephew of the illustrious patriot, Daniel O'Connell, our hero, Dan O'Connell, enjoyed every advantage in his early Irish surroundings. He associated with the best and brightest in his native Ireland and also in his adopted state of California.

The O'Connells were of unadulterated ancient Irish Milesian stock, bold agitators whenever freedom's rights were challenged and stout defenders in times of national struggle. An account preserved in English archives relates the story of another Daniel O'Connell, who turned back a Scottish invasion in the year 1245. Yet another Daniel from the noble O'Connell sept (clan) had been a leader of the exiled Irish Brigade—soldiers of fortune of the 17th and 18th century, the "Wild Geese"—who saw service in France, where he rose through the ranks to General, honored nobleman, and Count of France.

Dan O'Connell's Namesake: The Great Emancipator

The most distinguished of the O'Connells, Daniel, "the Great Emancipator" (1775-1847), was born in the townland of Carheen, near Cahirciveen in Co. Kerry. He was brought to Derrynane Abbey as a child and reared in the household of his uncle Maurice. When his uncle died, O'Connell inherited the estate and made it his home. Over the years, Derrynane became the meeting place of the O'Connells, a patriotic enclave, and the hub of Irish nationalism.

In Daniel the Emancipator's youthful days, Catholics had been denied an education in Ireland; so he was spirited out of his homeland by an uncle and on to the Catholic educational center of Louvain, France, to be schooled. From Louvain he transferred to St. Omers, a most congenial environment because of the many French-Irish there, descendants of the banished Irish "Wild Geese." When the French Revolution erupted, Daniel was compelled to take a temporary leave of his studies, and he returned to England in the company of other deportees. He completed his legal studies in London and was admitted to the Irish bar in Dublin in 1798. Coincidentally, the planned revolution of the United Irishmen exploded just as O'Connell was admitted as barrister. Had he been in Ireland the previous year, O'Connell probably would have become embroiled in the conflict because of the revolution's appeal to patriotic youth. Luckily for Ireland, O'Connell escaped the martyr's fate of patriots Robert Emmet, Wolfe Tone, and Earl Fitzgerald. At the youthful age of 23, he was a living witness to both a blood-letting French Revolution and an unsuccessful national revolt in Ireland. No doubt the loss of Ireland's bravest and best in violent conflict had a telling effect on his future plans.

Ireland endured a period of unparalleled humiliation and suffering following the ill-fated 1798 uprising. The Catholics were saddled by the English with all the blame and were too crushed to be able to offer either rebuttal or resistance. Savagely, the bright hopes of national independence were dimmed by the notorious Lord Castlereagh. Civil tribunals were closed and public gatherings were dispersed at the point of the bayonet. The outraged O'Connell vowed before God and his downtrodden countrymen to devote all his energies to his country and its altars, and to live for the emancipation of both. Although the pathetic loss of Ireland's noblest in the violent conflict of 1798 tore at his heart, this man of wisdom and chivalry was determined to undo his country's wrongs by peaceful means.

Throughout Ireland, O'Connell preached the gospel of "non-violence" as a means of redress. He stirred the hearts of his people and rekindled their hopes for this most distressful nation. For over a quarter-of-a-century O'Connell led his peaceful crusade far in advance of Ghandi's example. Like the fearless Indian pacifist of the next century, O'Connell dared to speak though surrounded by pointed guns and glistening bayonets even while under the watchful eye of Major Sire, the butcher of Dublin Castle, and the Saxon swordsman Lord Castlereagh. When O'Connell spoke, the boldness of the Celtic spirit in the youthful barrister filled the empty hearts of his downtrodden fellow patriots: "I would rather see the whole Penal Code reenacted than consent to the legislative extinction of Ireland."

What is less widely known is the fact that this Irish patriot was vitally influenced by the liberal principles of the Enlightenment and of the American Declaration of Independence, and the ideas of the founding fathers in particular: "...that governments must derive their just powers from the consent of the governed." O'Connell exposed England's most blatant disregard of this republican principle in the "Act of Union" of Ireland to Britain. In subjugated Ireland, the 'consent of the governed' was a myth reinforced by a well-equipped British army of 130,000 troops to assure the Act's passage. Yet in spite of such seemingly insurmountable obstacles, O'Connell persevered undaunted in his work to emancipate his country by peaceful means.

Dan O'Connell's Early Years

Our own Dan, the future immigrant to California, was a frequent visitor at the Emancipator's home at Derrynane, where his quick wit and jolly good humor made him one of the family. The youth closely resembled his patriot namesake in both physique and expression. Both spoke Gaelic, the language of their forefathers, a language rich in beauty of eloquence and dramatic delivery. Young

Dan was deeply influenced by the noble qualities of his illustrious grand uncle. Yet unlike the patriot who devoted all his energies to his native land, the youthful mantle-bearer looked to distant lands to fulfill his aspirations. He sailed the seven seas and sojourned in many ports until he found his heart's desire in the paradise of California on the Pacific. America's freedom and the hearty disposition of its people—the thousand and one charms which few can explain but all appreciate—captured his youthful imagination and held him in kindly bond all the rest of his days.

Like the education of his patriotic predecessor, the youth's early schooling had been directed in both Ireland and France by the Jesuits, whose philosophy left a lasting impression. Dan O'Connell's brief stay at the Jesuit school provided many happy memories. Throughout his many wanderings he never ceased to speak of his alma mater. Dan drank deep of life's cup in those early carefree days with his youthful companions, and rarely suffered a dull moment. While under the Jesuit's tutelage, young Dan also developed a keen appreciation of the classics, a penchant for poetry, and a philosophical outlook on life.

O'Connell's education was interrupted by the loss of his beloved mother and sister, who were drowned in the Grand Canal in Dublin. When the days of mourning had come to an end, Dan left the family residence in Ennis and enrolled in the prestigious Clongowes Wood College in Dublin, the headquarters of the Jesuit order in Ireland. Here he continued his classical studies in Greek and Latin and intensified his a strong passion for literature, a passion which guided his future ambitions.

To Far-off Lands

Young O'Connell was considered one of the greatest mixers and most delightful conversationalists of his era. Possessing a regal poise and dignified bearing, he was equally at home in the parlors of the rich and the hovels of the poor. It was said that he had no enemies, for he would permit no conflict to persist with any man. To be with him was to be happy, for he could produce humor like a conjurer and the laughter he evoked had no hint of acrimony.

His father, Charles, a prominent lawyer in Ennis, was offered a commission for his son in the English Navy. The youth, a seasoned swimmer and water-lover, set out to see the world as a man of the sea. But his seafaring days were cut short by a visit to a bachelor uncle in New York City. Fascination with the New World and the glamor of this bustling metropolis persuaded the youth to abandon the sea. However, the unexpected death of his uncle led to a further change in plans.

"Go west, young man" was a slogan that lured many adventurous youths to the Pacific Coast, and Dan, ever the intrepid one, was off again, this time around the Horn to California. He arrived at Santa Clara College in 1868, hoping that his previous association with the Jesuits might land him a teaching position. The students marveled to see the dashing young Irishman of strong athletic build, still clad in the brass-buttoned, handsome uniform of a midshipman in the British Navy. However, their curiosity was satisfied when the good Prefect, Father Varsi, informed the boys that the stranger was none other than Daniel O'Connell, grandnephew of the Irish patriot Daniel O'Connell, and that young Daniel had resigned from the British Navy to become a teacher at Santa Clara.

This Celtic wanderer with dignified carriage was soon on friendly terms with the boys. He confided that he had been compelled to leave the Navy on account of a duel with a Frenchman. Because the rules against dueling in the British Navy were strict, he had to (in his own words) "duck to avoid punishment."

His brief stay at Santa Clara was a time of great happiness since he was well-treated by the College President, Father Varsi, a man of culture and gentle manners. From Santa Clara Dan was dispatched to fill a minor professorship at old Saint Ignatius College in San Francisco, which was then located on Market Street, where the Emporium store stands today. Little is known of his duties at St. Ignatius, since the school records were destroyed in the fire of 1906.

Young O'Connell was a bohemian in the true sense of that often-misunderstood word: a man immune to the cares and worries of ordinary life, one who knew nothing of idleness, be it mental or physical. Moreover, he was a gifted writer, a student of literature, a poet of great depth, and a delightful raconteur. O'Connell's eloquence won the adoption of the name "Bohemian Club" at that group's first meeting in San Francisco on February 20, 1872. By coincidence, Boston's Papyrus Club, which was also bohemian in outlook, was spawned in the bachelor den of John Boyle O'Reilly, the famous wit, on December 14 of that same year.

Original Post Street home of the Bohemian Club, cofounded by the Master of High Jinks, Dan O'Connell. [Courtesy of the San Francisco Archives in the San Francisco Public Library.]

For more than 30 years, litterateur Dan O'Connell's delightful operas echoed life's "own sweet song" to the people of San Francisco. His *Songs from Bohemia* (1900) are a poet-lover's delight. In his lyrics, O'Connell was at his bardic best, tenderly conjuring forth either laughter or tears, as the humor led him.

Typical of O'Connell's poesy is this tribute to the humble drayman, the bane of the high-hatted coachman and his affluent fares:

The Captain that walks the quarter-deck,
 Is the monarch of the sea;
But every day, when I'm on my dray,
 I'm as big a monarch as he.

For the car must slack when I'm on the track,
 And the gripman's face gets blue,
And he holds her back till his muscles crack,
 And he shouts, "Hey, hey! Say, you!

Get out of the way with that dray!" "I won't!"
 "Get out of the way, I say!"
But I stiffen my back, and I stay on the track,
 And I don't get out of the way.

When a gaudy carriage bowls along
 With a coachman perched on high,
Solemn and fat, a cockade in his hat,
 Just like a big blue fly,

I swing my leaders across the road
 And put a stop to his jaunt,
And the ladies cry, "John, John, drive on!"
 And I laugh when he says, "I can't."

Oh, life to me is a big picnic,
 From the rise to the set of the sun;
The swells that ride in their fancy drags
 don't begin to have my fun.

I'm king of the road, though I wear no crown,
 As I leisurely move along,
For I own the streets, and I hold them down,
 And I love to hear this song:

"Get out of the way with your dray!" "I won't!"
 "Get out of the way, I say!"
But I stiffen my back, and I stay on the track,
 And I don't get out of the way.

According to O'Connell's biographer, William S. Harrison (himself a past President of the Bohemian Club), Dan O'Connell was prominent among the Club's founders, and all his life was the foremost exponent of the Bohemian Club's social ideals:

> I knew, and I think I understood O'Connell. Our friendship covered a quarter of a century of California growth. I saw him under all kinds of conditions of life. I knew him as a poet, litterateur, athlete, humorist, and Bohemian, and the more I saw him, and the better I knew him, the more I loved him.

O'Connell as a Journalist

It was hardly surprising that the literary O'Connell would drift into journalism. Here he found his true vocation, surrounded as he was by brilliant and genial companions whose appreciation of life found a response in his own nature.

After Dan gave up teaching, his first journalistic assignment was with the *San Francisco Chronicle.* Over the years he wrote for other daily and weekly publications. In 1871, he joined in partnership with social reformer Henry George to found *The Evening Post*, the first one-cent newspaper on the Pacific Coast. (George, it will be recalled, was the proponent of the Single Tax, a land tax which appealed to some of the brightest minds on the California scene. A well-known writer of the period once remarked, "Had the capitalists paid any attention to George's writings, they would not be in the mess they are today."

O'Connell's Celtic literary style, ready wit, and versatile pen distinguished his writings among his peers. His operatic works and novels, too, were worthy of a special place in the literary canon. However, largely because of his own indifference to commercial matters, his work suffered considerably more obscurity than it might have. His desire to spend money far exceeded his capacity to acquire it, which at times left him in short straits, and he was consequently left without funds to publicize his work. In any case, he wrote for the sheer joy of expression and for the joy of his fellow man. One of his best literary works was reputed to be the operatic libretto, *Bluff King Hal,* which was produced by the Bohemian Club and enjoyed a brief run at the Old Tivoli Theater.

The Domestication of O'Connell

In 1874, O'Connell married Miss Anna Ashley, the charming daughter of Senator Ashley. Their home of the O'Connell family, though modest, was a raucously joyful one. Their children, eventually numbering seven, worshiped their sweet-tempered father and inherited his optimism about life. No doubt that underneath O'Connell's jester's garb and constant good humor was a reverent and religious man, devoted to his family.

O'Connell's domestic talents did not end with being a loving husband and father. He took pleasure in the art of cooking with the same enthusiasm as his flair for literature and story-telling. He wrote a widely-circulated book called *The Inner Man,* which detailed the secrets of the culinary arts; in that gastronomic tome he declared that the key to good living was a well-appointed table.

In 1890, the O'Connell family took up residence in San Francisco's famous Octagon House in Cow Hollow, which was declared a historic landmark in recent years. The house was constructed by William McElroy in 1861 as a home for himself and his wife, Harriet. McElroy died nine years later, and his widow lived in the dream house until 1899. The house was then put up for rent, and the O'Connells were its first tenants. (The National Society of Colonial Dames of America, resident in California, now make this storied residence their headquarters.)

This rustic setting provided an ideal backdrop for O'Connell's lyrical ambitions. Here he wrote a "Grove Play" that was produced by the Bohemian Club. Club members often met at the house to plan these celebrated "High Jinks" pageants, of which Dan was the sire. The echoes of those convivial days linger in the voice of the cultured Bohemian as O'Connell bellows out his "Josephine":

She did not speak of ring or vow
But filled the cup with wine,
And took the roses from her brow
To make a wreath for mine;

She did not swear to love me true
Till earth should be no more,
She only said, "I'm struck on you,"
And then "Ah, me!" she swore.

She called another bottle up,
My glorious midnight queen!
She broke its neck and filled the cup,
My daisy Josephine!"

The Sage of Marin County

Only a cosmopolitan as diverse as O'Connell could find San Francisco unfulfilling. He was a man of magnificent physique and always kept in prime condition. Dan was in turn a fine boxer, wrestler, and angler, and he loved all kinds of outdoor life. It was only natural that such a fine athlete and outdoorsman, with an equally robust family, would find city life too confining. The O'Connells eventually relocated in Sausalito, on the North Bay, and settled in a chateau high above the harbor. The oak-covered promontory that rose abruptly from the shore and the towering redwoods that reflected in the clear waters of the bay formed a romantic setting for the O'Connell home in the Glen. The weekend campfires lit up the dark groves and highlighted the dim forms seated on logs outside the O'Connell family home, while the rich, deep voice of the poet broke the woodland silence as Dan recited:

Pleasant it was when the moors were green
  And the winds were soft and low
To lie amid some sylvan scene
  And watch soft shadows come and go.

A Strange Breakfast

Sausalito historian M.O. Moran relates a telling anecdote (Sausalito *News Letter*, September 26, 1936) that does much to illustrate O'Connell's personal character, when the woodland poet and self-made epicurean turned a chancy event into a resounding success. It seems that two businessmen were assigned to entertain the Grand Duke Cyril of Russia on his visit to the Bay area. Somewhat at a loss as to how to find grounds of common interest with a man so unlike themselves, and yet desiring to present him with creditable entertainment, they deliberated anxiously together. They were overheard discussing their problem in their favorite chairs at the Bohemian Club which went like this:

"It must be unusual," said Mr. Raphael Weill.

"A Sunday morning breakfast," suggested Mr. William Greer Harrison. "That seems to be in vogue among the artists."

"But where—here at the Club?"

"He has been banqueted three times at the Club already—that wouldn't be unusual now."

"The Palace Hotel?—the Maison Riche?—the Poodle Dog?"

"He probably knows the French restaurants by this time as well as we do, and he is stopping at the Palace."

"Well, then, where?"

"We must avoid being dull. We must not talk business to him. And that we're sure to drift into."

"Business is all right," protested Mr. Weill. "Maybe he would learn from us."

"No, he wouldn't want to. It wouldn't do at all; that's not his atmosphere. We'll take him to Sausalito."

"To Gaston Doumergue's? But that's a French restaurant, too, and that story about Doumergue's being a nobleman hasn't been proved to me yet."

"No. We'll take him to Dan O'Connell's for Sunday morning breakfast."

"Ah!" considered Mr. Weill.

"You know," explained Mr. Harrison to Mr. Weill, who delighted in delicate cookery and was famed as an amateur chef, "Dan is a *bon vivant*, a gourmet, an epicure. I have heard that the dishes he prepares in his Sausalito home are odes, madrigals, songs, hymns, as the fancy takes him. And you also know that wherever Dan is, there will never be any dullness."

"It's the solution!" agreed Mr. Weill. "I am with you on that."

The possibility of O'Connell's withholding his hospitality, of course, was not even considered.

It was not until Mr. Harrison (who insisted on covering the distance between the boat landing and their destination on foot) approached the house that the first misgivings arose in his breast. Somehow he had expected to see a dwelling considerably larger and more pretentious. The breakfast table was set out under the oaks, and the sheer simplicity of it sent another twinge of panic through his heart. The only decorations were two huge earthen bowls full of purple iris on the bare boards of the long table, around which were placed plates and bowls of a crude yellow crockery. Mr. Harrison soon realized that he had arrived during one of the journalist's financial lapses and that the madrigals, odes, and poetry in *haute cuisine* had simmered down to a kidney *saute*.

Now if there was one thing objectionable to Mr. Harrison's palate it was mutton kidneys, and in apologetic misery he glanced from Mr. Weill to the Grand Duke. But both gentlemen clearly were finding something attractive in the simplicity of color and arrangement, and in the gay, spontaneous service rendered by the Dan O'Connell's light-footed children, who had gathered the flowers and cooked the saute themselves, after the recipe of Thomas Newcomb, the first president of the Bohemian Club.

Although Mr. Weill pronounced the cooking excellent and proved it by taking a third helping, and although the Grand Duke Cyril declared that mutton kidneys were his favorite breakfast dish, Mr. Harrison remained nonplussed (though no longer apologetic) and satisfied his own hunger with rolls. The welcome extended to him and his guests had all the charm he had counted on. And it was with the memory of that breakfast still poignant that Mr. Harrison, in speaking of Dan O'Connell some years later, said:

> I have dined with him when the banquet was almost entirely intellectual, and the simple meal was made luxurious by the wealth of his humor and the beauty of his thought.

O'Connell, as an accomplished skipper with experience as a seaman in the Royal Navy, devoted much of his leisure time to cruising on the bay after he moved to Sausalito. A large white boat was fitted out for this purpose and manned by a crew of newspaper reporters, old buddies with a mutual love of the sea. Their rollicking adventures were officially known as the Roseleaf Social Yachting and Rescue Club. While the more timid salts set anchor on stormy days, neither wind nor rain was a deterrent to the Roseleafs; their staunch vessel ventured slowly through the turbulent waters of Raccoon Straits and set its prow in the direction of the Golden Gate and out into the open sea.

The acquisitive and pecuniary arts formed no part of O'Connell's life; and at times his pockets were empty and his cupboard almost bare. Yet a simple meal was made elegant by the wealth of his humor, and the richness of the thoughts that found expression in the rich organ tones of his voice. O'Connell looked upon debt as a mere accounting detail, to be paid or increased according to the current state of his finances; it never gave him the slightest concern or disturbed his splendid poise. The story of an overdue grocery bill, and the somewhat bizarre confrontation between merchant and debtor, sheds further light on the poet's character:

The grocer, a Mr. Schplatz, apparently had waited patiently for a bill to be settled and finally determined to call at the O'Connell home to make a peremptory demand for the money. The family was eating dinner when the grocer knocked at the door, and one of the children welcomed him in. Thereupon the indignant voice of Mr. Schplatz was heard resounding in firm, accented blasts, from the hallway to the dining room: "I've got a bill here against Mr. O'Connell and I vant my money!"

Without waiting to be called, Dan hurried to the front door and welcomed his visitor with effusive politeness:

> "My dear Mr. Schplatz," he said, grasping the astonished German by the hand. "You can't imagine how delighted I am to see you in my home at last. Really, I felt hurt that you never called on us earlier, and there's a custom of this house that I never permit to be overlooked. No stranger calling upon me for the first time has ever gone away without my having drunk his health, and so come in and let's clink glasses to better acquaintance."

The astonished grocer, silenced by the hospitable attitude of his tardy customer, was led ceremoniously to the dining room and introduced to the family and drinks were served. When Dan voiced another invitation:

> "Now, then, let me complete this delightful incident by insisting that you accept further hospitality of my wife and myself. There is a vacant chair and spare cover at my table. Do have dinner with us."

The grocer sat down and ate his meal, regaled by O'Connell's store of wit and anecdote. Dan then escorted his guest to the front door, declaiming:

> "Mr. Schplatz, your visit has been a real delight to me. I never carry any considerable amount of money about me and my check book is in my office. But if you can find it

> convenient to wait for a day or two, I will call personally and settle the account in full."

> Replied Mr. Schplatz:

> "Don't bodder yourself, Mr. O'Connell, I can vait, I can vait! Any time you like, Mr. O'Connell. Vat suits you suits me, goodnight, I don't care if it's six months!"

True to his promise, Dan paid the bill on the appointed day. There was a trifling balance coming to him in change which the grocer shoved across the counter toward him, but he waved it back with a deprecatory gesture:

> "No, no! he said, Keep the change. Oblige me. Yes, I know it doesn't belong to you. That is to say, not just now. But it soon will, for there is much likelihood that within a few days you will be compelled to transfer it to the other side of the ledger!"

Lord of the Manor

A real estate enterprise was established by two by Bohemian Club members, Payne and Brittian, to develop land in San Mateo County. The first order of business was to secure a promotion manager, and who could be more suitable than their trusted and able colleague, Dan O'Connell? Dan was by all account the most popular choice if (as it turned out) not the most ideal candidate. It was agreed that he must first sever any connections with other enterprises to avoid any conflict of interest. When the preliminaries were out of the way, the affable manager was installed in the imposing mansion.

It soon became evident that Dan's policies as a promoter were directed more in the interest of his many friends than in the promotion of real estate sales. Quite naturally, the recipients of Dan's hospitality were loud in their praise and showered their host with glowing adjectives as being the most suitable for the job on the basis of his nature, education, and dignity. However, despite Dan's eloquence and lavish sociability, the expenses far exceeded the intake, which didn't seem to cause him any concern. There were rumors that this project might have to be abandoned, but rumors of disaster were nothing new to Dan, bringing neither sigh nor sorrow nor remorse, for to Dan tomorrow was another day.

Poetic Tribute to Tom Moore

O'Connell had many moments of levity, but he never lost the haunting memories of the ravaged Irish land of his birth. His poesy rose to a new height in this tribute to Tom Moore, the Bard of Avoca:

The legends were dim and forgotten,
  Neglected the heart and unstrung,
And the sad, sweet lore of the nation
  Grew strange on her children's tongue,

When out of the ranks of the people
  Sprang a bard, like the flash of a blade,
And the world stood passive, and wondered
  At the weird, sweet music he made.

As the west wind, that breathes of the summer
  Wins the chilled buds to fragrance and bloom,
So the strains of the God-gifted comer
  Won the genius of song from its tomb;

From the old abbeys, ruined and hoary,
  From the castles that frowned o'er the sea,
He wove a romance and a glory
  As he chanted the hymns of the free.

What pathos he wrung from that shattered,
  That time-worn harp, when again
He swept its strings, breathing of sorrow,
  Of love and oppression and pain—

Of pain and of passion the deepest—
  Like wine, in the ripeness of years
The richer, because of the glimpses
  Of smiles through its burden of tears.

It began, as the promise of dawning
  Empurples the clouds of the night;
It grew till, like landscapes at noontide,
  The land was aglow with its light.

To-day it is mellow and tender,
Half mirthful, half sad, and all pure,

As it teaches the children of Ireland
  To be faithful, and strong to endure.

In the far battle-fields of the stranger,
  By the camp-fires of France and of Spain,
On the eve of the morrow of danger,
  The bivouac rang with its strain—

Now low, like the summer tides throbbing
  On the beaches of Ireland, and then,
Like the winter gales, raging and sobbing
  In the hearts of those strife-worn men.

O bard of our own land, thy laurels
  Are brighter than ever to-day,
As we tread the dark pathway of sorrow,
  And struggle toward Liberty's ray.

For the songs you have taught us have cheered us,
  And when we have conquered, be sure
The first toast, the first pledge of our freedom,
  Shall be to thy memory, Tom Moore!

In Memoriam

Above all others, Daniel O'Connell was the shining light of the Bohemian Club; nobody cherished more than he the Club's "never-say-die" philosophy, which teaches that there is but one final, fatal blow, and from all the lesser assaults one can come up smiling. But "Bohemia" itself became a place of deepest mourning when the final, fatal blow struck Dan.

On the 23rd of February, 1899, Dan O'Connell passed away at his home in O'Connell's Glen in Sausalito. He died, surrounded by his devoted wife and seven children. His bier was erected in the center of the Bohemian Club's green room. O'Connell lay in state in a casket garlanded by a mantle of orchids. Hundreds of mourners from all walks of life gathered to pay their last respects and reverently looked upon the face of their beloved bard. They remembered, wept, and quietly passed on. Funeral services were held at San Francisco's Saint Mary's Cathedral, the Mother Church of the archdiocese. Members of the Bohemian Club escorted Dan O'Connell's remains from their headquarters to the church where an

Sausalito memorial to Dan O'Connell, the poet. Inscribed on this monument is O'Connell's poem, "The Chamber of Sleep." [Courtesy of Jack Tracy, archivist of the Sausalito Historical Society.]

overflow gathering awaited. A long line of carriages followed the cortege to Calvary cemetery at the foot of Lone Mountain. There O'Connell's body was set before the tomb of William O'Brien, the Irish high King of the Comstock mines.

Few have been more sadly mourned than the always-merry, whole-souled poet "King of Munster." O'Connell's friends sought to sanctify his memory in a way he himself might have chosen:

On every hand thy debtors rise
The volume of their tribute pour!
For thou, so true in all men's eyes,
Had won love's universal prize,
Gentle heart that beats no more!

Following his funeral, friends assembled at his home to dedicate an oak tree to the bard. Sausalito erected a memorial to its illustrious citizen. Standing majestically on a pinnacle above the bay, a seat of granite is backed by a circular wall, on which is inscribed the last poem written by O'Connell: "The Chamber Of Sleep":

I have a castle of silence, flanked by a lofty keep,
And across the drawbridge lieth the lovely chamber of sleep;
Its walls are draped with legends woven in threads of gold,
Legends beloved by dreamland in the tranquil days of old.

And I lie in my Castle of Silence, in my chamber of sleep lie down,
Like the far-off echoes of forest, come the turbulent echoes of town,
And the wrangling tongues about me have now no power to keep
My soul from the solace exceeding the blessed Nirvana of sleep.

Lower the portcullis softly, sentries placed on the wall;
Let shadows of quiet and sadness upon my palace fall
Softly draw my curtains, ... let the world labor and weep—
My soul is safe environed by the walls of my chamber of sleep."

Contrary to popular belief, the Bohemian Club was not founded by wealth, but by journalists, artists, and writers—men, in fact, like O'Connell, some of whom were unemployed at the time. Once, O'Connell opposed an applicant for membership: "Because from what I gather, young man, you have nothing to do but stand behind your father's money, which is strictly an un-Bohemian occupation." Indeed the club's original nonmaterialistic philosophy fostered the spirit of true fellowship, regardless of one's station in life.

O'Connell's title "King of Munster" (referring to the Province of his birth) was bestowed on Dan early in his Bohemian career, and his many friends could vouch for the fact that he bore this title fittingly through many (and often strange) battles, and against discouraging odds. At the monthly "high jinks" of the Bohemian Club that followed Dan's funeral, D.M. Delmas, delivered a heart-warming tribute to their departed idol, closing most appropriately with these spirited lines:

> His epitaph shall outlast the chiseled tracery of crumbling granite or corroding marble, for as long as a votary of Bohemia kneels at her shrine, his bosom will heave with grief, and his eyes be drowned with tears as he mourns the loss of dear old Dan.
>
> The king of Munster is dead.
> Long live the king!
> O'Connell was a true Celtic spirit
> who left his mark wherever he roamed,
>
> That billowing band of the woodlands,
> The *maitre d'* of high jinks,
> The high priest of Hilarity,
> One of a kind, Daniel O'Connell, Prince of Bohemia.

Newspaper caricature depicting Dan O'Connell as the utopian visionary, Don Quixote.

Tom Maguire, the Irish-American Napoleon of impresarios. [Courtesy of the San Francisco Archives in the San Francisco Public Library.]

13

Tom Maguire: Napoleon of the Theater

Tom Maguire (1820-1896), the impresario of San Francisco's Washington Gulch, improbably rose from a New York City coachman and bartender to become a nationally famous theatrical promoter. Tom was also one of the handsomest men of his era. Tall of stature and dashing in manner, he dressed flamboyantly, sporting a massive gold chain and pendant dangling from his red velvet waistcoat, a diamond in his scarf, and a dazzling solitaire ring on his finger.

Before relating Tom Maguire's story, however, we first need to get a feel for the colorful world of San Francisco in which he naturally flourished.

The Living Theater of Gold Rush San Francisco

If ever the twain did meet, it was in the wedding of the dapper, daring, carefree chancers, like Tom Maguire, to the free-spirited, fun-loving, rip-roaring metropolis of San Francisco. When the knot of union was tied in the Gold Rush year of 1849, the city's eccentric festivities commenced and have never let up, even to the present day. San Francisco's guests, mostly uninvited, scrambled in from all over the globe. They were a mixed lot: prospectors, hawkers, kindly souls, and daring adventurers, saints and sinners (with the norm tending toward the latter). Their nationalities were as diverse: Mexicans, French, Germans, Italians, Scots and Gaels, Yankees, Chinese, Indians, and a polyglot mixture of tongues.

San Francisco always had a flair for the unusual—frolicking or reticent when need be, and a bit tipsy at times. The city seduced such characters as the cranky old skinflint, James Lick (1796-1876), who denied himself the merest morsel of comfort, yet became a generous benefactor to San Francisco. In 1862, Lick established the glittering showplace hostelry, "Lick House" with Corinthian columns, flagged marble floors, and gaslight chandeliers. For his own parsimonious needs, Lick pampered himself with only an attic room, thereby avoiding taking his meals in his posh dining room, an indulgence he considered too extravagant.

The rollicking city also tolerated such oddballs as Joshua Norton (1818-1880), the self-styled Emperor, because his style was surrealistically entertaining. San Franciscans amiably provided Norton with free meals on demand, cashed his worthless script without hesitation, and good-humoredly studied his preposterous proposals for zany (or madly inspired) public projects, like a Bay Bridge. The city also gave a respectful hearing to social reformer Henry George, who was obsessed with the idea of achieving a broader distribution of the world's wealth, while keeping society financially secure with his "Single Tax" system. A city which prospered on the hurly-burly insanities of the Gold Rush era could afford to be tolerant of strange ideas and even stranger characters.

Enter Tom Maguire

Such was the flamboyant style of San Francisco, the urban crazy-quilt canvas upon which Tom Maguire would project his imagination throughout his romantic life. But what of the man himself? San Franciscans were all dreamers of different varieties, but Tom Maguire was for real. He knew what he wanted and spared no effort to achieve it.

Tenaciously loyal to his friends, Maguire's enemies were few. His extravagant generosity was limited only by his resources. A gambler at heart, he lived his passionate life to the hilt. He sought no quiet streets or secluded rose-covered paths. Main Street was his beat. He could be as frolicsome as a lamb in springtime, but also as fearless as a grizzly bear when threatened. Although never one to be ruffled at the drop of a bowler, he also would never give ground when pushed. In his most colorful heyday, Maguire could be observed escorting society ladies down the center aisle at the theater with dignity and grace; yet before that same evening was spent, he would be standing eyeball to eyeball with a brawling gunman.

From his early years in New York City, Tom's career had its hectic moments, including his battle for the hand of "Little Em" (Emma), who would become his wife. Somewhat later, he challenged the bully of Park Row, a notorious rowdy named Dick Donnell. (Whether that flashy rascal had dropped the "O" in the bawdy Bowery or from the lashing of Tom Maguire, nobody seems to know.)

Tom's scanty formal education (he could not read) did not inhibit his ambition. Unlimited opportunities awaited the stout-hearted in the California Gold Rush Bonanza, then in full swing. He came with the early swarms of adventurers and argonauts, arriving in San Francisco in 1849. His first venture in the new surroundings was to open the Parker House Saloon. Later he also added a plush gambling den in the rear which he called "The Snug."

It was an opportune time for Maguire, the erstwhile gambler, as the first batch of prospectors who had struck-it-rich in the gold diggings drifted back to San Francisco, ripe for the fleecing. They wanted entertainment and were prepared to pay the price for it. They had their mentor in Tom Maguire who was equally committed to relieving them of their gold dust by providing the best that the miners' money could buy and that first-class talent could supply.

Show Business Was His Business

Maguire's connection with the theater began in New York City where he had a hack-stand near the Old Park Theater. Enamored by what he saw—the gaily-dressed patrons, the glamorous pageantry, and dazzling lights—he purchased an interest in the Theater Bar in order to share more profitably in the action. The experience he acquired as hackney driver, saloonkeeper, and theater buff had much to do with his rise to fame, if not to fortune, in California.

Maguire found his gold mine without ever leaving the muddy streets of San Francisco's Old Plaza. People were stage-struck and starved for any entertainment. Maguire shared their feelings and spent lavishly in bringing the finest performers that money could buy. His whole soul's ambition was to provide San Franciscans with first-class entertainment and the best theatrical talent. No actor or actress was beyond his consideration, no salary too high to pay.

Tom's first enterprise, to repeat, was the Parker House Saloon. After he had amassed some capital, he converted the upstairs into a theatrical showplace and dubbed it "The Jenny Lind" after the Swedish Nightingale.

But disaster struck Maguire in 1850, when the theater burned to the ground. Undaunted, he rebuilt and started again from scratch. The theater was gutted by yet another fire before the year was out, and once again Maguire rebuilt. As one contemporary observed, "He began to build again before the ashes were cold." Where he got the money, nobody seemed to know, nor did they care. Perhaps the little-known gambling Snug in the rear of the saloon raked in more chips than the lavish theatrical enterprise.

Maguire, the Theatrical Impresario

Tom developed a passionate love of grand opera. In 1855, he took over the San Francisco Hall of Minstrels. He lavishly remodeled it and changed its name to Maguire's Opera House. From that day on his name would be eulogized in the annals of his beloved city and in the hearts of the argonauts themselves. Maguire is said to have lost over $100,000 in his first grand opera staging, but his reward was in the people's enjoyment. Tom was a gambler at heart: the greater the odds, the more he seemed to enjoy himself. Bringing Shakespearean drama to a city of primitive, muddy streets and plank sidewalks would stun the purser of Monte Carlo, but not Maguire.

Tom's proteges in the 1870s were David Belasco and James Herne, and he brought the greatest performers from throughout Europe, New York, London, Paris, and Milan, to stage San Francisco's most breathtaking minstrel shows, dramas, and operas. His magic circle of stars were: John McCullogh, James O'Neill, Edwin Booth (from the tragic Booth family), "Eugenio Bianchi" William Lyster, and other greats. He imported, by way of Panama, whole opera companies and paid leading stars astronomical fees of $1,000 a night. Typical entertainment billings might read as follows:

Tom Maguire's Jenny Lind Theatre on Kearny Street facing Portmouth's Square in San Francisco. [Courtesy of the San Francisco Archives in the San Francisco Publlic Library.]

Fun and Frolic

Grace and Beauty Plus

Eccentric Variety Spells

Laughter for Millions!

The *Alta California* of this period paid this tribute to Maguire and his productions:

> The walls of the Jenny Lind must be made to reverberate with the echoes of the honest and timely applause tonight, in token of a heartfelt welcome to a worthy benefactor, the founder of the magnificent temple of the drama—Mr. Thomas Maguire.
>
> On the very spot, where now stands the noblest and most inspiring edifice in the State, where now flourishes the theater, which for internal beauty, comfort and grandeur shall compare with the best in America, Mr. Maguire has witnessed his enterprise crumble in ashes and his future dissolve into the air.
>
> Surely this community owes Mr. Maguire a deep debt of gratitude, for the display of energy, which after a long series of endurances and disappointments has at length established in our midst one of the most permanent sources of good, one of the best correctives of our society and most efficient instruments of moral reform ever established in our city.

The Vicissitudes of Maguire's Fortunes

The depression of 1879 was Tom Maguire's temporary undoing. He had made enormous profits over the years, but spent them with a free hand. Creditors began dunning him for their money. His business manager tried to negotiate, but with less money coming in, Tom could not meet his daily obligations.

Down, but not out, Maguire saw an opportunity. The growing city was much in need of a City Hall, and Maguire proposed to sell his building to the city fathers for that purpose. His asking price was $200,000, though he claimed it was worth much more. This intriguing offer became the talk of the town, with some supporting the deal as being in the city's best interest, and others vehemently opposed. Senator David Broderick, a political bigwig, spoke in support of the proposal; Broderick's endorsement may have tilted the scales, for the city finally accepted the deal. This windfall allowed Maguire to get off the hook and pay off all his debts.

His credit now restored, Maguire stepped once again smiling into the limelight. He built a new theater and christened it "San Francisco Hall." Junius Booth, Jr., another member of the ill-starred theatrical family, was installed as manager. Within ten years after his first appearance on Montgomery Street, Maguire was undisputed master of the theater in California. He operated theaters in Stockton, Sonora, Marysville, and Sacramento. He had actually opened his first theatrical subsidiary in Benicia, under the influence of his Bear Flagger friend Robert Semple (1806-1854), who was already laying plans to have the Capitol situated in this unique location. Tom must have shared Semple's ambition, because here in Benicia he built the finest gin mill in the entire state, the first grog shop to provide musical entertainment along with hard whiskey and soft punch.

Maguire also formed stock companies and transported full theatrical troupes to the far-off, unruly gold fields. He went on talent-scouting missions to the East Coast and to Europe. Even without formal training, he was a competent judge of good music and talented singers.

All good things come to their proverbial end; and so too were Tom's glamorous years fading fast away. To avoid financial disaster, he joined in partnership with Lucky Baldwin (1828-1909), who had made his fortune in real estate and the Comstock.

The partnership eventually soured. Maguire and Baldwin built the historic Baldwin Hotel and added the new Baldwin Theater. In deference to Tom's flair, the building was crafted in ornate style, with gilt scrollwork, velvet draperies, and satin drop-curtains. Tom presented plays in the glittering Baldwin up to the year 1882, after which Baldwin decided he had had enough of Maguire's extravagance and pulled out of the partnership.

The Passion Play Postponed

Maguire even dared to produce the Passion Play because of its success in Bavaria, but San Francisco was not the right place. Catholics were appalled at seeing Christ and his mother on stage, and Protestants saw it as sectarian Catholic propaganda. In order to avoid certain confrontation, the Board of Supervisors met in executive session and passed an ordinance, under extreme pressure, banning the production from the stage.

Nonchalantly, the flamboyant maestro Maguire not only ignored the artistic prohibition, but set about making plans to stage the Passion Play during Easter Week. This timing inflamed an already explosive situation. Maguire presciently engaged the well-known actor James O'Neill, the father of playwright Eugene O'Neill, to play Christ. On the evening of the performance, the police moved in and arrested Christ-O'Neill as he was about to go on stage and carted him off to jail. This exiting extemporaneous drama partly compensated an already pent-up audience for the abrupt cancellation of the production. Why the police did not arrest the cheeky perpetrator Tom Maguire was quite obvious: their chief objective was merely to postpone the controversial performance until tempers cooled and reason prevailed.

In the pulsating, Gold Rush city, where the unexpected was commonplace, and even more so when it involved such well-known figures as the entertainment czar Tom Maguire, San Franciscan's took it all in stride. The city's benign attitude has always reckoned that things will be even more hilarious, if not better, tomorrow.

Exit Tom Maguire

By now, Tom prudently felt he had worn out his welcome in San Francisco. He made an abrupt exit from the scene and returned to his old haunts in Manhattan. New York was the tragi-comic stage where he spent his final years in theatrical rooming houses, reminiscing and regaling his cronies with his earlier escapades, always dreaming of a triumphal comeback.

In 1896, Maguire may have succumbed to old age (no one ever knew his exact birthday) or he may have died like the true lover of the theater—of a broken heart. Either way, Tom's death concluded a dramatic life which may be judged to be one either wisely lived by a fool, or foolishly lived by a sage.

As for money, Maguire took no care except for his immediate needs. He romantically imagined himself the undefeatable warrior, garmented in purple and gold with a green cockade, even though there were unseen holes in every pocket. He gloried in the ornate theater with its elaborate frescoes, cotton bog carpets, and dazzling chandeliers. Most of all he delighted in the reverberating applause and laughter of the audience. His life was a one unbroken dream of prancing steeds and golden chariots dashing through pillars of fire, with trumpets blaring.

An ill-informed but laudatory article in the old *San Francisco Call* in the year 1886, some time after Maguire had made his hasty exit from the local scene, is credited with adding some ten years to the failed impresario's life: "Mr. Tom Maguire has moved into a magnificently furnished house in New York City. The California ex-manager is said to be the best dressed man in that city."

The Measure of the Man

How best to summarize the larger-than-life character that Tom Maguire played so convincingly? We can confidently assert that if, indeed, there was the slightest vanity in the flamboyant Maestro, it amounted to but miser's pinch. And if fortune had allowed Tom Maguire a final wish of naming his own life's drama, he would surely have chosen to be remembered as the "Napoleon of the Theater." Truly, his melodramatic career, both behind and in front of the scenes, earned Maguire that imperial title.

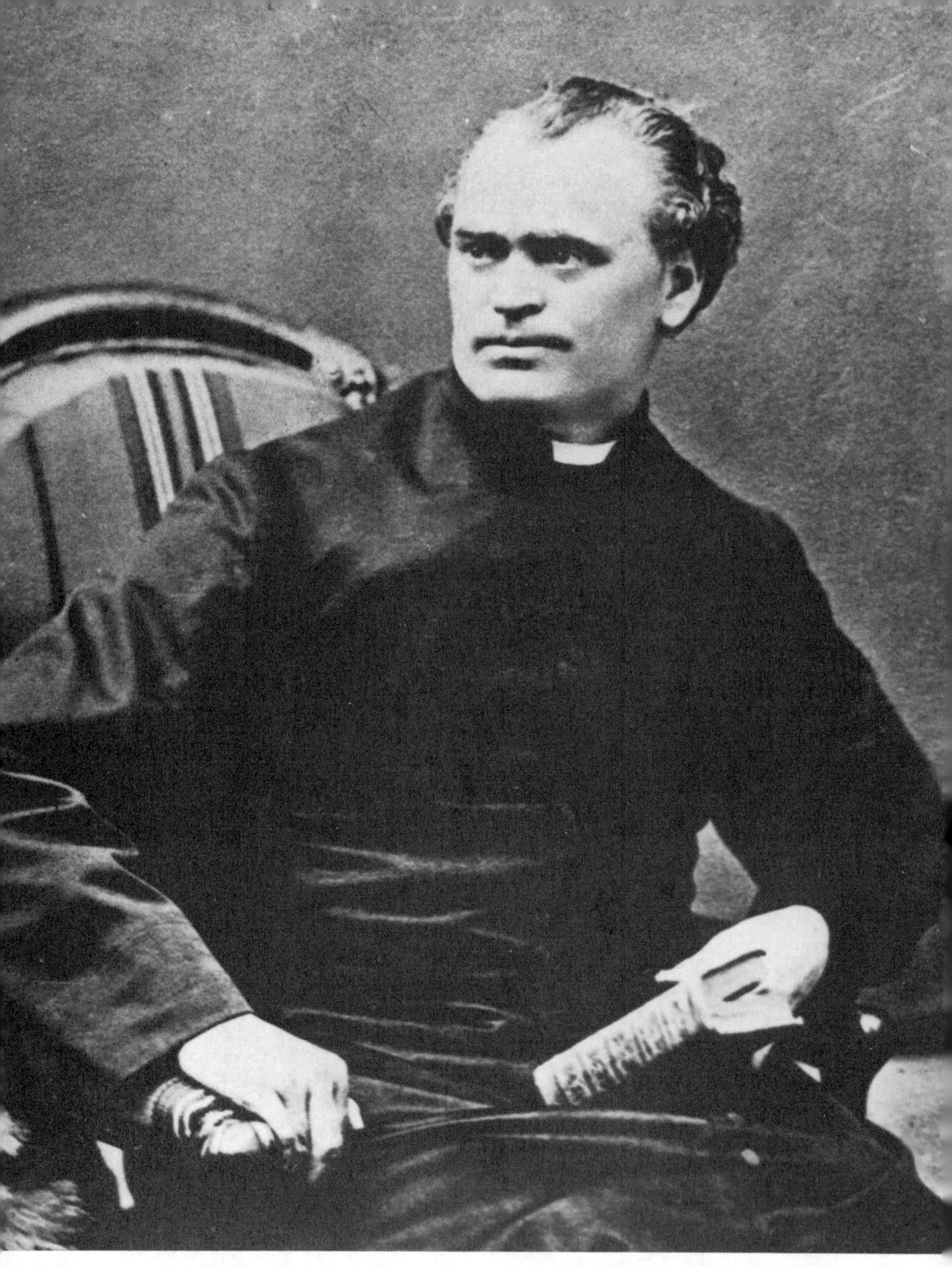

Bishop Patrick Manogue (1831-1895), apostle of the Mother Lode and first bishop of Sacramento. [Courtesy of Father James Bengal, pastor emeritus of St. Mary's of the Mountains.]

14

Patrick Manogue: Apostle of the Comstock

The colorful and character-rich era of the California Gold Rush has been painstakingly prospected and penned by early historians. In more recent times, this era has also been so thoroughly dredged and panned that sources of additional material might be judged well-nigh exhausted. However, strange to relate, little has been recorded of the influence during this tumultuous period of the Catholic Church, whose uninterrupted history and growth easily rivals the romantic glow of the Gold Rush itself.

Though largely unknown to the outside world, the unsung annals of sacrifice by godly women and men, like the Irish priest Patrick Manogue (1831-1895), were deeply engraved in the grateful hearts of rugged '49ers. These early Christian apostles, such as Padre Manogue, measured their wealth not in gold and silver, but in the good they could render their fellow men and women and in the honor and glory to their heavenly Master. It was a strange and worldly setting in which they found themselves pursuing their priestly labors: the California gold fields were a polyglot melting pot made up of many nationalities and beliefs. For a time it seemed that the one common interest was greed and the pursuit of gold.

Those early soul-seekers like Manogue soon discovered that their new parish was indeed a demanding domain, neither mapped nor fenced. Their itinerant parishioners were oftentimes wherever they could be found, constantly on the move, like the shepherds' flocks roaming the hills or hidden from view in the mountain valleys.

However, unlike the miner and the shepherd, these Christian pastors could expect no material compensation for their labors. They trusted in nature and sheer luck for bread and board. Despite the trying conditions and the harsh environment in which they toiled, these dedicated servants went about their daily tasks with unshakeable faith in the heavenly Father, in whose cause they had wholeheartedly enlisted.

One of the most noteworthy of those early clerical nomads in California was "*Le Gros*," big-hearted Patrick Manogue, who set aside his miner's gear and picked up his bible. Manogue was destined to become one of the most renowned missionaries of the Gold Rush period. Born in Ireland on March 15, 1831, he was the youngest of seven children born to Patrick and Catherine (Costigan) Manogue. He spent his first days in a thatched cottage in Dysart, County Kilkenny.

The name Manogue is of pure Irish origin. It echoes with saintly memories in the ecclesiastical annals of Ireland. One of the most renowned members of the clan was Cleardin O'Maneog, the holy Bishop of old Loughlin, Prince Piety of Ossorage (Ossory).

Father Manogue's Early Days

For a lively biography of the saintly Manogue—an account that brings Manogue's life and times to life with imaginative, reconstructed dialogue—the present author is indebted to Floyd Anderson's *Gold Rush Bishop* (Milwaukee: The Bruce Publishing Company, 1962). From Anderson's biography we learn of many fascinating anecdotes about Manogue, such as the following.

In California's rugged gold country, sitting on a log outside his cabin in Moore's Flat, chatting with Father John Shanahan, who was the first priest to visit the region, youthful Pat Manogue related in his own words the strange turn of events that led to the diaspora of the Manogue family, and how and why they came to California:

"Start at the beginning," said Father Shanahan. "When were you born, and where—in Ireland, I judge?"

"Oh, yes, at Dysart in County Kilkenny, on March 15 in '31," and Manogue added with a grin, "My brothers and sisters always said I was too early for Saint Patrick's day."

Padre Shanahan probed for more information: "How did you happen to come to the States and then to California?"

"It's a long story, Father; but to keep it short: our parents died when we were very young. My oldest brother, Michael—who met me in Nevada City—came to America to settle in Connecticut. As he could, he sent for the rest of us. I was 17 when I came, and I stayed here and worked in the mills. Then I went to Saint Mary of the Lake in Chicago to study for the priesthood."

"How did you like it?"

"I loved it! It was hard work, but I didn't mind that."

"Then how did you happen to leave?"

"Sickness. A bad cholera epidemic hit Chicago and spread to the seminary and a lot of us became very ill. When it was all over I was in pretty bad shape. It was felt that I should try to regain my health before continuing on in my studies. Michael had gone to the gold fields, working in Nevada City, and the others came out here, too. James was in Moore's Flat, as was Tom Dooling, Mary's husband."

"The idea appealed to me. It seemed just the thing to build me up again. James asked me to join him in partnership with his friends, so that I could make enough money to continue my studies. You know, there's more to California than precious metals. It is a little thing, but see how those roses grow with only little attention. This is fertile country, especially in the Sacramento Valley. When the gold is gone, this will be good farming country."

Mining in Moore's Flat

Those were hectic days in the isolated California region of Moore's Flat, where miners flocked to make their fortunes quickly—before too many others came. They spent their days swinging picks and sledgehammers, prying apart the rocks that held the precious metal, or digging tunnels underneath the rich California hills. Exhausted from the hard toil, they threw themselves on their rough-hewn bunks to sleep and rest for the next day's work. In a pursuit where hard work was the rule, Manogue distinguished himself as one of the most industrious in the camp. L.J. Hanchett, one of his partners in their mining claim, stated, "I have never seen a harder worker. Pat Manogue was a man of great frame and strength, who worked tirelessly from morning till night, drilling, blasting, and shoveling as hard as any."

But in one respect young Pat was different from all the others. Instead of collapsing into bed at the end of the day or gossiping with the boys, he would sit outside the cabin and read until nightfall forced him to retire indoors to continue his studies by lamplight. In his other spare moments, rare as they were, he took time to plant roses by his cabin and lugged pails of water from the creek to nourish them.

These extra chores seemed rather peculiar to the other miners; there seemed no earthly reason for undertaking any more physical exercise, for the men were already exhausted from the day's strenuous exertions. Newcomers to the fields were even more mystified by this handsome, dark-haired Irish giant who seemed so mild and good-natured. His quiet demeanor was even an invitation to trouble on one occasion.

Desperadoes on the Trail

Most of those who came to the mines were honest, hard-working individuals. But there were others—gamblers and unscrupulous, hardened characters—ever ready to prey on others and make their fortune without the inconvenience of having to work for it.

Down the trail one day slipped two desperadoes looking for an easy mark. When they spotted the Manogue's cozy cabin with a mild-looking man outside reading a book, they laid down their packs to size up the situation, quickly assuring themselves of easy plunder. They picked up their bags again and walked up to Pat's cabin. As they drew near, Pat put down his book and stood up.

"Good afternoon to you," he called. The two men put down their packs without uttering a word and then stepped apart, both in front of Pat, but each a little to either side.

"This is a nice cabin you got here," said the leader.

"That it is," answered Pat.

"We came to take it over," said the desperado in charge. "We bought it from Jack McBride in Sacramento. We paid for it and he said we could move right in."

"Did he, now?" said Pat, softly. "Strange, isn't it, that there's never been a Jack McBride in Moore's Flat?"

"That's the name he gave us," the thug insisted, "and we paid for it in gold." He moved to the side so that he and his partner could get the jump on Pat when they were ready to make their move. "This cabin is just as he described it to us. Built on the side of a hill above the camp, even to the flowers by the side door.

"Did he tell you what kind they were?" asked Pat quietly.

"Uh...let's see, now," stammered the other.

"You gentlemen wouldn't be the kind to know flowers, would you now?" said Pat. "They're roses that I planted myself, and carried the water from this stream. So Jack McBride described the flowers to you, did he?"

"Are you calling us liars? There's one way to settle this...."

As he spoke, the thug was planning to jump the fearless miner, but he never got the chance to finish his sentence. Pat reached out and grabbed the first desperado around the neck with his huge hand. The other hand—in fact, a fist by this time—caught his partner square on the jaw and sent him tumbling into the brush. Then Pat cuffed the other on the side of the head and also sent him sprawling to join his partner. The leader twisted on the ground, trying to pull a pistol from his hip pocket, but by that time Pat was standing over him. He grabbed the criminal by the shoulder and jerked him to his feet. He snatched the gun from the stunned man's pocket and threw it into the stream nearby. Then he heaved the other thug to his feet and relieved him of his weapon in like manner.

> "I've heard of claim-jumping," joked Manogue with a wry smile, "but this is the first I've heard of cabin-jumping! We have a weekly court here in Moore's Flat and it meets at sundown. By rights I should bring you down there. One of my partners is the judge, and my guess is that he'd give you about a month's hard labor, real hard, like building a road. But maybe you have learned a lesson. Get on the trail and head back to where you came from, and don't ever come back to Moore's Flat again!"
>
> The two characters looked at each other, picked up their packs, and disappeared from sight running down the trail. Pat Manogue then picked up his book and resumed his studying.

Miners' Adjudicator

During his mining career, Manogue the congenial Celt, gained quite a reputation as a peacemaker among the boisterous men. When a dispute arose between the prospectors, they usually turned to the scholarly Pat Manogue for mediation. "Let's leave it to Pat and see what he says," the old-timers would say. All the diggers had confidence in the big, kind-hearted man, and Pat never let them down.

A group of men once approached his cabin and entreated him for his opinion: "Pat, we've got a problem; maybe you can help us solve it."

> "If I can, I will," he answered. "Let's talk about it."
>
> As they sat around the fire, Marvin Kelly, the leader of the group, outlined the problem, "You know the claims we

have, and the one Fred Jackson's group has. The two are side by side. We have been tunneling along a line that seems to be the main body of ore, but all of a sudden it had dipped and is going under Fred's claim."

Pat nodded, "I know those claims. You've been working the other end of the claim, haven't you, Fred?"

"That's right, Pat."

"Then, what's the problem?"

"This is the problem," said Fred, "Where the main ore body seems to be on my claim, it's covered by a thick overlay of rock. The only practical way to reach it is through the Kelly tunnel. To start a tunnel from our side, that would be quite expensive and take a lot of time."

Marvin Kelly added, "This is on the Jackson claim, thus any gold found there belongs to them. But the problem is how to get to it."

"That's right," answered Fred Jackson, "and that's what we are asking you about, Pat. How are we going to work this out fairly and squarely for both sides?"

Pat smiled. "You give me the easy ones, don't you?" Manogue analyzed the problem and how it might be addressed in different ways, finally concluding, "All these seem rather complicated answers to what could be a very simple problem."

"That's what's bothering us!" said Kelly, "We're really friends together and we want to stay friends. We want some simple arrangement that we will all understand, that will be fair to everyone, and so we won't be fighting over it in the future."

Pat nodded, "That's what I had in mind. As I understand it, the prospects of both claims are pretty equal."

"That's right; sure thing; we all feel that way," replied Jackson and Kelly.

> "Then why not put all the claims together in one claim and make all of you partners? All of you can work together on the two claims, pool the profits, and all share alike. Then it would seem to me everyone would benefit and no one would lose."
>
> After some thought, one said, "Sounds good to me!" The others were quick to agree.
>
> Marvin Kelly confided in Pat afterwards, "That's exactly what I was hoping you would suggest, and so was Fred. But if we had suggested it, some of the other fellows might have thought we had something to gain. This way, coming from you—we knew they would agree. Many thanks, Pat!"

All the miners were grateful for their kindly, fair-minded neighbor, who gained their respect and confidence above all others; and he treasured their faith in him.

From Miner to Minister and Missionary

Pat Manogue's burning goal in life was to become a priest—"A good priest," as he told Bishop Alemany when they first met in Virginia City. But deep in his heart, known only to himself, was an even greater commitment to become a miner's priest: a dream that became a reality in time. In the meantime he continued his studies in his cabin and saved his earnings in the mines to pay for his future tuition in the seminary.

In the early 1850s, on one of Pat's rare visits to San Francisco, he told Bishop Alemany:

> "I think it might take a few years to accumulate enough money for what I have in mind; but I would like to continue my studies at the Seminary of Saint Sulpice in Paris. That is, if I'm accepted for your diocese and if you have no objection."
>
> "I have no objection, of course," smiled the Bishop, "but I may be a bit curious why Saint Sulpice instead of All Hallows in Dublin or one of the other Irish seminaries."

"I have heard that Saint Sulpice is among the best and also that it is hard. This may sound odd or different, but I'd rather make it the hard way than to have it too easy. Then I'll be sure that is what God wants me to do with my life."

With the Bishop's blessing, the big miner returned to Moore's Flat to complete his preparations for his journey to Europe.

Grass Valley showed more signs of becoming a permanent settlement than Nevada City, and the newly-arrived pastor, Father Dalton, made it his headquarters. Grass Valley was destined to become a thriving town, the first diocese in the mining region was established there. In 1856, Bishop Alemany paid a visit to Grass Valley, and Pat Manogue was on hand to greet him. During their meeting, plans were completed for the miner's entry into Saint Sulpice in Paris.

It was a sentimental moment when the miners gathered to say farewell to their friend and confidant. The big miner, Pat Manogue, having already disposed of his share in the mining claim, began making preparations for the long journey, he packed his bags that day and sat quietly outside the cabin taking in the view of Moore's Flat for the last time. In the meantime, the miners gathered in the meeting hall to prepare a surprise party for him. How to get him to the hall without revealing their intentions was the problem. Finally someone hit on the idea of creating a disturbance. The plot was perfect: one of the miners came running up the path:

"Pat! Pat!" he called. "They want you down at the hall right away. Caldwell and Hanchett are having an argument and nobody can settle it but you."

"Caldwell and Hanchett?" thought Pat, "That's hard to believe; they're such good friends."

But the big man dutifully went running to the miners' hall down on the flat. As he turned the corner, he saw the two men arguing violently.

"What's this all about?" cried Pat.

Both of the men shouted all the louder now. "I'm going to do it!" came from one, and "Oh, no, you're not!" from the other.

"All right, stop it!" said Pat very firmly. "What's all the fuss about?"

"Judge Caldwell wants to do it, and I have as much right as he does," grumbled Hanchett.

"Then why don't you do whatever it is that you want to do?" said Pat, "and tell me why you two good friends are quarreling like this in the middle of the road."

"Here," said Caldwell, grabbing one of Pat's arms, and Hanchett the other, "We'll show you what it's all about."

They walked him down to the miners' hall, where stood the man who had called Pat. He opened the door for them. The hall was dim for but a few seconds, when suddenly it was ablaze with light from the coal oil lamps turned up high.

"Surprise, surprise!" rang the rough voices through the building. "This is a party for you, Pat, and this was the only way we could think of surprising you."

Toasts and merrymaking followed, as everyone offered their congratulations to Pat for the new life he was embarking on. But they were saddened to see him leave them. Judge Caldwell summed up the feelings of all when he said, "Pat, you go with our blessings and best wishes. I can honestly say I have never seen you in anger and no matter what happened, you were always pleasant, always kind, always charitable."

A substantial purse was presented to Pat by the miners. He was obviously touched by the kindness and generosity of his fellow workers:

"I thank you from the bottom of my heart," he began, "I am very grateful to you for the financial aid you have given me toward my studies for the priesthood. But even more grateful am I for your friendship, your kindness, during the many months I have worked by your side." He paused and added with deep sincerity, "If I can reach my goal of becoming a priest, and with the help of God, I will make every effort to do so, I promise you I will come back to Moore's Flat and say mass here for all of you. Where my future life as a priest is to be spent, I do not know; but I could ask nothing better than to be allowed to spend it among miners like you."

The Long Journey to Paris

The next morning, the brawny miner felt a twinge of sadness as the stagecoach bounced along the rocky mountain trail to Sacramento. From there he would board the river boat to San Francisco, to discuss his future plans with Bishop Alemany before leaving for New York. His schedule included a stopover in Ireland to visit relatives before reaching the Continent. Then it was on to Paris for the beginning of the fall term at the seminary.

At first, Manogue found his new seminarian's way of life a bit strange, but he quickly adapted. His big Celtic frame, even more conspicuous in a black cassock, was a familiar sight along the banks of the Seine. His fellow students nicknamed him the big American, as he related to them the many exciting tales of life in the California gold mines. His stay in Europe was not entirely confined to his studies for the priesthood; he found time to visit the tomb of St. Theresa in Spain and found inspiration in being where other martyrs had sealed their faith with their blood.

Manogue completed his studies at Saint Sulpice within four years, and he was ordained a priest by Cardinal Francis Morlot on December 21, 1861. During his stay in Paris, he had been constantly in correspondence with Bishop Alemany, letting him know of his eagerness to return to California to undertake his priestly ministry in California. The Bishop gave him permission to visit Ireland on his way back, and suggested that while there he pay a visit to All Hallows College in Dublin. There Manogue was cordially welcomed by the college president, Msgr. Woodlock, who gave him the latest news of the California Mission and of the new consecrated Bishop O'Connell. Marysville, he learned, was now a new vicarate, with

Eugene O'Connell, former president of All Hallows, as its first Bishop. O'Connell was consecrated a Bishop by Cardinal Cullen in 1861, the very year that Manogue was ordained a priest.

> "O'Connell will welcome you back to California," said Msgr. Woodlock.
>
> But Father Manogue smiled and said, "Yes, but I have been ordained for the San Francisco archdiocese."
>
> The prelate then pulled from his desk drawer a letter from Bishop O'Connell stressing his desperate need for priests. "Very likely, the new Bishop may approach Archbishop Alemany to seek your services. You have a long journey home to California. I thought you might consider it carefully on your way, if the request does come."

Home Again in California

As soon as Father Manogue arrived in San Francisco, he called on Archbishop Alemany and related all that had happened and about his own desires.

> The Archbishop smiled and said, "You need not worry, Father. While you were ordained for the California missionary, both Bishop O'Connell and I thought that you would be assigned to the Marysville vicarate. That is where your home was, and that is where your work should be."

After a brief rest, Father Manogue boarded a river boat for his return to Sacramento, and from there on the rickety stagecoach to Marysville, where he would spend the remainder of his life administering to his beloved miners and their offspring. It was no doubt a nostalgic and happy reunion when the "big miner," attired in his new garb of black suit and Roman collar, greeted his old pals at the miners' hall. Yet even more dear to Pat was making good on parting commitment to the miners: "I promise you I will come back to Moore's Flat and say Mass for you." That he did.

In his first meeting with Bishop O'Connell, Father Manogue expressed his desires in his usual straightforward manner:

"I do not know what assignment you have in mind for me, but I would welcome the opportunity to work among these miners of the Marysville Vicarate, in any part of the area, no matter how wild."

"That's what I had in mind," said the Bishop, "And perhaps the most difficult part, in the Nevada Territory." The Bishop then spoke of a promising gold strike that was made near Virginia City in the Nevada Territory and continued, "You know what happens when a few miners make a strike. Everyone hurries there to try to make a fortune overnight.

Father Manogue nodded, "When I was at Moore's Flat, there was always the constant temptation to run this way or that as reports of strikes came. There was always the feeling that your pot of gold might be at that end of the rainbow; and sometimes it was, but more often it was not."

The Bishop warned the young priest as he prepared to leave for his assignment, "This will not be easy, Father; you will have the whole of Northern Nevada as your parish, with your headquarters in Virginia City. We will not be able to help you with finances. You have no church, no rectory; and probably for some time you will be the only priest in the Territory."

"I know, Bishop," answered Father Manogue, "but I also know the miners. If you help them, they will be most generous. I'm sure that the support will be coming."

The Bishop stood up, "I know you want to go to Moore's Flat to say Mass for your friends there. You will need to get a good horse, for you have much riding to do. Come and see me again before you leave for Virginia City, and God be with you."

A Stranger in Virginia City

In 1862, when the young priest first arrived in Virginia City he found it a city in name only, a tangled "settlement" of tents and wooden shanties formed most of "downtown." Some of the miners had cut tunnels into the mountainside to make rooms for themselves, and some of the larger caverns could accommodate from ten to fifteen men. While most did their cooking outside, some improvised by cutting a crude hole through the top of their caves for a stovepipe. Unlike Moore's Flat where he knew most of the miners, Virginia City was completely strange to Father Manogue when he rode down the winding trail to find a home and begin his missionary work.

It was Father Manogue's good fortune to meet up with another Irishman by the name of Matt Foley, a stableman, who offered a stall for the pastor's horse. How to procure a suitable residence for the Pastor himself was another matter. He looked over the sprawling mining settlement and turned to Foley, "What I'd like is a place to stay with some nice Irish family, at least until I can find a building to use as a rectory."

> "That will not be easy," said Foley. "Don't forget, Father, we're a couple of years newer than the camps on the other side of the mountains, and there are not too many families here as yet." He thought for a few moments and then had a solution, "I know just the place, if she has a room to spare," and sent him on his way up the grade to Mrs. Terry Byrnes.

Father Manogue walked up the dusty trail to the house Matt Foley had indicated. His admiration for blooming roses almost ruined his chances. As he approached the front door and bent over to examine the flowers more carefully, he didn't hear the door open behind him. Suddenly a woman's voice cried:

"If it's all the same to you, my good man, I'll trouble you to leave my roses alone!" In her hand she held a threatening broom, as though poised to sweep him out of the yard. Before he could respond, she added with exasperation, "Usually it's only the small boys who steal my roses; but a grown man!"

> He grinned and tipped his hat and bowed gravely, saying, "Allow me to present myself. I assume you are Mrs. Byrnes?"

"I am," she answered. "and who might you be, and what are you doing here?"

"To answer your last question," said the priest with a smile, "I was admiring your beautiful roses. I've always enjoyed roses, and when I saw how nice yours were, I couldn't help looking them over. As to who I am, I'm the new parish priest of Virginia City, named by Bishop O'Connell to live here and cover the whole Nevada Territory."

The broom dropped from her hands, "Oh, my goodness! I didn't know you were a priest, Father."

"Don't let that bother you, Mrs. Byrnes," he reassured. "What I came for is this. I need a room to stay in until I can arrange for a small house as a rectory. Matt Foley down at the livery stable thought you might have a room to spare."

"Of course, Father; come in, come in." She took his hat and coat and in typical Irish fashion set the kettle on the kitchen stove. She poked up the fire and turned toward the priest. "Won't you have a cup of tea, Father? You must have had a long and dusty ride. You know, Father, we do have a room we planned to rent. Not big and fancy. Mining camps are rather rough places."

"Don't let that worry you. I spent three years at Moore's Flat, working in the mines and living in a cabin there. I'm used to roughing it." Father Manogue was well-satisfied. The room, though small, was neat and clean. Now he had a 'rectory.'

Terry Byrnes offered to help the priest find a suitable location to say Mass. The most appropriate place turned out to be a big canvas tent near the stagecoach stop. On Sunday morning, Father Manogue celebrated Mass in the tent-the first one in Virginia City. The large turnout was a mixed congregation of Catholics and non-Catholics, who came on foot and by horseback. His first sermon was short and direct, "We should have a church where we can all pray for each other, and especially for the men who face the hazards of the mines."

There was joy throughout the mining community when the word spread that a priest was now stationed in Virginia City. Father

Manogue rode out to inspect his vast territory, seeking out Catholic families and others who might need his pastoral comforting. He would stop at the nearest camp when darkness came; he often slept at a trading post in the barroom, with his saddle for a pillow and a blanket drawn about him.

On one occasion as he rode along the trail to the next camp, he met a party of riders going in the opposite direction. They were looking for a priest and recognized Father Manogue from a description one of them had been given: "as tall as a steeple when he stands up."

> "We left Pioche early this morning," said one of the riders. "Mike McClellan is dying there and has been pleading for someone to find a priest for him. Are you going that way?"
>
> "I wasn't, but I am now," said the priest with a smile. "Give me some directions and I'll be on my way."
>
> He had been riding all that day and into the night by the time he spotted a campfire at the bottom of the gulch. As he guided his horse along the trail to the miner's cabin, a voice shouted, "Stop where you are!" In the light of the fire, he could see a bearded miner with a pistol in his hand. "What do you want?," he demanded.
>
> "I'm Father Manogue, a Catholic priest, on my way to Pioche. I apparently missed the trail."
>
> "There are no priests around here! I think you are a claim-jumper." Another voice chimed in, "I think so, too. Where are your partners?"
>
> "I have no partners," said the priest. "I tell you, I'm a priest, stationed in Virginia City!"
>
> "Virginia City? That's almost 300 miles away from here, and you expect us to believe that!"
>
> "Yes, I expect you to believe it. I got a message this morning that Mike McClellan is sick in Pioche, very sick, and is hoping a priest will come; and that's why I'm here. While I'm stationed in Virginia City, all the Nevada

Territory is my parish. If you know priests at all, you would know they'll go anywhere to answer a sick call."

"Maybe he ain't lyin', Jack. I do hear they go out of their way any time they are called."

"I don't know about that, Steve; but anyway, stranger, you can get off your horse and come down by the fire. Where did you get that message about Mike McClellan?"

"A few miles east of Fergusson's trading post. How far is Pioche from here?"

"Not too far," replied Jack, "You'll never find it on your own in the dark, though."

As they chatted, Father Manogue spotted a violin by the cabin door. "A violin out in the wilds of Nevada? Who plays it?"

"I do," said Jack, "I used to play a little."

"Mind if I try?" asked the priest. With that he reached up, took the violin, placed it under his square jaw and began to draw the bow across the strings. As he played some old Irish melodies, he could see their suspicions receding.

After he finished, Jack spoke again, "Anyone who can play like that couldn't possibly be a claim-jumper. Sit down and have a bite with us and then we'll take you to Pioche to see the sick man."

Later, the three rode down the trail together until they reached the Pioche camp. Father Manogue stayed with McClellan and administered the last rites while his former hosts rode back to their cabin.

Manogue's Kitty

When Father Manogue returned to Virginia City, he made plans to build a small church. Terry Byrnes knew everybody in the camp and set out to introduce the new pastor. He insisted that their first point of call be the Silver Dollar Saloon. Somewhat suspicious, the priest inquired, "What is this all about?" Inside, Terry introduced Father Manogue to the owner, Mike McGourn, and the bartender, Jim Neely: "Mike, will you tell him what you've done."

> "Rather, it's what you've done, Terry," grinned Mike, "but here's the story, Father:
>
> This bright Irish friend of yours comes in here with a little box all sealed up except for a hole in top. "Put this one on the bar," he told me.
>
> "What for?," says I.
>
> "For Father Manogue and the new church he'll be building."
>
> To make a long story short, Terry persuaded every saloonkeeper to put those boxes in the bars.
>
> "Manogue's kitty," interrupted Terry, "that's what we call it, Father, and we ask the boys to sweeten the kitty before they take their drinks."
>
> Father Manogue laughed. "I'm grateful to you, Terry, and to you, Mike, and all the lads up and down the street as well as to the customers. It will bring our church nearer, that's for sure."

The church was built in the summer of 1863, a wooden structure costing more than $12,000. That first church, known as St. Mary's in the Mountains, continued to serve the needs of the miners and their families for many years. The mines prospered and soon Virginia City was a bustling town, boasting a population of more than 3,500 inhabitants. Father James Croke, from the Diocesan headquarters in San Francisco was dispatched to lighten the load on Father Manogue in that momentuous year (1863) until a permanent assistant could be secured. Father Croke was later replaced by Father George Rigby, a priest from the Diocese of New York on loan to Eugene O'Connell, (the Vicar Apostolic of Marysville and later first Bishop of Grass Valley).

Father Manogue's original "St. Mary's in the Mountains Church," (1864) was replaced in 1868 by a brick church. The rebuilt third St. Mary's Church (above, 1877) is still in use as a parish church. [Courtesy of Father John Mc Shane of St. Mary's in the Mountains.]

On a cold, wintry day as the two priests were sitting close to the pot-bellied stove, when someone knocked on the door. Father Manogue opened the door and ushered the visitor inside:

> "Father," said the man, "Mrs. Morgan is dying up in the hills. She says she wants a priest, but her husband says he'll kill any priest who tries to enter the house."
>
> "I know Morgan," Father Manogue replied, "He's a tough character, all right."
>
> The man hesitated a minute and then said, "You know, Father, Jack Morgan is pretty tough and he means what he says. Shall I ask a few of the boys to come along?"
>
> "No, I don't think that will be necessary. This is a case where a group would make more trouble. I think I can talk to Jack Morgan."
>
> The priest bundled himself up against the wind and rode up to the cabin on the hill and boldly walked up to the door and knocked. Morgan answered the door, a cocked pistol in his hand.
>
> "I understand your wife is seriously ill. I've come to give her the last rites of her church," explained Father.
>
> "No priest will enter my house!" roared Morgan as he jabbed the pistol into the priest's ribs. Father Manogue looked over the man's shoulder into the one-room cabin. Ignoring the gunman, he called out, "I've come." "Thank God!" the woman cried, "Thank God!"
>
> "Get out!" snarled the miner as he jabbed the gun harder into the priest's ribs. The big clergyman suddenly sidestepped, slapping away the gun as he struck a hard right to the man's jaw. Morgan collapsed outside the cabin from the blow. The priest stepped inside and administered the last rites of the church to the woman. Father Manogue then picked up the man as he would a child, carried him into the cabin and laid him on a bearskin rug by the fire.

"He'll be all right in just a few minutes," he said to the woman, then mounted his horse and rode away.

A Bigger and Better Church

Father Manogue was a successful builder and administrator as well as a dedicated missionary. The fabulous wealth from the Big Bonanza and other mines attracted hundreds of prospectors and workers to Virginia City. This led to the need for a bigger church. The new structure, a spacious brick edifice costing $65,000—an enormous sum for those days—was completed in 1868. Had it not been for the wise counsel and money raised by people like John Mackay and his wife, Jerry Lynch, Ned Doule, and others of the priest's committee, the task would have been impossible.

Magnificent as it was, however, this new church was but short-lived. Seven years later, on October 16, 1875, Virginia City went up in flames. With the permission of the pastor, Father Manogue, the beautiful church was dynamited to keep the fire from spreading. However terrible the fire, there was a bit of ironic humor to hearten the parishioners. When the church took fire, an old Irish lady rushed over to the Comstock shaft where John Mackay was working like mad and implored him to come and save the church. "Damn the church!" he yelled. "We'll build another one, if we can keep the fire from going down these shafts!"

True to his word, Mackay saw to it that another equally grand edifice was built. John Mackay was said to be the most generous of the Bonanza Kings, but there is ample evidence to suggest that his three partners, Fair, Flood, and O'Brien, were also not found wanting. The new church, of Gothic design was constructed on the same spot as the blackened ruins of the old one. It was dedicated to Saint Mary's in the Mountains in August 1877. That same church is still functioning and stands as a memorial to the long-gone miners and their beloved pastor.

During this same period, Manogue built two schools: St. Joseph's for boys and St. Mary's for girls, plus an orphanage and a convent for the sisters. Both schools were run by the Sisters of Charity from San Francisco. These were the first educational institutions in Nevada.

In 1875, Father Manogue began the construction of St. Mary's Hospital. The Mackays were its principal financial supporters.

Mackay, in fact, had been introduced to his future wife, Louise Bryant, widow of Dr. Edmond Bryant, by Fr. Manogue, who also married them in November of 1875 in St. Mary's Church. The friendship between the priest and the Mackays flourished over the years. Mrs. Mackay purchased the land for the hospital grounds and donated it to the Sisters of Charity.

A New Diocese

For several years, Manogue was the only priest in the vast territory of 175,000 square miles, an area larger than the British Isles and far more rugged. With the constant growth of mining and the steady influx of new parishioners, a new diocese was created in Grass Valley in 1868, with Eugene O'Connell as its first bishop. There were by now seven priests working in the Nevada Territory. Father Manogue was appointed Vicar General of the new diocese in that same year.

There was enthusiastic joy in Virginia City when the people learned that their big-hearted pastor had been named a bishop. During all those years, no individual was more highly respected than Father Pat Manogue. He was looked upon as a man who understood men, not only among members of his own faith, but of all classes and creeds. He was equally at home in a miner's cabin as among the more affluent, in their well-appointed dwellings His interest extended to all the people of Virginia City, young and old, rich and poor, pagans, Christians, and Jews. The Indians respected him, too, because of his concern for them. True to his Irish Catholic upbringing, he often gave Irish names to the Indian children he baptized. Thus there were as many copper-skinned Michaels, Patricks, Timothys, Marys, and Bridgets as in the litany of the Irish saints: one old Piute couple he baptized as Adam and Eve. Generations of Indians, in turn, brought their children and grandchildren in to be baptized. The medallions and rosary beads which Father Manogue gave the Indians were treasured for many years.

On January 14, 1881, Father Manogue was consecrated Coadjutor Bishop of Grass Valley at a ceremony conducted by Bishop Riordan in St. Mary's Cathedral in San Francisco. He served in that position for the next three years. Following Bishop

O'Connell's retirement on St. Patrick's Day, March 17, 1884, Manogue was installed as the second Bishop of Grass Valley.

Cathedral of the Comstock

During his term in Grass Valley, Bishop Manogue was preoccupied with the spontaneous growth of Sacramento, the state capital. He petitioned Rome to change the diocesan headquarters to what he envisioned would become the city of the future. The fact that Sacramento was then a part of the archdiocese of San Francisco presented no apparent problem in such a vast territory, geographically endowed and blessed by the hand of nature. In due course, permission was granted by the Holy See to create the new Diocese of Sacramento with Patrick Manogue as its first Bishop.

Shortly thereafter, plans were made for the new Cathedral, to be known as the "Cathedral of the Blessed Sacrament." Bishop Manogue personally directed its construction in his methodical way. When it was dedicated on July 1, 1889, the magnificent edifice it was hailed as the largest church west of the Mississippi.

Legend has it that most of the money was solicited from his long-time friends of gold-mining days. There were many non-Catholics who contributed most generously: Mrs. Leland Stanford, the wife of the founder of Stanford University, and one-time Governor of California, presented Bishop Manogue with a painting of Raphael's Sistine Madonna, copied from the original owned by the Emperor of Austria. Mrs. Charles Crocker, curator of the Crocker Art Gallery, donated six stained glass windows in the nave of the Cathedral depicting the way of the cross in miniature. *The History of Sacramento County,* published in 1890, noted: "For grandeur, architectural magnificence and artistic finish, it has no equal in the West and is a noble addition to the attraction of California from a scenic standpoint."

The massive structure is a work of beauty. Viewed from outside, the great dome reaches to a height of 170 feet, and the bell tower to a height of 217 feet. All of the woodwork, including the pews, were executed of native California redwood and cedar.

The great bells are of special interest. The largest one that tolls the hour weighs some 8,000 pounds; it was a gift of Bishop Manogue himself. It tolled for the first time at his funeral on March 6,1895, and for the last time to announce the death of President Harding in

The Cathedral of the Blessed Sacrament, built by Bishop Manogue.
[Courtesy of Sirlin Studios in Sacramento.]

1921, after which its hourly ringing was replaced by a Seth Thomas clock.

Nearly all of the beautiful stained glass windows were made of white sand from the Monterey Peninsula. They depict the history of the Church from the beginning: with Peter receiving the keys to the kingdom. Saint Paul is depicted preaching to the Athenians, and Saint Patrick converting the Irish.

The *Sacramento Union* commented:

> There is no feature in the interior of the building which is calculated to excite so much admiration as the magnificent windows, which form so great an attraction to the eye. The plainest and the most unpretentious of them are beautiful and some of them are simply superb. All of colored glass are of the finest workmanship known in that art.

His Later Years

Bishop Manogue delighted in reminiscing with the younger priests on the rich history of the gold country. He spoke of the big fire of 1875:

> I remember well the day, for we had to dynamite our beautiful church to save the rest of the town and the mines on which the men's livelihood depended. We built another church, of course. You'll find it a beautiful one. The people call it, 'The Cathedral of the Comstock.'

He paid a farewell visit both to the St. Sulpice Seminary in Paris, his alma mater, and to his Irish homeland in 1890. He died on February 27, 1895. The Cathedral was crowded when his funeral mass was said on March 6. The only adornments on the bier were a wreath from the local Jewish synagogue, alongside a miter and crosier presented by the children of Mrs. James Fair.

The big-hearted Celt's epitaph was written long before the tolling of the final bell, when on one occasion he had ridden without letup for more than 100 miles over the mountain to prepare a man for death. The man had been sentenced to hang for a crime, and unfortunately for one he did not commit. After talking with the condemned man, the priest became convinced of his innocence. Time was of the essence, since the fatal hour was near at hand.

Father Monogue turned to the condemned man and in a whispered tone said, "Keep on praying, I am on my way to speak to the Governor." With that he jumped on his horse and rode away in the darkness, on a bitter Nevada winter night. The Good Samaritan was at the point of exhaustion when he finally arrived at the home of Nevada's Territorial Governor. Stiff from the long ride and nigh frozen from the cold, he literaly tumbled in, when the Governor's wife opened the door. As soon as he regained his composure, the priest introduced himself in his usual easy manner:

"I'm Father Manogue from Virginia City."

"Virginia City!" exclaimed the Governor. "Why that's a hundred miles from here!"

"True enough, Sir," replied Manogue, "but the importance of my mission left no alternative but to meet you in person and here I am."

The Governor listened with rapt attention to his plea and soon reached the same conclusion about the condemned man's innocence. He granted a reprieve. When the good news reached Virginia City, there was wild rejoicing, and even more when the man was eventually set free.

For over 20 years, Father Manogue kept in touch with his grateful flock, travelling on foot or horseback in summer's heat and winter's snow with the unwavering dedication of a faithful shepherd:

The cheery voice and kindly word
 Will be no more on the Comstock heard
But who of us can ever forget?
 The labors will be remembered yet.

They never will forgotten be,
 By those who loved and honored thee
Though death its mantle over thee cast
 And all the cares of life are past.

The pallid reaper cannot sever
 Fond memories that last forever."

The flourishing Diocese of Sacramento is a living testimonial to the farsighted Bishop Manogue who established this See on the Banks of the Sacramento River. His memory is perpetuated in the beautiful Cathedral, modeled after the Church of the Trinity in Paris. It towers over downtown Sacramento and provides an atmosphere of prayer and contemplation in the bustling capital of California. It also epitomizes what the big-hearted Celtic miner desired most of all to be: a "priest, a good priest."

Catherine Hayes, Irish singer, brought opera to California of the Gold Rush era. [Courtesy of the Society of California Pioneers.]

15

Catherine Hayes: The Swan of Erin

Irish songstress Catherine 'Kate' Hayes (1825-1861) was born in the shadow of the walls of Limerick and was cradled to the rhythm of the murmuring Shannon tide. According to an article that appeared in the *Limerick Journal* in 1985, Catherine was born to John and Mary Hayes on October 29, 1825, at the family residence, No. 4 Patrick Street. It was a trying period for the Hayes family, who were deprived of their only breadwinner when the father took off unexpectedly, never to return. In the ensuing years the family struggled doggedly to eke out a living. Somehow they managed to survive the horrendous Irish famine.

However, despite the hardships and tribulations that the Hayes endured, Kate, the darling of her family, was destined to soar to fame and fortune on the wings of her voice. Following a successful concert tour of Europe and a brief stay on the East coast of America, Kate arrived in San Francisco to joyous acclaim in November 1852. She gave 50 performances in California, 40 of them in San Francisco. Her vocal talents during this tour earned her a huge fortune in money, jewels, and gifts. When finally, on July 8, 1854, she bade a tearful farewell to thousands of California admirers, she was literally engulfed in an ocean of flowers and trinkets. Musically, like Orpheus, she had won over the hearts of the entire populace.

This tall, winsome Irish beauty was a lady of elegance and refinement, with nut-brown hair, radiant complexion, and blue Irish eyes. As one romantic rhymster put it:

Her hair had a meaning, her movements a grace.
You turned from the fairest to gaze on her face:
Such a blue inner light from her eyelids out broke.
You looked at her silence and fancied she spoke.
The weak and the humble, the bold and the rude,
She took them as she found them, and made them all good.
If you praised her as charming, some asked what you meant,
But the charm of her presence was felt where she went.

It was the River Shannon, famed in song and romance, that providentially led to the discovery of this aspiring vocalist. As it so happened, the Bishop of Limerick, Reverend Edmond Knot, was discoursing with the Earl of Limerick and other friends on the balcony of the Earl's riverside mansion in the fading twilight of a summer's evening. By a happy chance, at the same time an old weatherbeaten barge was slowly wending its way up the Shannon. A gentle breeze blowing in the opposite direction bore aloft the enchanting melody of an Irish lullaby. The charming voice was that of a young maiden by the name of Catherine Hayes. The Bishop immediately sought out the young virtuoso and requested that she pay him a visit. On hearing her voice for the second time, he was so entranced that he initiated a trust fund in order to provide professional tutoring for the talented songstress.

For her musical education, Miss Hayes was chaperoned to Dublin where she was placed in the capable hands of Signor Antonio Sapio. After preliminary voice training in Dublin, she then went on to Paris in 1843, where she continued her schooling under the instruction of the renowned Manuel Garcia, world-famous as the singing master of Jenny Lind, the Swedish Nightingale. Soon Miss Hayes made her triumphal European debut in the La Scala opera house in Rome under the direction of Felice Riconi. Following her performance in *The Barber of Seville,* she was called back to receive wild plaudits beneath the bright lights no less than twelve times. In Florence and Genoa her reception was equally enthusiastic. She went on to brilliant performances at Marseilles in 1844 and then at Elvira in 1845.

Miss Hayes made her first appearance in England at the Covent Garden Theatre in London as *Linda*. Hundreds of fans queued up to hear her. She also performed at Her Majesty's Theatre, and she was honored by being summoned to sing at a command performance for Queen Victoria at her residence in Buckingham Palace.

The jubilant high point of Kate's young life was her return visit to her native land, where she appeared in concert with the Dublin Philharmonic Society, followed by a performance at the Royal Theatre. She next traveled to Cork City in 1850, where she delighted all with a wildly successful engagement.

From Cork to Limerick, her native city where her meteoric rise to stardom had begun, Kate gave several concerts. In March of 1850, in her hometown of Limerick she performed a stellar recital at the old Theatre Royal on Henry Street. Her inspired rendition of Bellini's *Norma* brought down the house. It was an even more nostalgic occasion for the hometown star when she sang at Saint Mary's Church where she had been baptized.

Catherine Hayes in America.

In 1851, Miss Hayes, accompanied by her mother, set sail for America, which was fast becoming a cultural mecca for aspiring artists. On September 23, 1851, Kate made her first appearance in the New World at Tripper Hall, New York. She followed this gala event with many delightful performances in other cities on the East coast and in Canada.

However, a more lucrative adventure still awaited the enchanting Irish singer in far-off California, already affluent and burgeoning in its third golden year, where fabulous fortunes were still being plucked from the hills of the Gold Country. Such an impresario's opportunity was not lost on the great showman P.T. Barnum, who was quick to engage the "Irish Linnet," as Kate was fondly nicknamed. Barnum was eager to have Kate and himself cash in on the sure-fire cultural bonanza. The *Alta California* was the first Western newspaper to publicize the story of Miss Hayes' proposed itinerary in the Golden State. A preliminary announcement of her musical tour appeared in its October 21, 1852 issue:

> Mr. Barnum has contracted an engagement with Catherine Hayes, for sixty concerts to begin under his direction in California, Cuba, and the U.S. and the British Provinces of North America. Mr. Barnum is to pay Miss Hayes $50,000 and also to divide the profits of the concerts with her. Signor Mengis and other artists are engaged and the party is to sail for this state in November. It is fortunate that the Prince of Humbugs, as he is justly styled, should be thus interested in the movements of Hayes.

The shrewd showman Barnum was keenly aware that the many culturally deprived Midases who had struck-it-rich in the California gold mines longed for quality entertainment and were willing and able to pay handsomely for it. With dollar signs dazzling his eyes, he engaged the renowned *chanteuse* and sent her on her way to San Francisco. With the astute promoter W.A. Bushnell as her press agent, the star was in capable hands. Kate was chaperoned by her mother, Mary, who had accompanied her on the long journey to America the previous year. Understandably, the mother enjoyed the affluent life style made possible by her daughter's meteoric rise to fame and fortune.

The *Alta California* played up the cultural bonanza big in a second article, dated October 31, 1852:

> Miss Catherine Hayes—the great Irish Cantatrigo (*cantatrice*) is actually on the point of leaving for the Pacific Coast. Her agent is in town, energetically engaged in making preparations for her appearance, which we learn will be during the month of December. Her renown in the musical circles of Europe, and indeed the world, is built upon her own peerless powers which have entranced her listeners wherever she has appeared.
>
> Miss Hayes is a native of Limerick, Ireland and is about twenty-seven years of age. She has a most elegant and graceful personality and manner and wins the heart at once, not only by her voice but by the native simplicity of manner that takes the heart by storm at first sight. Her voice is a soprano, clear and rich, of affluence in its

> intonations and cadences which gives it a complete control of all the chords of sympathy and admiration. She is only equaled as a songstress by the Swedish Nightingale, and there are thousands who drew the comparison in favor of the 'Swan of Erin.'

Public excitement reached fever pitch once it became known that Kate's ship had cleared the Golden Gate. Crowds converged on the waterfront as the old square-rigger anchored in the sheltered cove beneath Telegraph Hill. Cheer after cheer went up as Kate stepped ashore in a downpour of rain and made her way to the gilded carriage that whisked the singer and her mother to the Oriental Hotel. An enthusiastic crowd of admirers followed her on foot to her hotel and let loose with a tumultuous round of applause when their idol made a brief appearance on the balcony and bowed in grateful acknowledgment.

Kate's first performance in the booming city of San Francisco was booked for November 30, 1852. To prevent speculation in tickets, her agents, led by Mr. Bushnell, decided it would be best to sell the tickets at auction. When the day of the sale came, crowds gathered at the site and a lively competition began. The auctioneers announced that the best seats would be offered first and knocked down to the highest bidders. Starting at $50, the bids rose quickly to a $100, then $150, then $200, and higher yet. The auctioneer was quick to point out that choice seats for the Jenny Lind concert in New York sold for $600. When the crowd responded with a roar, it was evident San Francisco would not be outdone in the bidding frenzy.

The bids continued to escalate by increments of $25 and $50, with cheers hailing each offer. The enthusiastic din almost drowned out bids of $800, $850, $900, and, incredibly, $1,125. At this point, George Green, foreman of the Volunteer Empire Engine Company (known as "Broderick" in the political heyday of Senator David Broderick), shouted at the top of his lungs, "One thousand one hundred and fifty dollars!" amid a deafening roar from the crowd. (That ticket was later framed in crimson and gold and became a memento of civic pride.) The lavishly decorated box for the first night was occupied by California Governor Bigler and the Chief of the city's volunteer fire department. At half past seven, the Empire Engine Company, togged out in full regalia and led by a brass band, escorted the celebrated songstress to the theater. Local residents had never witnessed such an outpouring of enthusiasm as that which greeted the Limerick-born star on her opening night at the ornate American Theater.

A star was indeed born when Kate Hayes made her San Francisco debut amid a phantasmagoria display of exotic frills and dazzling lights. She was a radiant figure of beauty, grace, and charm. The "Irish Linnet"—then thirty-two—was described in contemporary doting accounts as dignified, of medium height, fair of face, with blue eyes, bright auburn hair, and an expression of intelligence. Her opening number, from the *Barber of Seville,* was greeted with thunderous applause by the packed house. This aria was followed by such delightful airs as *Kathleen Mavourneen, The Harp that Once through Tara's Halls,* and *The Last Rose of Summer.* She concluded with the heart-rending *Emigrant's Lament,* which brought down the house of nostalgic sentimental exiles.

Again and again, she was called back for encores before the blazing stage lights and was showered with bouquets of flowers, some with hefty pouches of gold attached. At the finale of her performance, the members of the Empire Fire Engine Company arose on cue and let loose with three earsplitting cheers. Outside the theater, the firemen formed an honor guard in two lines, one of which took the lead in front of the star's carriage and the other brought up the rear. A huge crowd followed again on foot and congregated outside her hotel to serenade their Queen of Song, letting loose with cheers that reverberated over the City's hills. From that moment on the town belonged to Catherine Hayes.

The morning after Kate's triumphant concert, the *Alta California* enthusiastically reported:

> Long and loud were the cheers which greeted her entry.... Miss Hayes sang the sweet and plaintive invocation, *'Ah, mon fils!'* one of the most touching gems of Meyerbeer's music. Her voice is naturally a mezzo-soprano....It is sweet, mellow, lacking if anything, power....Her voice is admirably cultivated, flexible, and the delightful shake or quaver which she introduces with so much effect, imparts a softness or tremolo to her plaintive songs, soothing and agreeable to the listener.

Amusements.

SAN FRANCISCO HALL.

POSITIVELY THE LAST CONCERT BUT ONE!

MISS CATHRINE HAYES
Has the honor to announce that her

LAST CONCERT BUT ONE

will take place on

Thursday Evening, March 17. 1853

PROGRAMME.

Part I.

Donizetti's favorite Opera of

LA FIGLIA DEL RIGGIMENTO!

Marie......................................Miss Cathrine Hayes
Sulpizio......................................Herr Mengis
Marcheza......................................Miss Emily Coad

The first act is on a road, near a village; the second in an inn of a village; and the third, in the drawing-room of the Marchioness.

ACT I.

Overture......................................Orchestra
Recitativo Canto Militaire......................" Dans le service."
SULPIZIO.
Recitativo duetto......................" Apparve alla luce."
MARIE AND SULPIZIO
Recitative and Aria......................" Ciasch 'un lo Dice."
MARIE.

ACT II.

Recitative and Aria......................" Bello e vaso."
SULPIZIO.
Recitative, Aria and Trio......................" Conivan partir."
MARIE, MARCHESA AND SULPIZIO.

ACT III.

Recitative and Aria......................" La Richezze."
MARIE.
Recitative and Grand Terzetto Finale Rataplan......................
MARIE, MARCHESA AND SULPIZIO.

Part II.

Selections from the favorite Comic Opera,

L'ELISIR D'AMORE.

Overture—" Le Medicine sans Medicin"......................F. Herold
Grand Orchestra.
Cavatina—" Udite o Rustici,"......................Donizetti
Herr Mengis.
Cavatina—" Ah non e'vero"......................Donizetti
MISS CATHRINE HAYES.
Barcarrola—" Io Son rico"......................Donizetti
Herr Mengis.
Duetto—" Quanto Amore"......................Donizetti
MISS CATHRINE HAYES AND HERR MENGIS.

Musical Conductor......................MR. GEO. LODER

Tickets $5, $3 and $2. Seats may be secured at the Hall THIS MORNING. mh17

Announcement of a St. Patrick's Day Concert (1853) in San Francisco, featuring Kate Hayes' operatic medley.

The Metropolitan Theatre in San Francisco (1854), the scene of some of Catherine Hayes' operatic performances. [Courtesy of California State Library.]

> Miss Hayes was ably assisted in the duet from *Norma* by Herr Mengis, baritone, prior to which Signor Herold executed a *fantasia* on the piano with much taste and skill. Altogether the concert was highly successful. There was much enthusiasm and altogether too much noise and uproariousness. Some younger sons of Erin became so excited as to toss hats and money upon the stage, which however enthusiastic it may seem, could not but be regarded as extremely bad taste.
>
> The program also contained an interpretation of *The Last Rose of Summer,* a scene from *Don Pasquale,* and several ballads.
>
> Her ballads being most exquisitely rendered were repeatedly encored. At the close Miss Hayes was escorted to the Oriental Hotel by a torchlight procession composed of a body of our firemen, and serenaded.

Kate Hayes had the distinction of introducing genuine opera to San Francisco. Her first-ever full-costume scenes established her as the definitive word in fashion. Never before had the fair sex been seen out and about in such numbers, a change chronicled with delight by the local press. The shops were crowded daily with women in search of silks and velvets, cozy mitts, embroidered shawls, and variegated fans. Merchants cheerfully dressed their windows ever more elaborately. Market Street became one great thoroughfare of glamor, and the air was heavy with sweet perfume. Shop windows displayed Kate Hayes coats, and flower vendors sold Kate Hayes corsages.

Not to be outdone, the men also spent lavishly on new finery. They bought frilled shirts, embroidered waistcoats, and silken scarves. The inimitable Yankee "Doe" Robinson was inspired to dramatize the hilarious and colorful era in verse:

San Francisco for excitement,
 Has forever something new.
Here's employment for the workingman
 And pleasure for the blue.
For the music of the Monte Room,
 The light of other days,

We now have San Francisco Hall
And Erin's Swan, Kate Hayes

Whenever and wherever the songstress appeared in public thereafter, she became the center of attention. Glowing adjectives were showered on Miss Hayes at every opportunity. She captivated one and all with her beauty and gracious personality.

The San Francisco Irish, who were already quite numerous and most anxious to show their appreciation, called upon Miss Hayes *en masse* and presented her with a special token of their affection: a massive card case of pure California gold, with a written stripe attached, reading: "Emblematic of your own Green Isle and the land of your sojourn." On a shield in the center was engraved the inscription, "Miss Catherine Hayes, from a few of your countrymen residents of San Francisco, February 5, 1853." The case was elegantly adorned with scenes of Ireland on one side and California on the other.

In December 1852, Miss Hayes initiated a special series of costume recitals, in which she sang famous opera arias. Among them were the highly-favored *Barber of Seville, Lucia de Lammermoor, Don Pasquale.* For many of those early settlers, Catherine's performances in the old San Francisco Hall on Washington Street were special occasions for social gatherings and family reunions. Night after night, they came with an air of excitement, dressed in their Sunday best, despite the price of admission, which was double that of most other entertainments.

It was considered quite appropriate for out-of-town organizations to converge on the stage when the opportunity arose and make known their identity and from whence they came. Calaveras County's rugged men drew special attention when they somehow floated on to the stage a massive garland of flowers, with a jewel of great price attached, which landed squarely at the feet of their idol. On another occasion, when the more enthusiastic showered the performers with gold nuggets, one of these baubles struck the conductor's shoe and ricocheted into the audience.

The star reciprocated all the attention with dignity, benevolence, and generosity. Kate contributed in full measure to the practical wants of the San Francisco community by performing gratis for the Firemen's Charity Fund. As a result of Miss Hayes' dedicated efforts, the fund reached the amazing total of $105,000 before she departed San Francisco. On the occasion of the Firemen's Charity Ticket Auction, first choice was knocked down to Sam Brannan, the newspaper publisher, for a bid of $5,000.

The firm of Tobin and Duncan, two early Irish entrepreneurs, combined business with pleasure in this flowery salute to the celebrity singer:

> A joyous welcome was given last evening to the Swan of Erin: the beauties of San Francisco clustered together to listen to the thrilling melody of one whose world wide fame had already given her a place in our hearts. Bright eyes looked brighter in the arena of fashion and women's loveliness shone forth on every side.
>
> The scene was a daguerreotype of our young state, a picture of wealth which even the Atlantic side could not rival. Shawls of the richest crepe, exquisite in embroidery, and of every hue from the snowiest white to the darkest crimson were beautifully displayed, a feature of luxury known only to the golden land. Diamonds flashed amid silks and velvets, and mechlin kerchiefs fanned the perfume-laden air, while the matchless *Casta Diva* was borne upon the entrancing vibrations! It was an evening long to be remembered, a triumph of the stranger songstress well worthy of her fame.

In the Gold Fields

Kate Hayes, while vacationing with her mother in the California Sierra Nevada mountains, visited the mining country in 1853, and gave concerts in Virginia City, Grass Valley, and Sacramento. The well-heeled argonauts were starving for world-class entertainment. One of the most noteworthy of the star's many performances took place in Sacramento, which injected new life into an old community that in earlier years was known as the Embarcadero. The *Sacramento Union* newspaper devoted a column to the particularities of yet another auction that was held to dispose of tickets for admission to the concert performance by Catherine Hayes. The frantic bidding was held in the Orleans Hotel lounge, which was filled to capacity long before the appointed time. When the auctioneer announced that there were only 400 seats available for the first performance, he almost incited a riot among the huge gathering. An Irishman was the first to voice his disappointment. He emphasized that there were that many of the star's countrymen and that in all fairness they should be given first choice. There were others present, were equally perturbed, who had travelled long distances and were prepared to pay any price to hear the charming Irish songstress. Despite the squabble, the final say was reserved for the auctioneer, who was not in the least intimidated in asserting his authority.

The Ticket Auction

The first choice ticket was knocked down to the Sutter Rifle Company with a high bid of $1,200. When it was announced that the box would be occupied by Captain John Sutter, the gathering uttered a sigh of contented relief. Indeed, the box would be no ordinary seat, but a full sofa, elaborately upholstered in green velvet and trimmed in crimson and gold, positioned directly in front of the podium. At the appointed time in the evening of the concert, the Sutter Rifle Company escorted Captain Sutter to the theater, bedecked in full regalia and led by a brass band with banners flying and torches blazing.

The graceful beauty thrilled the audience with operatic arias, but it was the popular numbers that completely captivated them. The packed house adored her and called her back for repeated encores. When asked the secret of Miss Hayes' outstanding success, a pioneer resident of Sacramento answered, "Her grace of manner and becoming dignity made friends of her audience before she opened her lips to sing."

Following a most successful concert tour of the Mother Lode country, Kate returned to San Francisco, the scene of her California debut. Continuing on the concert route during the fall of 1853 with her manager W.A. Bushnell at her side, she then ventured to South America to perform another tour of concerts, returning to California in 1854 to spend another three months in her favorite city. Her farewell concert, often remembered as the most awe-inspiring of all, was given on July 7, 1854.

Kate finally departed from San Francisco on July 8th for the last time and set sail for Australia, and later to Rome, where she married her faithful manager, W.A. Bushnell, in September 1857. She finally returned to the British Isles. There she passed away prematurely, in Sydenham, London on August 11, 1861.

Catherine "Kate" Hayes, the "Swan of Erin," took San Francisco by storm from the day she sailed through the Golden Gate in 1852. She dethroned the then reigning queen of song, Signora Biscaccianti, and captured the hearts of the Argonauts of that early Gold Rush city. Lavishly and tirelessly she poured her soul into concert after concert, sometimes at the rate of three a week. Each performance, resplendent in full costume, Miss Hayes sang to an enthralled infant city that was destined to become the cultural and entertainment center of the West.

Kate Hayes' musical genius was enthusiastically acclaimed throughout California. The Golden State had lured many of the world's outstanding performers, but the Swan of Erin was the *Prima Donna* of them all. The success of this pioneer soprano is unsurpassed in the musical history of San Francisco. In an era of fine artists, this Irish-born *diva* was without peer in the theatrical world.

William S. O'Brien (1826-1878) rose from saloonkeeper to silver baron.
[Courtesy of the Bancroft Library, University of California at Berkeley.]

16

William Shoney O'Brien: The Jolly Millionaire and Silver King

Call it one man's good fortune or simply the Luck of the Irish, if you will, but in either case Billy O'Brien (1826-1878) was indeed the right man in the right place at the right time.

O'Brien's principal endowment was his congenial Irish personality, one without a trace of vanity, and lacking either the interest or apparent talent in making money. It was only by the rarest of chances, through a series of incredibly lucky incidents based largely on his wonderful disposition, that this Irishman with the accidental Midas touch went on to amass a prodigious fortune. As some of his close friends were fond of saying, O'Brien became a millionaire in spite of himself. In his salad days, he appeared out of place rubbing shoulders with his wealthy peers, preferring the company of old cronies from his less affluent past. He was more at home in the beer-smelling cardroom of McGovern's saloon on San Francisco's Kearny Street than he was in the decorous and palatial Lick House, with its gilded adornments and well-heeled gentry.

The town of Abbeyleix, in County Laois, birthplace of William S. O'Brien. [Courtesy of Michael O'Connor, Dublin historic post card collector.]

O'Brien's Early Irish Roots

Little is known of O'Brien's early boyhood in Ireland, beyond the fact that his family belonged to the working class, and that Billy, like so many of his unfortunate countrymen, was forced to emigrate. His American biography states that he was born William Shoney O'Brien in Abbeyleix, Queen's County (County Laois or Leix) in the year 1826 and that he arrived in America in 1845. He settled first in New York City, where he worked as a clerk in a grocery store. He became an American citizen on November 3, 1845, at the age of 19.

Abbeyleix, O'Brien's birthplace, took its name from a religious foundation established by the Clan O'Moore in 1183. This monastery was one of the most successful institutions of its kind in all Ireland. In fact, the monastery's opulence induced Pope Nicholas IV to levy on it an ecclesiastical tax to help fill the coffers of a war chest intended to prevent the Saracens from seizing the Holy Land. The abbey continued to flourish until the Reformation when it was confiscated by Queen Elizabeth in 1562 and granted as a political favor to the Earl of Desmond. It was subsequently assigned to Sir John Vessey, ancestor of its present-day occupants who acquired title under the name of Lord DeVesci.

The beautiful wooded demesne on the banks of the winding River Nore is now open to the public as one of the showplaces of modern Ireland. The tomb of Malachi O'Moore, preserved in a shaded garden, is the only extant memorial to that renowned Gaelic clan who resisted the English invader for a century or more. Their rallying cry, "*Remember Mullaghamast!*" recalls the ghastly slaughter of the O'Moores and their cohorts by deceit and treachery.

The grisly story runs as follows. The O'Moores were invited to the great fort under the guise of a friendly assemblage that turned out to be the very opposite. As each of the O'Moores entered the fort, anticipating a welcoming hand, they were brutally set upon by fully armed English soldiers and murdered in cold blood. The treacherous encounter inspired the oft-repeated Irish phrase, "Never trust a horse's hoof, the horn of a bull, or the smile of a Saxon."

The loss of the O'Moores deprived the Irish of leadership, without which they could not effectively pursue their hoped-for resistance to the English. In the intervening years 30,000 or more acres of the most fertile land in Ireland were confiscated. The evicted owners were replaced by English settlers. Deplorable conditions followed in the wake of the 17th-century Cromwellian plantation and resettlement of Ireland. These depredations uprooted the Gaelic Irish for years thereafter and drove many of them to the New World. In later years, similar conditions were to uproot families like the O'Briens, who immigrated to America.

O'Brien in San Francisco

Following his little-documented sojourn in New York City, O'Brien was lured to join the hordes of onrushing gold-seekers to

California. He secured a berth on the old brig *Torolinta,* bound for California, by working as a deck hand on the precarious journey around the Horn. On September 23, 1849, O'Brien stepped ashore in San Francisco.

When O'Brien, the future millionaire, landed in San Francisco he was a pathetic, sorry-looking figure. He wore shabby clothing, and his shoes were so badly worn that a sympathetic bystander gave him a pair, a practical gift that he never forgot. When Dame Fortune finally smiled on O'Brien, he made repeated efforts to find the donor of the shoes in order to reward him appropriately. But to his utter disappointment, his every attempt to find the Good Samaritan proved futile.

It appears that the youthful O'Brien was in such penury when he arrived that he was obliged to help unload the ship's cargo in order to buy enough food to sustain himself. But thereafter fortune continuously smiled on Billy O'Brien. This amiable Celt would find the pot of gold he had never wished for at the end of a western rainbow he had never dreamed of.

O'Brien's first business venture began in 1851, some two years after his unpromising arrival in California. He entered into a partnership with a man named William Hoff in the mercantile trade. It was during this period that he became acquainted with another Irishman by the name of James Flood, a New Yorker born of poor immigrant parents. Like O'Brien, Flood had braved the trek to California to seek his own pot of gold. Their chance meeting developed into a lifelong friendship and business partnership.

By trade James Flood was a carriage-maker who took up carpentry for a short period after arriving in San Francisco. His initial venture, a livery stable, prospered for a time, but failed during the city's first depression, in the same period in which O'Brien's own enterprise collapsed. Undaunted, the pair decided to begin all over again. O'Brien came up with the idea of going into the liquor business, which would not be vulnerable to sudden fluctuations in demand, since men drink in bad as well as in good times (albeit for different reasons). The two Irishmen opened a saloon on Washington Street, the heart of the original San Francisco business district, and called their establishment the "Auction Lunch." It proved to be a popular watering hole, located close by the

Washington market, and the new Mining Exchange, which was patronized by San Francisco's leading financiers.

In those days, it was the custom for saloonkeepers to provide a free lunch for their patrons. The Auction Lunch Saloon set out an impressive spread of victuals, the equal of any other popular restaurant of the period. Flood tended bar, while O'Brien, the more affable of the pair, presided over the well-stocked lunch counter. Business grew steadily from the outset, offering drinks at two for a quarter (others charged two bits straight), and a hearty free lunch to boot. Soon O'Brien was able to hire an assistant and to devote himself exclusively to his role as meeter and greeter. It was a perfect partnership: Flood, the shrewd businessman, served drinks and watched over the till, while O'Brien solicited business out front.

O'Brien, the former barefoot boy, was now in his glory, flamboyantly dressed in broadcloth and high silk hat, greeting prospective customers with a grin as broad as Broadway. O'Brien was a carefree, happy-go-lucky character, who showed little interest in accumulating money. He was content to leave business transactions in his partner's capable hands, and this arrangement worked to the advantage of both. Within ten years, the Flood-O'Brien partnership amassed a fortune.

From Saloonkeeper to Stockbroker

Over the years, Flood and O'Brien had developed friendships with the local stockbrokers who frequented their saloon. They became intrigued by this shortcut to acquiring wealth without a large investment. The Irishmen determined to learn the intricacies of the stock market. Eventually they sold the Auction Lunch at a fabulous profit and then moved around the corner to Montgomery Street, where they established their new enterprise as the brokerage house of Flood and O'Brien.

It was during this time that two mining speculators from Virginia City, named John Mackay and James Fair, arrived in San Francisco. By chance again, they met Flood and O'Brien. Both Mackay and Fair were Irish-born: Mackay a Dubliner and Fair from County Tyrone. They had already amassed their own fortune from the mines. Now they were seeking investors to share in an even more lucrative venture. As a result of the meeting, all four Irishmen joined in partnership to seek control of the booming Hale and

Montgomery Block, the commercial center of San Francisco in the days of William S. O'Brien. [Courtesy of the San Francisco Archieves in the San Francisco Public Library.]

Norcross Mine, in the sun-browned hills of the great Mother Lode country. Contrary to well-established business method whereby each party is bound by a written document bearing signatures, the agreement was on a mutual word-of-honor basis. Mackay, the wealthiest, put up three-eighths of the total investment. Flood and O'Brien pooled their money to match Mackay's share. Fair contributed the remaining quarter share. Flood was appointed President, O'Brien and Mackay were trustees, while Fair became Superintendent.

From Stockbroker to Millionaire

The Irishmen's partnership reaped a fortune and paid out dividends of some $200,000 in the single year of 1869. The success of the big Bonanza mines electrified the entire West, and many looked upon the four Silver Kings, Mackay, Fair, Flood and O'Brien, as the fount of unlimited prosperity for the Pacific Coast. Their new venture into banking was Flood's idea; Mackay and O'Brien were in favor, while Fair assented with no particular enthusiasm. The enterprise was incorporated as the Nevada Bank, with a paid-up capital of $5,000,000; the four magnates as directors owned all but a few shares of stock. Their capital quickly doubled to $10,000,000, and a branch opened in Virginia City.

O'Brien owned a quarter share in the banking firm, and purchased a seat on the San Francisco stock exchange, a seat he rarely occupied. Reluctantly, he joined his wealthy peers at fashionable Lick House or the Palace Hotel. But he felt more like a fish out of water than a metropolitan tycoon. He by far preferred a game of Pedro in the smoke-filled backroom of McGovern's Saloon on Kearny Street with his old cronies than sitting in on the shareholders' meetings on profit-and-loss reports of the banking company.

O'Brien was no gambler at heart, so the stakes in his card games were kept low to accommodate his less affluent buddies. It was also his custom during the Pedro game to keep a stack of silver by his elbow, with the understanding that any less fortunate soul down on his luck could reach in and help himself. When his pile was quite diminished, Bill would signal the bartender, slip him a couple of gold pieces, and the kitty would be replenished. It was his custom to retire early and give his left-over kitty to latecomers.

O'Brien's lifestyle was often criticized by those who regarded him as uncouth because he associated with the lower class and frequented Irish saloons. But those who were more intimately acquainted with him recognized O'Brien as a man of dignity, profound humility, and generosity. Although millions of dollars came his way, he cared naught for wealth, and it did little to change his unpretentious ways. Indeed, he would have been quite content with the camaraderie of the Auction Lunch crowd for the remainder of his life.

The gregarious instinct characteristic of the Irish was O'Brien's in a special manner. At family gatherings and social functions, he was the epitome of a cultured gentleman, with more than a touch of class. Gertrude Atherton, the aspiring literary matron, noted, "When

William O'Brien entered the gas lit ballroom of the Occidental Hotel with his sister, Marie Coleman, on his arm, his patrician figure, silvery grey hair and dark set eyes drew the attention of all." Mrs. Coleman was an uncommonly handsome woman, tall, blond, and dignified, with the bearing of an Irish princess. Both O'Brien's sisters, Marie Coleman and Kate McDonough, were women of beauty and charm and were for many years prominent figures in San Francisco society. O'Brien was more than proud of his two charming sisters and showered them with every luxury, from costly jewels to the latest in Parisian fashions. Gilded carriages were at their disposal, with high-hatted coachmen at the ready. O'Brien's generosity extended also to all his relatives and to the many members of the Coleman and McDonough clans who had migrated to San Francisco over the years.

O'Brien himself remained a confirmed bachelor and died leaving the bulk of his fortune to his sisters and their children. It was only in death that the full extent of O'Brien's generosity came to light. He had set aside a considerable sum to be apportioned among Catholic and Protestant orphanages and other charitable organizations. The inventory of his estate included more than a quarter of a million dollars in promissory notes from many old-time friends, on which he apparently made no effort to collect. A short time later, his brother Patrick (thought to be dead) showed up in San Francisco and contested O'Brien's will. An out-of-court settlement was reached wherein Patrick and his daughter, Mary O'Brien, were given $600,000 and relinquished any additional claim.

Although O'Brien was the oldest and the most inconspicuous of the four partners, he was always the most popular. Though he shunned his share of the business responsibilities at times, he nevertheless contributed far more to the partnership than that for which he was credited. For always the peacemaker, the mild-mannered, softspoken Billy O'Brien did much to calm the troubled waters whenever the Bonanza Kings were in disagreement. He never allowed himself to get embroiled in any of their disputes. Thus he maintained the respect of his three associates down through the years.

O'Brien never forgot the decisive turning point of his fortunes when he arrived down at heel in San Francisco. It was his custom, every year after he rose to affluence, to gather together as many fellow passengers who came with him on the *Torolinta* as he could locate and serve them an elaborate banquet in honor of the occasion. The year 1877 would see his final bash, the last of the *Torolinta* reunions. He chartered a boat and took 50 of his old buddies on an outing to Angel Island in San Francisco Bay. It was a sumptuous affair in the typical O'Brien manner: the happy revelers were serenaded by a twelve-piece band, interspersed by speechmaking and singing and toasts all round. The hilarious party continued into the night and refused to let up even on their return trip, with the guests singing "O Susanna" and drinking all the way. The celebration was to be O'Brien's last. Near the end of 1878 his health began to fail and he sensed that he did not have long to live. An architect was commissioned to design a mausoleum in Calvary Cemetery as his final resting place. He moved to the residence of his nephew, James Coleman, in San Rafael in the spring of 1878, where he passed away on May 2 at the untimely age of 52.

Out of respect for his memory, the San Francisco Stock Exchange closed, and business came to a virtual standstill as thousands mourned the loss of a dear friend. Funeral services were held at St. Mary's Cathedral, with Archbishop Alemany, O'Brien's lifelong friend, officiating. The requiem mass was attended by many the city's leading men and women. The Society of California Pioneers (of which O'Brien was a life member), the fire department, the San Francisco Association of Brokers, and numerous civic and fraternal organizations, were all represented by large delegations. The funeral of the Bonanza King has been described by one contemporary as a popular demonstration in which thousands of San Franciscans, who had known him for years, came to pay their last respects. The flag floating at half staff over the Nevada Bank, the stately citadel of the Bonanza King, was visible in the distance as a long line of carriages and hundreds of marching feet escorted their kindly benefactor on his final social outing, to Calvary Cemetery on Lone Mountain. The barefoot boy from Abbeyleix thus became a legend in his own time. The "Jolly Millionaire" to some, the "Prince of Humility" to others, Irish-born William Shoney O'Brien was gone, yet remained alive in the colorful spirit of California.

Tom Hayes (1820-1868) rose from a San Francisco squatter to become a civic-minded philanthropist. [Courtesy of the Bancroft Library, University of California at Berkeley.]

17

Tom Hayes: The Beloved San Francisco Squatter

Of all the Argonauts who ventured to California, few left a legend more colorful than that of Irish-born Tom Hayes (1820-1868). He blazed an adventurous rags-to-riches trail, rising from squatter to land baron, track sweeper to railroad tycoon, and from timid crowd-watcher to fearless mob-controller. Tom Hayes moved in and staked his claim for a quarter section in the sand dunes—now the site of San Francisco's posh Civic Center. He dispensed with the formality of asking official permission. The area has been known from that day to this as Hayes Valley; and who with even the slightest knowledge of this hardy pioneer would say nay to his claim?

The Hayes Ancestral Homeland

Thomas Hayes was born in Rosscarbery, County Cork, in 1820, son of Timothy Hayes and Mary O'Mahony. The ancestral home of the Hayes clan, Corca Laoide, is located in southwest Cork. The Gaelic surname *Ohaoda* (or *Ua Aedha*) was anglicized as Hayes, Hays, or Hughes. Clan members scattered to Limerick and South Tipperary, where they are numerous today. From this area also came Catherine Hayes, the "Swan of Erin," who is the subject of another chapter on the California Irish. The O'Mahony roots can be traced to the same region. They were descendants of nobility, with High King Brian Boru (the *Ard Re* himself) on the maternal side.

In the 1840s, living conditions during the Potato Famine were so intolerable for the native Irish that the Hayes family was compelled to emigrate to America. Timothy and his wife Mary, together with their young family, made their arduous voyage to the New World and settled in New York City. There the father found work and the children attended school.

That the children acquired a substantial education is evidenced by Tom's first job as a clerk in U.S. Customs. He gained valuable experience in the Customs House and became adept in American government procedures and business practices. He also became involved in local politics, and was elected Alderman for the Fourth Ward at an early age. Hayes also took an active interest in the plight of his beleaguered countrymen. When a movement to advance the cause of Irish freedom was initiated, young Hayes became one of its most passionate spokesmen. He even accompanied Michael O'Connor, Editor of the *Irish Volunteer*, to Canada to enlist Irish-Canadians in a revolutionary movement to drive the British out of Ireland. That attempt petered out for lack of support and direction. Only somewhat discouraged, Hayes returned to New York.

Hayes California-Bound

Like so many others, the Hayes family caught the fever of the Gold Rush; Tom and Michael headed out to California. By all accounts, Tom, the subject of this narrative, was already a man of considerable stature in the business community, with a sizable nest egg to his credit. He shrewdly purchased a quantity of select merchandise that he felt would be in demand in California and had it shipped to the Port of San Francisco. The brothers themselves booked passage on the brig *Torolinta* (famous for Billy O'Brien) around the Horn, arriving in San Francisco on July 1, 1849.

During the administration of President Polk, the American frontier was expanding ever westward. The annexation of Iowa and Texas opened up vast amounts of land for new settlers. Yet it was hardly surprising that even this opportunity was overshadowed by the thrill and temptation of the California Gold Rush. Many there were who had previously settled in the Midwest to engage in farming but hastily pulled up stakes again to head for the beckoning California mines. In the year 1849 alone, over 100,000 fortune-hunters converged on California. From the Hayes brothers' standpoint the timing was just right. When their consignment of goods arrived, the demand was such that they were able to dispose of the complete inventory in short order and reap a huge profit. With a considerable amount of cash on hand, the Hayes brothers were able to take advantage of the opportunities that the new territory had to offer.

The Magic Well

Shortly after his arrival in San Francisco, Hayes explored the wilderness skirting the Bay. Unoccupied then, the sand dune ridges were interlaced with scrub oak, red birch, chaparral, and tufts of wild grass. The surrounding hills then abounded in wild life: grizzly bears, raccoons, squirrels, and flocks of wild birds. As Tom made his way through the shifting sands, he was startled by the sound of a gurgling spring, its crystal-clear waters trickling through a grassy mound. He stopped to quench his thirst, like the stranger that came to the well of Saint Keane:

> A traveller came to the well of Saint Keane
> And joyfully he drew nigh
> For from cock crow he had been travelling
> And there was not a cloud in the sky.
>
> He drank of the waters so cool and clear
> For thirsty and hot was he
> And he sank to rest on its grassy brim
> 'Neath the drooping willow tree.

Wells—hallowed and venerable from ancient Druidic times—carried over their air of holy mystery as a symbol of reverence in early Christian Ireland, and many wells still bear the names of Irish saints (or their pre-Christian counterparts). In more recent times the well has been associated with romance, and the fair maiden has tiptoed down the path more often to meet her lover than to fill her pail. So it was, too, with Hayes' Spring in San Francisco.

Public use of a good spring called for cooperation in those pioneer days of old San Francisco. There is much to suggest that the gurgling spring in the sand dunes forever changed the life of Tom Hayes and helped seal his romance with the city of his adoption.

The original well was at the site of the present City Hall. The stream gradually burrowed its way beneath the sand to emerge again in the area of Seventh and Howard Streets. Over the years it formed a lagoon that became a haven for fish and wild waterfowl. (An Irishman named Patrick Rowan built a wooden bridge over the stream and charged a toll for man and beast. Many claimed Rowan's toll bridge was the City's first bridge.)

The well was reopened when the new City Hall was built in 1878. The contract to do the work was let to yet another Irishman by the name of Charles Delaney, according to an article in the *Alta California*, dated September 27th, 1878:

> Contractor Delaney has finished the well at the new City Hall at a cost of $1,500. In about a fortnight the City Hall will be free from the exactions of Spring Valley Water Co.

Even in those days, it seems someone was always battling City Hall or vice versa. It is of particular interest that the well provided almost a thousand gallons a day and served the needs of the local residents for many years.

Hayes, thrilled with his discovery of the spring, began studying the old Spanish land grants. To his amazement, he discovered that there were hundreds of acres in the heart of the city as yet unclaimed. His research led him to believe that it was possible to acquire city land at little or no cost. None too timid, to say the least, the intrepid Hayes moved in and took for himself a full quarter section (160 acres) without asking anyone's permission. He had the land surveyed and mapped and filed his claim, with a description of the perimeters attached, with the office of the City Assessor.

The tract was placed on the assessment rolls, and Hayes received a tax bill in due course, like all other property owners. Strange as it seems, he failed to pay the tax when due. The property was duly sold for delinquent taxes, but Hayes had it bought by a friend who deeded it back to him. This odd transaction made his title all the more secure; who now could possibly dispute his claim? No one did. All rights and title to the tract were now vested in him, and his claim was confirmed by the Van Ness Ordinance, which became law in 1855. Ironically, the original map of the Hayes property was one of the few to survive the fire of 1906. The document, bearing the date of March 8, 1860, is still preserved in the City Recorder's Office.

A Home in the Sand Dunes

When Hayes built his own residence, the big white house, it was the first in his Hayes Valley. He chose a clearing close by the well, near the site of the present Davies Symphony Hall, San Francisco's present-day performing arts building, and dubbed it "Travellers' Rest." The name seemed most fitting for this oasis in the sandhills, the only one for miles about, with only the silent city of Yerba Buena cemetery nearby. Perhaps the cemetery incited jokes about "Travellers Rest," for a short time later Tom changed the name of his wilderness abode to "The Hermitage."

The Hayes residence was a stopping place for equestrians on their way from Portsmouth Plaza, the beginnings of San Francisco, to Mission Dolores. Hayes always greeted visitors himself with the typical Irish hospitality of a Lord of the Manor. As one of his callers kindly remembered, "Hayes' greeting was always warm and sincere. When he reached out and grasped the visitor's hand, it was a feeling the recipient never forgot." The riders always got refreshments and a friendly chat while their horses rested.

With the added complement of German lager beer, the Hayes residence gained city-wide attention. Two newcomers from Germany opened a small brewery in the area of the present intersection of 14th and Valencia Streets, and from that time on there was always a good supply on hand at the Hayes house. On warm days a keg of beer was placed in the well to cool, awaiting the arrival of thirsty travelers. In those days nearly all the residents rode horseback, and the gaily attired *dons* and *senoritas* imbued the procession with a colorful style as they trotted their way through Hayes Valley on their way to Mass at the Mission Chapel.

San Francisco's First Recreation Park

In 1861, Hayes constructed the city's first outdoor recreation park on his property, and it immediately became quite an attraction for the locals. It was a favorite spot for outdoor picnics and other gatherings until superseded by the more sophisticated Woodward

Gardens on Valencia Street in 1866. The area was sheltered by a ring of shrubs and evergreens planted by Tom and his brother Michael. An enclosed pavilion was added later, a practical convenience where young mothers could care for their babies in comfort while the robust fathers and sons played ball and pitched horseshoes in the open park.

In 1863, the Irish threw a rip-roaring celebration on St. Patrick's Day in Hayes Park. Well aware of the Irish vote, the State Legislature in Sacramento adjourned for the day and made their way to the park. Following suit, the San Francisco Board of Supervisors set aside their agenda and took part in the St. Pat's festivities. The Irish were already a power in both state and city politics, and two of the most prominent, Hugh Farley and Edward Dunne, were selected to address the gathering. The platform consisted of a flat-bed dray, decorated with Irish bunting topped by a green banner and bearing the words, "*Eirean Go Bragh.*" The speakers extolled the virtues of the good Saint Patrick, who had brought the Faith to Ireland and had driven out the snakes. They lambasted John Bull and his hirelings and calling for the freedom of Ireland amid ringing cheers.

The day's highlight was an historic hurling match between teams with patriot names: "The Emmets" *vs.*"The Wolfe Tones." Many in the gathering were startled when they heard the clash of sticks and the accompanying uproar in the distance; the hill was soon filled with spectators watching the hilarious combatants. One old-timer was heard to say, "We thought we had seen everything; but the old town will never be the same again."

With the increase in population, Hayes Park became the Hyde Park of California, the stumping ground for upcoming politicians. One of the most noteworthy was Leland Stanford, who campaigned for Governor in the Park. Stanford was opposed by an astute Irishman named John Conness, born in Abbey, County Galway, who ran on the Union Democratic ticket. No doubt Conness would have been elected but for the split in the Democratic Party in which another Irishman, McConnell, was put forward by the Independent Democrats. (Stanford won with 50,036 votes. Conness was next with 32,750, and McConnell a close third with 30,944.)

The City's First Transportation

The increase in San Francisco's population also brought about a strong demand for city land, and as a result Hayes became a man of considerable wealth. His interests next turned toward providing a system of transportation for the growing city. At the time there was only a plank road called "Mission Road" connecting the town with Mission Dolores, plus the trail through Hayes Valley, frequented by the equestrians on the way to the Mission. Another trail led over the hills from the plaza by way of Polin Springs to the Presidio. A committee was formed with Hayes as President, assisted by his brother Michael, a successful real estate man, J.P. Haven, Peter Donahue and Frank McCoppin, later Mayor of San Francisco. The organizers were all men of stature and accomplishment.

In 1860 the *San Francisco Directory* features the following entry:

> This road, incorporated in 1859, extends from Market Street to Mission Dolores, a distance of three miles. The capital is $250,000. The laying of rails commenced June 7th, and the road was completed July 4th, 1860. This enterprise is one of considerable importance to the growth of San Francisco. Real estate has been much more valuable, and the comfort and health of the inhabitants advanced in a remarkable degree. These results, so widely known and appreciated in the Atlantic States are certain to follow in this City from the construction of the Market Street Railroad. President Thomas Hayes, Secretary, S.C. Simmons, Directors, Thomas Hayes, Peter Donahue, Michael Hayes, J.P. Haven, H.A. Cobb, and Frank McCoppin.

Additionally, the work in building the railroad provided much-needed local employment. Its completion stimulated the first land boom in the area. A problem arose in clearing the tracks of drifting sand, which piled up so high at times that the trains sometimes had to be stopped while the tracks were being cleared, sometimes by Tom himself. This problem was eventually solved by planting shrubs and encouraging native growth.

Evidently, it was a most successful undertaking, for the *San Francisco Directory* picks up the story again in 1863 with the following note: "Travel over the Road to and from the Mission,

Hayes Valley and the Railroad in the early days of San Francisco.
[Courtesy of San Francisco Archives in the San Francisco Public Library.]

Hayes Park and intermediate points, since its opening, has been immense and beyond calculation." The railroad's leading carriage was appropriately dubbed "Tom Hayes."

Hayes: a Man for all Seasons

Nor was the railroad Tom's only contribution to San Francisco's planning. When the residents of the western part of the city stared out their windows on that fateful morning in the year 1906, they well might have thanked the old pioneer that their homes had been spared. His vision in planning the spacious thoroughfare called Van Ness Avenue (whose breadth is exceeded only by Market Street) prevented the flames from reaching the opposite side. Van Ness had been designed under the direction of Hayes by the Dublin-born engineer, Jasper O'Farrell.

Besides his many contributions of time and property to the City and State, Hayes served as Captain of the National Lancers, a military company in the perilous days of coping with rough-riding vigilantes. Fully committed to upholding the law under any circumstance, he put his life on the line many times in preserving order. On one occasion, he guarded the jail against an impending vigilante attack. He rallied his men and stood guard all night to hold off the raging mob. In later years he bore the title of Colonel in the State Militia.

In 1852, Tom Hayes was elected to the Board of Aldermen, forerunner of the present Board of Supervisors, and served as County Clerk from 1853 to 1856. He was Chairman of the Committee appointed to prepare the City's first charter, which paved the way for the all-important Van Ness Ordinance of 1855, which clarified property rights. The names of Tom and his brother Michael grace the timeworn pages of the Society of California Pioneers, of which Tom became a member in 1854 and Michael in 1868.

Known to his many friends as "Old Hickory," Tom was affectionately described by his associates as hospitable, sincere, generous, and a true friend, as well as a man possessed of great wit and a princely disposition. His untimely death came as a shock to his relatives and friends and to the citizens of his beloved San Francisco.

The Passing of Tom Hayes: His Legacy

Tom Hayes died a bachelor on June 23, 1868. His will made provisions for a several trusts to benefit his father, who was still living, and for other kin. The rest of the estate was left to his many other nieces and nephews, kept in trust until they came of age. Besides Michael, who accompanied Tom to San Francisco in 1849, Tom had two other brothers, Timothy and John, and also two sisters, Margaret and Hannah. Timothy lived in Rosedale, New York for some time before he came to California, engaged in farming near the present city of Livermore, and died in 1901. John came to California some years later and acquired land near Redwood City; his place later was named Hayes Ranch. He died in 1903. Margaret lived with her father in Rosedale, New York. Hannah married John Fitzgerald and also lived out her life in New York State.

The will, dated May 29, 1868, was written in Tom's own handwriting. In light of the value of the estate and the number of relatives involved, it is almost inconceivable that both Tom and his attorney would have felt at ease with such a hastily prepared document. It may have been only a temporary measure, drawn up on the spur of the moment because Hayes was scheduled to go to the Democratic Convention shortly thereafter. The will was filed in Probate Court on August 18th, 1868, by the executor, Henry F. Williams. For one reason or another, probate dragged slowly through the courts and the settlement was still unfinished when the executor died in 1903.

Hayes' wealth was estimated at a quarter of a million dollars, no mean figure for those days. What became of it all, no one knows, for most records were destroyed in the fire of 1906. A copy of the will was recovered by an heir living in New York and was admitted to Probate under the Lost Instruments Act. A niece, Katherine Hayes Allen, living in Sacramento, filed a petition in Probate Court many years later (1931) on her own and others' behalf. However, her claim was denied.

Tom passed away aboard ship on his way to New York to attend the 1868 Democratic Convention. His body was returned to San Francisco for burial in Calvary Cemetery at the base of Lone Mountain, close to where he spent his carefree days in the big white house amid the sand dunes.

In an expression of the sympathy and sorrow of the people of his adopted city, the San Francisco Board of Supervisors adopted the following resolution:

> *Whereas*: the remains of the late Colonel Thomas Hayes are to be interred in this City on the 27th day of March inst.;
>
> *And whereas* Colonel Hayes was one of the earliest and most active and useful of the pioneer residents of San Francisco, having arrived here in July '49, and having at once made San Francisco his home, and having continued until his death, encouraged and helped to build up all its material, moral and educational interests, and having always displayed an exceptional hospitality and charity;
>
> *And whereas* as he was from the earliest times, employed in many offices in this City of honor and responsibility, commencing with a Deputy Sheriffship, under Colonel Jack Hayes, having been County Clerk for two terms, and

President of the Charter Convention of this City, which paved the way for the Van Ness Ordinance and the Consolidated Bill, and other public benefits.

Whereas: in all his official acts, he sustained the character of an upright, honest, and honorable officer and whereas, he was assistant Board of Alderman in the year 1852, which was one of the progenitors of our present Board of Supervisors.

Now, therefore, in consideration of the premises, it is hereby resolved by the Board of Supervisors of the City and County, that a vote of sympathy, respect and condolence be passed by this body upon the death of the late Colonel Hayes, and that a copy of this resolution be presented by the Clerk to his afflicted Family, and that this Board attend his funeral in a body, and wear the usual badge of mourning for thirty days.

Adopted unanimously
by the Board of Supervisors
on March 21, 1870.

(*signed*)

Thomas H. Selby, Mayor
Winkle, Harold, McCarthy, Ashbury, Badlam, Story,
Strader, Adams, Canavan, Kelly, Flaherty
Jno. A. Russell, Clerk

Sad to say, the Valley and the Street which bear Hayes' name today stir up few historical memories among the Bay Area's millions. Although the man and his many accomplishments have been largely washed from memory by the swift river of History, nonetheless, the pioneering achievements of Irish-born Tom Hayes can never be separated from the greatness which is California.

James Stephens, cofounder of the Irish-American Fenian Brotherhood, which inspired agitation for Irish independence against the British even in the gold fields of California.

18

The Fenian Rebels of the Mother Lode

In 1859, high upon the eastern ridge of Sun Mountain, a new community called Virginia City was in the making. A Virginia native nicknamed "Ole Virginny" had discovered a rich vein of placer gold and thereby inspired the town's geographically puzzling name. Irish influence abounded on the Comstock and in Gold Country towns (Irishtown, Irish Hill, Irishmans Bar), and the Irish predominated among Virginia City's foreign-born prospectors and laborers. Not only were the Celts the most numerous, but also the most vocal and best organized. Each mining camp (such as Carson City, Austin, Silver City, and Gold Hill) boasted some kind of Irish organization: either the Irish Benevolent Society or a branch of the Fenians. The Fenians were a revolutionary association of Irish patriots, devoted to freeing Ireland from British rule. They proudly borrowed their name of *Fenians* from that heroic band of legendary Irish warriors who rallied around King *Finn* and his son Oisin.)

Ireland's fight for independence and the problems of Anglo-Irish relations have involved America continuously from its own beginnings. After the English drive to colonize North America, the Irish and other oppresed colonists united in common cause to free themselves from subservience to the British Parliament. English propaganda to the contrary, this alliance of the Irish (on both sides of the Altlantic) and other Americans became even more tightly knit during the 19th-century Fenian movement and the American Civil War. It ultimately led to Ireland's Easter uprising of 1916.

Background of the Fenian Brotherhood

In 1858, the militant Irish Republican Brotherhood was organized simultaneously in both Ireland and America by such survivors of the Irish struggle of 1848 as James Stephens (its founder in Ireland), John O'Mahony (its American founder), Charles Kickham, and Jeremiah O'Donovan Rossa. The American "Fenians" were supported by the Irish-American group, the *Clan na Gael*.

The Fenians were led by remarkable men. John O'Mahony, an Irish founder of the Young Ireland movement, had fled his native Ireland after the failed 1848 Ballingarry uprising, sojourned in Paris' revolutionary republican climate, and next embarked for America. O'Mahony's chief objective was to assist in raising regiments of Irish-American Fenians modeled after the American militia system. Another Fenian leader, Major Thomas Sweeney, a U.S. Army veteran, was appointed Fenian Secretary of War. And West Pointer Charles Teevan served as Fenian Adjutant General. Such capable officers guaranteed that the Fenian organization was disciplined and well-coordinated.

The insurrectionary specter of the Fenians alarmed the British authorities. The thought of an Irish-American army functioning openly in the former English colony shook the very foundations of the British Empire. *The London Times* bluntly expressed its fears: "No Irishman could have invented such a scheme, no Yankee would ever have believed in it, but put American exaggeration and Irish credibility together and you have Fenianism." British fears were amply confirmed with the opening of the Fenian Congress in Cleveland, Ohio in 1866. *The Cleveland Herald* detailed the Congress' anti-British pro-Irish independence manifestoes, and the story made its way westward into the columns of the *Sacramento Union*, much to the delight of the California Fenians.

The American-Irish Fenians' plans were temporarily derailed by the Civil War. Yet they found themselves at an even greater advantage when the war ended; for the war had provided the Fenian organizers and sympathizers valuable military experience, plus the gratitude and good will of the American government. Indeed, President Lincoln did nothing to dampen their spirits, knowing only too well that the Union needed the spirit of the fighting Irish within its ranks.

When the American Irish saw that their ancient English antagonist across the Atlantic was opposed to the Union cause, they were motivated to enlist for the North by the thousands. Throughout the war, the Fenians were an army within an army; they openly organized their own military formations within those of the Union army itself. The eventual victory of the Union forces, composed of large numbers of Irish, was a great boost for the Fenian patriots. In their own eyes, and in the eyes of many Americans, the Fenians were patriots and heroes.

With added determination, the Fenians now began their anti-English agitation where they had left off at the start of the Civil War. Toleration of their activities during the war and their purchase of military supplies afterward (not to mention the benign silence of the American authorities) led Britain to suspect an official approval of the Fenians' cause. Blatantly, Thomas Sweeney, held the dual ranks of both Union Army Major and Major General of the Fenians. Furthermore, Sweeney provocatively led a Fenian delegation to Washington requesting war materials from then Secretary of War Edwin Stanton. To counter the expansion of Fenianism in the United States, British Lord Russell took the initiative and lodged a complaint with the American government. Russell's warning seemed to fall on deaf ears in Washington.

Anglo-American relations had deteriorated considerably during the Civil War. Secretary of State William Seward used the opportunity to express the Union's bitterness toward Great Britain that was prevalent at that time. The breach was widened when the Secretary appeared at Irish gatherings, supporting the repeal of the English Act of Union which had forcibly 'united' England and Ireland as one nation ruled from Great Britain.

Britain was frustrated in its attempts to stem the tide of the Fenian movement by curbing American cooperation; she was forced to act on her own. Secret British agents were dispatched to America, and eventually they succeeded in infiltrating the Fenian movement. The British government became even more alarmed when it learned of a bold Fenian scheme. The Fenians were planning to seize English ships in American ports, divert them for an invasion of Canada, drive the British out, and unite Canada with the United States. England realized that this was no disorganized Irish peasant revolt when it discovered the huge Fenian arsenal.

The Brotherhood's Acting Secretary numbered the Fenian Brigade at 8,000 enlisted men, with 15,000 rifles, 16,500 accoutrements and 120,000 pounds of ammunition. Fenian William Roberts spent a fortune to cache weapons in depots with sympathizers along the Canadian-American border between St. Albans and Oswego. Sacks Harbor was home to 2,000 stands of arms, while Platts Point played host to 1,200 more—in all, some 20,000 rifles. Another Fenian contingent claimed to have 15,000 sabers, huge stocks of ammunition, and a vessel in New York harbor.

The English diplomats at first found the American Johnson administration slow to halt the Fenian plan to invade Canada. Their disappointment was evident in an article in *The London Times* of April 26, 1866:

> Mr. Stanton, Secretary of State, would let the Fenians make war how they pleased and even give them help. Such is the bitterness toward England.

The Fenian Invasion of Canada

The Fenian invasion began on June 1, 1866, a year after the end of the Civil War. Col. John O'Neill led his Fenian army across the Niagara River into Canada, tore down Fort Eire's Union Jack, and replaced it with Erin's Green flag, an act that stirred 50,000 more Irish to volunteer for service. However, a naval task force under Captain Bryson prevented Fenian reinforcements from crossing the river to support O'Neill's advance, and President Johnson issued a proclamation against the movement. Undaunted, O'Neill managed to rout the besieging Canadian militia, but upon being informed of the advance of British regulars, O'Neill prudently ordered a retreat back to the United States on June 3. The Fenian attack on Canada had failed, but the incursion had contributed a tremendous boost for Fenian morale. This bold Fenian band's expedition roused the confidence of the Brotherhood throughout America and Ireland.

The Fenians of the Comstock

The boldness of the Fenian organization on the American Eastern seaboard galvanized its Fenian counterpart in the West. Virginia City Fenians had organized back in 1864, paving the way to establish a California statewide Brotherhood in 1866, the year of the Fenian invasion of Canada. California Fenians displayed militant patriotic utopianism in resurrecting the ancient spirit of Finn's warrior band. The first Fenian convention was held in Gold Hill on May 13 of 1866 with delegates from Virginia City, Carson City, Austin, Unionville, and other mining communities in attendance.

Irish miners and Fenians from Virginia City on the Comstock. The California Fenians were organized around 1864.

What stirred up the Comstock Fenians? James Stephens (1825-1901), one of the Fenian founders and chief organizers, had only recently escaped from jail in Ireland, a feat acclaimed in both Ireland and America. Born in Kilkenny City in 1825, Stephens as a young man had joined the Young Ireland Movement and was wounded in the last battle at Ballingarry in 1848. A report of his death was circulated, and his friends carried out a mock funeral. This ruse enabled Stephens to escape first to France and then to America. He gave up a promising journalistic career in the United States in order to channel his energies in founding of the Irish Republican Brotherhood with the aid of John O'Mahony, Michael Doheny, and Colonel Corcoran of the Fighting 69th New York Regiment.

In 1859, Stephens had returned to Ireland, where he worked to duplicate his success. Stephens was a born organizer, and by 1863 he had firmly established the Fenian movement in Ireland, England, and Scotland. With John O'Leary, Charles Kickham, and others, Stephens founded a Fenian movement newspaper called *The Irish People.*

But what this intrepid Irish revolutionary feared most, "the informer," struck again. Stephens was arrested and thrown into jail, and his Fenian newspaper suppressed. He was arraigned before a magistrate on November 15, 1865, but staunchly refused to make a case or recognize English law in Ireland: "I have employed no lawyer on this case and I mean to employ none because in making a plea of any kind, I should be recognizing English law in Ireland—I defy and despise any punishment that could be inflicted upon me." (Stephens refusal to recognize the English court encouraged similar defiance during the later so-called Black-and-Tan War of 1919-22.)

Before Stephens could be brought from prison to trial, a fellow Fenian by the name of John Breslin carefully planned and carried out his escape. As a hospital steward in Richmond jail, Breslin was able to obtain and copy a key to Stephens' cell. With this the Fenian opened the door to his freedom. Stephens' escape was most humiliating to the English constabulary, who offered a thousand pounds for his capture.

Now imagine the news of the Fenian leader's escape reaching the California gold mines! A spontaneous celebration erupted. A torchlight parade was staged on May 18, 1866. This march proved to be one of the most spectacular events in the history of the Gold Rush.

At 8 o'clock in the evening, as the red flame of the setting sun went down over the hills, some three hundred Virginia City Fenians fell into line and marched south on C Street, the main thoroughfare. Overhead, a shower of rockets and fireworks blazed. The Comstock had never witnessed such excitement. The Fenians crossed the Divide on their way to Gold Hill to join the local chapter.

The Fenian torchlight procession that flowed through Virginia City and Gold Hill resembled a river of fire. The defiant crowd marched to the musical accompaniment of the Metropolitan Band, which played "The Wearing of the Green" so raucously that it drowned out the cheers of the multitude. There they were joined by members of the local Fenian chapter, who redoubled the parade's enthusiasm. The marching throng shook the hills without letup and then reversed its direction for the return journey to Virginia City. As the parade neared the head of the ravine, a deafening roar of cannons shook the rustic battlements of old Fort Homestead as a greeting to the Fenians. Then the cheering crowd set off yet another pyrotechnic display to light the night skies.

As the procession entered Virginia City once again, the main street assumed a carnival atmosphere, with colorful decorations and Irish-green bunting. As it passed the Delta Saloon on C Street, Jimmy Malone turned up the lights. This revealed a magnificent transparency above a picture of the Goddess of Liberty, who carried an Irish flag and sat atop a prostrate British lion, with a broken chain in her left hand. The picture's legend read:

IRELAND AS SHE SHOULD BE

Malone's neighbor, the Adriatic Saloon, not to be outdone, burned a row of candles behind a transparency which bore the following legend:

JAMES STEPHENS...

HE IS COMBATTING THE SAME ENEMY IN IRELAND

THAT WASHINGTON DID IN AMERICA

Other signs displayed similar sentiments:

ENGLAND:

PIRATE OF THE SEAS, ROBBER ON LAND!

IRISH REVOLUTIONARY BROTHERHOOD... PIONEERS OF REPUBLICANISM IN EUROPE

THE FENIAN BROTHERHOOD WILL SOON WRITE ROBERT EMMET'S EPITAPH.

The speakers' platform was set high on the second story of the McLaughlin Building, where a tumultuous crowd gathered for an hour of speechmaking. One of the main speakers was the Honorable Judge James Meagher, a member of the Virginia City chapter of the Fenians. After James Murphy of Gold Hill had spoken, another strong supporter of the Fenians, Col. Charles Sumner, though not Irish, took the podium, as did Attorney William Woodburn. Woodburn, though not a member himself, added fuel to the Fenian fire by wishing the order every success He enthusiastically supported the planned Fenian invasion of Canada, which he hoped the Irish revolutionaries would conquer and make part of the United States.

Twelve days later, on June 1, 1866, local Fenians would have renewed cause to celebrate because of the Fenian invasion of Canada. (Word of the invasion, however, did not reach the mines until June 6th.) The news provoked another celebration on the Comstock, and it instigated a milder sort of invasion at the local level. Fenians from Virginia City, Gold Hill, and other camps paraded down Gold Canyon to Dayton for an evening of revelry. They began by firing off rifles, power blasts, pistols. They beat on anvils, rattling cans, blowing horns—anything and everything to celebrate the long-awaited battle with the British. It was enough to make old John Bull shake in his hobnailed boots. Things started getting out of hand when the fired-up celebrants began making bonfires out of piles of lumber. Some concerned bystanders notified Dayton's Volunteer Fire Department. Soon horses, pulling pumpers

Thomas James Clarke, patriot-martyr. The link between Irish Fenians and the cause of Irish independence during Easter, 1916.

and hose carts, came galloping to the scene with bells jangling. But once the fire laddies realized the patriotic reason behind the conflagration, they set aside their gear and themselves joined the celebration. Soon the firemen were drinking toasts to the Irish. It was only a matter of time before Fenians and firemen, merchants, and miners broke out into song, and they kept it up for the better part of the night. Most made it home, while others passed out and slept it off in the sagebrush. The *Territorial Enterprise* version of the celebration ended on a happy note, "All quiet on the Carson front by all accounts."

The American Fenians & Shamrock Power

In retrospect, even though the Fenian expedition into Canada was not a military success, it was, nonetheless, a great moral victory for the Brotherhood in both America and Ireland. Win or lose, the Fenians had succeeded in fielding an army. They had marched right into Canada to challenge the might of the British Empire. This blatant incursion, in utter contempt of the British authorities (and, upon reflection, without much common sense), did encounter belated interference from the American government. The year of the Fenian invasion, 1866, was, however, an American election year. The Johnson Administration was plagued by the problems of Reconstruction, and though it reluctantly moved against the Fenians, it mightily feared of losing the Irish vote. Since the Democrats were courting the Irish vote at the same time, neither party desired to risk the wrath of the Shamrock.

The Fenians relished their political position. They had previously won the good will of most Unionists because of their heroic role in the Civil War. Now they could easily succeed in portraying England as the common enemy.

The Inspirational Legacy of the Fenians

The tale is longer, but suffice it to say that the Fenians had won a great moral victory that would inspire Irish nationalism for generations. The efforts of Isaac Butt (of Co. Donegal) in reviving the cause of Repeal against the Act of Union reflected this spirit, as did the work of his successor, Charles Stewart Parnell. Parnell, prevailed in uniting Fenians, peasant, and parliamentarians in a coalition that eventually broke Anglo-Irish control of the land.

The legend of the Fenian movement, one of the most daring attempts to rescue the Irish homeland from British control, is colorfully related in the stirring ballad, *The Bold Fenian Men*:

Oh see who comes over the red-blossomed heather,
 Their green banners kissing the pure mountain air,
Heads erect, eyes to front, stepping proudly together,
 Freedom sits throned on each proud spirit there.

While down the hills twining,
 Their blessed steel blades shining

Like rivers of beauty they flow through each glen;
From mountain and valley,

'Tis Liberty's rally,
Out and make way for the bold Fenian Men!
Side by side for the cause have our forefathers battled
Where our hills never echo'd the tread of slave.

On many a green hill where the leaden hail rattled,
Through the red gap of danger they marched to their grave.
And we who inherit
Their names and their spirit

Will march 'neath the banners of Vict'ry then,
All who love Saxon law,
Native or Sassenach must
Out and make way for the bold Fenian Men!

Both the Irish and the American wings of the Fenian movement carried on the torch of Irish freedom and independence handed down from the nationalist struggles of 1798 and 1848. After their abortive Canadian invasion of 1866 and their later Irish uprising of 1867, the Fenians kept alive the flame for 50 years until the Rising of Easter, 1916. For example, the flame passed to Tom Clarke (1858-1916), who was born the year the Fenians were founded, went to America in 1879, joined the *Clan na Gael,* and returned to foment revolution in Ireland. His mission failed and he was imprisoned for 15 years. After his release in 1898, he married Kathleen Daly, a daugher of a Fenian leader, helped revive the Irish Republican Brotherhood (which led to the I.R.A), and prepared for the Rising. He fought at the Post Office during Easter Week and was executed in 1916. The martyr Tom Clarke was thus a living Fenian link in a chain of Irish and American events that led to Irish independence.

The Fenian saga also involved the innovative use (from 1861-1915) of public funerals for the Fenian dead to fan the flame of freedom and nationalism. The first such burial in 1861 honored Young Irelander, Terrence Bellew McManus, who had escaped from political prison in Tasmania and settled in San Francisco. McManus' coffin was conveyed from San Francisco to Dublin, where his funeral procession was larger than O'Connell's 14 years earlier. Fenians like McManus and Clarke, in different ways, helped: "God Save Ireland!"

James Concannon (1847-1911), founder of the Concannon Vineyards in Livermore, California. [Courtesy of the Concannon family.]

19

The Concannons: California's Gaelic Vintners

For the Irish, history is usually stranger than fiction. Imagine the implausibility of an immigrant Irishman like Jim Concannon (1847-1911) founding a thriving California wine dynasty! But such a Gaelic vintner's saga is a sober reality. The traditions established by the patriarch Jim Concannon and his ingenious family have set their roots in California as firmly as the sturdy vines that flourish in the rich loam of San Francisco's East Bay, the sun-drenched Livermore Valley.

Over a century of development in California and the Livermore region, in particular, has borne witness to the vitality of this closely-knit Irish-American family, the Concannon clan. This togetherness is reflected in their relaxed and amiable dispositions in a family portrait taken on the front porch of their residence in the year 1870. The Concannons' winemaking enterprise was no ordinary achievement in pioneer days, when suitable cuttings had to be selected, packaged, and shipped from far distant Europe, which took months to reach California.

In the competitive art of winemaking, the Concannon name and label have become distinguished, and they have been bolstered by more than a hundred years of quality wine production. Today this meticulously groomed vineyard nestled between rolling hills offers a pleasant respite to the eyes of many a tired motorist traveling from the inland California plains to the San Francisco Bay area. These luxuriant Livermore vineyards are in marked contrast to the pioneer James Concannon's stark birthplace on Aran Island, a wind-blown rocky region of Ireland where grass existed only in small patches and grapevines only in grand imaginations.

The Aran Islands: Home of the Concannons

The first known inhabitants of the Aran Islands were the half-legendary "Firbolgs," who settled there in the dim mists of time before 200 B.C. and built immense fortifications, some of which still stand. Shortly thereafter (by historical standards) the islands became the cradle of monastic Christianity. The three islands (Inishmore, Inishman, and Inisheer) were the center of the early Irish church and the venerable refuge of the saints of old. Saint Enda came to Aran in 483 A.D. and established the first monastery. His school became famous not only in Ireland, but in Europe as well, at times attracting as many as 3,000 students. Many eminent Irish saints of the 5th and 6th centuries served their novitiate at Saint Enda's, and the Islands became known as "Aran of the Saints."

In 546 A.D., Aran was declared an independent state by the kings of Ireland, and it continued to flourish for a full millennium, until the Tudor Queen Elizabeth put an end to its sovereignty in 1557 and granted the islands to Sir John Rawson of Athlone. The Lynches of Galway took possession in 1650, only to have the islands besieged by a fleet of 2,000 Cromwell's soldiers. Under the leadership of one Robert Lynch, the gallant defenders held out for more than a year until they were offered acceptable terms.

The islands were eventually forfeited and most of the buildings and churches torn down to make way for a massive Cromwellian fortress. A portion of the fort was set aside as a concentration camp for 'Papist' priests captured on the mainland, who survived on a subsistence allowance of sixpence a day, each and every day a battle against starvation, and no prospects of a reprieve.

These rugged Aran Islands stand out in majestic splendor, rising in terraces from the shoreline to the towering cliffs, a kaleidoscope of serene beauty on clear days and awesome grandeur in stormy weather, changing color at will according to the season and time of day. When visiting the islands for the first time, the stranger steps back into another world and era: climate-hardened natives dressed in homespun garments and speaking a strange language known as Gaelic, which was common to all of Ireland before the strangers came. It's a place where time stands still as people live out a life little changed from that of their forebears of centuries long gone. On certain days the visitor can observe a vanishing way of life, as weather-beaten fishermen head out to sea in frail *curraghs* (boats made of canvas bound on a wooden frame), similar to those used by their hardy ancestors. These native fishermen reflect the spartan atmosphere in their attire: gray tweed trousers, white homespun vest, fluffy knitted cap, and rawhide shoes.

The Concannon Ancestral Home and Roots

According to the ancient Irish chronicles known as the *Annals of the Four Masters*, the ancestral home of the Concannons was in County Roscommon, from whence they were driven during the English conquest in the second half of the 17th century. The Livermore, California branch of the Concannons' was first noted in the picturesque village of Spidal in County Galway. From there they relocated to the Aran Islands where James the founder of the Concannon Winery was born. A James Concannon married Mary O'Flaherty, who bore him two sons, James and John. John moved to Inishman (the middle island), married and had two sons named Peter and James. James married Margaret, the daughter of Jonathan O'Flaherty, who bore him thirteen children. One of the thirteen, named Patrick, married Mary Meagher, and they had five children, one of whom was the previously mentioned James (Jim) Concannon, founder of the Livermore Vineyard and century old Winery. James was born on Saint Patrick's Day in the year 1847 in Inishman, where he lived until 1864, when at the age of 17 he set out for America. Like most Aran lads in the early 19th century, Jim Concannon grew up near poverty and with little formal education. The only instruction he received was from an itinerant teacher who conducted classes outdoors in the shelter of stone walls when the weather permitted or in his parents thatched cabin when it was too cold or stormy outside. What he did learn however, he used to good advantage during the ensuing years in his many and various exploits in both the United States and Mexico. Besides Gaelic, the language of his forefathers, he studied and mastered both English and Spanish, in the following years.

Concannon in America

It was a tremendous change in many ways from the remoteness of Aran and a parochial way of life to the bustling City of Boston and the attendant charisma of the New World, but the youth took it all in stride. Much to his delight, Concannon found the great city home to thousands of his countrymen, who like himself had fled their impoverished homeland in search of freedom and opportunity. There was "bread and work for all," as the song goes, but the intern adjustment proved awesome in every aspect and presented a challenge to even the stout-hearted. James was overly concerned as he beheld young Irishmen, many in their teens and men advanced in years, working their hearts out in stifling factories, warehouses, and weather beaten docks to eke out a marginal existence. At that same time he made up his mind that he wanted no part of this degrading environment, and he determined to venture out on his own, come what may.

As luck would have it, Jim Concannon found work as an employee of the newly established Singer Sewing Machine Company in Boston. Although the wages were not to his liking, he persevered until he earned enough money to take him to Augusta in the State of Maine, where a well-to-do uncle, named Peader, lived. After arriving in Augusta, James found work as a bellboy in a nearby hotel, and he parlayed that lowly job into a position as general manager. His enthusiasm and deportment on the job were so impressive that he was offered a partnership in the business. However, indoor life was never to his liking, and so he declined the offer.

Concannon's love of the outdoors and the freedom to roam at will in a manner reminiscent of his care-free days on rocky Aran was such that he was willing to start all over again in some outdoor occupation. An avid reader, young Concannon was intrigued by the adventurous tales of the California Argonauts and the lure of the broad expanses of the American West. Once he made up his mind to follow in their footsteps, it was only a matter of time and preparation for the precarious westward journey. In the meantime there were more important matters to be taken into account. James was already in love with a young lady named Ellen Mary Lowe, whom he hoped some day to make his wife. By coincidence he was also making plans for a return trip to Ireland unbeknownst to anyone. Despite his American good fortune, Concannon was homesick for his native Aran, rocks and all. He revelled in the very thought of it many times a day and dreamed of it at night while he slept. His main concern was that if he went to far-away California he might never again have the opportunity to visit his beloved Aran. The solution was quite obvious; he brushed aside any thoughts of the westward journey for the time being and concentrated on his return visit to Ireland and the placid isolation of the rocky islands.

A Trip to Ireland and Aran, Concannon's Birthplace

Concannon had by now acquired an American Yankee's business acumen which propelled him to higher office in the city of Augusta. He was able to use this shrewdness to good advantage upon his return visit to Aran. The first thing that caught his eye was a bumper crop of potatoes which were only a glut on the local market with no means of disposal. To transform this difficulty to his advantage, James went over to the Irish mainland with the determined goal of finding a market for the surplus potatoes. He was heartened to discover certain areas where the tubers were in scant supply and inhabitants even anxious to acquire an amount suitable to their needs. Concannon hurried back to Aran to spread the good news and help make arrangements for shipping the surplus crop to a ready market. It was a joyous occasion for the natives when the first *curragh* (boat) crammed with potatoes set out for the mainland. This was followed by others in quick succession. For Jim Concannon, who departed Aran as a raw-boned and illiterate youth of 17 years and returned home an astute merchant prince, it was a dream come true. The Yankee deal put money in the Islanders' pockets and partly reimbursed Jim for the expenses incurred in his negotiations.

Following this brief stay in Aran, James returned to America in high spirits and to Augusta where his Irish colleen, Ellen Mary Rowe, awaited him. Ellen was a native of Castlecomer, County Kilkenny. They had first met following his arrival in the city of Augusta in 1864. James and Ellen were united in marriage in

Augusta, Maine in the year 1874. As part of their honeymoon the newlyweds journeyed across the prairies and over the mountains to begin a new life in the great American West. What a life it turned out to be! A career that epitomized the opportunity of the American dream in all its embellishments. It was an adventure that spanned a period of some 36 years, one that involved Jim Concannon in sheep herding in the uplands of Oregon, initiating the rubber stamp business in both California and Mexico, pioneering wine making in California, and implementing sanitation in Mexico City, all the while managing time to father a family of ten robust children.

Westward-Bound

The Concannon newlyweds arrived in Oregon following an adventurous overland trek. At first James engaged in sheep herding for a period on the vast western ranges. Like most Irish, people accustomed to the intimacy of family and friends, the young couple found the sparsely populated territory far too lonely and decided to seek a more desirable environment. Soon they were on the move again destined for the booming Gold Rush city of San Francisco, where they found things much to their liking. For Jim in particular, who had acquired a delicate constitution, the equitable climate and bracing air was a welcome respite from Maine's extremes of hot summers and freezing winters. He had a particular rapport with outdoor life and began selling books from door to door, in the employment of Anton Roman, the publisher of Bret Harte's delightful works. In book selling he found no quick fortune and decided to look for something better.

The rubber stamp business had made its debut on the East coast where the new invention found a ready market. Jim Concannon was quick to foresee the unlimited possibilities of a gadget that had already proved its worth in other areas and negotiated an exclusive franchise for the San Francisco Bay region with the Shipley Rubber Stamp Company who pioneered the product. Concannon first worked the stores and offices in San Francisco, which proved such a success that he branched out taking the whole Pacific coast from the Canadian to the Mexican border and from the Rocky Mountains to the Pacific. He serviced the vast territory by whatever transportation was at his disposal: by train, stagecoach, horse and buggy, horseback or on foot. He even ventured into Mexico where the rubber stamp was something unheard of. During this time he learned to speak Spanish as he went about, and his fluency enabled him to inaugurate the rubber stamp business in Mexico, which by all accounts proved to be more lucrative than California. With his new-found wealth, he returned to the family residence in San Francisco Mission District to share his joy and new prosperity with his wife Ellen and their growing family, which already numbered two sons and two daughters. Convinced that the city was no place to rear the children, James next set out on his own in search of country property. His favor fell on the sunny Livermore region in San Francisco's East Bay, where land was to be had at a reasonable price. He purchased 47 acres of prime land for $1,200, which included a small cottage into which Jim moved his wife and family. Some years later he acquired additional acreage adjacent to the original property. Concannon's fluent Spanish won him close contact with the *Californios* and he quickly acquired a working knowledge of the art of viticulture. As a result of more study, following his return to California, he came to the conclusion that both the soil and climate of the Livermore Valley compared favorably with those of the celebrate winegrowing region of Bordeaux in France. Concannon garnered the attention of the University of California which assisted him in more advanced studies of grape growing and winemaking. Over a period of time he imported only the choicest vines from the Burgundy and Sherry regions of France and planted them in his Livermore ranch. This systematic planting gave birth to a winery that was destined to become famous. Concannon received more encouragement from the Reverend Joseph Alemany, the first Bishop of California, who sought an adequate supply of sacramental wine to meet the needs of a growing Church. The Bishop's difficulties with the English language were no problem for Concannon who spoke fluent Spanish, and this common language helped to cement their lifelong friendship.

Concannon's Sojourn in Mexico

Many years are needed before a vineyard can reach the productive stage and begin to repay the owner. In the meantime, however, Concannon, had to provide income for his growing family. To free up his own time, Concannon brought out his brother Martin from Aran, instructed him in the art of grape growing, and placed him in charge of the infant vineyard while he himself returned to Mexico.

Besides his involvement with winemaking, evidently Concannon had other important ventures in mind. When Jim first went to Mexico City, he found that the streets were being cleaned in medieval fashion, each merchant or householder cleaning only the zone in front of his entrance. Concannon made his way to the seat of government and requested an audience with the city officials and presented his proposal to sweep the streets in a modern manner that would insure them a clean city at all times. After examining the proposition the Mexican officials decided to abandon the old ways and give the zealous Irishman's modern mechanical street-sweeping system a try. To the delight of all the inhabitants this new system proved so successful that it changed the face of the picturesque Mexican capital and greatly enhanced Concannon's reputation. When the opportunity presented itself, he sold the concession to a French entrepreneur at a handsome profit, and went on to pursue his primary objective: the study of viticulture.

Ambassador at Large

During his earlier years in Mexico when Concannon was developing the rubber stamp business, he had availed himself of the opportunity to study the soil, climate, and the growth of the various crops. Now that he was partially free from business cares, he took over where he had previously left off and travelled throughout Mexico to complete his study in the art of grape growing and winemaking. This latest survey, coupled with his experience in Livermore, led him to the conclusion that Mexico ideally suited for viticulture.

At this same time, Concannon caught the attention of the celebrated Mexican dictator, Porfirio Diaz, who saw in him a young man of good character who had already won the admiration of Mexican businessmen. James went directly to the powerful Dictator with his proposition that Mexico could become, by virtue of its amenities, a wine-producing country. Diaz studied the Irishman's prepared report from every angle and eventually granted its approval. Amid considerable fanfare, Concannon was awarded the concession of supplying his choice of grape cuttings to the Mexican growers. The contract specified that he too was given the task of instructing the owners in how to plant and cultivate the vines, for which he was well paid. Of even greater significance, President Diaz dispatched a cavalry escort to accompany the young Irishman, not merely for his personal safety but as much to impress the natives with the national importance of his mission.

At Home in Livermore

To fulfill his contract with Mexico, James Concannon recruited a large crew and put them to work in Livermore to prepare the selected cuttings for shipment to the neighboring Republic. He then dispatched his brother Martin, who had already gained sufficient knowledge of viticulture, to Mexico to oversee the planting and care of the vines. Martin took a particular interest in the model vineyard at Cayala, the hacienda of Senator Senor Raigosa who had close family ties with President Diaz. Cayala soon became the showplace of viticulture in Mexico. With the operations in both new California and old Mexico in the charge of the Concannon brothers, it was a grand day for the "Men of Aran." In the meantime Martin, like his more illustrious brother, also took up the study of Spanish to make easier his communications with his Spanish-speaking employees.

The growth and development of the Concannon operation in Livermore was so rapid that James was no longer able to attend to the rubber stamp business in Mexico. As a result, he sent for a younger brother, Tomas Ban (White Thomas) Concannon, who he learned was whiling his time away doing nothing in particular. James tutored the younger Concannon in the rubber stamp technology and gave him charge of the operation in Mexico. Tomas Ban was to attain notoriety far beyond his dreams on the Irish scene in later years, and the highlights of this story add to the colorful Concannon saga.

Tomas' primary interest was in the study of Irish folklore, legend, and poetry. When he learned that the two patriotic women in Belfast, Ethna Carbery and Alice Milligan, were starting a national magazine called the *Shan Van Vocht*, he became one of its first subscribers. Upon his return visit to Ireland from Mexico, he collaborated with the good ladies in launching a succession of famous cultural *feiseanna* (or feasts), where prizes were awarded for the best dancers, singers, storytellers, and Gaelic drama. With his interest in everything Irish and Gaelic, Tomas contributed most of the funds for its upkeep and promotion. This Irish cultural idea was later promulgated by the Gaelic League, founded by Douglas Hyde, and eventually the movement spread throughout all Ireland. Tomas Concannon gave up a profitable business in Mexico, became the first organizer of the Gaelic League, and founded branches in every corner of the land.

Assessing Tomas' contributions to the revival of Ireland's culture, an Irish publication of the period noted:

> Thomas Ban proved himself to be such a fine speaker, and magnetic exhorter, that the Belfast girls pleaded with him to stay in Ireland, and carry the Gaelic ideals to the ends of the land. He was too valuable an asset for Gaelic Ireland to lose at this juncture. He gave up a lucrative business in Mexico, remained in Ireland, became the first Gaelic League Organizer, carried the message of the League to every corner of Ireland, and everywhere founded branches. Tomas kindled the fire in almost every town and hamlet of the north, south, east, and west nursed it to flame—all but sacrificing his youth, his strength, and his health in the great work.

Since our story more concerns not Tomas Ban's career, we now pick up again the thread of James Concannon's life. Concannon, always a hard taskmaster in his business dealings, was possessed of a soft and tender Irish heart in matters of human concern and he particularly nurtured a love of Ireland and Aran that grew stronger with the passing years. This is borne out in his letters from his home in Livermore, from Mexico, and various parts of America: his constant longing for even a glimpse of rocky Aran. He loved Irish people above all others and loved Ireland with a passion that even his own countrymen could scarcely comprehend. Whether at home or on the road James Concannon carried the latest edition of *The Irish World* newspaper, then edited by the renowned Patrick Ford. Concannon had the newspaper delivered to his home every week so that his children might embrace the Irish spirit and grow up respecting and loving the land of their mother and father. His door and family's hearth was always open and his hand extended to any Araner and Irelander who came their way.

One telling anecdote relates how Concannon dearly loved the Gaelic language. When the family knelt for the recitation of the

Rosary not a word of English was spoken; the prayers were always in Gaelic. Another family story tells of how James took his eldest daughter, Mary (May) to Ireland so that she might be instilled with Irishism and Gaelicism. In Galway, he pointed out the decaying buildings and broken wharfs, saying, "There can be no prosperity in a land ruled by aliens."

At the age of 60 while at home in Livermore James Concannon suffered a stroke and for several days it was a matter of life and death. After a partial recovery, he put his affairs in order with both man and God and then announced with a determined spirit, "I'm going to Ireland." His alarmed family raised strenuous objections and rightly so for a man in his condition about to travel such a distance. The family doctor was consulted and gave his opinion, "If you make such a journey, it will kill you." Concannon answered, "I'm sorry, but I've set my heart on seeing Ireland, and I'll see it no matter what the consequences." The good doctor consoled the frightened family. "He has his heart set on it, it will kill him if he does not go."

Away Concannon went in high spirits. He visited his beloved Aran, walked among the grey rocks and down to the shore to hear again the lashing waves and the crashing sea. His stay in Aran had an invigorating effect on both mind and body. With renewed energy and great expectations James journeyed to Dublin where the Oireachtas was in session and addressed them in Gaelic, the language of his heart's desire. While there, he conversed with Ireland's noblest; Douglas Hyde, Padraig Pearse, Arthur Griffith, Alice Mulligan, and others he had long admired. With joy in his heart and a prayer on his lips James Concannon returned to America and to Livermore to spend his remaining days in quiet repose. He passed away shortly thereafter.

Concannon's life's story bears out the truth that he was a man of strong convictions, sound principles, and high ideals. He said and did what he considered just and right and taught his children to do likewise. He would relate instances of how he met and faced up to situations that he could have avoided by compromising his principles. An example of his integrity was his hair-raising encounter with a gun-toting desperado on his way through Arizona. He had put up for the night in the only hotel in town frequented by cattle rustlers and rowdies of every hue. While he sat in the lobby, in strode one of the wild ones, and let out with an oath: "line up at the bar, drinks are on me." All obeyed as ordered except one, Jim Concannon, who continued reading. That was enough for the desperado, who drew from his hips not one but two guns and descended on the lone holdout.

> "Stranger, did you hear my request?"
>
> "I did."
>
> "And you ain't going to obey."
>
> "I thank you for your invitation. But I'm not in the habit of drinking."
>
> "Then by the Eternal, you're now going to get the habit! Stand up, about face, and march to the bar. Name your p'izoen and then drink it!"
>
> "I thank you. You and your friends can have your drink; but I regret I cannot join you."
>
> With that he thrust the guns in Concannon's face and barked, "Stand up and march!"
>
> "If you're headstrong enough to shoot me because I refuse to drink with you, I'm sorry for both you and myself; but you cannot frighten me into doing what I don't wish to do."

The wild, reckless fellow lowered his guns, shoved them into the holders as the frightened customers looked on, went back to the bar, finished his drink and took off without saying another word.

Jim explained the incident to his children:

> This was not stubbornness on my part, but I felt if other men could make me do things I did not want to do, there would be no self-respect left in me.

Concannon's sense of justice was exemplary at all times even where his own family was involved. When his son Bob committed a breach of rules at Saint Mary's College that called for his

James and Ellen Mary Rowe Concannon with their brood of ten children at the Concannon home in Livermore in 1868.

dismissal the President of the college hesitated to enforce the rule when a member of this righteous family was involved. Instead he sent for the boy's father, and laid the case before him in his office, saying, "Now, I want you to say what I should do."

Concannon replied, "Your rule lays it down, doesn't it, without reservation, that Bob's act calls for expulsion." The President answered, "But in this case the boy is James Concannon's son." Said Jim, "It matters not whose son he is. You have no choice in the matter, and neither do I." And he sorrowfully led the boy out of the school.

James Concannon took life seriously, being careful of what he said and did, both at home and in public. Beneath that grave countenance beat a warm Irish heart ever ready to extend a helping hand for those in need. His legion of admirers acknowledged that California had not known a man more honest and dependable than James Concannon. Honor was his guiding light which endeared him among businessmen in both California and Mexico. They said of him, "No written, legal contact was ever more valued by us than James Concannon's simple word." In all his life he was never known to wrong a fellow man, nor use a fellow being solely for profit.

It is of little wonder that when he passed away, at the age of 64, the Livermore Valley became one vast mourning chapel. Concannon's end came following several strokes which sapped his strength and muted his speech. But apparently the strokes did not diminish his intellectual ability, as he continued to discuss family matters and to put in writing things that had previously escaped his attention. It was a happy ending too for the Aran boy who had lived life to the fullest, surrounded by his loving wife Ellen and all of his ten children except James when the end came. Funeral services were held at St. Michael's Church in Livermore where the family worshiped over many years. A requiem high mass was celebrated by Father Power, a close friend, assisted by Father Riordan of Livermore and Father McAuliffe of Pleasanton. Honorary pallbearers included old-time residents and family friends: Patrick Connolly, Peter McKeany, John Sweeney, Daniel Murphy, George Beck, Carl and Ernst Wente, and S.C. Mcleod. The attendance at the funeral was said to be the largest ever seen in Livermore up to that time.

The Second Generation

When the old patriarch James Concannon died in 1911, the Concannon winery became the property of his five sons in equal shares, as provided in his will. All of them except Joseph received a college education, no meager achievement in those pioneer days. Joe, anxious to see a bit of life before he settled down, enlisted in the U.S. Cavalry as a buck private in 1909 at the age of 26. Like his illustrious father who aspired to do all things well, Joseph worked up through the ranks to Captain, a title he retained after his return to civilian life. To all his old friends in Livermore, he was always "Captain Joe."

Joe was inducted into the army at Fort Columbia, Washington. Upon completion of his basic training he served with the 33rd Coast Artillery at Vancouver Barracks and then with the Field Artillery at Camp Kearney. Under Lieutenant (later General) George Patton, he took part in the Mexican-American conflagration (1915-16), commanded by General John J. (Black Jack) Pershing, the famous World War I hero. The Concannon family diary contains several letters from Pershing and Presidents Roosevelt and Truman addressed to Captain Concannon. At the behest of General Hershey, the Director of the Selective Service System, Captain Joe served on the Selective Service Draft Appeal Board headquartered in San Francisco, without pay during World War II.

Following the old patriarch's example, his wife Ellen assumed the dual role of family confidante and household guardian. She apparently had negative feelings about the military as a way of life for any of her sons. While Joe himself took great pride in his army career, he was shunned by the other members of this closely knit family clan. After much persuasion, Captain Joe acceded to his mother's wishes and returned to Livermore to help his other brothers in the general operation of the winery. Robert, a graduate of Santa Clara, took charge of the planning and day-to-day operations, while also serving as wine master. Joseph, the outgoing one, was placed in charge of public relations.

All went well at the Concannon winery until the coming of Prohibition in 1920. The anti-drink legislation so devastated the family business that four of the five brothers decided to seek other employment. Ironically it was Captain Joe, the prodigal son, who had the tenacity to stick with the winery, come what may. He bought out the other brothers' interests and took over as sole owner of the Winery. Fortunately, he received help from his brother-in-law, Carlo Ferrario, who owned a nearby winery. Later Joe married Nina Ferrario, Carlo's sister, who had come from Italy to live with her brother after their mother passed away. Joe Concannon and Nina were married in St. Michael's Church in Livermore, where both families, the Concannons and the Ferrarios, worshiped. Four children were born to them, one of whom they named James after his illustrious grandfather. James is now the owner and general manager of the renowned Concannon Winery.

The young couple, James and his bride, began life together in "Ravenswood" the former home of San Francisco politico Christopher (Blind Boss) Buckley, a choice area of Livermore. In 1921, this property reverted to the Redemptorist Missionary Order, which converted the ornate residence into a retreat house named Villa San Clemente. The former Buckley estate is now a city park and the big house, a museum.

The Concannon Winery never ceased functioning even during Prohibition, and today it claims the distinction of being the oldest winery in California in continuous operation. The Concannon altar wines, a favorite since the days of Bishop Alemany, found a ready market among the Catholic and Episcopalian clergy, whose loyalty kept the winery in business during the long dry period of Prohibition. Bishop Sweeney, of Honolulu, a protege of Bishop Alemany used Concannon wines almost exclusively in his Diocese. However, despite their support and that of other Christian communities, it was not enough to sustain the Concannon enterprise and Captain Joe found it necessary to seek other sources of income.

Fortunately for Joe a new industry was in the making where coal was discovered earlier an Irish engineer, Francis O'Byrne, while mapping a route for the San Francisco-Stockton Railroad. With an eye to the future Joe began investing in farm land and stock raising to meet the needs of the coming coal miners and their families. Over a million tons of coal were extracted from the hills within a few years, and the profits from the sale of meat and produce to the workers helped sustain the Concannon family enterprises until the repeal of Prohibition in 1933. When repeal came the Concannons were strategically positioned in the American wine market. They had on hand one of the largest inventories of wine in the entire state.

It was a day for rejoicing when that first shipment of California wine, bearing the Concannon label, cleared the Golden Gate, December 5, 1933, on route to Seattle, Washington.

The Distaff Side

All the Concannon girls did well, particularly May (Mary) the oldest daughter, a red head, and the apple of her father's eye. May was highly educated, and took her first position as a schoolteacher at the age of 18. She gained nationwide attention for her work in the Junior Red Cross which resulted in her being solicited by the University of California to accept an distinguished position. On orders from Washington, she was later sent to the Philippines and was installed as an administrator. She travelled all over that country by muleback or on foot, devoting her time and talents in the establishment of schools and clinics. It was only in later years that the word got around that many of her former pupils had become doctors, nurses, teachers, priests, and nuns. When Miss Concannon departed the Philippines, she turned over all the funds collected and the management of the various institutions which she had helped to establish to her former pupils. In later years, she flew all over the globe in her capacity as International Director of the Junior Red Cross. She was feted and wined and dined in world capitals and at home by Earl Warren, the then Governor of California and later the Chief Justice of the Supreme Court, who paid her a special tribute on behalf of the State and Nation at the time of her death.

The Third Generation

When Captain Joe Concannon died in 1965, his two sons, Joseph Jr. and James, took over the winery as equal partners. Joseph was educated at Notre Dame University where he became acquainted with Father Theodore Hesburgh, its affable President. In later years, when Father Hesburgh later paid a visit to his former pupil in Livermore, he was presented with a rare Moselle Concannon wine as a momento of his visit. Joe too, had made it big in his own field, much to the delight of his former teacher and mentor. A chip off the grandfather's block, Joe was recognized as one of the most knowledgeable and progressive viticulturists in the state of

California. Joe Concannon took the lead in research and development of a wide variety of choice vines and fine wines, and he served with distinction on the Board of the California Wine Institute. His great work, however, was cut short by his untimely death of cancer in 1978. His passing was deeply regretted by the people of Livermore and his many friends throughout the State.

The Concannon mantle then passed on to his younger brother, James, who was equally dedicated to preserving the Concannon name and tradition of winemaking. Besides his knowledge in the arts of grape growing and winemaking, James excelled in human relations in dealing with employees and their families. Within five short years, he organized a cohesive group of workers who shared a common goal with management in operating the Concannon vineyard and winery. For years, Jim, as he is affectionately known to all, provided a luscious Thanksgiving banquet for the workers and their families as a gesture of his personal friendship.

For each succeeding generation, and especially for the current proprietor, Jim Concannon, the Winery has been a way of life as much as a business enterprise. With an eye to the future, while also revelling in the past, he proposed setting aside land for a regional conglomerate: a perpetual vineland preserve for all aspiring viticulturists and wine-lovers, "the fruit of the land."

The 100th Anniversary celebration of the Concannon Winery in 1983, held in cooperation with the California Historical Society, was a milestone in the history of Northern California and the bountiful Livermore Valley in particular. As part of the festivities, a tour of the historic winery was conducted by Jim Concannon himself to stress the importance of the occasion.

The ornate Concannon residence built in 1883 is now a California Historical Landmark and a mecca for tourists and history buffs. A weather-beaten cider press, in use from 1894 to 1974, stands as a memorial to the hardy pioneer James Concannon who braved the wilderness in search of opportunity in the American West. The cellar also houses two huge casks (*circa* 1883), which are still in use. These vintage casks were shipped in an iron-bottom freighter around the Horn from Bordeaux, France to California. If these old relics could only speak, what colorful tales they could spin of this enterprising Irish clan that figured so prominently in the history of early California!

ESTATE BOTTLED

Concannon

1981

LIVERMORE VALLEY

SAUVIGNON
BLANC

GROWN, PRODUCED & BOTTLED BY
CONCANNON VINEYARD, LIVERMORE,
CALIFORNIA, U.S.A. ALC. 12.5% BY VOL.

Jasper O'Farrell (1817-1875), an Irish founding father of San Francisco.
[Courtesy of the Society of California Pioneers.]

20

Jasper O'Farrell
Father of San Francisco

O'Farrell as City Planner

Jasper O'Farrell (1817-1875), the Dublin-born engineer, was an Irish pioneer who quite literally shaped much of Northern California, and especially the San Francisco Bay Area. It was O'Farrell who conceived and designed the original plans for one of the world's major cities, San Francisco, queen of the Pacific. O'Farrell laid down his surveyor lines in a wilderness of drifting sand dunes and brush covered hills. Despite the difficulties, he improvised a plan in harmony with the rugged terrain, a plan that is unique among world cities.

As a man of creative vision, O'Farrell foresaw a bright future for San Francisco and predicted it would become the empire city of the west. That O'Farrell was indeed a man of clear vision and forthright judgment is borne out in his 1847 letter to his friend Abel Stearns in Los Angeles. He prophesied: "I have no doubt of it [San Francisco] becoming one day, and not very distant, the Empire City of the Pacific."

In keeping with his prediction, O'Farrell drew a map of a 110-foot-wide boulevard on a diagonal swath from the waterfront (the site of the present Ferry Building) to the bottom of Twin Peaks and thence to the settlement at Mission Dolores. For this prophetic and unorthodox design, he received the princely sum of $300. The San Francisco coffers were evidently skimpy in those pioneer days, for the contract which O'Farrell drew up in his own handwriting agreed to survey any number of city lots at $5 each. It read:

> To George Hyde, Esq.
> Alcalde or Chief Judge of San Francisco
>
> Sir:
>
> I hereby agree to survey lots of one hundred varas square each on and adjacent to the Southern boundary of the late Survey on that part known by the name of the Rincon. Establishing corners to each lot 8e8e. The number of lots to be one hundred or more if required. The whole to be executed in a satisfactory and proper manner at the rate of five dollars $5.00 per lot. To be paid as soon as the Survey is completed or within twenty days thereafter.
>
> I am, Sir, very Respectfully,
>
> Jasper O'Farrell, C E
>
> San Francisco, June 12, 1847
> The above approved
> George Hyde
> Premier Alcalde

From the information about O'Farrell that has filtered down from those early years, we can be sure of one thing: he was no fortune-seeker. Being the only qualified surveyor in San Francisco at that time according to the *San Francisco Examiner*, he certainly could have demanded much more for his services.

O'Farrell's Irish Background

The O'Farrells, "Princes of Annaly," were of pure Irish Melesian stock. A noble chieftain named Aughaile ruled over a vast Irish territory for many years, and from his rule it became known as the land of *Aughaile,* later anglicized to "Annaly." Aughaile's grandson, Fearghail, a courageous warrior, led his clansmen to victory under the banner of Brian Boru at the decisive Battle of Clontarf in 1014. He so distinguished himself that all of his descendants were called "*O'Fearghail,*" anglicized "O'Farrell." The name, with slight variants (like Farrell, O'Farrell, or Farley) is still flourishing in their ancestral territory, known today as County Longford.

Jasper O'Farrell was born in the old-world capital city of Dublin in the year 1817, where he resided until he reached the age of 24. He studied engineering in his native city, and upon finishing received an appointment as a member of an English surveying expedition that set out for South America. The company began the long journey in 1841, and after a harrowing passage around Cape Horn reached their destination on the west coast of the South American continent. This assignment lasted almost two years. Afterwards, young Jasper set out on his own to Mazatlan, Mexico where he readily found employment with a U.S. survey crew. This American expedition sailed north and set anchor in the old pueblo of Yerba Buena (San Francisco) on October 14, 1843.

It was a sleepy little hamlet that greeted the 26 year-old Irishman when he stepped ashore on that sunny afternoon. The only signs of life came from the little Mexican settlement nestling between the hills, which came into view as the old rigger rounded Telegraph Hill and anchored in the sheltered cove. This inner portion of the Bay was filled in with land some years later and forms the site of the present financial district in downtown San Francisco.

Shortly after his arrival, O'Farrell secured employment with the Mexican government, conducting extensive surveys in both Marin and Sonoma counties and putting to good use his previous experience with both the English and American survey expeditions. When California became a part of the United States in 1850, he continued his work under American jurisdiction.

For his services, O'Farrell was granted one section for every twenty he laid out, under an agreement with Thomas Larkin, United States Consul at Monterey. He discovered that large areas in

Sonoma County lay between the boundaries of the Spanish grants, and he delineated these in sections according to the American method. His old survey drawings still survive in county records and constitute the basis of present-day land titles.

The year 1846 ushered in many changes as American influence took hold. The first belligerent clash between the Americans and Mexicans was the colorful month-long Bear Flag Revolt (June 10-July 9, 1846). On June 15, the insurrectionists proclaimed a California Republic and raised a crudely designed flag with images of the bear and star upon it. The revolt's accomplishments were quickly overtaken by news of the outbreak of the Mexican War, which ended on January 13, 1847, when Governor Pio Pico accepted the terms of surrender given by General John Fremont. The terms of the treaty were in accordance with President Polk's desire for peace and conciliation. In 1848, Mexico ceded California to the United States under terms of the Treaty of Guadalupe Hidalgo which brought a lasting peace between the former antagonists.

Jasper O'Farrell seems to have been involved in at least one of these early military actions, according to a brief in the *Pioneer Register and Index*. In 1844, Captain John Sutter organized an expedition of two companies with O'Farrell as quartermaster. The little army marched the long trek to San Fernando, engaged in battle, and returned home after an armistice was declared in 1845.

Washington Bartlett became the first *Alcalde* (Mayor) of San Francisco under American rule, and one of his first acts was to commission a land survey for the little town. He sought out O'Farrell, who was on an assignment in Marin County, and hired him for the job. O'Farrell based his survey work on an 1839 drawing by Frenchman Jean Voight. Voight's original plan had covered only a very small area, roughly bordered by Dupont (Grant Avenue), Broadway, California and Montgomery Streets. In studying the Voight plan, O'Farrell quickly discovered that instead of crossing at right angles as intended, the streets were skewed more than two degrees. His first chore was to correct the error. This change became somewhat affectionately known as "O'Farrell's swing." Fortunately there were few houses there at the time, and the realignment created only minor disturbances.

O'Farrell's next assignment was to survey San Francisco's beach and submerged water lots around the half moon from Telegraph Hill to Rincon Point. This extension of city property had been granted by order of General Stephen W. Kearny, then military governor of California, residing in Monterey. The growth of the community, coming on the heels of the Yankee invasion, required more land development. It was now that the youthful engineer conceived an unorthodox plan which forever would set him above his peers.

O'Farrell's greatest triumph will always be his design of San Francisco's Market Street, a broad avenue bisecting the city at a diagonal angle, and from which all other streets radiate. He laid out Market Street as a broad avenue intersecting the city and opening up a direct route to the Mission Dolores settlement. This plan avoided the usual checkerboard or "grid" design, so that the streets north of Market followed the contours of the hills, and the streets to the south ran parallel and at right angles to the main artery. The San Francisco *Examiner* lost little time in paying tribute to O'Farrell, "There is little need to speak of surveyors since there is only one—O'Farrell," and the paper's tribute continued:

> Those early settlers who plotted Market Street as a broad line showed rare prescience. Most cities came by their artery by accident, but Market Street was laid out to be the city's axis, convenient as a road from which all other streets radiate. It's a street that should be honored, for it will ever be the main stem of San Francisco, the hub of the city from which other streets spring as the branches and foliage..

Not everyone was pleased with O'Farrell's survey, however. Citizens became irate when they discovered that the O'Farrell Plan cut through their property. A meeting was called in a warehouse on Kearny Street, to which O'Farrell was invited, to explain the new layout. It developed into a boisterous affair, with the most vocal participants accusing the engineer of wanton disregard for their property rights; some even cried, "Lynch him!"

O'Farrell sensed the explosive situation and made his escape, with the help of a friend, out the side door. He fled to North Beach and took a boat to Sausalito on the north side of the Bay. From there he made his way under cover of darkness to his retreat near San Rafael, and remained in the country until things quieted down. One by one the disgruntled property owners had a change of heart, and came to the conclusion that the new plans would benefit all in the long run. O'Farrell then returned to the city and, without further uproar, the plans were adopted. The man some people were ready to lynch became their hero.

Heartened by this public support, O'Farrell decided to devote his career to surveying. His shingle adorns the time-worn pages of the old *Californian,* San Francisco's first newspaper. It reads:

Jasper O'Farrell

Civil Engineer and Land Surveyor

By Appointment of Colonel R.B. Mason

Governor of California

Office Portsmouth Square San Francisco

How Bush Street Got Its Name

The extent of the work of mapping such an extensive city area proved too much for one person; Jasper was obliged to seek an assistant. His search uncovered many prospects, but none with professional experience. Finally he engaged a man named Bush, a New Englander who seemed to have jumped ship in San Francisco. Bush assisted O'Farrell for some time without any mention of payment by the latter. Enough was enough, and Bush finally confronted his employer and demanded, "Who is going to pay me, and when?"

"Don't worry! You'll be taken care of," O'Farrell answered.

The following morning, he approached his assistant. "Mr. Bush," he said, "You have been a good worker and a friend. Unfortunately, I can't pay you in cash; but how about something more rewarding—I'm going to name a street in your honor!"

Bush exclaimed, "You are?"

"Yes, I am!" O'Farrell replied.

And that's how San Francisco came to have a Bush Street. Incidentally, Bush Street runs nearby and parallel to O'Farrell Street, named for the Dublin engineer.

Building a Home

Besides his work in laying out the streets of San Francisco, O'Farrell made several a surveys in Marin County. One of his major projects in the latter county was mapping Nicasio Township, for which he acquired a parcel of land of almost 9,000 acres, which he in turn exchanged for land in Sonoma County near Sebastopol. One of his first acts was to name his Sonoma estate Annaly, the title of the ancient Gaelic patrimony of the O'Farrells in County Longford. He settled down, in this secluded domain, to the life of an Irish country gentleman, surrounded by family and friends. It was then that O'Farrell's kindliness and boundless generosity became known to all. The O'Farrell homestead was a mecca for the many who had no homes or incomes of their own. Through the Annaly portals passed friends, neighbors, and strangers and none went away empty.

In 1845, Jasper married Mary McChristian, a daughter of Patrick McChristian, a pioneer who came from Ireland directly to California. McChristian, a man of strong build, was no slouch to say the least; the two-fisted Irishman took an active part in the Bear Flag Rebellion. Some years later, O'Farrell and his father-in-law joined William Leary, Sam Morris, and Jacob Leese in a mining venture, and apparently struck it rich, making a combined profit of $75,000 within less than six months. However, profit or no, O'Farrell quickly tired of the mines and returned alone to his beloved Annaly in Sonoma.

It appears that all of those early Irish adventurers, without exception, had one thing in common—an abiding love of home, family, and friends. When Jasper settled down in Sonoma County, he brought out from Ireland his widowed mother, Mary O'Farrell, who lived with him and his family until her death in 1869. The close family relationship of the Irish is reflected in a letter from Mrs. O'Farrell to her son during his convalescence in a hospital. (Although a robust individual by all accounts, Jasper nevertheless

The home of Jasper O'Farrell, Annaly, near Sebastopol in Sonoma County. [Courtesy of the Society of California Pioneers.]

spent a considerable period in recuperation at the time this letter was written):

> March 21st
>
> My dear Jasper,
>
> We were anxiously looking forward to your letter, all glad to hear you were so much better.
>
> I hope to God, you will continue to improve and that you will be particular to take care of yourself.
>
> We were all very much amused at your description of your room at the hospital and am not surprised at one night giving you enough of it.

I hope you received the note from Mary enclosing the advertisement from the "Alta" office concerning some children that would be given to some charitable person, who would take them and bring them up. Perhaps you could take the boy and girl, they could be made useful here in a short time. You will be a better judge when you see them.

Mary says it would be well if you brought a package of good vaccine and get all the children done. Small Pox is very prevalent in Tabor Tapold.

I hope you will be home soon. We feel very lonely. Mimo says bring home plenty of candy.

The little fellow is walking now and quite pleased with himself. If not coming home, write soon.

Your most affectionate Mother,

M. O'Farrell

This letter from mother to son suggests how close-knit and caring the O'Farrells were. Yet despite this togetherness, they were willing to share their home with others less fortunate. Concerning children who had been thrown into the world with no home of their own, "Perhaps you could take the boy and girl," she wrote. "You will be a better judge when you see them."

A Successful Career

One of O'Farrells most important and earliest assignments was the surveying and mapping the proposed town of Benicia. This project was the brainchild of Robert Semple better known as Chairman of the first California Constitutional Convention, in 1849. Benecia made history when it became the State Capital in 1850. It was originally called "Francisca," but the name was changed so as not to confuse it with San Francisco. Incidentally, both names, Francisca and Benicia, were adopted in honor of Francisca Benicia

Vallejo, the wife of General Vallejo. In connection with the foregoing, a letter written by O'Farrell to Abel Stearns in Los Angeles is of particular interest:

Abel Stearns, Esqr.

Dear Sir:

I hope you have escaped all misfortune during the late troubles in your part of the country. Previous to the war breaking out, I wrote you and hope you received my letters. I have to repeat to you my thanks for the trouble you have taken in regard to the papers of my farm; however, I am all right, having purchased Berryessa claim.

I have got some extensive surveys to make here, particularly in the vicinity of the bay. I am now laying out the city of San Francisco and another city on the straits, named Francisca, belonging to Gen'l. Vallejo and Dr. Semple, to which I wish to attach a map of the whole bay with soundings. I remember having seen a survey of the bay with you, I therefore write to solicit a loan or a trace of this from you. I shall take care of it and at the same time obligate myself to return a finished map of the bay and adjacent county to you. By having that will save me the trouble of a survey; therefore you can judge the favor you will confer by letting me have it. If I can be of any service to you this way, you will please command. I am sorry my expedition to the north was not earlier—it should have been had I known the turn of affairs.

I am, Dear sir, yours respectfully,

Jasper O'Farrell

P.S.- You can give the map to Capt. Libbi or Smith, who will bring it to me.
June 12/47

After receiving a reply from Stearns, Jasper wrote again:

Abel Stearns,

Dear Sir:

I have to acknowledge the receipt of your favor of the ninth of April ulto. together with the accompanying map of the bay, for which allow me to return my thanks. I shall, as soon as I have time (being now rather pressed) make you a finished copy.

I have been so engaged as not to be able as yet to make a survey of your claim at the Mission, but I shall at the end of this week do so and act as you direct in every respect.

You have no idea of how fast the town, or rather city, of San Francisco is improving—houses springing up in every direction, wharfs being built, etc., etc. I have no doubt of it becoming one day, and that not very distant, the Empire City of the Pacific. Every day brings fresh arrivals from the Sandwich Islands—men of respectability and capital. The Pukes and Hoesers have given way and are as usual retiring before civilization. I have just completed the survey of a new city at the Straits of Carquinez—Dr. Semple and T.O. Larkin, proprietors.

I think if you would divide your land here in lots of from one hundred to fifty varas, you could sell them at an advantage. I shall do it by hearing from you. The town authorities are having lots surveyed as far as Mission Creek. one hundred varas square, the most of which and they are disposed of as soon...some have sold as high as one hundred dollars, and I...no doubt but that I co...get at least the...price for every one hundred varas lot where your land is situated.

Let me know your opinion of this, and believe me yours truly and respectfully,

Jasper O'Farrell
San Francisco
July 12/47

Again a brief note with no date:

Abel Stearns Esqr.,

Dr. Sir:

I have located your claim at the Mission and shall send you the corresponding documents in a few days.

If you feel inclined to dispose of the property by informing me to that effect and letting me know the price in money, I will, if not unreasonable, become the purchaser.

I am respectfully,

Jasper O'Farrell.

Besides his engineering practice, O'Farrell engaged in the cattle business as early as 1849. To protect his herd from the cattle-rustling, so prevalent in those days, he had his branding iron registered in Southern California as well as at his home grounds in Marin County. The certificate as recorded in the town of San Rafael reads:

This is to certify that this, the tenth day of April, A.D. 1849, Jasper O'Farrell presented for registry an iron, the figure of which is marked in the margin, which iron was registered in the Book of the City of Los Angeles on the twenty-second day of February 1846. I do therefore by these presents and the power invested in me, give him, the said Jasper O'Farrell, full and sole power to use said iron to brand cattle and horses in the district of San Rafael.
Given under my hand and seal, in my office at the Estero Americano this tenth day of April A.D. 1849.

Manuel E. McIntosh
1st Alcalde, San Rafael

O'Farrell and Captain John Sutter were friends from their first acquaintance. When Sutter contemplated cutting a canal to bring water to his ranch, he sought the advice of his trusted friend in a letter dated August 24, 1844, from Sutter's New Helvetia settlement:

> Mr. Farrell
>
> Dear Sir:
>
> I contemplated cutting a canal from the American Fork to lead the water to my establishment. I wish to commence operations as soon as possible. Before doing so, however, would be pleased that you would make an examination of the premises and inform me what modes would be the most advantageous to make the excavation, probable costs, etc., as I have been informed that you are a suitable person to apply to for such information. If not particularly engaged would be glad you come up as soon as convenient.
>
> Very respectfully,
> Your obdt. svt.
>
> J.A. Sutter.

Man of Integrity

O'Farrell was a man of principle who was disposed to put right before might on critical occasions. One particular example comes to mind in the case of General John Fremont who tried to portray himself as a leader without blemish. Such was not the case according to O'Farrell, who cited Fremont's part in the slaying of three law-abiding Mexican settlers in San Rafael. In his letter to the Los Angeles *Star*, dated September 27, 1856, he states emphatically that Fremont was directly responsible for the callous murder of the De Haro twins and an old man named Jose Berryessa. (The tragedy was widely publicized during the confrontations between foreign settlers and native Californians, an aftermath of the war between the United States and Mexico). O'Farrell's letter stands as testimony to his unrelenting efforts to place the blame where it belonged and to warn the nation of the consequences if such a man became president. (Fremont was the Republican candidate for President running against James Buchanan, a Democrat, and such an indictment was bound to have national implications.) Despite the consequences O'Farrell who had no political ax to grind felt honor-bound to warn the nation even if it meant putting his life on the line. In conclusion, he added: "I must say that I feel degraded in soiling paper with the name of a man who for that act I must always look upon with contempt and consider him as a murderer and a coward."

Despite his condemnation of such a leading figure as Fremont, O'Farrell was elected State Senator for both Sonoma and Mendocino Counties in 1859. He was a candidate on the Democratic ticket for Lieutenant Governor in 1862, but was defeated by the Republican ticket led by Leland Stanford. His defeat was primarily due to the split in the Democratic party. At that time the Democrats were divided into the Breckinridge Democrats (McConnell and O'Farrell) and the Union Democrats (John Conness).

A picture from a daguerreotype in the collection of the Society of California Pioneers shows O'Farrell as a rugged man with long, bony nose, dark, bushy hair and beard and with a challenging look in his Irish eyes. He is holding a rifle, a pistol, with a knife in his belt, but is sitting with a favorite dog's head in his lap. In a much later photo, he seems to have abandoned the frontier image of his youthful days. In its stead appears a well-dressed country gentleman, his side whiskers gone but still retaining the strong mustache and bushy goatee.

O'Farrell's Family

According to Prendergast's *Forgotten Pioneers*, Jasper had several children, one of whom, Gerald, was still living in San Francisco in 1935. Prendergast also mentions John J. O'Farrell as another son. Again, that there were several children is evident in the letter from Jasper's mother to him while he was recuperating in a hospital, which states that Jasper's wife, Mary, "says it would be well if you brought a package of good vaccine and get all the children done." It is known that he had a daughter named Elena (see letter below). Evelyn O'Farrell Dunne of Portland (Oregon), Jasper's granddaughter, never met her famous ancestor as he died before she was born. However, she remembers riding horses on his Sonoma estate when she was a girl, and she keeps a portrait of the old maestro on the wall of her living room in the fashionable district of Portland Heights. Also believed to be a descendant is Sheila O'Farrell Murray of San Francisco.

Although it is well over a century since the youthful surveyor drove the first stakes into the muddy flats of San Francisco Bay, the legend of Jasper O'Farrell never dims. As recently as 1980, in San Francisco's unofficial Court of Historical Review, presided over by the Honorable Judge Harry Lowe, local luster was restored to that raw-boned, bushy-browed pioneer surveyor who plotted Market Street, one of the great thoroughfares of the nation. A host of witnesses—including John Molinari (then President of San Francisco's Board of Supervisors), Arlo Smith (District Attorney), and Bernard Averbush (President of the San Francisco Boosters Club)—enthusiastically lauded the good deeds of their erstwhile benefactor and also highlighted his memory with an account of the important role that the Irish have played in San Francisco's history.

O'Farrell died suddenly at San Francisco's Semple Saloon on Hardie Place off Kearny Street on November 16, 1875. He was having a drink with an actor named McCabe when he collapsed in his chair and passed away before medical help could be summoned. His body was conveyed to the Occidental Hotel, where his remains were surrounded by mourning friends.

In a letter to his daughter Elena, a short time before his death, he spoke of a disastrous conflagration in the mines, concluding with these fitting sentiments:

> Many and many are they who went to bed last believing they were rich who woke poorer than the poorest. Such, dearest Elena, is the evanescent quality of the world's riches. Let it teach us to lay more store, more thought, on the wealth of the next, that once obtained can never pass away.

Little did Jasper O'Farrell know that this was to be his last note to his daughter, kindly words from a loving, God-fearing father. Let these words be the measure of the wise man who wrote them.

James Martin Miller, pioneer land baron of Marin County. [Courtesy of William J. Miller III of Corte Madera, California.]

21

Little Ireland: Marvelous Marin County

Just north of San Francisco, across the Golden Gate Bridge, lies Marin County, "Marvelous Marin" to its residents. Marin is ranked as one of the nation's most affluent regions, a sun-latticed community of palatial homes, vine-covered lanais, swimming pools, backyard barbecues, cliff dwellings, boat houses, and hot tubs. It hardly seems possible that this posh environment was once the domain of hard-working, Irish farmers like the Millers, who came west in search of land and dreams, long before the magic word "Gold!" had been shouted in these parts. However, a map of Marin County land grants recorded by Mexican officials between 1834 and 1846 confirms that the Irish already owned 69,000 acres of range land within rowing distance of the booming Metropolis of San Francisco.

Though our book focuses on detailed biographies of those who brought Ireland to the Golden State, it will be worthwhile in this last chapter to take in a rapid panorama survey of the many Irish who shaped the character and destiny of Marin County before concluding with the saga of one remarkable Irish family, the Millers of Marin, who illustrate the continuity of Irish contributions to California.

Remains of John Reed's original sawmill located in Marin's exclusive town of Mill Valley.

Mill Valley's John Reed & Inverness' James Berry

John Reed (Read) was the first land grantee and the first Irishman to set roots in Marin County. Born in County Dublin in 1802 or 1805, John came to California via Acapulco, Mexico in the year 1826. Reed stepped ashore on the North Bay into what was a veritable wilderness, the habitat of wild animals, birds, and bees. He chopped down trees and built a cabin for himself in the woods, where he lived alone until he met another newcomer, William Richardson, an English sailor. Richardson had jumped ship, smitten, as some say, by the charming *senoritas,* the daughters of prominent Spanish-Mexican Conquistadors who then held sway in *Alta California.* In 1834, a few years after he first set foot in Marin, Reed acquired the *Corte Madera del Presidio Rancho,* consisting of 7,845 acres in the area of the present Corte Madera-Larkspur townships that skirt San Francisco Bay. This transaction predated Richardson's acquisition of the *Sausalito Rancho* on the Marin headlands by some four years, making Reed the first non-Spanish settler to acquire land in Marin County. Reed's ingenious invention of a sawmill powered by water from a nearby creek, the first of its kind in the Bay Area, stands as a memorial to his ingenuity. Today, the aging timbers of the dilapidated old mill in "Mill" Valley are reminders of the primitive conditions that existed in Reed's time and of how he and other early pioneers improvised to create the things they didn't have.

In 1836, James Berry, of Anglo-Irish stock, became the second foreigner to own land in Marin County. His service as Colonel in the Mexican Army earned him an enormous grant of 22,525 acres in two parcels on Tomales Bay (near present-day Inverness) in the *Punta de los Reyes Rancho*. This acreage established Berry as one of the leading land barons of Marin County.

San Rafael's Don Timoteo Murphy of County Wexford

Irish-born Don "Timoteo" Murphy (1800-53) came in a close second to Berry with 21,680 acres in three *ranchos*: the *Santa Margarita*, the *Las Gallinas*, and the *San Pedro*, which included most of the present city of San Rafael and eastward to Point San Pedro on the Bay. Born Timothy Murphy in Coolaneck, County Wexford in 1800, he came to California by way of Lima, Peru, where he had lived for two years. Don Timoteo was in the vanguard of an adventurous troop searching for gold at the end of the rainbow. In 1828, he and 18 of his cohorts stopped off on business in the port of Monterey, the lazy Spanish colonial capital of *Alta California*. Attracted by the quaint old *pueblo* and the charm of its inhabitants, Murphy applied for permission to remain as a permanent resident. The Wexford bachelor showed a liking for the charming *pueblo* by enlisting in the local militia, which protected the town from marauders and ruthless gun-toting highwaymen. Murphy was a leader in stature as well as in name. He looked every inch the fierce Celtic warrior. He stood six feet two in height and weighed in at 250 pounds, with broad features and bushy auburn hair. When questioned about his size, he would joke that he was actually the runt in his family. History is silent about when Murphy left Old Monterey, or his later whereabouts, until he arrived in San Rafael before 1846. He died in 1853 and was buried in San Rafael Catholic Cemetery.

Drawing of Irish-born Don Timoteo's hacienda in Marin's San Rafael.

San Rafael owes its beginning and much of its early prosperity to this huge Celt, Don Timoteo Murphy, who served as its first *Alcalde* (Mayor) and as Indian Agent for all of Marin County.

John Lucas and other Irish Rancho-Land Grantees

Murphy's nephew, John Lucas, who gave his name to Marin's Lucas Valley, was another pioneer who helped mightily in the early development of Marin County. Lucas came to California at the urging of his famous uncle, and eventually he inherited a part of Murphy's fabulous real estate holdings, which included the 7,000 acre *Santa Margarita Rancho*. Lucas himself was born March 12, 1826, in the Parish of Edermine, County Wexford. He travelled directly by ship to California in 1852 to live with Murphy in San Rafael until he took possession of the above property in 1856. Lucas married Mary Sweetman, his childhood sweetheart from County Wexford, who bore him six fine children. Lucas went on to carve a niche for himself in California's history.

John Cooper, yet another Irishman, settled in Marin County on lands adjacent to John Reed's farm. Cooper held the 8,895 acres of the *Punta de Quentin Rancho* around today's San Quentin.

John Martin, a seasoned Irish farmer, arrived shortly after Cooper in search of land and he negotiated the purchase of the *Corte Madera de Novato Rancho,* in northern Marin County, comprising 8,878 acres.

Surprisingly, these Irish land acquisitions occurred at a time when the Mexican authorities frowned on *los extranjeros* (strangers) and foreigners, with few exceptions: notably the Irish. No doubt the cordial relationship that had long existed between Irish settlers and both the Spanish conquistadors and Mexicans grandees was a major reason for the hospitable exception. One typical example was that of the previously mentioned Irish-born John Reed, who secured a 7,845 acre land grant from the Mexican authorities a dozen or more years before California came under American rule.

After becoming a Mexican citizen, John Reed sought the hand of Hilarita Sanchez, the charming daughter of Senor Antonio Sanchez, Commandante the San Francisco's Presidio. In 1836, the handsome couple got married at the historic Mission Dolores adobe chapel. Reed's Irish mother sent the couple wedding presents from Ireland, and Reed regularly corresponded with Irish relatives. He died in 1843, was buried in San Rafael Cemetery, and left four children.

John Keys of County Fermanagh

Another Irishman connected with early Marin was John Keys. Keys struck it rich in the gold mines in less than two years. He then wisely invested his new-found wealth in Marin land in 1850, the year that California became a state. With the help of local Indians, Keys cleared the land, planted the first crops, and built the first house in what was then a wilderness.

A native of County Fermanagh, Keys had earlier set out for America at the invitation of an uncle who lived in New York State. When news came that gold had been discovered in far-off California, Keys was one the first to brave the uncertain journey to seek his fortune in the mines. Before doing so, however, he invested his savings in merchandise, sold it a hefty profit in San Francisco, and then headed for the mines. Following a successful mining adventure, Keys then returned to San Francisco with the thought of engaging in merchandising. But he changed his mind and went to Marin County. His favor fell on the quaint Bodega Township where he settled and took a lease on the nearby Smith Ranch. There, in 1851, he planted a crop of potatoes, which flourished in the sandy soil of Bodega Point. When the crop matured the following autumn, Keys hired field hands to harvest the tubers and get them ready for market. In the meantime, he purchased a barge, loaded it with spuds, and towed it across the Bay to the San Francisco waterfront. The potatoes were grabbed up by the hungry settlers who were willing to pay unheard-of prices for any kind of food.

On one of his round trips, John Keys found a scenic place that matched his Irish dreams on the ocean front near the present community of Tomales. He moored his craft, went ashore like the legendary Robinson Crusoe, but found not a creature in sight. He shouted at the top of his voice, but all he could hear was his own faint echo in the distance. In high spirits, Keys went into the nearby woods, retrieved some saplings for markers, and staked his claim in the accepted western manner.

Somehow word reached Keys (since he was evidently well known in those parts) that claim-jumpers had removed his markings and intended to claim his land as their own. Undaunted, Keys set out again for Tomales Bay, accompanied by a close friend, Alexander Noble, to challenge the intruders if they returned. The claim-jumpers never did showed up, so Keys and his friend restaked the parcel and built a cabin on the property by a running stream that cascaded down from the nearby hills. Their hastily constructed shack was the first house, if one could dignify it as such, in this backwoods district. The flowing stream, called "Keys Creek," discovered by the former miner and onetime potato farmer almost a century-and-a-half ago, continues to bear witness to the area's first citizen and the early Irish presence in Marin County. In that same year, John Keys married Catherine Miller, a daughter of the famous Irishman James Miller, who once owned all of what is today the delightful community of Terra Linda, which lies north of San Rafael on Marin's Highway 101. Although Keys retired from farming, he remained active in shipping until his death on August 14, 1873.

William Roland

William Roland, born April 9, 1835, was still another Irishman who made good in the mines and invested his earnings in Marin County property. With a light heart and a lighter purse, young Roland and three of his friends footed it all the way to the mines in windy and rainy weather. When they arrived in Gold County several days later, tired, hungry, and penniless, they were not in the least dismayed. Roland was the first to venture out on his own and staked his claim at Michigan Flat, a rich vein on the South Fork of the historic American River. As it turned out he could not have chosen a more bounteous location. Before a year had passed, he was able to dispose of his claim at a windfall profit.

After sealing that deal, Roland returned to San Francisco to plan his next move. He soon learned of the flourishing Irish community in nearby Marin County, a bit of the "Old Sod," where the Irish were at home among their own. He was impressed by what he saw and heard, and eagerly purchased 1,070 acres of grazing land near the town of Tomales, where he engaged in dairy farming and stock raising. While still single, he constructed a fine residence on the land with the intent of marrying and raising a family. No sooner said than done: "the farmer takes a wife." Young Roland met and married a nubile lass by the name of Maria Johnson, who bore him five fine children. A successful farmer and family man, Mr. Roland was held in high regard by all who knew him and by others whose lives he had enriched. To show their appreciation, the grateful citizens elected him to high office as a member of the Marin County Board of Supervisors in the hectic days of the Civil War.

Irish Settlers: The Nortons, Irwin, Manning, & Buchanan

The Irish Norton brothers, Eugene and Patrick from County Roscommon, were also examples of successful farmers in fertile Marin County. Patrick shipped to California by way of Nicaragua in 1858. He acquired a minor holding, by California standards, of 147 acres, which he creatively cultivated to yield more per acre than other more extensive operations. Eugene, the other Norton brother, had immigrated to America in 1850, and moved on to California in 1864. For a brief period Eugene lived with his brother Patrick in Tomales until he managed to save enough capital to invest in land that was to his liking. The timing was opportune for the fortunes of the Norton brothers. This was a period when land was being made available in the amount of 160 acre parcels to all qualified settlers when California became a state in the year 1850. In Marin County's cradle days, the Norton brothers were numbered among its most successful farmers and philanthropists. Their initiative and industry inspired others less fortunate than themselves.

Another Irishman in early Marin was James Irwin, a native of Belfast and born in the year 1832. He immigrated to America at the age of 19 and at first settled in the East coast port city of Baltimore. In 1853, he voyaged to California by way of Panama, and then journeyed on to San Francisco in the fall of that same year. Irwin moved to Marin County and lived for a period with John Reed at the *Corte Madera Rancho*. He managed to save enough money (with the help of a friend, most likely Mr. Reed) to buy 240 acres, bordering on San Francisco Bay. Irwin then built a house on the waterfront, where he lived with his wife and five children for the rest of his life.

Another successful Irish immigrant farmer to Marin was Andrew Manning, from County Longford. Manning was born in 1831, and came to America as a youth of 17 years. At the age of 22 he arrived in California, about the same time as James Irwin. Like so many of his countrymen, Andy was attracted to sunny Marin, and he likewise settled in the Tomales Township on a 540 acre farm. During one of his visits to San Francisco, he struck up an acquaintance with an Irish girl named Mary Kehoe from County Kilkenny. Following a brief courtship, they married and in quick succession became the parents of nine children.

Irishman John Buchanan was born in County Antrim in 1827. He immigrated to America in 1844 and settled for a time in Pennsylvania. In 1851, he came out to California to mine in El Dorado County, and a year later he returned to San Francisco with his pot of gold. He, too, followed his countrymen to Tomales, bought 350 acres, and spent the rest of his days farming on rolling slopes within view of the Pacific.

James Fallon of County Roscommon

The town of Fallon was the terminus of the old Marin County Railway and was named after Irish-born James Luke Fallon, who came to Tomales in 1859. Fallon was born in 1828 in County

Roscommon and at an early age he immigrated to Boston. Like thousands of other ambitious Irish youths, James was bitten hard by the gold bug and set out as an Argonaut by ship to California via Panama, landing in San Francisco in March 1853. He wasted little time after his arrival, took off for the diggings, and began prospecting in French Gulch in the fall of that same year. Six years spent slaving in the mines earned him an enviable fortune and respect when he returned to San Francisco in 1859.

Like most Irishmen of that early period young Fallon's was land-hungry. He followed the beaten Celtic path to Marin County and settled in Tomales. Here he purchased land and took up dairy farming and stock raising. The Fallon Creamery was one of the most successful enterprises of its kind in the early history of Marin County. In its heyday, the dairy produced an average of 30,000 gallons of milk a day, in addition to copious amounts of butter and cheese. James married an Irish lass named Delia Gunning, and they reared seven children. In later years, Mr. Fallon purchased additional acreage near Tomales, and went on to become one of the largest landholders in western Marin County. His son Tom became a man of high status, and served as Marin County Treasurer for many years. In more recent times, a grandson was elected County Recorder.

John Griffin & George Dillon

John Griffin was a native of County Limerick, who was born in 1830 and came to America while still a youth of 17. For a while, he took up residence in Savannah, Georgia, a city which boasted a large Irish population even before the American Revolution. After five years in Savannah, Griffin set out for California at the age of 22. He took up mining in Mariposa County and carefully set aside his earnings to invest in land. He also chose Tomales, by now a virtual microcosm of Ireland. He farmed in a secluded, sheltered valley which eventually took his name. John fell in love with a blue-eyed colleen named Ellen Malone, whom he had met in San Francisco. They married in June of 1856 and became the parents of six children.

George Dillon, who was also born in Ireland, trekked across the plains to California in 1856 and settled in Tomales Township, where he acquired 906 acres of good farm land. Besides farming and stock raising, Dillon established the first seaside resort in Marin County on

Bodega Bay, which attracted throngs of pleasure-seekers from the booming city of San Francisco. It is still known as "Dillon Beach."

Irish Settlers in Marin's Bolinas

Seaside Bolinas had its business birth in 1849-50, when the huge redwood groves were harvested to make the wharf pilings for the San Francisco waterfront. The denuded lands were then used for farming and stock raising. One of the first of the Irish to settle in Bolinas was David McMullen. Born December 27, 1826 in County Antrim, he came to California in 1856. He purchased 1,850 acres, some of which were still forested; the remainder he turned into a dairy farm. He married Mary McCurdy and fathered ten children.

Next to arrive was Hugh McKenna, another native of Country Antrim. McKenna was born in the picturesque seaside resort of Ballycastle on February 26, 1826, where he lived until 1845. Shortly after arriving in America at the age of 19, he enlisted in the United States Army, and served during the Mexican-American War. Following his discharge in 1848, McKenna briefly returned East to live in Kentucky. On March 1, 1849, he left with other Argonauts for California, where he engaged in mining for some six years, from 1852 to 1857. It was then he went to Marin County, settled in Bolinas among his many countrymen, and became a successful dairy farmer.

Henry Strain was another Irishman who chose Bolinas as his future home. Born in 1826 in County Monaghan, he came to California in 1852. Following his arrival, Strain went to the mines and took up prospecting near Placerville, which was then called Hangtown for obvious melancholy reasons. On Saint Patrick's Day in 1860, Strain showed up in Bolinas and celebrated the joyous holiday with the many transplanted Gaels residing there. He too fell in love with the remote area, where he engaged in business as a woodcutter and purveyor. Strain eventually found a more lucrative gold mine in the nearby hills: covered with live oak, ash and birch, which he chopped down and sold for firewood. At a later date, he acquired 250 acres on the sloping hills and in time became a prosperous dairy-farmer. There was always a plentiful supply of meat and milk for his wife, Marcella Dowd, and their eight children.

San Rafael

San Rafael owes its civic and commercial origins to our aforementioned Gael, Timothy (Don Timoteo) Murphy, whose two-story adobe was the only house in 1850 other than the original mission buildings. Marin was one of the original counties created by the California legislature in 1851. San Rafael was declared the County Seat of Justice, and Murphy's old adobe mud pile became County Hall. During that first winter, it was cold and damp, with nothing to break the chill but a wood-burning stove in the middle room. Mildew permeated the building and the moths fed on the clerks' files. The old adobe was a simple affair in comparison with today's majestic Civic Center, designed by the famed modernist architect Frank Lloyd Wright. All county business fell within the jurisdiction of the court, which assessed properties, collected taxes, set up road districts and election booths, and doled out all county monies. Some referred to the powerhouse court as a miniature Tammany Hall because the Irish received the first political patronage plums. Four roadmasters, James Miller (San Rafael), Timothy Mahon (Novato), William Murphy (Point Reyes), and John Keys (Tomales), were the first appointees under the newly-established county government.

By 1897, San Rafael had 3,500 residents. The Irish, too, had increased in numbers and strengthened their hold on the political machinery. The City Trustees were Edward McCarthy, William Miller, and Stan Moorhead, with William Doherty as Assessor, William Kinsella as Clerk, and John Healy serving as Marshal.

The big daddy of San Rafael was Don Timoteo Murphy, who stood tallest in both physique and legend among the pioneers of Marin County. The tale of his nearly-fatal battle with a brown bear in the San Anselmo Valley is but one of many yarns. While riding through the sheltered valley, Murphy's horse shied, throwing him directly in the bear's path. To save himself, he wound his brawny arms around the beast, wrestled him down by applying his weight of 300 pounds, and pounded a tattoo on the bear's stomach with his knees. At this point his riding companion, one Dominic Sais, joined the battle, belting the bear across the eyes with a leather thong. The combatants rolled over on to a mound, where the bear broke out of Murphy's grip and scampered away. The big Irishman got to his feet, shook himself, and turned in disgust to his friend. "Dominic," he said, "you Spaniards are well-meaning, but never again, as long as you live, get mixed up in an Irishman's fight." Later he confided that the leather jacket he wore, which was shredded by claw marks, was all that had saved him.

Timothy Mahon's "Mahon House," located on a quadrangle, was the San Rafael's first hotel. Already a fledgling politician and landowner, Timothy brought out his brother Edwin from Ireland and set him up in business. Equally ambitious as his brother, Edwin took up the study of law in his spare time and received an appointment first as County Treasurer, then as District Attorney, and finally served as Superior Court Judge of Marin County.

James Donahue, a son of Peter Donahue and the founder of the San Francisco Union Iron Works, built, with the help of another Irishman named Sweeney, San Rafael's first posh hotel and dubbed it "Hotel Rafael." A most elaborate establishment, the hotel boasted more than a hundred rooms and was surrounded by green lawns and shrubs. Tennis courts, billiard tables, carriage houses and stables provided recreation. The hotel became a celebrated landmark and served the community in fine style through the years.

Old Doc McCue, the Water Peddler

Until they came to Marin County, the Irish never had it so good. All were amazed at how quickly they climbed the social and political ladders of leadership. One of these nimble Celtic climbers was James ('Doc') McCue, the father of the County's water system. Doc McCue got his start by peddling water from a spring on his property door-to-door. He first carried the jugs by hand, and later acquired a horse and dray, on which rested the familiar water wagon tank. McCue's contraption caused quite a stir. Water wagons were already in use in the growing city of San Francisco, but they were a novelty in Marin. McCue's flowing well was finally harnessed, and continued as the principal supply until the Marin County Water Company was formed in 1877.

But old Doc McCue had a flair for more exciting ventures than water-peddling. He built a circus compound in Corte Madera on the John Reed *Rancho* and grazed his animals on the hills and marshes around the Bay. On weekends the noisy entertainment brought crowds from San Francisco and other points, and the old water baron retired with the title, "Mad-hat Doc McCue."

In Marin, October the 24th was set aside for the Timothy Murphy Day celebration. A carnival atmosphere prevailed, with bull and bear fights, calf-roping and greased pig contests, and hayrides for the young and not so young. Barbecues filled the air with a pleasant aroma; all ate heartily, with plentiful grog to wash down the victuals. An outdoor platform was erected for dancing. Irish fiddlers, led by Big John Kelly, provided the music, and the well-watered celebrants kicked up their heels to the lively beat.

Tiburon & the Reed Family

The affluent settlement of Tiburon (Spanish for "Shark"), close by the Golden Gate, owes its early development and affluence to John *'Don Juan'* Reed, the County's first English-speaking settler. Reed resided for several years in an adobe house in Marin's Mill Valley, and his daughter, Mrs. Deffenbach, lived there until 1880. From there, Reed moved to the Tiburon peninsula and built a large wood-frame dwelling overlooking the Bay, where he lived in contentment for the rest of his life.

Reed's son John inherited 2,061 acres of his father's estate and constructed the first mansion on the Tiburon Point, where he lived with his wife and two children. Reed's daughter, Hilarita, received 1,466 acres as her share. In 1872, she married Dr. Benjamin Lyford, who built the family home on Strawberry Point. The Lyfords took an active part in community affairs and donated the land for the building of Saint Hillary's Church, which today is an historic Marin County landmark. The first couple married in the newly constructed edifice was John J. Kelly and Elizabeth Gilroy. The Lyford home, which once stood on Strawberry Point, has vanished; the site now serves Marinites as a wildlife sanctuary.

Peter Donahue was largely responsible for the rapid development of Tiburon. Donahue extended his North Pacific Railroad from San Rafael to Tiburon, to connect with ferry boats from San Francisco. The first ferry, "The James M. Donahue," was named for his only son, who died in 1880.

Novato's Irish Gentry

Novato in northeastern Marin County is said, according to one account, to be named after an Indian convert who was baptized at

Mission San Rafael. In those early days it was a creekside town where small craft docked after a run on the bay. Novato then boasted a general store, a friendly butcher in a white-starched apron and bowler hat, and not a few blacksmith shops. But it was a poor town, indeed, until Peter Donahue laid the railroad and built a terminal which became known as the Donahue Station. History was made in Novato when a jovial President named Rutherford B. Hayes (1877-81) strode out onto a platform and tipped his silk top hat to the happy crowd, on his way to the County Fair in Petaluma.

Among Novato's distinguished citizens was an Irishman named John Redmond, who arrived on the scene in 1864. Redmond was born in 1819 and at first immigrated to South America, where he engaged successfully in merchandising. In 1863, he came to California and set out in search of farm land. He acquired a full section of 640 acres west of what was then called "Novato Corners" and began dairy farming. Redmond was said to be one of the most industrious settlers to take up residence in Novato Township. He married an Irish girl named Johanna Walsh, who bore him seven children.

The Twin Cities: Larkspur and Kentfield

Two Irishmen, William Murray and Patrick King, paid $4,500 for 1,233 acres of the area comprising the site of the present cities of Larkspur and Kentfield. A large Silicon Valley computer would be needed to figure out the astronomical sales value of that same area in today's real estate market, with 100-foot lots costing as much as $100,000 and homes averaging well over a quarter of a million dollars. Murray held on to his share and became a wealthy man, while King sold his land to an investment company at a considerable profit. An Irishman named William Costello bought King's home at Magnolia and King Streets, refurbished it, and named the house "Woodstock" after his ancestral home in Ireland.

The Blue Rock Inn in Larkspur was the brainchild of another Irishman, Jim McCormick, who was part-owner of a San Francisco brewery. The inn opened in 1887 and has been a favorite watering hole and feeding trough for generations. The Limerick Inn, too, merits a brief note in history. Every July 14th, trainloads of Frenchmen converged on this Larkspur landmark to celebrate Bastille Day. They came by ferry to Sausalito, transferred to the

Donahue North Pacific Railroad, and were picked up at the nearby station and brought to Larkspur.

Larkspur's first Council election was a stormy one. The more conservative demanded a vote recount when it became known that some polling places had stayed open after hours to accommodate late voters (who presumably had visited the local saloons and who, it was alleged, had voted more than once already). To make their point, the challengers cited a recent San Francisco election in which the largest block of voters in one precinct all lived at one address, which turned out to be a cemetery. The Larkspur recount found nothing questionable, and the first tally carried the day. The results did demonstrate clearly that the Irish were the favored politicians. W.J. Kennedy, J. Foley, James Bain, Frank Craig, and J.J. Murphy were elected Councilmen. The fact that the first session was held in the Lynch building left little doubt as to who was in the saddle.

Sausalito

Tourist-haunted Sausalito originally came into being as a summer town and as a convenient and delightful setting for family gatherings on weekends. The old County Road that led around the water's edge was a pleasant, scenic drive even in horse-and-buggy days. There was neither gas nor electricity, no paved streets or sidewalks, yet nobody complained. The town did have one outstanding amenity: clean, clear spring water, which was ferried over to San Francisco and sold by the gallon. Today this water source is the property of the Mountain Springs Water Company, where it is bottled and sold throughout Northern California.

The Sons and Daughters of Erin in Marin found an eloquent spokesman in Dan O'Connell (grand-nephew of the patriot orator Daniel O'Connell and the subject of an earlier chapter). O'Connell dispensed Irish hospitality at his hacienda in the Glen. As related elsewhere, the Bohemian O'Connell presided over the banquet like a bardic prince while his family served steaming trays of roast beef and venison. Captain Healy, the pilot of a local scow, was a constant visitor at O'Connell's. He charmed other visitors with his melodious voice and danced an Irish hornpipe for a finale.

James V. Coleman, President of the North Coast Railroad, entertained the Sausalito cliff-dwellers with his steam-powered yacht, the *Queen of Sausalito*. The powerful craft churned the Bay to a foamy white and sprayed onlookers like a rain forest when it turned against the wind.

Nicasio

Marin's Nicasio Township was divided into five separate parcels and surveyed by Jasper O'Farrell, the famous Dublin-born engineer who designed the streets of San Francisco. A Spanish Californian from Santa Barbara, Pablo de la Guerra, was granted the largest amount of land, Lots 1 and 5, a total of 30,843 acres. John Cooper acquired Lots 2 and 4 comprising 16,293 acres, while O'Farrell was given Lot 3 in lieu of payment for his services as surveyor. The town prospered when the narrow-gauge railway came in 1870, and the Wells Fargo stagecoach stopped at Nicasio Station to pick up passengers. Irishman James Miller built the town's first hotel and donated land for the building of a new courthouse. A new post office was constructed to meet the needs of a growing community, and here too was conceived the first installment plan for the purchase of land ("A little down and a little per month"), a novel scheme which made it easy to own land.

Lucas Valley

Lucas Valley now forms the site of the fashionable community of Marinwood. John Lucas, for whom it was named, was (as previously noted) Timothy Murphy's nephew and came to California and San Rafael in 1852. Lucas, like Murphy, was born in County Wexford and lived with his uncle in the adobe for a while after his arrival.

John Lucas was himself the son of a fearless hero of the Irish insurrection of 1798, Harry Lucas, who joined the movement at the age of 22. He had fought under brave Father Murphy and was severely wounded by a musket ball which struck his jaw. His agony was great as he lay concealed in the bushes which shielded him from the hated British yeomen who murdered others in cold blood. An old woman, so decrepit as not to attract attention, brought him food in the dark of night. Miraculously, he recovered and his jawbone healed. Harry Lucas lived to a ripe old age and raised an enterprising family which included John, the immigrant to San Rafael.

In 1855, John made a return trip to Ireland to fetch his bride, Mary Sweetman, who was also from County Wexford. He acquired more than 2,000 acres of the Santa Margarita Rancho from his uncle Don Timoteo. He then constructed an imposing residence on the land and settled down to a long and fruitful life. John and Mary were the parents of six children.

An Irish Family Saga: the Millers of Marin

Today's easy-living Californians owe an enormous debt to an earlier era's pioneers, a heroic breed of men and women who risked everything to find a new land to the West. These settlers handed down to their descendants a spirit of "true grit," courageous endurance, and enterprise. Such virtues were notable in the pioneer Miller family of Marin. The Millers are a fascinating example of the contributions made by Irish families throughout California. Irish families, usually unsung by historians, made their communities strong and humane by leading lives of quiet integrity and industry. They reared their children with love and educated generation after generation to take pride in honest work and love of country.

By telling part of the story of one such California Irish family—the Millers of Marin—we can appreciate the continuity of Irish contributions to America made possible by the freedom of California, the Land of Irish Dreams. The enduring and energetic Celtic stamp on five generations of the Miller family remains, as noted by the late historian Florence Donnelly, "indelibly affixed upon Marin County history, geography, its physical development and the pioneering spirit of its people."

The Miller Family Tree

Today in Marin County's town of Corte Madera there lives in vigorous retirement William James Miller III, a fourth-generation Irish American descendant of the County Wexford immigrant family of James Martin Miller (1814-1890), a founding father of Marin County. The Miller family traditions are kept alive by this energetic great-grandson, whom the present author interviewed at his home in Marin.

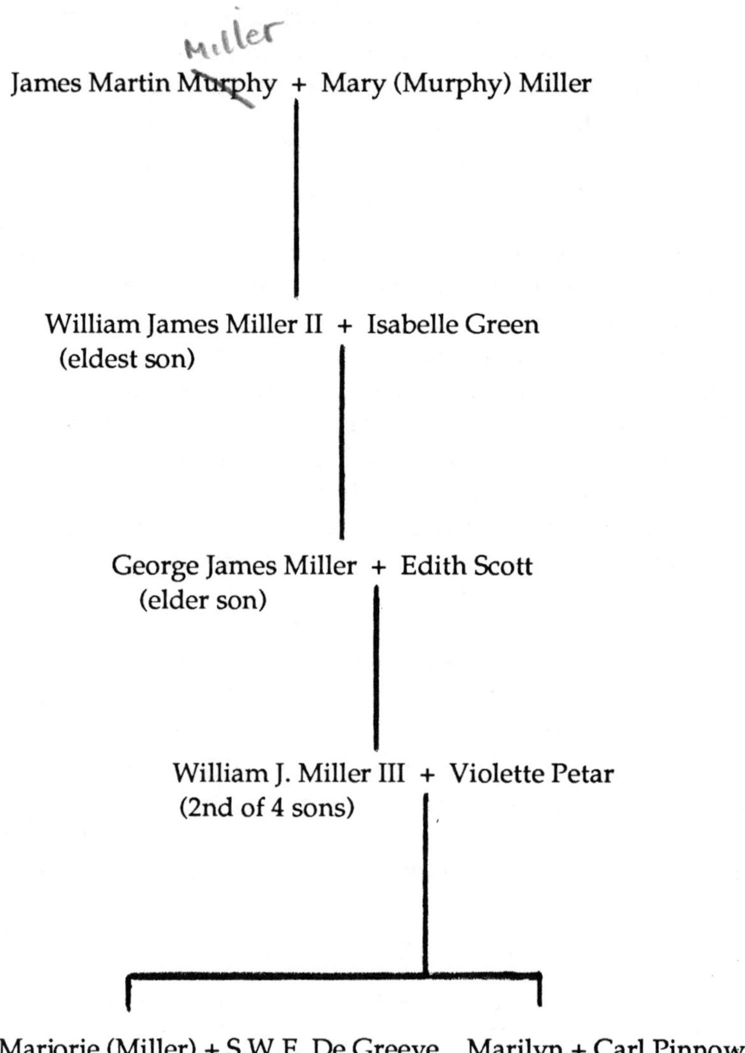

Partial Family Tree and Genealogical Chart of the Millers of Marin.

Three generations of James M. Miller's descendants.
Top left: William James Miller II (son of James M. Miller);
Top right: George James Miller (son of William James Miller II;
Bottom center: William James Miller III (son of George James Miller.
[Courtesy of William J. Miller III.]

William Miller's Irish family tree is indeed impressive not only for his forebears but also for his own successful children who form a fifth generation of Millers. The original progenitor and patriarch of the Miller family tree was William Miller's great-grandfather James Miller, who had been born in County Wexford in the townland of Upton, Parish of Livermore on May 1, 1814. In 1828, young James Miller was another "Oisin" who emigrated from Ireland to Canada with his parents, William and Catherine Duff Miller, to the New World. The Millers endured an ocean crossing and tramping to farmlands in frigid Canada, where James Miller married Mary Murphy in 1834. After leaving Canada, they endured soul-testing years tilling malarial farmlands in Missouri. Still seeking their Promised Land, in 1844 William Miller's great-grandfather and grandfather (William James Miller II). took part of an historic "first" overland wagon-train trek that helped to settle California and Marin.

As our contemporary William Miller III relates his family's historic pioneering achievement: "The Miller-Murphy Party of 1844 were the first immigrants to bring their wagon train all the way from Missouri to California without the loss of a single person." William Miller, the custodian of his family's saga, draws on a rich store of memories:

> I can recall the stories of my grandfather, William J. Miller, who was 12 when he made the trek.
>
> I can also reconstruct some of the incidents pertaining to the Millers both from the memories of my father, George James Miller, eldest son of William J. Miller, as well as from the memories of Theresa and Bernard Miller.

The heroic tale calls to mind the title of Irving Stone book on how the West was won: *Men to Match My Mountains*. On May 18th, 1844, 13 covered wagons carrying 26 men and 8 women and guided by gritty mountain man Elisha Stevens, departed westward from Council Bluffs to the cry of "Wagons, ho!" With James Miller were his wife, Mary Murphy Miller, their four children (including their son William James Miller II), and Mary's father, Wexford-born Martin Murphy, Sr. They would endure inclement weather, stoically withstand thirst and starvation, arduously trek across prairies, ford

Mary Murphy Miller, wife of James M. Miller & daughter of California pioneer, Martin Murphy, Sr. [Courtesy of William J. Miller III.]

rivers, and scale mountains to reach America's Golden Land of California and realize their dreams.

Marinite William Miller's great-grandfather and grandfather, then, were members of the legendary Murphy-Miller Party (also described in Chapter 6). These Irish adventurers displayed the "true grit" of rugged pioneers in making the arduous trek by covered wagon train from Missouri to the rugged Rockies and High Sierras before reaching California in the winter of 1844.

Coincidentally, the Murphys and the Millers were also neighbors back in County Wexford. The Millers, as previously mentioned, had immigrated to Canada when James Martin Miller was 14 years old, and they settled in Frampton, just outside Quebec, in the same neighborhood as Martin Murphy, Sr. While living on the farm, young Miller had married Mary Murphy (who had come to Canada with her brother in 1828), and they lived near Frampton until 1841. Both families soured on Canada's prospects and migrated with their numerous offspring to the state of Missouri.

There they purchased land in Holt County (a settlement that became known as Irish Grove), which was particularly suited for diverse farming and reminded them of their native Wexford.

The Millers Reach Irish Marin by Wagon Train

Our Marin family historian, William Miller III, relates that Missouri, with its malarial plagues, was too oppressive, and soon the Murphys and Millers hit the trail again, this time with California as their destination.

James Miller (our storyteller William Miller III's great-grandfather and, as mentioned, a member of the Murphy-Miller Party) was, then, the first man to reach Marin County by the overland route. His son William James Miller II, who was twelve at the time, preserved part of the story in the family archives:

> My father was Captain of the party and everything was done with military precision.
>
> The crossing of the plains through the intense heat and the tortures we suffered at times from the alkali and scarcity of water were indescribable...And there were times when the hide of the buffalo or the riata was used to make soup for our hungry and fatigued wanderers.

After eight agonizing months blazing a grueling overland route, the families arrived safely in California. On the one hand, Martin Murphy, Sr. and his family (see Chapter 6) were attracted to the sunny farmlands of Santa Clara County near Morgan Hill. The Millers, for their part, continued on to Marin County, where in 1845 they were welcomed by the Irish Don Timoteo Murphy of San Rafael. The two transplanted Celts became fast friends when Don Timoteo learned that young Miller came from near his old home in County Wexford. The flexible Millers learned to speak Spanish fluently (no doubt with a brogue!) and, like Irish chameleons, adapted themselves to the Hispanic customs and culture of the San Francisco and Marin area.

Later, relates William Miller III, the two Irishmen—James Miller and Timothy Murphy—struck a bargain that would one day make history. The deal consummated the transfer of 680 acres in

Murphy's *Las Gallinas Rancho* to James Miller. (Miller's family had camped out on these very lands the first night they arrived in Marin.) The Grant Deed from one Irishman to another—the first such deed recorded in English in Marin County—was a milestone in the California Irish Experience. Written in language none could misunderstand, it reads: "Granted, Bargained, Sold, Aliened, Remised, Conveyed, Confirmed, and Released." A copy of the deed, recorded on November 8, 1850, can still today be found in the old book of Marin County land grants.

When James Miller's and Mary Murphy Miller's family arrived in Marin, it consisted of a son William J. Miller II (then 12 years old) and three daughters. The family increased to number 10 children: William J., Kate, Mary, Martin, Ellen, Julia, Frances, Therese, Bernard, and Josephine.

In Marin James Miller prospered by farming upon his *Las Gallinas Rancho* land. Through hard work, he bred cows, cattle, horses, and mules. After building his family a shake house, he replaced it first with an adobe home, and then a far more impressive mansion, "Miller Hall." Miller Hall stood near Miller's farm offices and his extensive dairying business. By 1864, the dairying enterprise had expanded to such a large scale that Miller was marketing butter and milk to San Francisco. In 1880, the *Marin County History* reported the following facts about the success of Miller's shrewd investments: "Besides owning a considerable quantity of real estate in the thriving town of San Rafael, he is the proprietor of no less than 8,000 acres of land in different parts of Marin County."

Great-grandson William Miller III relates that in 1849 James Miller, his son William Miller II, and their *vaqueros* made headlines in early California journals by smelling a profit and driving 150 head of cattle from their ranch in San Rafael all the way to Marysville in the Mother Lode and swapping beef for gold at a dollar a pound. James Miller also financed the first private school in San Rafael at 4th and A Streets, where the descendants of the early pioneers received their first lessons. In August of 1858, he bought 1,000 acres in Tomales Township at $2.00 an acre. The following year he paid $50,000 for the rest of the big ranch. When the railroad was constructed through *Las Gallinas Rancho*, Miller's Station was also set up. What has been written earlier in this book of the success of the

Miller Hall, James Miller's mansion in San Rafael, built in 1853.

Martin Murphys, the landed gentry of Santa Clara, could be repeated of Miller, one of the largest Marin County landowners.

Miller Hall, mentioned above, was Marin County's fabulous mansion and a showplace of Irish hospitality, which served as home for the Miller family through the years that witnessed the expansion of the Miller holdings. It was while living as a guest in Miller Hall that historian Rev. Hugh Quigley wrote his eulogistic history, *The Irish Race in California and on the Pacific Coast* (1878). A colorful portrait of Miller Hall was written by William J. Miller II: "It was the mecca of the young aristocrats of the county and many delightful functions were held there. In the large fireplace in the spacious parlor the coffee pot always swung on the crane and delicious refreshments were served by the young folk." In early writings, Miller Hall was described as "a dwelling of magnificent proportions lying four miles north of San Rafael on the Petaluma Road." The setting was extolled in verse some years later by a family member, Fannie Miller, a talented writer of note, who described the Miller estate as "Valley, fairest of the fair." In 1929, a group of local investors purchased the property from the Miller heirs. Today the site has become part of the wealthy Marinwood development.

Irish patriarch James Martin Miller's adventurous life came to an end on November 25, 1890 after a long bout with illness. His funeral services were conducted directly across from Miller Hall at St. Vincent's orphanage, a palpable memorial to Miller's generous charity and philanthropy.

Marin & the Descendants of James Martin Miller

The Irish-American offspring of patriarch James Miller and Mary Murphy Miller also left their mark upon Marin County and California. Many of the Millers reared sizable families, whose children were a credit to their ancestors' nobility. (Again, the source for much of this Miller family saga is William J. Miller III's recollections and writings.)

William James Miller II: Marin Civic Leader

The previously mentioned William James Miller II was the eldest son of the pioneer James Miller. After graduating from Santa Clara University, William Miller left the home ranch and moved to San Rafael, where he opened a real estate and insurance office. He married Isabella (Belle) Green and had two sons, George James Miller and William Alphonso Miller. William Miller II accomplished notable works in San Rafael. He built a large home, erected the Marin Hotel, and constructed an entire business block. His political career was conspicuous. After serving as a member of the San Rafael Board of Trustees, he became a Representative of the California State Legislature in Sacramento from 1869-70. He also served as Mayor of San Rafael for six years. He was a strong proponent of making Nicasio the County seat, but the electors chose San Rafael by a slim margin: one vote.

The second son of William James Miller II was William Alphonso Miller, who married Martha Forsyth of Santa Rosa. They had two sons Don A. Miller and Milton Miller. William Alphonso worked for the Southern Pacific Railroad as Chief Engineer in San Jose, California.

George James Miller: New Frontiers in Alaska

William Miller II's first son was George James Miller, the father of William James Miller III, our family historian and source. George Miller married his childhood sweetheart, Edith Scott, a native of San Francisco. He worked in lumber as a gauger, time keeper, and accountant. After working in Shasta County in the 1890s, George and Edith pioneered in pre-Gold Rush Alaska and engaged in trading and shipping. After gold was discovered in Alaska (and reminiscent of the Miller family talent for cashing in on opportunity) George opened a store to provide groceries, wagons, and supplies to the mines. His enterprise landed him a job with the Northern Commercial Company as manager of several Alaskan stores. The adventurous Irish Millers lived in such exotic out-of-the-way spots, haunted by Indians and Eskimos, as Nome, Kotzebue, Golovin, Mouse Point, Fairbanks, Tanana, Barrow, Dawson, Skagway, and Nenama.

While in Alaska, three sons were born to George and Edith Miller, including William James Miller III (our source), who was born in Tanana in 1909. The lure of the Golden State eventually brought back George J. Miller and family to California. His diverse and remarkable background equipped him to become Secretary with the San Francisco Board of Trade, where he served with distinction until his retirement in 1938. The George Millers divided their retirement between their San Rafael and Bolinas properties.

William James Miller III: the Family Historian

Corte Madera's William James Miller III, our guardian of the Miller family archives, was the second son of George and Edith Miller. After being educated in San Rafael schools, he worked for 10 years for Shell Oil Company first as a salesman, then as a travelling auditor working out of San Francisco, Susanville, Auburn, Marysville, Sacramento, Placerville, and Rio Vista. He resigned his job to go into the dairy business. Meanwhile he had married his childhood sweetheart, Violette Petath of Marin County's scenic Bolinas in 1939. On land that now houses the Audubon Canyon Ranch and Bird Preserve near Bolinas Lagoon, the William Millers for 15 years produced hay for dairy feed and livestock for milk and beef. They marketed their beef and milk in San Francisco. After selling the ranch business, Miller went to work representing the San Joaquin Valley Hay Growers Association. He serviced the area from the Golden Gate to Southern Oregon and from the Pacific Ocean to western and central Nevada until retiring in 1974..

The next generation of Millers was born to the William Millers while on the dairy farm. They had two daughters Marilyn, born in 1942, and Marjorie, born in 1943. Each daughter attended college and married. Marilyn married Carl W. Pinnow and they opened a business in Napa. Marjorie and her husband (Stanley W.V. de Greeve of San Anselmo and Bolinas who has a business in San Rafael) were married in the same church in Bolinas as had the William Millers; they also had two daughters.

These particulars of family history, prosaic though they may at first appear, carry the deepest of human hopes and dreams and bear testimony to the humane and successful legacy of but one California Irish family, the pioneering Miller clan.

The Irish Legacy in Marin & California

The names of these and many other early Irish pioneers are alive and embedded in the hills and valleys, the meadows and moorlands of Marin County. These Irish place-names and memorials include Dan O'Connell's "Chamber of Sleep" in Sausalito and the town of Fallon in west Marin. Such Celtic names range from McClure's Beach by the bay to the broad expanses of Lucas Valley. From Patrick King's Larkspur, Bill Murray's Kentfield, and Timothy Murphy's San Rafael, to the aging timbers of Reed's old sawmill in Mill Valley and the roaring waves that crash against Dillon Beach. Like the early Pilgrims who came to America, the Irish who settled in Marin County also came from an farming upbringing. They also cleared the land, cultivated the soil, and planted the first crops in the bountiful soil of California. Whether rural or urban, Irish families formed a dynamic part of the State's progressive spirit and continue to contribute their vitality and varied talents to the modern polyglot culture of California.

Selected Bibliography of Works on Irish & Irish-American Studies

Adams, W.F. *Ireland and the Irish Emigration to the New World from 1815 to the Famine.* New Haven, 1932.

Anderson, Floyd. *Gold Rush Bishop.* Milwaukee: The Bruce Publishing Co., 1962.

Bancroft, Hubert Howe. *History of California.* 7 Vols. 1886-90.

——. *Chronicles of the Builders of the Commmonwealth.* 7 Vols. San Francisco: The History Company, 1891-92. [See Vol. 3, *Chronicle of the Kings,* 1891.]

Begley, Monie. *Rambles in Ireland.* Old Greenwich: Devin-Adair Company, 1977.

Biever, B.F. *Religion, Culture, and Values: Native Irish and American Catholicism.* New York, 1976.

Birch, Rev. P. *Saint Kieran's College.* Dublin: M.H. Gill and Son, Ltd., 1951.

Blake, J.W. "Transportation from Ireland to America, 1653-60." *Irish Historical Studies* 3 (March 1943).

Blessing, Patrick J. "West among Strangers: Irish Migration to California, 1850-80." Ph.D. dissertation. Univ. of California, Los Angeles, 1977.

Bottigheimer, Karl S. *Ireland and the Irish.* New York: Columbia University Press, 1982.

Brown, T.N. "Origins and Character of Irish-American Nationalism." *Review of Politics* 18 (July 1956): 329 ff.

Bulfin, William. *Rambles in Eirinn.* Dublin: M.H. Gill and Son, Ltd., 1920.

Burchell, Robert A. *The San Francisco Irish 1848-1880.* Berkeley: University of California Press, 1980.

Byrne, Stephan. *Irish Emigration to the United States.* New York, 1873.

Colum, Padraig. *Cross Roads in Ireland.* New York: The Macmillan Company, 1931.

—— (ed.). *A Treasury of Irish Folklore: The Stories, Traditions, Legends, Humor, Wisdom, Ballads and Songs of the Irish People.* 2nd Rev. Edition. New York: Bonanza Books, 1983.

Concannon, John Joseph & Cull, Francis Eugene (eds.). *The Irish American Who's Who.* (In cooperation with The Ancient Order of Hibernians.) Pearl River, New York, 1984.

——. *The Irish Directory.* Pearl River, New York, n.d.

Concannon, Mrs. Thomas. *Women of Ninety-Eight.* Dublin: M.H. Gill and Company, 1920.

Considine, Bob. *It's the Irish.* New York: Doubleday & Co., 1961.

Cooper, Brian E. *The Irish-American Almanac & Green Pages.* 2nd ed. New York: Pembroke Press Publishers, 1987.

Corkery, Daniel. *Hidden Ireland: A Study of Gaelic Munster in the 18th Century.* 2nd ed. Dublin: Gill & Macmillan, 1979.

Corrigan, Rev. William. *The History and Antiquities of Ossory.* Dublin: Sealy, Bryers and Walker, 1905.

Cotter, James H. *Tipperary.* New York: The Devin-Adair Company, 1929.

Crimmins, John D. *Early Celebrations of St. Patrick's Day.* Published by Author, 1902.

Crowley, George T. "The Irish in California." *Studies* 25 (1936): 451-62.

Cullen, L.M. *An Economic History of Ireland since 1660.* New York, 1972.

Cunningham, George. *Roscrea and District.* Roscrea: The Parkmore Press, 1976.

Cunningham, Florence R. *Saratoga's First One Hundred Years.* Fresno: Valley Publishers, 1967.

Curtis, L.P. *Anglo-Saxons and Celts: A Study of Anti-Irish Prejudice in Victorian England.* Bridgeport, Connecticut, 1968.

Daly (M.H.M.), Rev. John. *The History of St. Patrick's Parish and Church.* San Francisco: St. Patrick's Parish, 1976.

D'Arcy, William D. *The Fenian Movement in the United States, 1858-1886.* Washington, 1947.

Davis, Burke. *George Washington and the American Revolution.* New York: Random House, 1975.

Davis, W.H. *60 Years in California, 1839-1889.* San Francisco: J. Leary: 1889.

De Breffny, Brian (ed.). *The Irish World: The Art and Culture of the Irish People.* New York: Harry N. Abrams, 1977.

——. *Ireland: A Cultural Encyclopaedia.* London: Thames & Hudson, 1983.

Delaney, Mary Murray. *Of Irish Ways.* New York: Barnes & Nobel Books, 1980. [A good popular introduction to Irish culture.]

DeVoto, Bernard. *The Year of Decision 1846.* Boston: Little, Brown and Company, 1943.

Dickson, R.J. *Ulster Emigration to Colonial America.* London, 1966.

Diner, R. *Erin's Daughters in America.* Baltimore, 1983.

Donnelly, Florence. "The Reed Family Story." *San Rafael Independent Journal* (Nov. 6, 1965).

——. "Marin's Irish Don." *San Rafael Independent Journal* (Feb. 26, 1966).

——. "The Story of the Millers of Marin." *San Rafael Independent Journal* (July 10, 1971).

Dowling, Andy. *Johnstown, Galmoy and Urlingford Parishes.* Freshford, Kilkenny: Wellbrook Press, 1978.

Dowling, P.J. *The Hedge Schools of Ireland.* Dublin: Talbot Press, 1935.

Doyle, David Noel. *Ireland, Irishmen and Revolutionary America.* Dublin and Cork: The Mercier Press, 1981.

Doyle, David Noel & Edwards, O.D. (eds.). *America and Ireland, 1776-1976.* Westport, Connecticut, 1980

Duff, John B. *The Irish in the United States.* Belmont, California: Wadsworth Publishing Co., 1971.

Duffy, Francis. *Father Duffy's Story.* New York: George H. Doran and Co, 1919.

Dwyer, John T. *Condemned to the Mines.* New York: Vantage Press, 1976. [Story of Grass Valley's Bishop Eugene O'Connell.]

Egan, P.M. *Illustrated Guide to the City and County of Kilkenny.* Kilkenny: Egan Printing Company, n.d.

Fallows, M.R. *Irish Americans*. Englewood Cliffs, New Jersey, 1979.

Feehan, John. *The Landscape of Slieve Bloom*. Dublin: The Blackwater Press. 1979.

Fennelly, Teddy. *100 Years of G.A.A. (Gaelic Athletic Association) in Laois*. Portlaois: The Leinster Express, 1972.

Flannery, John Brendan. *The Irish Texans*. San Antonio: University of Texas Press, 1980.

Flower, Robin. *The Irish Tradition*. Oxford: Clarendon Press, 1947.

Gaffey, James P. *Citizen of No Mean City: Archbishop Patrick Riordan of San Francisco (1841-1914)*. San Francisco: A Consortium Book, 1976.

Gleeson, Rev. *History of Ely O'Carroll Territory or Ancient Ormond*. 2 Vols. Kilkenny: Robert Books; reprinted 1982.

Gmelch, George. *The Irish Tinkers*. Menlo Park, California: Cummings Publishing Company, 1977.

Gordon, M.A. "Studies in Irish and Irish-American Thought and Behavior." Ph.D. dissertation. Univ. of Rochester, 1977.

Graham, Hugh M.A. *The Early Irish Monastic Schools*. Dublin: The Talbot Press, Ltd., 1923.

Grant, John. *The Poems of Ossian*. Edinburgh, 1926.

Greeley, Andrew M. *That Most Distressful Nation: The Taming of the American Irish*. Chicago, 1972.

Green, Alice Stopford. *History of the Irish State to 1014*. London: Macmillan and Company, 1925.

Griffin, William D. *A Portrait of the Irish in America*. New York: Charles Scribner's Sons, 1983.

Gwynn, Denis. *Young Ireland and 1848*. Cork: Cork University Press & Oxford: B.H. Blackwell, Ltd., 1949.

Hafen, Leroy R. *Broken Hand: The Life of Thomas Fitzpatrick: Mountainman, Guide, and Indian Agent*. Lincoln: University of Nebraska Press, 1981 (1931).

Hale, Dennis & Eisen, Jonathan (eds.). *The California Dream*. New York: Collier Books, 1968.

Hart, James D. "Irish in California." In Hart's *A Companion to California*. Rev. ed. Berkeley & Los Angeles: Univ. of California Press, 1987, pp. 239-240.

Hayden, Mary & Moonan, George A. *A Short History of the Irish Race*. Dublin: Talbot Press, 1921.

Hayes, Edward. *The Ballads of Ireland*. Vol 1. Boston: Patrick Donahoe, 1855.

Hayes, Richard. *Biographical Dictionary of Irishmen in France.* Dublin: M.H. Gill and Son, Ltd., 1949.

Hennessy, Maurice N. *The Wild Geese: The Irish Soldier in Exile.* London, 1973.

——. "The Wild Geese of Eire." *Town & Country Magazine* (May 1988). [Photo essay on modern descendants of the Wild Geese around the world.]

Hogan, John. *Saint Cirian of Ossory.* Kilkenny: Journal Office, 1876.

Holland, Rev. W.P.P. *History of West Cork.* Skibbereen: Southern Star Ltd., 1949.

Howell, Charles Fish. *An Irish Ramble.* New York: Greenberg, 1929.

Hutchenson, W.H. *Two Centuries of Man, Land and Growth in the Golden State*. Palo Alto: American West Publishing Company, 1967.

Jenkins, Brian. *Fenians and Anglo-American Relations during Reconstruction.* Ithaca & London: Cornell University Press, 1960.

Johnson, Paul. *Ireland: A Concise History.* London: Granada, 1980.

Jones, Plummer F. *Shamrock Land.* New York: Moffat, Yard and Company, 1908.

Joyce, W.L. *Editors and Ethnicity: History of Irish-American Press, 1848-83.* New York, 1976.

Keep, G.R.C. "Irish Migration to North America in the Second Half of the 19th Century." Ph.D. dissertation. Trinity College, Dublin, 1951.

Kickham, Charles Joseph. *Knocknagow*. Dublin: James Duffy and Company, Ldt., 1887.

Knobel, D.T. "Paddy and the Republic: Popular Images of the American Irish, 1820-60." Ph.D. dissertation. Northwestern University, 1976.

Leadabrand, Russ; Lowenkopf, Shelly; & Patterson, Bryce. *Yesterday's California.* Miami, Florida: E.A. Seemann Publishing, Inc., 1975.

Leamy, Margaret. *Parnell's Faithful Few.* New York: The Macmillan Publishing Company, 1936.

Lee, Thomas Zanslar (ed.). *The Journal of the American Irish Historical Society*. New York: American Irish Historical Society, 1897.

Levine, Edward M. *The Irish and the Irish Politicians: A Study in Cultural and Social Alienation.* Notre Dame, 1966.

Lewis, Oscar. *Silver Kings: The Lives and Times of Mackay, Fair, Flood and O'Brien, Lords of the Nevada Comstock Lode.* New York, 1947.

——. *San Francisco: Mission to Metropolis.* Berkeley: Howell-North Books, 1966.

Loftis, Anne. *California: Where the Twain Did Meet.* New York: The Macmillan Publishing Company, 1973.

Lotchin, Roger W. *San Francisco 1846-1856: From Hamlet to City.* New York: Oxford, 1974.

Lover, Samuel. *Rory O'Moore.* New York: The American News Company, n.d.

MacManus, Seumus. *The Story of the Irish Race.* New York: Devin-Adair Company, 1944.

Maguire, John Francis. *The Irish in America.* New York: David J. Sadlier and Company, 1880 (1868).

McCabe, Seosamh. *Historical Notes on Laois and Place-Names of Bally Roan.* Portlaoise: The Old Laois Society, 1975.

McCaffrey, Lawrence J. *The Irish Diaspora in America.* Bloomington, 1976.

——. "Irish America." *The Wilson Quarterly* 9 (Spring 1985): 78-93.

McCarthy, Justin H. *Ireland Since the Union.* Chicago: Belford, Clarke and Company, 1887.,

McCormack, Lily. *I Hear You Calling Me.* Milwaukee: Bruce Publishing Company, 1949. [Story of John McCormack.]

McDowell, R.B. *Ireland in the Age of Imperialism and Revolution, 1760-1801.* Oxford, 1979.

McGee, John Whalen. *The Passing of the Gael: Our Irish Ancestors, Their History & Exodus.* Grand Rapids, Michigan: Wolverine Printing Company, 1975.

McGee, Thomas D'Arcy. *History of O'Connell and His Friends.* Boston: Donahue and Rohan, 1845.

——. *The History of the Irish Settlers in North America.* Boston: Patrick Donahoe, 1855.

McGloin (S.J.), Rev. John B. *California's First Archbishop.* New York, 1966.

McGowan, Joseph. *History of the Sacramento Valley.* 3 Vols. New York: Lewis Historical Publishing Co., 1961.

McGroarty, John S. *California: Its History and Romance.* Los Angeles: Grafton Publishing Company, n.d.

McMaster, John Bach. *Benjamin Franklin.* New York & London: Chelser House, 1980.

McNamee, Mary Dominica. *Light in the Valley (Notre Dame in California).* Berkeley: Howell-North Books, 1967.

McWade, Robert M. *The Uncrowned King: Charles Stewart Parnell.* Edgewood Publishing Company, 1891.

Meehan, Patrick F. *The Members of Parliament for Laois and Offaly, 1801-1918.* Portlaiose: The Leinster Express, 1972.

Miller, William J. "Millers Came in Wagon Train." (1976).

——. Typescript MS. to author on Miller Family Genealogy.

Miller, Kerby A. *Emigrants and Exiles: Ireland and the Irish Exodus to North America.* Oxford-New York: Oxford University Press, 1985. [Brilliant study of Irish emigration to America.]

Moody, T.W. & Martin, F.X. (eds.). *The Course of Irish History.* New York: Weybright and Talley, 1967.

Murphy, Cecelia M. "The Stevens-Murphy Overland Party of 1844." Unpublished M.A. Thesis. University of California at Berkeley, 1941.

Murphy, Richard C. & Mannion, Lawrence J. *The Society of the Friendly Sons of Saint Patrick in the City of New York.* New York: J.C. Dillon and Company, 1962.

National Board A.O.H. *History of the Ancient Order of Hibernians and Ladies Auxiliary.* 4 Vols., 1923.

Neider, Charles. *The Great West.* New York: Bonanza Books, 1958.

Nolte, W.N. "Irish in Canada, 1815-1867." Ph.D. dissertation. University of Maryland, 1975.

O'Brien, Michael J. *A Hidden Phase of American History.* Freeport, N.Y, 1919. [Irish role in the American Revolution.]

——. *Irish Settlers in America*: A Consolidation of Articles from the *Journal of the American Irish Historical Society.* 2 Vols. Baltimore: Genealogical Publishing Co., 1979

O'Brien, Pat. *The Wind in Your Back: The Life and Times of Pat O'Brien by Himself.* Garden City, N.Y, 1964.

O'Connor, R.C. "The Irish in California." *American Irish Historical Society Journal* 1 (1916): 200-211.

O'Donoghue, D.J. *The Geographical Distribution of Irish Ability.* Dublin: O'Donoghue & Co., 1906.

O'Donovan, Donal. *Dreamers of Dreams: Portraits of the Irish in America*. Bray, Co. Wicklow: Kilbride Books, 1984.

O'Farrell, P. "Millennialism, Messianism and Utopianianism in Irish History." *Anglo-Irish Studies* 2 (1976).

O'Grady, Joseph P. *How the Irish Became Americans*. New York, 1973.

O'Hanlon, Rev. John. *History of Queen's County*. 2 Vols. Dublin: Sealy, Bryers, and Walker, 1905.

——. *Irish American History of the United States*. New York: Murphy & McCarthy, 1920.

O'Hanlon, Rev. J. *Irish Emigrant's Guide to the United States* (1851). New York, 1976.

O'Laughlin, Michael C. *Irish Settlers on the American Frontier, 1700-1900*. Kansas City: Irish Genealogical Society, 1984.

O'Mahoney, John. *History of Ireland*. Brooklyn: Kirker, 1857.

O'Mahoney, Katherine O'Keefe. *Famous Irishwomen*. Lawrence: Lawrence Publishing Company, 1907.

O'Sullivan, Sean. *Irish Wake Amusements*. Cork: The Mercier Press, 1961.

O'Sullivan, T.F. *The Young Irelanders*. Tralee: The Kerryman Ltd., 1944.

Phelan, James D. *Travel and Comment*. San Francisco: A.M. Robertson, 1923.

Postgate, R.W. *Dear Robert Emmet*. New York: The Vanguard Press, 1932.

Potter, George. *To the Golden Door: The Story of the Irish in Ireland and America*. Boston: Little, Brown & Company, 1960.

Prendergast, Thomas F. *Forgotten Pioneers: Irish Leaders in Early California*. San Francisco, 1942.

Quigley, Rev. Hugh, *The Irish Race in California and on the Pacific Coast*. San Francisco: A. Roman & Co., 1878.

——. *The Cross and the Shamrock*. Boston: Patrick Donahoe, 1853.

Quinn, Arthur. *Broken Shore: The Marin Peninsula in California History*. Inverness, CA: Redwood Press, 1981.

Quinn, Elena. *The History of Downey, California*. Downey: Elena Quinn, 1973.

Reynolds, Frank L. *Ireland's Important and Heroic Part in American Independence and Development*. Chicago: John P. Daleiden, n.d.

Roberts, Edward F. *Ireland in America.* New York: G.P. Putnam's Sons, 1931.

Robinson. W.W. *Los Angeles (From the Days of the Pueblo).* Los Angeles: California Historical Society, 1981.

Roche, James Jeffrey. *Life of John Boyle O'Reilly.* New York: The Cassell Publishing Company, 1891.

Russell, Diarmuid (ed.). *The Irish Reader.* New York: Viking Press, 1946.

Sandburg, Carl. *Abraham Lincoln: The War Years.* New York: Charles Scribners Sons, 1946.

Sarbaugh, T.J. "Irish Republicanism vs. 'Pure Americanism': California's Reaction to Eamon de Valera's Visits." *California History* 69 (Summer 1981).

Saul, Gerord Brandon. *Traditional Irish Literature and Its Background.* Lewisburg: Bucknell University Press. 1970.

Schrier, Arnold. *Ireland and the American Emigration, 1850-1900.* Minneapolis: University of Minnesota Press, 1958.

Shannon, William V. *The American Irish.* New York: Macmillan Company, 1963.

Smith, Cecil Woodham. *The Great Hunger.* New York: Harper and Row, 1962.

Smith, Charles. *The Ancient and Present County and City of Cork*. Cork: Guy and Company, n.d.

Starr, Kevin. *Americans and the California Dream, 1850-1915.* New York: Oxford Univ. Press, 1973.

——. *Inventing the Dream: California through the Progressive Era.* New York: Oxford Univ., 1985.

Stivers, R. *Hair of the Dog: Irish Drinking and American Stereotype.* University Park, Penn., 1977.

Sullivan, Sister Gabrielle. *Martin Murphy Jr: California Pioneer 1844-1884.* Stockton: University of the Pacific, 1974.

Sullivan, T.D.; A.M.; & D.B. *Speeches from the Dock.* New York: P.J. Kennedy, 1882.

Sunnyvale Historical Society. *Proposal for the Erection of California Landmark No. 644*, May 1966.

Tepper, Michael. *New World Immigrants.* 2 Vols. Baltimore: Baltimore Publishing Company, 1980.

Thebaud, Aug. J. *The Irish Race in the Past and Present.* New York: P.J. Kennedy, n.d.

Thompson, William Irwin. *The Imagination of an Insurrection: Dublin, Easter 1916*. New York: Harper & Row, 1972.

Tierney, Mark. *Croke of Cashel.* Dublin: Gill and Macmillan Ltd., 1976. [Story of the founder of the Gaelic Athletic Assoc.]

Tracy, Jack. *Sausalito, Moments in Time.* Sausalito: Windgate Press, 1983.

Waller, Francis. *The Poetical Works of Thomas Moore.* New York: P.F. Collier, 1880.

Walsh (S.J.), Rev. Henry L. *Hallowed Were the Gold Dust Trails: The Story of the Pioneer Priests of Northern California.* Santa Clara: University of Santa Clara Press, 1946.

Walsh (F.S.C), Brother Hilary D. *Borris-in-Ossory: An Irish Parish and Its People.* Kilkenny: Kilkenny Journal, Ltd. , 1969.

Walsh, James P. (ed.). *The San Francisco Irish, 1850-1976*. Edited for the Irish Literary and Historical Society. 2nd ed. San Francisco, 1978.

—— (ed.). *The Irish: America's Political Class*. New York, 1976.

Whalen, Richard. *The Founding Father: The Story of Joseph P. Kennedy.* New York: New American Library, 1964.

White, James. *My Clonmell Scrap Book.* Dundalk: Dundalgen Press, 1907. [Anthology of Irish readings.]

Whiteridge, Arnold. *Rochambeau.* New York: Collier Macmillan Co, 1965.

Whitney, David C. *The Colonial Spirit of '76.* Chicago: J.G. Ferguson Publishing Co, 1974.

Wittke, Carl. *The Irish in America.* Baton Rouge: Louisiana State University Press, 1956.

Wright, R.L. (ed.). *Irish Emigrant Ballads and Songs.* Bolling Green, 1975.

Yeats, William Butler (ed.). *Irish Folk Stories and Fairy Tales.* New York: Grosset & Dunlap.

——. "The Wanderings of Oisin." In Yeats' *The Celtic Twilight*: and a Selection of Early Poems. New York: Signet Classics, 1962.

Young, John P. *San Francisco: a History of he Pacific Coast Metropolis*. 2 Vols. Chicago, 1912.

Younger, Calton. *Ireland's Civil War.* New York: Taplinger Publishing Company, 1969.

Zimmermann, G.D. *Songs of Irish Rebellion: Political Street Ballads and Rebel Songs, 1770-1900*. Dublin, 1967.

[Photo by Scott Buschman]

About the Author: Vision & Challenge

Irish-born in County Leix, Patrick J. Dowling was lured to the "New Ireland" of California a half-century ago. Active in San Francisco business life and cultural affairs, Pat pioneered in establishing an all-Irish Library and Archives in 1975.

Both as Director of the Library of San Francisco's United Irish Cultural Center and as an independent researcher, Pat has devoted himself to preserving Irish lore and learning for Irish Americans. His own goal is to establish an institute to promote a rebirth of Irish-American awareness in their Irish family roots, culture, and heritage.

This book is part of Dowling's larger Irish dream: ***to challenge Irish Americans to help him fund programs that use all the media (books, libraries, TV, and movies) to explore the Irish experience***:

> ***I have written this history to awaken Americans and the American Irish to their forgotten heritage both in Ireland and California and to help inspire a renaissance of Irish history, culture and achievements.***

Dowling's Vision and Irish-American Dream

Pat Dowling is enthusiastic about the exciting possibilities of launching a wide variety of Irish-based programs in America. Today, every other major ethnic group has taken an interest in exploring their own roots. The time is now ripe, says Dowling, to stir up a more lively sense of Irish roots and identity among the 40 million Americans who claim Irish descent.

Americans and Irish Americans who are sympathetic to this cause are encouraged to take practical steps to assist Pat Dowling's programs: these will focus on Ireland's historical contributions and the amazing achievements of Erin's sons and daughters in America.

Dowling's new programs will be varied. We need to: conduct oral history interviews, write helpful guides to orient Irish Americans to their genealogy and history, sponsor conferences and network with likeminded groups and individuals, produce TV documentaries and home video-cassette programs on topics that promote understanding of the Irish-American experience, ***and establish a central clearing house for all these projects, namely an Irish-American institute, museum and archives*** (for photographs, artifacts, correspondence, computer information data bases, etc.).

How Can You Help Expand Irish-American Awareness?

If you are sympathetic to Pat Dowling's programs to expand our awareness of the Irish-American experience and history, you can help in several practical ways:

* Send in suggestions, information, photos, etc., for Pat's new historical books on the Irish in California, America, and abroad.
* Express your interest in helping Pat create an Irish-American institute and museum.
* Contribute your donations of money to help fund Pat's future Irish-American projects.

Send donations & suggestions to Patrick Dowling at:

Golden Gate Publishers
173 Cerritos Avenue
San Francisco, CA 94127
Telephone: (415) 585-8091